Praise fo

Neil Cohn is diving deeper into comics & the brain than anyone I know now.

Scott McCloud, author of *Understanding Comics*

This trailblazing collection provides an excellent starting point for anyone interested in the study of cognition and visual narrative. Drawing on an array of disciplines and approaches, from linguistics and psychology to anthropology and art education, *The Visual Narrative Reader* investigates such intriguing topics as children's drawings, manga, ancient Maya art and Australian sand narratives. It is also one of the few recent contributions to the field of visual studies that is truly international in scope. Highly recommended.

Kent Worcester, Professor of Political Science,
Marymount Manhattan College, USA

For years Neil Cohn has been doing his own leading edge work on the structure and cognition of visual narratives. Now he has assembled a collection of studies, both seminal and new, from across disciplines and cultures, to challenge our assumptions about how humans create and comprehend images. More than just an important resource for comics scholars, this anthology might well be a catalyst that transforms the nature of comics studies.

Randy Duncan, Professor of Communication, Henderson State University,
USA and co-author of *The Power of Comics*, second edition (Bloomsbury, 2015)

Anyone interested in visual narrative will be very grateful to Neil Cohn for compiling this collection of diverse knowledge by insightful researchers from a variety of disciplines. Even though I've been involved with comics and other forms of visual storytelling for most of my life, this book, like all of Cohn's works, gives me great new insights and points of view.

Carl Potts, Former Executive Editor, Marvel Comics and Author of *The DC Comics Guide to Creating Comics: Inside the Art of Visual Storytelling*

While formal, cognition- and language-oriented research should be among the fundamental building blocks for all studies into comics and sequential art, it is too often marginalised or even completely overlooked. This volume finally collects in one reader comprehensive overviews of diverse established approaches; as well as several of the most essential and fruitful contributions to the field. Its special focus on cultural variation provides important and unique perspective. *The Visual Narrative Reader* should set a new and indispensable standard for all linguistic and interdisciplinary research into visual narrative.

Stephan Packard, Junior Professor of Media Culture Studies, Freiburg University, Germany and President of the German Society for Comics Studies

The Visual Narrative Reader situates comics within the broader context of visual language and uses approaches from cognitive science to offer new insights into the ways that comics work. Neil Cohn has assembled an overview of an expanding field that will provoke and enlighten comics readers and cartoonists alike.

Matt Madden, author of *99 Ways to Tell a Story: Exercises in Style*

This volume breaks new ground: No one before has tried to organize scholarship on visual narrative into a coherent collection. Neil Cohn is perfectly suited to this task. The result is a great resource for students, scholars, and anyone interested in the science of how we understand stories told with pictures.

Jeffrey M. Zacks, Professor of Psychology and Radiology, Washington University in St. Louis, USA and author of *Flicker: Your Brain on Movies* (2014)

This multi-faceted collection looks beyond just comics to trace visual narrative through history and across cultures: it provides a rich foundation for understanding how we acquire, interpret, and communicate through visual language, and details how discrete visual language systems reflect and serve the particular cultures within which they develop. Whether read on its own or as a companion to Cohn's *The Visual Language of Comics* (essential reading for any student of comics), this collection will challenge readers' ideas of how comics and other visual narratives are taught, learned, and used in everyday communication.

Alexander Danner, co-author of *Comics: A Global History, 1968 to the Present* (2014)

The Visual
Narrative
Reader

The Visual Narrative Reader

Edited by Neil Cohn

Bloomsbury Academic
An imprint of Bloomsbury Publishing Plc

B L O O M S B U R Y

LONDON · OXFORD · NEW YORK · NEW DELHI · SYDNEY

Bloomsbury Academic

An imprint of Bloomsbury Publishing Plc

50 Bedford Square	1385 Broadway
London	New York
WC1B 3DP	NY 10018
UK	USA

www.bloomsbury.com

BLOOMSBURY and the Diana logo are trademarks of Bloomsbury Publishing Plc

First published 2016

© Neil Cohn and Contributors, 2016

Neil Cohn has asserted his right under the Copyright, Designs and Patents Act, 1988, to be identified as the Editor of this work.

British Library Cataloguing-in-Publication Data

A catalogue record for this book is available from the British Library.

ISBN:	HB:	978-1-4725-7790-0
	PB:	978-1-4725-8559-2
	ePDF:	978-1-4725-7791-7
	ePub:	978-1-4725-7792-4

Library of Congress Cataloging-in-Publication Data

The visual narrative reader / edited by Neil Cohn.

pages cm

Includes bibliographical references and index.

ISBN 978-1-4725-7790-0 (hardback) — ISBN 978-1-4725-8559-2 (pb) —
ISBN 978-1-4725-7792-4 (epub)   1. Semiotics—Psychological aspects.   2. Visual literacy.
3. Visual education.   4. Readers.   5. Sequence (Linguistics)   6. Cognition.   7. Psycholinguistics.
I. Cohn, Neil, editor.

P99.4.P78V57 2016

302.2'2—dc23

2015019464

Typeset by RefineCatch Ltd, Bungay, Suffolk
Printed and bound in India

Contents

Part II Psychology and Development of Visual Narrative

7 *Manga* Literacy and *Manga* Comprehension in Japanese Children *Jun Nakazawa* 157

8 What Happened and What Happened Next: Kids' Visual Narratives across Cultures
Brent Wilson 185

Part III Visual Narratives across Cultures

12 Linguistic Relativity and Conceptual Permeability in Visual Narratives: New Distinctions in the Relationship between Language(s) and Thought *Neil Cohn* 315

Online resources can be found at www.bloomsbury.com/Cohn-Visual-Narrative

List of Illustrations

Notes on the Contributors

John Bateman is a professor of linguistics in the English and linguistics department of Bremen University, specializing in functional, computational and multimodal linguistics. His research interests include functional linguistic approaches to multilingual and multimodal document design, semiotics and theories of discourse. He has been investigating the relation between language and other semiotic systems for many years, focusing particularly on accounts of register, genre, functional variation, lexicogrammatical description and theory, multilingual and multimodal linguistic description, and computational instantiations of linguistic theory. He has published widely in all these areas, as well as authoring several introductory and survey articles on multimodality, multimodal linguistic film analysis and automatic natural language generation. His publications include *Multimodality and Genre* (2008), *Multimodal Film Analysis* (2012), with Karl-Heinrich Schmidt, and *Text and Image* (2014).

Neil Cohn is an internationally recognized scholar for his research on the overlap of sequential images and language in cognition. He received his doctorate in psychology from Tufts University in 2012, working with renowned linguist Ray Jackendoff and psycholinguists Gina Kuperberg and Phillip Holcomb. His postdoctoral work has included fellowships at the University of California, San Diego, at the Center for Research in Language and the Institute for Neural Computation, in collaboration with cognitive neuroscientist Marta Kutas. Also a comic artist, he began working in the comic industry at age fourteen, and is the illustrator/author of *We the People* (2004) with Thom Hartmann, *Meditations* (2005), and the illustrator of *A User's Guide to Thought and Meaning* (2012) with Ray Jackendoff. His pioneering work on the cognition of 'visual language' has been most extensively explored in his books *Early Writings on Visual Language* (2003) and *The Visual Language of Comics* (2013). His work is online at www.visuallanguagelab.com.

Charles Forceville is associate professor in the media studies department of the Universiteit van Amsterdam. He studied English at the Vrije Universiteit Amsterdam, where after graduating taught in the English, comprative literature, and word and image departments. Forceville was programme director of the Research Master Media Studies from 2004 to 2012 and chairs the ACLC project AIM/Rhetoric in

Multimodal Discourse. In addition to having published many articles and chapters, he co-edited *Multimodal Metaphor* (2009) with Eduardo Urios-Aparisi, and *Creativity and the Agile Mind* with Kurt Feyaerts and Tony Veale. His research adopts concepts from cognitive linguistics and relevance theory to examine the structures in multimodal texts, especially metaphor, narrative and argumentation.

Pascal Lefèvre is a special guest professor in the arts at LUCA School of Arts (campus Sint-Lukas Brussels). He studied social sciences and American studies at the University of Leuven (KU Leuven). While working as a researcher at the Belgian national broadcasting corporation (BRTN), he started publishing and organizing conferences. From 1996 to 1999, he was attached part-time as a scientific advisor to the Belgian Centre of Comic Strip Art in Brussels. Since 1998, he has been lecturing on comics and visual media at various Flemish university colleges of art (in Brussels, Antwerp and Genk). In October 2003, he completed his PhD in social sciences (communications) at the University of Leuven. He conducted research for various organizations, such as the folklore museum Het Huis van Alijn in Ghent and the artist agency SMartbe. Lefèvre has numerous publications and has presented at various conferences worldwide: selected publications are *Pour une lecture moderne de la bande dessinée* (with Jan Baetens), *The Comic Strip in the Nineteenth Century* (co-edited with Charles Dierick), *Bande dessinée et illustration en Belgique. États des lieux et situation socio-économique du secteur* (with Morgan Di Salvia). He is a member of the international editorial board or consultative committee of various academic journals such as *Image [&] Narrative*, *International Journal of Comic Art*, *SIGNs (Studies in Graphic Narratives)*, *European Comic Art*, and *Journal of Graphic Novels and Comics*. His work is online at: page sites.google.com/site/lefevrepascal/home.

Nancy Munn is Professor Emerita of Anthropology and of Social Sciences at the University of Chicago. She received her PhD in 1961 from the Australian National University. Her work focuses on exchange, cultural space and time, and symbolic analysis. She is best known for her extensive and pioneering work based on field research in Papua New Guinea and Central Australia. She is the author of many works, including the books *Walbiri Iconography* (1973) and *The Fame of Gawa* (1986).

Jun Nakazawa is a professor of the Faculty of Education at Chiba University in Japan. He received his BA, MA and PhD (Psychology) from Hiroshima University. His primary research looks at human development processes, especially from early childhood to adolescence, in various fields such as cognitive and social development. In addition to his extensive research on developmental psychology in general, Nakazawa has been among the first to empirically examine the development of children's understanding of comics and sequential images, research that he has been doing for over twenty years. He is the co-editor of *Applied Developmental Psychology* (2005).

Jesper Nielsen is Associate Professor at the Institute for Cross-Cultural and Regional Studies, University of Copenhagen. He received his PhD in 2003 on a dissertation discussing the imperial iconography of Teotihuacan in the Maya area in the fourth century. He specializes in the iconography and writing systems of ancient Mexico (including the Maya, Olmecs and Teotihuacan), and has published extensively in international peer-reviewed journals and monographs, just as he has presented papers and given workshops in Mexico, Canada, Germany, Holland, Poland, Belgium, and in several other countries. Another area of his research is the early colonial period (fifteenth to sixteenth centuries), and more specifically how religious ideas and imagery from the indigenous cultures of Mesoamerica merged with those of the Euro-Christian tradition. Dr Nielsen is also the author of two books, one on the ancient Maya and the second a biography of one of the most famous Maya archaeologists, both written in Danish.

Mario Saraceni teaches at the University of Portsmouth, and previously worked in Bangkok, Thailand, and at the University of Nottingham, where he received his PhD in 2001. His dissertation on comics using discourse theory was among the first research to explicitly connect the study of comics with linguistic theory. His research primarily focuses on issues related to the rules and the roles of English as a transnational and de-Anglicized language, especially from political and ideological perspectives, and in the applicability of systemic functional linguistics and of multimodality for (critical) discourse analysis. He is the author of *The Language of Comics* (2003) and *The Relocation of English* (2010).

Eric Stainbrook was born and raised in rural Pennsylvania and was a fan and collector of comics from a young age. He graduated from the University of Pittsburgh with a degree in creative writing, from Northeastern University in Boston with a Master's in writing and linguistics, and from Indiana University of Pennsylvania with a PhD in composition. His doctoral dissertation, from which portions of his chapter were drawn, is titled *Reading Comics: A Theoretical Analysis of Textuality and Discourse in the Comics Medium*. He currently resides in Winston-Salem, North Carolina, where he teaches college composition and creative writing.

Søren Wichmann is a senior scientist at the Max Planck Institute of Evolutionary Anthropology, Leipzig, an institution with which he has been affiliated since 2003. He has also held positions at the University of Copenhagen, Universidad de Sonora, Leiden University, and Kazan Federal University. Although originally trained in comparative literature at the BA and MA levels, Wichmann has worked as a linguist throughout his professional career, first specializing in Mesoamerican languages and writing systems, and then increasingly addressing more general topics, including quantitative methods in historical linguistics and language typology. His more than one hundred and fifty publications reflect a broad range of cross-disciplinary interests and include papers in journals such as *Language, Journal of Linguistics, Annual Review of Anthropology, Current Anthropology, PLoS ONE, Human Biology,* and *Communications in Computational Physics.* In 2011, Wichmann co-founded a journal, *Language Dynamics and Change.*

Janina Wildfeuer is a postdoctoral research fellow for multimodal linguistics in the Faculty of Linguistics and Literary Science at Bremen University, Germany. She teaches classes in multimodal, interdisciplinary and applied linguistics and researches film, comics, and other documents within several projects exploring the notion of multimodal discourse. Her publications include the monograph *Film Discourse Interpretation: Towards a New Paradigm for Multimodal Film Analysis,* published in 2014 with Routledge, as well as several contributions and papers on the analysis of multimodal artefacts such as film, comics and multimodal discourse.

David P. Wilkins is an anthropological linguist whose main interest is the human capacity for meaning-making, no matter what the modalities may be. Since 1982, he has worked with Australian Aboriginal communities in central Australia, and more recently began work in Far North Queensland. He has worked for Aboriginal-controlled community schools, helping them establish culturally appropriate education programmes. In the early 1990s, Wilkins taught at UC Davis and later the State University of New York at Buffalo, and then spent seven years as a senior researcher at the Max Planck Institute for Psycholinguistics in Nijmegen, where he undertook fieldwork-based cross-cultural research on the relationships between language, culture and cognition. He returned to live in Sydney in 2006 and has worked as a consultant.

Brent Wilson is Penn State School of Visual Arts professor emeritus. His research includes studies of visual cultural influences on children's artistic development, cross-cultural studies of children's graphic narratives, Japanese teenagers' dōjinshi/manga and comic markets, studies of children's interpretations of artworks, and Internet ethnography and pedagogy. He has authored four books; four-dozen book chapters, chapters in conference proceedings, and research monographs; and over a hundred research and evaluative reports. During the 1970s, he developed the first National Assessment of Educational Progress in Art; in the 1980s, he did the research for and drafted *Toward Civilization: A Report to the President and Congress* (on the status of arts education in the US); and in the 1980s and 1990s, he evaluated k-12 professional development programmes funded by the Getty Education Institute for the Arts (which culminated in the publication of *The Quiet Evolution: Changing the Face of Arts Education*); and also in the 1990s, he served as a researcher for the President's Committee on the Arts and Humanities. He received the Manuel Barkan Award for outstanding contributions to the literature of art education, the Edwin Ziegfeld award for contributions to international art education and research, and the Lowenfeld award for his studies of children's art. He delivered the Ziegfeld Lecture at the Osaka Congress of the International Society for Education through Art in 2008. Solo exhibitions of his artist-books and folios have been held in Taipei, Hong Kong, New York, and Utah. Wilson received a PhD in art education from the Ohio State University (1966), an MFA in painting from Cranbrook Academy of Art (1958), and a BS in art and education from Utah State University (1956).

Preface

I have never been one to let a good idea go to waste. A few months after my book *The Visual Language of Comics* went to the printer, I began reflecting on the many interesting and important papers that helped shape my theories on the structure and cognition of visual narrative . . .

For example, David Wilkins's paper, 'Alternative Representations of Space' about Australian sand narratives (which has become Chapter 10 of this book) provided me with important contrasts to many of the assumptions our culture holds about drawings and sequential images. Over a decade ago, when I first read it as a third- (or more) generation photocopy, I was astounded by the way it both supported my ideas and dramatically changed the way I conceived of drawings and visual narratives. It was a revelation. Yet most people did not know of this paper because it was almost impossible to find, even via interlibrary loan. I have heard that even amongst some scholars, it was a paper of legend – many knew of it, but few had actually read it.

In a similar vein, in the forty years of work by Brent Wilson (Chapter 8), I found evidence supporting the idea that imitation is the engine for learning to draw, that sequential image creation is not a developmental inevitability, and that drawing development might differ cross-culturally. Equally important was my discovery of research by Jun Nakazawa (Chapter 7), who has spent over twenty years in his native country of Japan studying how children understand comics and their educational benefits. While some scattered experimental studies of visual narratives appeared in the American cognitive science literature, here were two scholars with decades of work examining these issues directly. Yet again, despite their huge role in shaping my theories, I found that most other researchers of comics and visual narrative rarely mentioned their work; many had no idea that they existed.

There seemed to be several of these types of papers and bodies of literature; significant findings that were very influential (to me), but not widely recognized. One of the challenges, I thought, was that they often came from diverse academic fields or geographical places. Wilson was in art education. Wilkins was an anthropological linguist. Nakazawa was a developmental psychologist, whose papers were mostly in Japanese. Other works were in dissertations, but never converted to books or papers, and some accessible only on microfiche!

Nevertheless, it seemed to me that it was important that people should be able to glean the insights from these writings directly, and not just from seeing them listed in bibliographies. I resolved to rectify this problem, and the result is the collection you are about to read.

Here, I hope to make accessible several seminal papers and summaries of literature that deserve to be included and appreciated for their contribution to the study of visual narrative. In many cases, they should be considered seminal, foundational research for this overall field. Some of these works were hard to find. Some of them deserve more notice (in my opinion). Others have been created newly for this collection in order to enhance, enrich, and challenge further studies as this field grows within the interdisciplinary cognitive sciences.

*   *   *

I intend this collection to serve several purposes. First, it is meant as a resource for researchers so that the chapters can provide references for further studies (see also the final section on Further Reading). Wherever possible, I have urged the authors to write accessibly for readers across disciplines, so as to provide an introduction to topics that may or may not be familiar.

Second, the book can be used as a 'Reader' for classes. Many of the chapters offer overviews of research spanning several decades, and/or provide key background for various topics of interest to those learning about drawing, comics, or visual narratives. In many cases, the classes I teach discuss these or other papers by these authors already – now they are all in one place. If you are an educator, I hope this collection will be as helpful to you as it will be for me.

Finally, I hope that the topics in each chapter will be fascinating to *anyone* interested in this growing field of study of the visual language of comics and visual narratives. My own passion for this work is fuelled by a fascination with how visual narratives work – from structure and cognition to culture and social contexts – and thus editing this volume was a pleasure for me. I had the chance to read and to grow excited about the prospect of its contents exciting others. Hopefully, this collection allows you to learn something new, gain an alternative perspective, and/or motivate you to probe further.

*   *   *

Let me close with something of a confession. While I am very proud of the works collected here, I am also disappointed with regard to those that are absent. I wish that this Reader was five times larger and bursting with chapters about every facet of structure, cognition, development, cross-cultural and historical variation, and all the sociocultural implications of visual narrative imaginable. Unfortunately, at present, such a book could not be compiled because insufficient research exists as yet. I therefore hope that the chapters in this book serve as an inspiration and a challenge to others, in the same way that many of these works inspired me, so that some day in the near future we will indeed be able to have that tome. Hopefully, it will be sooner than we think.

Neil Cohn
La Jolla, CA
March 2015

1

Interdisciplinary Approaches to Visual Narrative

Neil Cohn

1. Introduction

Drawing is a uniquely human capacity for expressing meaning. Other animals convey meaning through verbalization and bodily motions (like humans) along with other species-specific modalities of expression. In addition, other species have been shown to use tools, at least to a rudimentary degree. However, no other animal combines these abilities, by manipulating the world with tools (even a finger) to convey meaning the way that humans do when drawing. This unique capacity for image-making is pushed further by the use of *sequential* images to convey meanings beyond single expressions. Sequential visual narratives date at least as far back as cave paintings and have appeared in numerous cultural artefacts – woven into tapestries, painted on pottery, and drawn in sand, among others. In contemporary industrialized society, we find static visual narratives most prominently in comics, but also in instruction manuals, illustrated children's books, and various other contexts.

Despite this historical depth and societal prevalence, concerted efforts to study these sequential images have only recently begun in earnest. The primary questions here are: how do we understand visual narratives? How are they structured and comprehended? What is the relationship between their structure and other aspects of human expression, like language?

2. Visual language theory

In my own work, I have attempted to articulate an approach to an understanding of visual narrative that establishes this expressive capacity as a cognitive phenomenon parallel to that of spoken or signed languages (Cohn, 2013b). As described above, humans as a species have only three primary ways to convey our concepts communicatively – we create sounds through our mouths; we move our bodies, especially our hands and faces; and we draw images, using our fingers or other tools. While other modalities could be imagined as biologically possible (perhaps emitting smells or secreting mucus?), these are our only ways to convey meaning to each other. These meanings are not just novel forms though – in all channels we use systematic patterns stored in our long-term memories: Words and idioms are systematic patterns of sound mapped to meanings. Gestural emblems are systematic meaningful manual expressions (like 'OK' or 'thumbs up'), in contrast to the novel gesticulations that often accompany speech (McNeill, 1992). Drawings also use systematic patterns, whether as conventional ways of drawing people, houses, or stick figures, or the more complex patterned styles of superhero comics or Japanese *manga*. All of these forms are systematic patterns of a form (sound, body, graphics) mapped to meanings.

In addition, all of these modalities can express meaning in ordered sequences. Not all sequences might make sense, though. We use a system of rules and constraints – a 'grammar' – to ensure that sequences are coherent, and to limit production of incoherent sequences that might violate those constraints. For example, in the verbal modality, the sequence *George walked to the kitchen* is coherent, but *George to walked the kitchen* is not, despite only changing the position of two words (*to* and *walked*). The same thing occurs in sequential images. For example, Figure 1.1(a) shows a coherent sequence of a man swinging from vine to vine in a jungle, but the reversal of two panels in Figure 1.1(b) renders it less coherent.

Thus, continuing this overall theory, the combination of meaningful forms using a grammar in ordered sequences, begets a type of language: Structured sequential sounds become *spoken languages* of the world. Structured sequential body motions become *sign languages* (as opposed to just the individual forms of gestures). And, structured sequential images become *visual languages*.

A 'language' therefore involves a specific combination of three cognitive structures: a *Modality* (sound, body, graphics) that expresses *Meaning* using systematic forms

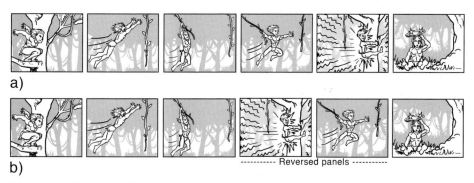

Figure 1.1 Coherent (a) and incoherent (b) versions of a sequence of images.

(a 'vocabulary'), ordered with a *Grammar*. Though we have the potential for all modalities to become full languages, not all individuals develop each modality into a full language. Most everyone gestures or doodles (limited vocabulary, no grammar), but not everyone can communicate fluently in sign language or create a coherent sequence of images in a visual language (full vocabulary, full grammar). Note also, that written language is not a natural 'visual language'. Writing is the conversion of the verbal modality into the visual form, for an unnatural (albeit useful) type of modified expression. We know it is unnatural, because children do not write naturally without explicit instruction – they must be taught how to write, and in fact most of primary education is dedicated to this!

Whether or not these channels become full languages, all of these systems combine in *multimodal* interactions. We gesture while we speak and we use text combined with images to communicate. These interactions that go beyond a single modality reflect our natural manner of communication. Thus, this broader theory goes against the idea that 'language' is an amodal system that flows into different modalities with no consequence on its structure, but rather it posits that humans are built with *one expressive system* that manifests conceptual information in three complementary modalities, each of which has its own properties and structures.

In addition, having this capacity does not mean that all humans will develop the same externalized systems given this internal biology. Just as spoken languages and sign languages differ around the world, we should expect that different visual languages manifest in unique cultural contexts. For example, such diversity can explain why distinct systems arise in the visual languages found in 'comics' of different countries (like the systems distinct to American superhero comics versus Japanese *manga*), in the visual languages used in different sociocultural contexts (like in comics versus illustrated picture books or instruction manuals), and in the visual languages completely disconnected from comics, like the sand narratives of Australian Aboriginals (Green, 2014; Munn, 1986). That is, the abstract principles that govern the broader human capacity for 'visual language' manifest in different ways depending on their cultural contexts.

Thus, 'visual language theory' places drawings and sequential images directly on par with other expressive modalities in terms of their structure and cognition. This parallelism warrants a second level of comparison with regard to processing in the mind/brain. Here, I have proposed a '*Principle of Equivalence*' (Cohn, 2012, 2013b), which says that *we should expect that the mind/brain treats all expressive capacities in similar ways, given modality-specific constraints.* In other words, the brain uses common cognitive resources across all of these expressive modalities, and the places where structure or processing is different should be motivated by the properties of the modalities themselves. Clearly, sound and graphics vary greatly, and these departures will motivate certain affordances for how they structure the creation of meaning. Thus, the job of research is to identify which aspects of structure and cognition overlap between various domains and which ones remain unique to their respective modalities.

3. Studying visual narratives

Whether one wants to buy into the full theory of 'visual language' or not, any study of visual narratives that purports to describe how people produce and comprehend sequential images must be grounded in the cognitive sciences and the questions motivating the aforementioned theory. As such, the study of sequential images can benefit from following the methods and disciplines for studying 'language' found within the interdisciplinary union of linguistics, philosophy, anthropology, cognitive science, and psychology (as well as others). Across these disciplines, three primary methods of research form a model for the study of sequential images: theory, experimentation, and corpus analysis.

3.1. Theory

The oldest and most frequent method of studying visual narratives is theorizing about their structure. Theories can develop either bottom-up or top-down, and feed into the empirical research done in experimentation and corpus analysis (Cohn, 2014a). Bottom-up theories are usually *observation-driven*, motivated by researchers noticing a particular trait in the structure of a visual narrative, and then rigorously analysing that element. For example, imagine if a researcher noticed that authors consistently used a certain type of panel-to-panel relationship, like depicting one panel of a person followed by another zooming in on that person's eyes. The researcher may then theorize how this convention came about, how it operates, and whether this type of relationship (*large view–zoomed view*) extends to other patterns beyond a figure and eyes. Top-down, *theory-driven* research posits abstract principles about generalized structure, often occurring when ideas are imported from one domain (such as linguistics or discourse) and applied to another (like visual narratives), or from making connections between different ideas. For example, a researcher might theorize that there is a narrative pattern of *large view–zoomed view* based on the fact that panels in general can show different viewpoints, and thus such a pattern is likely to occur. This top-down theorizing could then be followed by observation-driven research seeing if this intuition is correct. Both directions of inquiry can yield interesting insights, and most often they are used in combination with each other.

Many theories about visual narrative's structure have been offered by academics, but the ideas with the most traction have often emerged from the creators of visual narratives themselves. For example, Anglo-American theoretical scholarship often attributes its impetus to the influential book *Understanding Comics* by theorist and comic artist Scott McCloud (1993), who himself was inspired by comic artist Will Eisner's (1985) seminal *Comics and Sequential Art*. However, practitioners theorizing about the building blocks of visual narrative understanding goes back at least as far as the 1800s. The Swiss educator Rodolphe Töpffer (1845), often credited as one of the recent progenitors of modern comics (Groensteen, 1997), reflected in depth on various aspects of his newfound craft, including making comparisons with language. From a 'language' perspective, the insights of actual creators of visual narratives should make sense, since those 'fluent' in a system should have intuitions beyond those looking in from the outside.

Not all theoretical work originated in the insights of creators though. Serious academic inquiry seems to have arisen around the late 1960s and early 1970s when European scholarship began to use the popular foundations of *semiotics* to investigate the makeup of visual narratives like comics. These works followed the 'structuralist' traditions derived from pre-1950s linguistics (Saussure, 1916), which were then applied across various fields to decompose cultural system into their minimal units. In the context of comics, this included identifying the minimal 'morphemes' of visual images up through the narrative structures of sequential images (summarized in D'Angelo and Cantoni, 2006; Nöth, 1990). Several contemporary European theories have followed, succeeded, or rebelled against, this tradition (e.g., Groensteen, 1999; Miodrag, 2013).

Theories about visual narratives arose in research from several different countries (for example, see the recent collection edited by Miller and Beaty (2014) for works in French), but we here explore the growth of such work in the scholarship from Germany. In Chapter 2, 'Linguistically Oriented Comics Research in Germany', Janina Wildfeuer and John Bateman summarize an ever-growing body of literature from Germany that has persisted from the 1970s through the present day. They describe the progression of German theories about comics from their foundations in the structuralist tradition, through to their integration with more semiotic and linguistic approaches. The result is an extensive review of many important approaches to the structure of comics never previously detailed for an English-reading audience.

Theories often break down visual narratives into several component parts. Broadly these include: 1) How the form and meaning of individual images is constructed, 2) How images in sequence connect with each other, and 3) How text and image combine to form a larger multimodal expression. This collection explores theories related to each of these primary aspects of visual narrative structure.

First, we can ask the simple question: How do people understand that images are meaningful? This question involves both understanding perceptual systems (how we recognize visual objects in general) and the ways in which patterns of graphic information are stored in cognitive structures (how we understand drawings in particular). In Chapter 3, 'No Content Without Form: Graphic Style as the Primary Entrance to a Story', Pascal Lefèvre explores these basic aspects of the nature of drawings and how they convey meaning, entwined with the unique characteristics of graphic style. His approach ranges from a discussion of the biological properties of the visual system to detailing how graphic style involves both coherency and narrative functionality in contributing to the larger understanding of sequential images. The result is one of the first papers attempting to integrate stylistics and visual narratives with regard to graphic representation specifically.

Beyond the form of images, it is no trivial matter how lines and shapes create meaning. While this comprehension may involve seemingly basic aspects of scene perception and object recognition, the meanings conveyed in visual narratives often veer into the more abstract and complicated, and even seemingly simple images may engage complex underlying conceptual processes. In Chapter 4, 'Conceptual Metaphor Theory, Blending Theory, and Other Cognitivist Perspectives on Comics', Charles Forceville discusses how more complicated meanings arise from the mapping of different domains of understanding. The field of *cognitive linguistics* has described conventionalized mappings between domains as *conceptual metaphor* (Lakoff and Johnson, 1980), which are subsumed under the larger process of *conceptual blending* (Fauconnier and Turner, 1998, 2002). This work in linguistics has stressed that these complex mappings between domains are a ubiquitous part of everyday language usage. However, over the past two decades, Forceville has spearheaded an analysis of this type of meaning-making in multimodal expressions (Forceville and Urios-Aparisi, 2009), with focus over the last decade especially directed to visual narratives like comics. Here, he summarizes his work and that of others as constituting a 'cognitivist' approach to comics.

Beyond individual images, theories of visual narratives have also sought to explain how meaning might be comprehended across a sequence. Some work has examined how readers navigate across panels distributed in a page layout (Cohn, 2013a; Cohn and Campbell, 2015), while a few theorists have speculated on how meaning is acquired via whole pages (Barber, 2002), and the functional roles that page layouts play in a narrative (Caldwell, 2012; Groensteen, 1999; Peeters, 1991). Nevertheless, the main theories of sequential image understanding have focused on the meaningful relations between juxtaposed images. In English works, these theories primarily began with McCloud's (1993) categorization of 'panel transitions', which described how elements change between images, such as shifts in characters, spatial location, time, etc. While subsequent research has shown that linear panel transitions are not enough to account for the full sequential image understanding (Cohn, 2010, 2013c; Cohn, Jackendoff, Holcomb and Kuperberg, 2014; Cohn, Paczynski, Jackendoff, Holcomb and Kuperberg, 2012), psychological experimentation has shown that meaningful relations between images do seem to impact some aspects of visual narrative comprehension (Cohn et al., 2012; Magliano, Miller and Zwaan, 2001; Magliano and Zacks, 2011).

Following McCloud's (1993) original taxonomy, several dissertations in English in the early 2000s pointed out their similarity to notions of *discourse coherence* from linguistic theories. 'Coherence' is the continuity that allows an utterance or discourse to be meaningful, facilitated by the cues that indicate connections between one sentence and another. Like McCloud's panel transitions, classic work in the discourse literature yielded taxonomies categorizing the various ways sentences link together (Halliday and Hasan, 1976, 1985). For example, sentences may relate to each other through reference via pronouns, by deleting or substituting words or phrases, by repeating words, or through connective words like *and*, *therefore*, or *because*. This collection highlights two different approaches that describe how McCloud's panel transitions link with notions of discourse coherence.

First, Mario Saraceni's (2000) dissertation 'Language Beyond Language' used discourse theories to operationalize McCloud's panel transitions; he later summarized this material in a short monograph (Saraceni, 2003). However, his particular focus on sequential images appears in his paper 'Relatedness: Aspects of Textual Connectivity in Comics' (Saraceni, 2001), originally published in Jan Baeten's (2001) collection *The Graphic Novel*. This work is important because it attempts to operationalize McCloud's transitions and notions of inference across the dimensions of semantic associations and repetition of characters. It is reprinted here in Chapter 5 in hopes that the additional exposure brings more focus to Saraceni's ideas.

Another dissertation, 'Reading Comics' by Eric Stainbrook (2003) also attempted to describe McCloud's transitions and many other aspects of the structure of the visual language of comics in terms of discourse theory. Having never been previously published, a concise summary of this work appears in Chapter 6, 'A Little Cohesion between Friends; Or, We're Just Exploring Our Textuality'. Here, Stainbrook summarizes the key aspects of his dissertation, supplemented with more recent theorizing about the visual language found in comics. He reinterprets McCloud's original taxonomy of panel transitions in terms of discourse connectives and insightfully discusses non-narrative examples of sequential images. However, a key discussion of Stainbrook's chapter also raises a final aspect of visual narrative: the connections between images and written language to form a broader communicative whole. Indeed, most visual depictions exist in *multimodal* interactions that require us to understand not just images or text on their own, but to integrate those two streams of information into one cohesive whole – possibly with emergent meaning arising from their union.

Multimodality runs as an important undercurrent throughout many of the works in this collection. The study of multimodal interactions may be considered as an important goal for the study of visual narrative to strive toward. It both reflects the natural characteristics of human communication, and its description requires a detailed understanding of the structure of each individual modality in order to also discuss their combination.

3.2. Experimentation

Beyond theoretical structure, since the 1950s, the growing fields comprising the cognitive sciences (linguistics, psychology, cognitive neuroscience, etc.) have stressed that comprehension of any media, whether linguistic or visual, must be traced to patterns found in the brain. Thus, in order to truly understand the comprehension of visual narratives, we must directly connect with aspects of cognition. Such a shift alters the question under study from, 'How are visual narratives structured?' to 'What goes on in the mind/brain that allows us to comprehend a sequence of images?' These questions cannot be answered by theorizing alone and require empirical study through psychological experimentation, an endeavour which has only recently begun in seriousness (for summaries of some research, see Cohn, 2013b, 2014b).

If such structure arises only as a facet of cognition, an important next question must be, 'How do we acquire the abilities that enable us to understand and produce sequential images?' The stereotypical belief seems to be that this ability is universal: Everyone is able to comprehend visual narratives and they require little to no special training to be understood. Under this view, comprehending sequential images would rely on general cognitive capacities like perception, attention, event segmentation, etc. This preconception may arise from the presumed similarity between sequential images and the perception of everyday events. The logic goes something like this: Since visual narratives use images that convey actions and events sequentially, and we perceive actions and events in daily life, shouldn't the understanding of visual narratives just draw upon these same cognitive mechanisms?

The chapters in Part II of this collection provide evidence that this assumption may be limited, and they summarize several decades of research on the comprehension and production of visual narratives from across the world. First, in Chapter 7, '*Manga* Literacy and *Manga* Comprehension in Japanese Children', the developmental psychologist Jun Nakazawa summarizes over twenty years of Japanese research on how kids and adults understand *manga*, extending beyond the scope of his previous review in English (Nakazawa, 2005). His work has shown that understanding the elements within and across sequential images is conditioned by both age and experience reading comics. In addition, this work summarizes years of research on the role of visual narratives like comics as educational material. Overall, these Japanese studies suggest that information is conveyed more effectively in multimodal visual narratives than as text alone, and that the reading of *manga* benefits various educational fields, especially literacy.

Chapter 8, 'What Happened and What Happened Next: Kids' Visual Narratives Across Cultures', summarizes the work of Brent Wilson, an artist and researcher of art education who has examined the development of children's drawing ability for over four decades. Wilson's work staked out the iconoclastic position that drawings were structured similarly to language (Wilson, 1974, 1988; Wilson and Wilson, 1977), rebelling against the dominant paradigm of art education that decried imitation (e.g., Arnheim, 1978). Here, he reviews his years of research, discussing both published and previously unpublished work on children's drawing abilities, their production of sequential visual narratives, and the sociocultural contexts that arise around their drawing practices. Throughout, Wilson shows that the ability to produce visual narratives is tied to exposure to graphic systems throughout a culture. This view is distinctly similar to language: drawing is based on acquired patterns appropriated from the environment of a learner.

3.2.1. Corpus analysis

Just as there is no single, universal spoken language, the idea of 'visual language' intrinsically expects that graphic systems are not universal either. Rather, because they arise from the patterns found the brains of a community of individuals, we should expect systematic properties in visual narratives both within and across cultures. Here, we find a tension between the biological and the cultural – to what extent are visual narrative systems universal, and to what extent are they culturally relative? In order to fully examine whether structures of visual narratives might be universal or bound to culturally distinct systems, we need wide-ranging cross-cultural studies documenting the systems of drawing and visual narratives across the world. Corpus analyses can range from simply coding various properties of the world's visual narratives (whether in comics or other contexts) to the anthropological investigation of existing and historical cultures. In this effort, it is especially important to study the visual narratives of non-Western industrialized societies, or else we run the risk of believing that widespread cultural appropriation (or influence) is universal, when it may not be. The works comprising Part III of this book push beyond the visual narrative traditions in 'comics' to examine two such traditions in Chapters 9 through 12.

First, Aboriginal communities in Central Australia have visual narrative systems drawn in the sand that combine with speech and an auxiliary sign language (Cohn, 2013b; Green, 2014; Munn, 1986). Sand drawings are an especially good contrast to the visual narratives found in comics because they are drawn in real-time exchanges, appear also in daily conversation, and use structures very different from the spatially juxtaposed sequential images found in comics. The anthropologist Nancy Munn offered the first comprehensive analysis of these systems, adeptly showing the systematic and language-like properties of sand stories created by the Warlpiri (previously written 'Walbiri') of Central Australia. While Munn's initial analysis came in the form of a 1962 paper (Munn, 1962), she provided an excellent introduction to these systems broadly in her book, *Walbiri Iconography* (Munn, 1986). She has kindly allowed an abridged version of Chapter 3 of this book, 'The Walbiri Sand Story', to be reprinted as Chapter 9 of this collection. This contribution discusses the visual vocabulary of these sand narratives at length.

A more cognitive approach to Australian sand narratives was undertaken in work by the linguist David Wilkins. Wilkins' work with the Arrernte – a neighbouring community of the Warlpiri – further probed these individuals' understandings of their systems and how they are acquired by children. The result is his 1997 paper, 'Alternative Representations of Space: Arrernte Narratives in Sand', which is now reprinted here in Chapter 10. This chapter provides several challenges to the orthodoxy of how we think about both individual and sequential images, and it should be considered a seminal work in the broader endeavour of visual narrative understanding.

The visual narratives from a second non-Western society are analysed in Chapter 11, providing an additional dimension to this study: history. In 'Sequential Text–Image Pairing among the Classic Maya', authors Søren Wichmann and Jesper Nielsen expand on their earlier work (Nielsen and Wichmann, 2000) describing the multimodal interactions and sequential images found on pottery from the sixth- to ninth-century Mayan culture of Mesoamerica. The authors' careful and linguistically inspired methodology illuminates the fairly regularized structures of this graphic system and shows how text–image combinations across sequential images often share properties with contemporary visual narratives like comics.

Finally, an intriguing question with cross-cultural research is: does variation in an expressive system (like language or drawing) affect other aspects of cognition? A similar question has been posed in language research under the idea of *linguistic relativity* – the idea that the language you speak influences the way you think. In the final chapter of the book, 'Linguistic Relativity and Conceptual Permeability in Visual Narratives', I explore how this notion of linguistic relativity might change given the perspective of drawings and sequential images constituting 'visual languages'. This discussion involves two questions: 1) do the structures of verbal and visual languages influence each other? and 2) do verbal and visual languages influence more general aspects of cognition like perception or attention? Given that cognitive research on visual narrative is still fairly new, such questions cannot be answered outright. Thus, while this chapter describes several places that evidence may arise, it more importantly serves to pose these questions and establish potential paths to investigate them.

3.3. Putting it together

These three methodologies of theory, experimentation, and corpus analysis frame an interconnected approach for the broader understanding of how visual narrative is structured and comprehended in human cognition, and how it manifests in the world. Each approach offers a unique viewpoint with different types of data, and the method of research largely depends on the questions asked by a researcher. Yet, a full research program does not take these methods in isolation, and all of these approaches can complement each other (schematized in Figure 1.2). For example, in order to understand the patterns and regularities in sequential images, we might create a theoretical model that outlines structures and makes predictions for how sequences of images are understood. These principles can then be tested using psychological experimentation to see, if in fact, these constructs are psychologically real (an important test for *any* theory of cognition). These theoretical constructs can also be used to examine a corpus of examples from across the world: do different cultures convey information in sequential images in the same ways? Corpus analysis and experimentation can also inform each other: imagine if some aspect of sequential images occurs more often in Japanese *manga* than in American comics – might we expect that readers of Japanese *manga* would then comprehend that structure with more proficiency than readers of American comics? Such differences in comprehension should be measurable in psychology experiments.

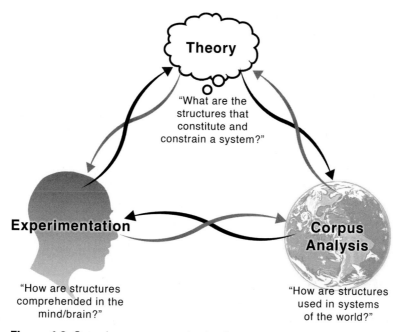

Figure 1.2 Complementary methods of research.

In this way, all of these methodological approaches can combine to offer a broader understanding of the cognition of visual narratives. While these methods frame the primary ways that (visual) language can be studied, they are not the only ways. For example, the advances in technology over the past forty years have coincided with sophisticated computational modelling aimed at simulating the cognition and/or development of linguistic abilities. Similar computational approaches can be pursued in the study of visual narratives, and indeed some work has begun to explore such methods (e.g., Guérin et al., 2013; Laraudogoitia, 2008, 2009).

These methods may also contribute to, and be enriched by, studies of the sociocultural contexts and implications of visual narratives. Researchers of sociolinguistics study how the use of language factors into its understanding and treatment. For example, though all languages are equal in terms of their cognitive status, some 'dialects' may be privileged over others within a given society. For example, the English of white middle-class Americans is considered 'standard' and given more status than regional variations (Bostonian, Texan) and languages spoken by minorities (such as African American Vernacular English). In a similar vein, we can ask: are some graphic dialects privileged over others? Also, how do people who prefer one visual language perceive others (e.g., how do readers of superhero comics perceive the style and storytelling in *manga* and vice versa)? These and other questions can best be answered in a sociocultural approach that grounds itself in the methods of theory, experimentation and corpus analysis.

4. Onwards and upwards

It is my hope that this collection of works can begin to further frame the issues regarding visual narratives in the context of the mind. The work presented throughout this volume summarizes an incredible collection of knowledge from over the past forty years by only a handful of researchers across the globe. In this regard, such work will hopefully be appreciated for its breadth of insights and, perhaps, for being more extensive than many may have assumed. But we should not stop there; this work should be treated as the start of a bigger conversation. Through the act of compiling these diverse perspectives, we can hopefully see the emergence of an interconnected field of study capable of addressing questions that transcend the disciplinary divides of each individual contribution. Altogether, these works establish a basic framework from which research can grow in the broader quest to understand visual narratives and their connections with other expressive systems.

References

Arnheim, R. (1978). Expressions. *Art Education*, 31(3): 37–38.
Baetens, J. (2001). *The Graphic Novel*. Leuven: Leuven University Press.

Barber, J. (2002). *The Phenomenon of Multiple Dialectics in Comics Layout.* Masters Thesis, London College of Printing, London.

Caldwell, J. (2012). Comic panel layout: a Peircean analysis. *Studies in Comics*, 2(2): 317–338. doi: 10.1386/stic.2.2.317_1

Cohn, N. (2010). The limits of time and transitions: challenges to theories of sequential image comprehension. *Studies in Comics*, 1(1): 127–147.

Cohn, N. (2012). Explaining 'I Can't Draw': parallels between the structure and development of language and drawing. *Human Development*, 55(4): 167–192. doi: 10.1159/000341842

Cohn, N. (2013a). Navigating comics: an empirical and theoretical approach to strategies of reading comic page layouts. *Frontiers in Psychology – Cognitive Science*, 4: 1–15. doi: 10.3389/fpsyg.2013.00186

Cohn, N. (2013b). *The Visual Language of Comics: Introduction to the Structure and Cognition of Sequential Images.* London: Bloomsbury.

Cohn, N. (2013c). Visual narrative structure. *Cognitive Science*, 37(3): 413–452. doi: 10.1111/cogs.12016

Cohn, N. (2014a). Building a better 'comic theory': shortcomings of theoretical research on comics and how to overcome them. *Studies in Comics*, 5(1): 57–75. doi: 10.1386/stic.5.1.57_1.

Cohn, N. (2014b). The architecture of visual narrative comprehension: the interaction of narrative structure and page layout in understanding comics. *Frontiers in Psychology*, 5: 1–9. doi: 10.3389/fpsyg.2014.00680

Cohn, N., and Campbell, H. (2015). Navigating comics II: constraints on the reading order of page layouts. *Applied Cognitive Psychology*, 29: 193–199. doi: 10.1002/acp.3086.

Cohn, N., Jackendoff, R., Holcomb, P. J., and Kuperberg, G. R. (2014). The grammar of visual narrative: neural evidence for constituent structure in sequential image comprehension. *Neuropsychologia*, 64: 63–70. doi: 10.1016/j.neuropsychologia.2014.09.018

Cohn, N., Paczynski, M., Jackendoff, R., Holcomb, P. J., and Kuperberg, G. R. (2012). (Pea)nuts and bolts of visual narrative: structure and meaning in sequential image comprehension. *Cognitive Psychology*, 65(1): 1–38. doi: 10.1016/j.cogpsych.2012.01.003

D'Angelo, M., and Cantoni, L. (2006). Comics: semiotics approaches. In: K. Brown (ed.), *Encyclopedia of Language and Linguistics* (2nd edn, Vol. 2: 627–635). Oxford: Elsevier.

Eisner, W. (1985). *Comics and Sequential Art.* Florida: Poorhouse Press.

Fauconnier, G., and Turner, M. (1998). Conceptual integration networks. *Cognitive Science*, 22(2): 133–187.

Fauconnier, G., and Turner, M. (2002). *The Way We Think: Conceptual Blending and the Mind's Hidden Complexities.* New York: Basic Books.

Forceville, C., and Urios-Aparisi, E. (2009). *Multimodal Metaphor.* New York: Mouton De Gruyter.

Green, J. (2014). *Drawn from the Ground: Sound, Sign and Inscription in Central Australian Sand Stories.* Cambridge, UK: Cambridge University Press.

Groensteen, T. (1997). Töpffer, the originator of the modern comic strip. In: C. Dierick and P. Lefèvre (eds), *Forging a New Medium: The Comic Strip in the Nineteenth Century* (pp. 28–71). Brussels: VUB Press.

Groensteen, T. (1999). *Systeme de la bande dessinée*. Paris: Presses Universitaires de France.

Guérin, C., Rigaud, C., Mercier, A., Ammar-Boudjelal, F., Bertet, K., Bouju, A., . . . Revel, A. (2013). *eBDtheque: A Representative Database of Comics*. Paper presented at the Document Analysis and Recognition (ICDAR), 2013, 12th International Conference.

Halliday, M. A. K., and Hasan, R. (1976). *Cohesion in English*. London: Longman.

Halliday, M. A. K., and Hasan, R. (1985). *Language, Context, and Text: Aspects of Language in a Social-Semiotic Perspective*. Victoria, Australia: Deakin University Press.

Lakoff, G., and Johnson, M. (1980). *Metaphors We Live By*. Chicago, IL: University of Chicago Press.

Laraudogoitia, J. P. (2008). The comic as a binary language: an hypothesis on comic structure. *Journal of Quantitative Linguistics*, 15(2): 111–135.

Laraudogoitia, J. P. (2009). The composition and structure of the comic. *Journal of Quantitative Linguistics*, 16(4): 327–353.

Magliano, J. P., Miller, J., and Zwaan, R. A. (2001). Indexing space and time in film understanding. *Applied Cognitive Psychology*, 15: 533–545.

Magliano, J. P., and Zacks, J. M. (2011). The impact of continuity editing in narrative film on event segmentation. *Cognitive Science*, 35(8): 1489–1517.

McCloud, S. (1993). *Understanding Comics: The Invisible Art*. New York: Harper Collins.

McNeill, D. (1992). *Hand and Mind: What Gestures Reveal about Thought*. Chicago, IL: University of Chicago Press.

Miller, A., and Beaty, B. (2014). *The French Comics Theory Reader*. Leuven, Belgium: Leuven University Press.

Miodrag, H. (2013). *Comics and Language: Reimagining Critical Discourse on the Form*. Jackson, MI: University Press of Mississippi.

Munn, N. D. (1962). Walbiri graphic signs: an analysis. *American Anthropologist*, 64(5): 972–984.

Munn, N. D. (1986). *Walbiri Iconography: Graphic Representation and Cultural Symbolism in a Central Australian Society*. Chicago, IL: University of Chicago Press.

Nakazawa, J. (2005). Development of manga (comic book) literacy in children. In: D. W. Shwalb, J. Nakazawa, and B. J. Shwalb (eds), *Applied Developmental Psychology: Theory, Practice, and Research from Japan* (pp. 23–42). Greenwich, CT: Information Age Publishing.

Nielsen, J., and Wichmann, S. (2000). America's first comics? Techniques, contents, and functions of sequential text–image pairings in the classic Maya period. In: A. Magnussen and H.-C. Christiansen (eds), *Comics and Culture: Analytical and Theoretical Approaches to Comics* (pp. 59–77). Copenhagen, Denmark: Museum of Tusculanum Press.

Nöth, W. (1990). Comics. *Handbook of Semiotics* (pp. 472–475). Indianappolis, IN: University of Indiana Press.

Peeters, B. (1991). *Case, planche, et récit: Lire la bande dessinée*. Paris: Casterman, 1998.

Saraceni, M. (2000). *Language beyond Language: Comics as Verbo-Visual Texts*. Doctoral dissertation, University of Nottingham, UK.

Saraceni, M. (2001). Relatedness: aspects of textual connectivity in comics. In: J. Baetens (ed.), *The Graphic Novel* (pp. 167–179). Leuven, Belgium: Leuven University Press.

Saraceni, M. (2003). *The Language of Comics*. New York: Routledge.

Saussure, F. de (1916). Course in general linguistics. Translated by Roy Harris. Chicago, IL: Open Court Classics, 1972.

Stainbrook, E. J. (2003). *Reading Comics: A Theoretical Analysis of Textuality and Discourse in the Comics Medium*. Doctoral dissertation, Indiana University of Pennsylvania, Indiana, PA.

Töpffer, R. (1845). *Enter: The Comics. Rodolphe Töpffer's Essay on Physiognomy and the True Story of Monsieur Crépin*. Translated by E. Wiese. Lincoln, NE: University of Nebraska Press, 1965.

Wilson, B. (1974). The superheroes of J. C. Holz: plus an outline of a theory of child art. *Art Education*, 27(8): 2–9.

Wilson, B. (1988). The artistic tower of Babel: inextricable links between culture and graphic development. In: G. W. Hardiman and T. Zernich (eds), *Discerning Art: Concepts and Issues* (pp. 488–506). Champaign, IL: Stipes Publishing.

Wilson, B., and Wilson, M. (1977). An iconoclastic view of the imagery sources in the drawings of young people. *Art Education*, 30(1): 4–12.

Part I

Theoretical Approaches to Sequential Images

2

Linguistically Oriented Comics Research in Germany

Janina Wildfeuer and John Bateman

1. Introduction

In the 1960s and 1970s, there was a significant increase in the analysis of diverse cultural artefacts such as advertisements, fashion, photography and film that was largely inspired by the early semiotic work of Roland Barthes (Barthes, 1977). These early structuralist descriptions of cultural products and behaviours of all kinds were felt in Germany as elsewhere. Within linguistics, this led many to look beyond the traditional boundaries of the sentence, giving rise to the nascent field of textlinguistics (cf. de Beaugrande and Dressler, 1981). This involved inputs from explorations of the formal semiotic and literary treatments of narratives (Todorov, 1966; Greimas, 1966) as well as the goal of covering more extensive ranges of 'naturally occurring' language use.

Much of this use occurred in contexts where linguistic accounts alone would evidently not cover the entire communicative event – most typically in document types such as advertisements and comics where the non-verbal contribution is impossible to overlook (cf., in the German context, Kloepfer, 1977; Spillner, 1982; Posner, 1986). A growing number of moves to follow Barthes in opening up a broader range of cultural artefacts for 'linguistic' investigation then ensued and, as part of this drive, approaches in both linguistics and semiotics began to consider combinations of verbal and graphical material as integral components of unified acts of signification.

Several German research projects focusing both specifically and illustratively on comic strips and comics consequently emerged in the 1970s and 1980s, demonstrating an increasing awareness that broadly semiotic treatments of comics, for which Eco (1964) is commonly cited as an initial point of crystallization, offered new possibilities for understanding the medium. Most of these early approaches accordingly positioned themselves within semiotics as much as they did within linguistics, and there was also a range of proposals made for general semiotic accounts that included detailed considerations of the position of language and linguistics within them as well (Koch, 1971). It was consequently quite usual to see textlinguistic and semiotic approaches in combination – indeed, separating these facets is often made difficult due to the entangled historical relationships of linguistics and semiotics as fields of endeavour. In many respects, the disciplinary boundaries of semiotics and linguistics are inherently blurred, making semiotics 'transdisciplinary' almost by definition (cf. Posner, 2009); a brief overview of semiotic approaches to comics more broadly can be found in D'Angelo and Cantoni (2006).

Early work exploring comics from this perspective is noteworthy for several reasons, one of which is to counter the now common belief that attention to multimodality and multimodal artefacts is a novel enterprise. Looking back to the early state of textlinguistics and to empirical approaches to semiotics, both of which received particularly detailed attention in Germany in the 1970s and 1980s, shows that the exploration of complex combinations of verbal and graphical materials was already a very active area at that time. This movement lost momentum considerably in the 1990s, however, perhaps due to changing research priorities or a perceived lack of return on the early investment of effort that resulted from running up against some challenging foundational difficulties, some still current today. Although a general consensus on the nature of the phenomena under investigation was achieved relatively quickly, methods for taking the investigation further and making contact with broader research questions were lacking. Indeed, it has only been with the resurgence of multimodal semiotic and linguistic accounts that has occurred internationally since the early 2000s (cf. Kress, 2000; O'Halloran, 2000; Kress, 2003; Norris, 2002; Scollon and Scollon, 2003) that attention has returned to the detailed analysis of multimodal artefacts and performances in force. As we shall see, this applies to the study of comics as well as multimodal artefacts in general.

In this chapter, we review this development of a textlinguistic, semiotic perspective on comics in Germany, examining both earlier and more contemporary approaches and giving an indication of the kinds and range of materials studied. The accounts we have selected will be presented chronologically, setting out the main methods, theoretical orientations and results achieved. Moreover, we will place each approach described against the broader background of their semiotic and linguistic roots, thereby showing more of their interrelations and dependencies. To help us in this discussion, we begin the review with a brief characterization of some of the major concepts from linguistics, semiotics and other related fields, such as narratology, on which the individual approaches build. Then, following our chronological tour, we conclude with a summary outlook of how we see the field in Germany developing further. Important here will be the reaction of researchers to the very much broader acceptance of both multimodal and text-oriented concerns now unfolding within the international research community at large.

2. Orienting concepts

Many of the accounts we describe here either orient themselves explicitly to the semiotic, linguistic and aesthetic-literary concerns that emerged during the 1960s and 1970s or build on these earlier precursors. For this reason, it will be useful before we start to introduce some of the primary conceptual dimensions this involved. Our discussion will of necessity be rather brief, but will nevertheless enable us to make several more general comments relating and distinguishing the individual approaches as we go through them below. This should also allow connections to be drawn without prior knowledge of the semiotic constructs invoked – although, of course, there is certainly considerably more useful material that could be invoked to deepen the discussion.

When considering input from semiotics – the general study of signs and signification – accounts of comics either draw on specific components of Saussure and Peirce, the commonly recognized 'founding fathers' of semiotics as a field who developed their models around the beginning of the twentieth century (Saussure, 1915; Peirce, 1931–1958), or on explicit attempts to take those foundations further. This included the work by Barthes and Eco mentioned above as well as accounts in the German context such as Koch's (1971) attempt to offer a general framework for semiotics building on then emerging notions of embodied perception and multiple orders of sign systems. Koch's approach will be of relevance to us below since several semiotically inspired research projects in the German context drew on his account and he also adopted comics as one example of a field of application. The actual uses of semiotic frameworks we describe vary considerably, however, ranging from Wienhöfer's (1979) or Packard's (2006) detailed applications of aspects of the sophisticated machinery provided by

Peirce, on the one hand, to rather more superficial adoptions of the basic dimensions offered by Saussure, on the other. It is also unfortunately by no means uncommon to see terms misused or abused.

The Saussurean categories in particular have often been adopted in rather simple, and not always accurate, fashions – a situation made worse by the fact that Saussure does not provide adequate foundations for semiotic systems involving visual aspects, nor for connected discourse or text, both critical aspects for engaging with comics appropriately. More usable notions of discourse and text capable of supporting detailed analysis only began to be developed in linguistics in the 1980s and so accounts applying Saussurean semiotic categories to comics before this had relatively little to build upon. Some of the negative evaluations we see today concerning the relevance of semiotics to the study of comics still draw on this earlier state of the art, despite substantial advances that have been made since in both linguistics and semiotics.

The basic notions from Saussure that appear in comics-related research can be described relatively easily. In particular, we will see in the discussions below use of the following distinctions or dichotomies: (i) the signifier–signified pairing, (ii) the syntagmatic–paradigmatic distinction, (iii) the distinction between *langue* and *parole*, as well as (iv) some rather more general mentions of the conventional nature of sign systems – discussed by Saussure in terms of language being a 'social fact'. Most of these distinctions have found their way into everyday technical usage, reflecting the immense influence that Saussure's ideas had as one of the primary contributing streams of thought leading to structuralism. Given this, oft made claims of the irrelevance of Saussure today are in many ways overstated.

The signifier–signified distinction divided any sign into two necessarily linked components, or facets: the material cue or realization or expression of the sign (signifier) and the 'psychological' corresponding content (signified). Although this is sometimes given less emphasis, these categories are then *essentially* linked with Saussure's further dimension of syntagmatic–paradigmatic relations. Signifiers and signifieds enter into a web of inter-relationships, either forming structural configurations (syntagmatic) or patterns of associations or alternatives (paradigmatic). In short, syntagmatic descriptions set out structural configurations and paradigmatic descriptions define the choices that a language user has for filling and organizing those structures. For Saussure, the abstract language system, or *langue*, is defined precisely in terms of these webs of connections. This means that signs do not exist in isolation, only as systems of 'differences'. This is the first basic feature of Saussurean semiotics that can easily be overlooked by those attempting to apply it to new fields, such as comics: only *alternations* are significant and meaning-bearing – individual elements only achieve sign status by occurring in contrast to other elements or organizations that might have occurred but did not.

The other term in the *langue–parole* pair, *parole*, is the second place where discussions readily run into problems – the issues in this case are more subtle, however, and stem directly from the historical context of Saussure's work. Saussure's primary aim was to carve out an object of inquiry for the development and application of, what were to become, linguistic methods. The *langue–parole* distinction played a crucial role in this: systematicity and linguistic theorizing about that systematicity were exclusively the concern of *langue*, which then stood in sharp contrast to *parole*, which covered the actual phenomenon of speaking, talking, writing, and so on. Even up until the late 1950s and early 1960s, naturally occurring language was considered to be replete with mistakes, self-corrections, hesitations and other distracting features that only served to hide the 'underlying' regularities considered to be the proper object of study of linguistics.

This view has now been modified and in many respects refuted, but for those working with the early Saussurean categories – and this includes, as we shall see, many of those who have subsequently applied the terms to comics – this leaves a problem. Comics are commonly held to unfold in sequence (taking at least some of their meaning from this property) and so have often been characterized more as 'discourse'. Unfortunately, when this is aligned with Saussurean *parole*, the Saussurean model offers little guidance on how to continue because *parole* is precisely where idiosyncratic, context-specific and individual differences appear and so is not subject to the kinds of systematicity that marked out Saussure's main contribution both to linguistics and to semiotics in general. Focusing then on comics 'as *parole*' in the Saussurean sense opens the door to more *ad hoc* accounts separated from the important methodological precision that Saussure developed. This has in some cases been taken so far as to invite rejections of semiotic 'idealized formalisms' as such – a position we see expressed in the German context by Frahm (2010) below, who then retreats (and must retreat) to valuing individual texts and their individual interpretations despite reoccurring claims of generality.

By the 1970s, sufficient linguistic research had been conducted into the nature of texts and discourse to make it clear that there is in fact considerable systematicity at the level of text as well. Thus even at the level of text and discourse we begin to find aspects that conform more to notions of *langue*, albeit exhibiting rather different properties to those found in treatments of syntax. The consequence of this is that addressing text and discourse should by no means be thrown back to a pre-Saussurean methodological uncertainty. Abstractly, this can be summarized in the observation that the following proportionality, still observed in many discussions, is no longer tenable:

discourse:grammar :: *parole:langue*

Accounts employing such categories need to be aware of this and to repoint their argumentation accordingly; we pick out some consequences of this for comics research below.

The increasing focus on text and discourse that took hold in the 1970s and 1980s led another property of semiotic systems to receive attention: that is, the recognition of the *dynamic* nature of text interpretation. Semiotically, this is better anchored in the work of Peirce, and his well-known notion of 'unlimited semiosis', than in the quite deliberately static (i.e., 'synchronic') account of Saussure. Peirce's model includes many statements concerning how interpretation of signs must proceed, relating different ways of being signs to the general process of increasing knowledge about the world. This required a far more general notion of the 'sign' as such, covering both verbal and visual ways of making meaning as well as general semiotic relationships between sign materials and (both natural and conventional) interpretations. In contrast to Saussure's view of the sign as a double-entity, Peirce emphasizes that signs are always constituted by a three-way relationship between a perceptible sign vehicle (called the Representamen), the object, state or event in the world invoked by the sign (the Object), and the interpretation of the sign-vehicle in the process of semiosis (the Interpretant). Peirce also takes this far beyond the well-known icon, index and symbol trichotomy that is often cited or used in both visual and verbal research.

Many of the implications of Peirce's scheme are only now gradually working their way into redefinitions and reorientations at the heart of semiotics, and there is much still to be done; a very readable general introduction to Peircean visual semiotics can be found in Jappy (2013). One example of the continued relevance of Peirce's semiotics for the study of comics is the position accorded to *materiality*. Whereas the direction of research begun by Saussure moved steadily towards a structuralism in which questions of the material with which alternations could be signalled were de-focused, Peircean semiotics insisted from the outset that attention be paid to the materiality of the semiotic process. This central role of materiality in Peircean semiotics is still not as generally realized as it needs to be – particularly by those who attempt critiques of semiotics when it is applied to semiotic systems beyond language (cf., e.g., Rippl, 2004). Such critiques are then actually only discussing (certain views of) Saussure rather than semiotics as such. It would therefore be more appropriate for such critiques to talk of new orientations in semiotics rather than moves supposedly 'beyond' or 'post' semiotics – indeed, the international state of the art in semiotics includes developments in which the treatment of multimodality is inherently associated with the central role played by materiality (cf., e.g., van Leeuwen, 1999). Developments such as these need to be brought into discussions of semiotics and particularly of visual semiotics relevant for comics far more centrally than has hitherto been the case.

Returning to the developments in textlinguistics, several of the primary concerns of German textlinguistics have also made their way into discussions and analyses of comics. For example, from early on, German textlinguistics has addressed issues of text types and text typologies (e.g., Sandig, 1972; Gülich and Raible, 1972), attempting to draw out both what distinct types of texts there are and how these can be identified linguistically by combinations of specifiable linguistic properties. Very detailed work of this kind has been, and continues to be, done. Generally, such work follows the goal of being able to relate particular contexts of use, and categorizations of such contexts, with linguistic and structural properties of the texts that appropriately appear in such contexts. This approach has then also found application in attempts to define and characterize various kinds of visual communication (e.g., Sandig, 2000), comics now among them; one example of this will be seen in the work of Knieja (2013) below.

Finally, there are also further areas which have been drawn on for comics, each introducing their own sets of terms and practices – these include pedagogy and didactics, narratology, psychology, psychoanalysis and literary analysis. All of these have strong representatives in Germany. Pedagogy and didactics played an important role in earlier German comics research, while currently significant input is coming from the growing area of transmedial narratology, itself building on the many foundational works on narratology produced within the German context (cf., e.g., Stanzel, 1979; Martinez and Scheffel, 1999; Fludernik, 2009). Some of this latter work overlaps with our concerns here – although, at the same time, it tends to be already more established in the international narrative research community than is the case with German comics research in general and revolves around classic narratological questions such as whether there can be said to be a 'narrator' in visual media at all.

3. A broadly chronological review

We will now describe the accounts selected for this overview in chronological order, starting with a range of approaches from the 1970s and a summary of works from the 1980s and 1990s, which is shorter due to the comparatively small number of approaches from that time. We then finally come to a more comprehensive summary of the 2000s and the current state. Our focus will be on German approaches to comics that have been articulated within a broadly linguistic or semiotic perspective and so, in this respect, our review will differ from several other useful overviews that have appeared previously (primarily in German).

There is a considerable amount of work to report upon – one overview of German comics research given in the early 1980s by Knilli et al. (1983), for example, lists 601 German-language publications on comics in the period 1947 to 1983 (511 articles and 90 books). The overview sets out lists of publications according to author, type of approach, provides extensive bibliometric information and already documents a considerable diversity in addressed topics, ranging over production issues, the kinds of audiences intended for comics (e.g., market analysis), ideological evaluations, potential effects on readers, the history of the medium as such, as well as more abstract theoretical accounts. Overviews have also appeared in the context of chapters in doctoral dissertations. These often give insightful historical and critical overviews of the state of the art at their respective times of production (e.g., Hünig, 1974; Riedemann, 1988); the discussion offered by Riedemann is particularly informative in this respect and we will draw on it ourselves in our presentation below. A further comprehensive overview of German (and English) works on comics since 2008 and a useful tool for reference work is given by the international bibliographic database, the *Bonner Online-Bibliographie zur Comicforschung* (English: Bonn Online Bibliography for Comics Research), available at http://www.comicforschung.uni-bonn.de/.

For our overview, we will facilitate comparison and contrast by identifying the particular data addressed by each approach – i.e., what kind and range of comics artefacts were analysed, the kinds of methods that were invoked and the analytic units that these methods presume. We will not, however, restrict our description by subject matter or the particular comics that are analysed. By explicitly raising questions of method and analytic units, we already bias our discussion in order to ask to what extent the individual approaches meet the requirements of *empirical* research. As we will emphasize more in the final sections of this chapter, we consider an appropriate combination of theoretically well-founded approaches with empirical methods an essential prerequisite now for further progress.

3.1. The 1970s: an early boom

Immediately following on the re-setting of the research agenda initiated by Barthes, Eco and others, a host of publications appeared in Germany taking comics and visual narrative as their primary focus. Such work often began with a didactic or pedagogical function – as in the work of Riha (see below), Pforte (1974b), Kagelmann (1976) and others. This was caused by the strongly negative evaluations of comics as 'light literature', *Trivialliteratur* and so on, that had previously been widespread. According to such views, comics offered, at best, a 'primitive way of expressing thoughts' and, at worst, actively contributed to a decline in ethical and moral values. As briefly discussed in Bateman (2014: 91), evaluations of this kind were common across many countries and cultures up until the 1960s and Germany was no exception in this. A range of such views are summarized, for example, by Welke (1974) and Riedemann (1988: 41–42), and are still regularly picked up for discussion and critique in introductions to comics and similar visual narratives (cf. Sackmann, 2010).

This prejudicial evaluation gradually gave way in Germany as elsewhere. Comics began to be accepted in the education process and, subsequently, as literary or artistic products in their own right as well. Thus, although we will not focus on the educational use of comics in German research here in particular, several of these approaches are nevertheless relevant for our current concerns to the extent that they also attempted to offer detailed analytic tools for characterizing the form and reception of comics. An important source of input was foundational work in the semiotics of verbo-visual artefacts also emerging at this time. Indeed, in the late 1960s and early 1970s several semioticians in the German context attempted to derive systematic and more inclusive models of semiotics analogous to attempts such as those of Umberto Eco and others in other countries. Another semiotic issue that began to receive attention at this time was the manner in which different kinds of semiotic systems – for comics in particular text and image – could work together. Comics have always been at least partially defined as being a communication form in which image and text productively combine, either as a form of symbiosis, as 'complementary' semiotic systems (Oomen, 1975; Kloepfer, 1977), as a medium-specific form of 'interaction' (Schnackertz, 1980), and so on. Indeed, forty-two per cent of the German publications surveyed by Knilli et al. already considered aspects of the text–image relationship, showing that this central feature of comics has always been prominent in studies in the field.

As more detailed characterizations of the technical complexity of comics as a communicative medium emerged, there was also increasing acceptance of the need to include aesthetic considerations in comics analysis. This can be seen to correlate progressively with more semiotically oriented approaches of other, often non-linguistic kinds, more related to cultural interpretation and art historical questions than to textlinguistics. This also involved a gradual shift from describing the contrasting elements of image and text as something special from and different to 'normal' literature, paving the way for the cross-medial and cross-genre explorations that form a substantial part of today's research agenda.

3.1.1. Baumgärtner (1970)

In a collection of papers about theoretical approaches to 'light fiction' (cf. Zimmermann, 1970), Alfred Baumgärtner's contribution deals with comics as a (graphical) semiological system, following the Saussurean concept of *langue* and at the same time adding notions of Barthes's (1973) mythology. Baumgärtner's analytical focus lies on the example analysis of a single Tarzan story from Burroughs' 1969 book *Tarzan of the Apes* as a case study, for which he delivers numerical counts of all images with regard to their size and format, their arrangement on the page and their relation to the verbal text. With a short discussion of two example pages and the application of the theoretical concepts, Baumgärtner provides a description of comics as information carriers which involve certain peculiarities for the reception process as a time-limited operation between product and consumer.

Baumgärtner first distinguishes between different uses of verbal text inserts: text in captions, text in bubbles as the representation of either manifest or uncertain thoughts, and text in large capitals. These elements are described as part of the so-called surface structure of the comic as a picture story dominated by images and partly filled in by verbal text offering additional information (cf. Baumgärtner, 1970: 74). This picture story operates with a repertoire of signs whose meaning is mostly determined by conventions that must be learned by the recipient and which is thus similar to other semiological systems in the Saussurean model. As a consequence and furthermore following Barthes (1973), Baumgärtner describes comics as a semiological system of *graphical* signs which combine signifiers and signifieds within an associative whole (cf.

Baumgärtner, 1970: 74). He thereby follows the general trend of applying Saussurean theory to other than verbal units without further addressing resulting questions, such as that of how syntactical configurations can be described systematically, for example.[1]

Instead, and in order to learn more about this system, Baumgärtner suggests a more detailed analysis of the deep structure of the comic on three levels of description: those of characters, spaces, and events in and of the comic – well-known categories of every narrative. By working out, for example, how the visual and physiological representation of characters from the Tarzan story reflects their hierarchical position within the comic's constellation of figures, he defines the semiological system as 'second order' – that is, according to Barthes (1973), a myth that builds upon a semiological chain of interpretation. Whereas the visual characteristics of Tarzan without the specific context of the story depicted in the comic would refer to a young man with athletic appearance, they produce on the second level a further associative or connotative connection with a strong and winning character. We illustrate this twofold process of meaning construction in Figure 2.1. This association can only take place within a connotative second order interpretation process building on the first order, denotative construction of meaning.

The same process of interpretation can then be described for both the level of the comic's spaces as well as that of its events, for which Baumgärtner respectively describes first a symbolic meaning without any specific context and a secondary meaning. For this, he later uses the term 'paradigmatic relationship' (Baumgärtner, 1970: 75) in contrast to the syntagmatic descriptions within the particular context of the story. This distinction then prompts him to describe the semiological system of the graphical signs as not representing and reproducing reality, but using this reality

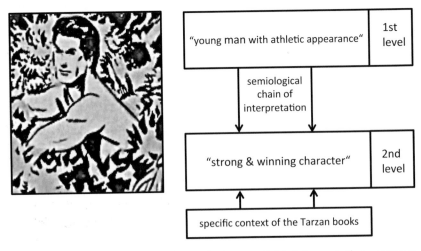

Figure 2.1 Graphical illustration of the twofold interpretation process according to Baumgärtner (1970).

to construct an entertaining story which can only be understood by learning the conventions of the system and its use of the sign repertoire – a position showing many interesting similarities to that developed earlier, for example, in film theory. Nevertheless, Baumgärtner's approach subsequently falls behind its initially promising attempt to systematically describe the features of comics. His primary goal of taking into consideration the relationship between product and consumer is also not really achieved – a fact at least partially attributable to deficiencies in the applicability of Saussurean terms to non-verbal artefacts and their concrete analysis.

3.1.2. Koch (1971)

Walter Koch's *Varia Semiotica* argues that the establishment of structures at increasingly abstract levels is a necessary feature of 'understanding' and acting in the world, occurring whenever any continuous set of stimuli is mapped to a more restricted set of equivalence classes. Thus, for Koch, semiotics and its tasks begin with basic perception, no matter how biologically simple. The construction of more sophisticated possibilities for meaning, and eventually social and cultural interpretations, builds on finding higher-order structures. This early statement of levels of abstraction aligns well with several semiotic positions, particularly socio-semiotic accounts, pursued today.

Probably the most important theoretical viewpoint developed by Koch is then as summarized in several diagrams in which he explicitly shows the 're-use' of properties derived from linguistics across levels of abstraction (Koch, 1971: 31, 43); a somewhat refined summary of Koch's proposals building on his figures is given in Figures 2.2 and 2.3. The first figure shows how Koch builds on Saussure's idea that the language system might provide a 'template' for other semiotic systems but takes this further showing an early version of the idea that the organization of semiotic systems exhibits 'fractal' properties – i.e., similar structural organizations and relationships that reoccur at different 'scales' (cf. Martin, 1995). Koch sees this as a way of importing fine-grained structures and methods into the description and analysis of a range of semiotic domains, including dance, mass media, film, theatre, music and many more.

The principal properties assumed offer methods for composing hierarchical structure, thereby showing interesting parallels to several proposals for the essential properties of language still circulating today. Four main categories are proposed: morphemes, 'logemes', 'syntactemes' and 'textemes'. These may readily be placed in correspondence with current linguistic terminology and are relatively unproblematic in principle, although how precisely they may be related to one another and characterized is another matter. Significant for us here is that Koch repeats these categories along six levels of abstraction, among which verbal language occurs in the middle (as level 3: hierarchical construction). The other levels are: (1) the referential (and structured) world itself, (2) semantics, and three 'manifestation' levels: (4) phonemes, (5) graphemes and (6) 'representemes' (cf. Figure 2.3).

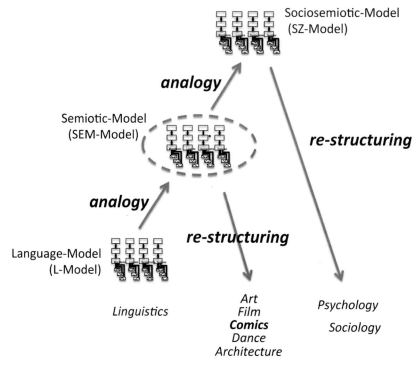

Sociosemiotic-Model
(SZ-Model)

analogy

Semiotic-Model
(SEM-Model)

re-structuring

analogy

re-structuring

Language-Model
(L-Model)

Linguistics

Art
Film
Comics
Dance
Architecture

Psychology

Sociology

Figure 2.2 Koch's (1971) view of the relationship between the semiotics of language, of semiotic systems in general, and their socio-semiotics.

After a few linguistic examples, Koch proceeds directly to a short comic strip to illustrate the framework in action. For Koch, the 'genre' of comic strips is considered to be a language system in its own right (Koch, 1971: 38), in which the sequence of panels is a 'text' and the individual panels are 'syntactemes'. Reoccurring visual elements are seen as capable of picking up and developing topics and are characterized accordingly as 'logemes' (i.e., words in an analogical sense). When these elements appear in various forms, for example, when a particular character is depicted in various postures, these are 'allologemes', also in analogy to the notion of allophones in linguistics (i.e., variations in acoustic detail that do not effect the linguistic identity, or -emic status, of the element). Individual graphical components of these figures are considered to be morphemes on the visual level, manifested through the 'representemes' of individual strokes and shadings, angles and so on.

Koch applies this framework to two examples relevant for us here: a short comic strip and, as an example of several instances of 'mass communication' analysed, a somewhat longer extract from an early Superman comic by Jerome Siegel and Joe Shuster ('Superman and the dam', *Action Comics #5*, 1938). Here, Koch's main aim is illustration and to offer support for the suggestion that his model reveals interesting features of the artefacts analysed; the detail provided is therefore rather less than would be required for more empirically well-founded research and remains descriptive rather

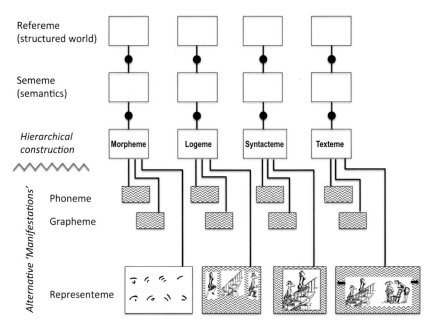

Figure 2.3 Refined graphical summary of Koch's (1971) generalized semiotic model with four main categories (shown horizontally) echoed at six levels of abstraction (shown vertically).

than predictive. However, as we shall see, several researchers subsequently adopted this framework and attempted to set out those technical elements corresponding to the different categories and their levels of abstraction in considerably more detail.

3.1.3. Hünig (1974)

Wolfgang Hünig builds explicitly on Koch's framework, applying it and developing it in detail for a more extended comics example. His principal aim is to derive an account that is capable of capturing the comprehension process of a reader when confronted with visual narratives such as comics. And, in order to do this, he characterizes in semiotic and narratological terms the structures employed in a selection of comics material. Hünig is very clear here in his rejection of the notion of 'visual phonemes', i.e., independently distinguishable units that may be brought together independently of context to establish meaningful larger-scale visual units. By commuting (i.e., exchanging) simple visual forms, he demonstrates that the 'meanings' produced can change in a nonmonotonic fashion, echoing earlier arguments by, for example, Gombrich and others (cf., e.g., Bateman, 2014: 47); he accordingly places *textual* interpretation as his central point of departure (Hünig, 1974: 5–6). This leads him to consider narrative structure as a central method of access to comics analysis, relating also to narratological concerns and earlier approaches to stories, in particular that of Propp's (1968) account of folktales.

The wish to conduct a textlinguistic analysis necessarily brings about the problem of characterizing just what elements and units can be found in comics to carry the meanings they construct. Thus Hünig, as many both before and after him, begins by attempting to characterize just what technical elements are operative in comics. For this, he draws both on semiotic and perceptual sources – particularly theories of Gestalt perception, which provide an appropriate description for the recognition of larger forms on the basis of overall properties of the visual material rather than on a strict composition on the basis of smaller units. Hünig also attempts to demarcate his object of study more finely by distinguishing types of comics – this facet inherited from textlinguistics is important as it allows for the fact that different forms of visual narrative may require differing treatments or show differing properties. The nature of such forms is thus made an empirical question. Hünig proposes two text sorts: narrative texts and 'humorous' texts, although, as we shall see criticized by Riedemann below, this distinction does not appear to operate at a suitable level of abstraction since it is unclear why narrative texts cannot also be humorous. Nevertheless, given these distinctions and the adoption of Koch's general types of semiotic categories (textemes, syntactemes, logemes, morphemes, realizations), Hünig proceeds to detailed analysis by segmenting his objects of investigation along the dimensions defined.

To demonstrate the applicability of the method, Hünig begins with an analysis of the comicbook *The Adventures of Phoebe Zeit-Geist* (Michael O'Donoghue and Frank Springer, 1965–1966), consisting of thirteen episodes in which locations and the involved participants (partially) change. The analysis then characterizes the events involved in order to identify units and participants, thus providing an overall text-segmentation of the analysed data. In form, this is very similar to the account proposed by Propp, involving a relatively small number of narrative 'functions' distributed around the text in reoccurring sequences (Hünig, 1974: 79). By these means, Hünig argues both that the general method is applicable and that, in particular, the Phoebe Zeit-Geist story is constituted by a reversal of the superhero genre in which the main character has none of the usual capabilities attributed to superheroes and is mostly defenseless and subjected to a range of indignities and abuse. Hünig also characterizes the relationships between the narrative functions he proposes and their realization in comics form, considering for example the number of panels that particular functions are allocated and so on. On the basis of this result, Hünig then goes on to consider a corpus of Tarzan comicbooks in order to evaluate whether the method is as general as hoped.

Hünig's goal of characterizing how readers comprehend visual narrative required validation of the categories and analyses by relating the account to the behaviours and responses of actual readers. For this, he conducts a series of recipient studies in which, first, participants had to read selected episodes of the Phoebe Zeit-Geist story with the text components removed and then briefly summarize what they had seen on a single sheet of paper; second, the same participants read the episodes as published and similarly produced a summary of what they had read on a single sheet of paper; and third, the same participants were asked, without being informed previously that this would be part of the task, to produce a third summary, this one twice as long as the second. The goal was to relate the events described in the summaries to the narrative structures analysed by Hünig and to see where misunderstandings due to lack of information arose and which information was included or not depending on the length of the summary to be produced. The results showed that, without the verbal components, recipients made mistakes involving jumps in location and time and sometimes in the ordering of events.

Although showing several clear weaknesses in experimental design, Hünig's attempt as such reflected a very early orientation to an empirical investigation of comics reception and the use of analytic models for making experimental predictions and for explaining observed behaviours. The division made between interpretations based solely on the visual and on the verbo-visual material also allowed some of the details of the visual form and their consequences for narrative comprehension to be explicitly addressed.

3.1.4. Riha (1974)

Karl Riha's short contribution to a collection of papers all dealing with comics as an aesthetic object in the classroom (cf. Pforte, 1974a) mainly focuses on technical features of comic strips which, as media-specific elements, contribute to their sequentiality. Riha does not build on semiotic or linguistic descriptions of these specificities, but rather provides an individual discussion of medium inherent characteristics such as speech bubbles and the juxtaposition of images. The approach can thus be classified as one of those works that focus on questions of the distinctiveness and typological classification of comics, mostly in contrast to other literary works that might be discussed in school. The analysed data comprise on the one hand widely cited examples of early comic pages or strips, such as the *Yellow Kid*, the *Katzenjammer Kids*, *Little Nemo* and *Krazy Kat*, which serve to demonstrate the historical differentiation and thus separation of comics from similar artefacts, and on the other hand some 'randomly chosen examples' from criminal (*Detective Marc Danger*) and adventure comic stories (*Superman* and *Tarzan*).

The starting point of the discussion is then the lack of approaches dealing with technical and formal characteristics and the analysis of structural patterns and practices in comics. According to Riha, it is only these features which constitute the comic's medium specificity. By highlighting differences between caricature series (caricatural drawings in more than one image), picture stories and comic strips and working out the respective relationship between images and verbal texts in these text forms, he emphasizes that only a synthesis and integration of these two sign systems (images and verbal text) constitutes the 'real' comic strip. This comic strip then represents a new way of integrating and accumulating sensory stimuli by a process of 'densification' which, as a consequence, leads to changes in function and quality of the text.

Riha highlights this juxtaposition and interconnection of text and image as a specific feature of comic strips which has consequences both for the layout and structuring of the strip or page as well as for the reading and interpretation process. Particularly the latter is then mainly constituted by the interaction of two reading operations which overlap and complement each other and stimulate interpretation by means of an alternation of image and verbal signs. Riha illustrates this alternation both on the level of the panel as well as with regard to the layout of the whole page, which he claims is normally read following the typical Z-reading path (cf. Riha, 1974: 160).

Riha makes explicit in this regard that this analysis is not only concerned with the question of sequentiality in comic strips, but also asks for perceptual-psychological as well as sociological aspects. This interdisciplinary examination then makes it possible to find out more about the manipulation of the reader, not only by the content, but also and mainly by the structure of the comic page.

3.1.5. Kloepfer (1977)

Rolf Kloepfer's text in a collection of articles on sign processes and their semiotic analysis deals with the general notion of complementarity of language and images in multimedia or multicodal communication. His underlying hypothesis highlights a dynamic and polyfunctional relationship between these two codes, which mutually influence each other in their functions within a text. For his description of two short strips from Schulz's *Peanuts*, Kloepfer explicitly refers back to Peircean semiotics in order to critique static and descriptive approaches, emphasizing instead the dynamic and procedural character of finding and (re-)evaluating signs and their interpretations. He not only discusses the distinction of the three Peircean sign types icon, index and symbol, but also widens his view to pragmatics-oriented approaches, such as those of Morris (1938) and Eco (1972).

Initially, Kloepfer describes the *Peanuts* comic strips as a picture story but, in contrast for example to Riha, does not refer to questions of media specificity or differences to advertisements, which he analyses as further multicodal artefacts. He explains that a traditional reading of the images in the comic results in the analysis of iconic signs which, according to Eco (cf. 1972: 213), construct a similarity to the perception of the object shown in the image. This helps the reader recognize the boy with a striped sweater and specific facial expressions and gestures as Linus, since the comic has introduced the character having this name. By repeatedly recognizing these codes and similar depictions throughout the comics, the dominantly iconic code is then transferred successively into a dominantly symbolic code, conventionalized within the specific context and with the specific features given by the comic (see Figure 2.4).

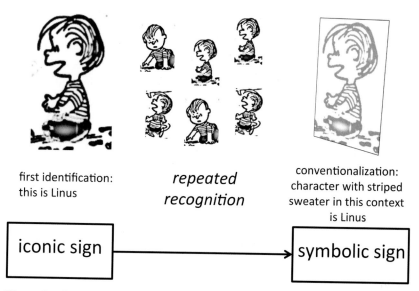

first identification:
this is Linus

repeated recognition

conventionalization:
character with striped
sweater in this context
is Linus

iconic sign ⟶ symbolic sign

Figure 2.4 Transfer of the iconic code into a symbolic sign by conventionalization according to Kloepfer (1977).

This process of transformation is a dynamic process of active and partly unlimited semiosis in the Peircean sense (see above), in which signs are read and decoded by the recipient. This is then at the same time a learning process for the recipient who, as a reader of the *Peanuts* comics, learns about the characters by reading iconic signs and, in a next step, transfers them into symbolic codes. The verbal code as an indexical sign then helps the reader to identify the iconic signs as representing the intended symbols. Language and image thus clearly interact and *reciprocally work together* as the context guiding this transfer.[2]

Kloepfer emphasizes that this interaction and mutual interdependence cannot be analysed by a static reading of the individual codes, but only by taking into consideration the decisive qualities of the specific text type. In the *Peanuts* example, image and language undergo opposing sign processes in which the image code is improved and qualified to express more complex propositions, whereas the language code is being reduced (cf. Kloepfer, 1977: 142). Although not providing further terminology for describing this semiotic reading and interpreting of the relationship between image and language, Kloepfer mostly strikes out in a new direction by highlighting the dynamicity of this relationship and its interpretation. By referring back to Peirce and his description of active semiosis, and at the same highlighting the inclusion of pragmatics-oriented accounts, this is an innovative discussion of the traditional process of decoding signs, which, in contemporary semiotics, is now combined with inference processes and abductive hypotheses about the most plausible interpretations.

3.1.6. Krafft (1978)

In his still often cited *Comics lesen: Untersuchungen zur Textualität von Comics* (English: *Reading Comics: Investigations on the Textuality of Comics*), Ulrich Krafft explicitly situates comics in relation to notions of text by pointing out the need for contextual analysis. With the analysis of more than sixty-five different examples from comics mostly from the 1960s and 1970s and partly adopted from previous work on comics (cf., e.g., Pforte, 1974a), Krafft delivers one of the first convincing empirical examinations of the applicability of textlinguistic concepts for the analysis of comics. For this, he takes as a starting point both the linguistic trend then emerging of finally taking units into consideration that go beyond sentence boundaries as well as considering a distinctly analytic semiotic approach, contrasting with those of art studies, for example.

In order to be able to work out the specific features of comics, Krafft explicitly emphasizes that all individual panels of a comic are always embedded within a specific context and at the same time give context to other panels. They are thus elements *of* a text and should be analysed *as text* and, consequently, are the result of a text segmentation process initiated by the author. This brings to bear several properties crucial for an understanding of text that we will also see picked up below.

Going back to fundamental approaches within textlinguistics at that time, Krafft draws parallels to the analysis of a verbal text as the primary sign that is analysed according to its units and their functions for the text. Panels in comics and further smaller units are then similar to these verbal units and can be described with the help of methods established within textlinguistics, such as the examination of tenses in texts or of 'macrosyntactical' signals (cf. Weinrich, 1976; Gülich and Raible, 1972). Among these, Krafft focuses on so-called reference chains (*Verweisketten*), which give rise to qualities of cohesion and coherence. These cohesive references between panels construct the textuality of a sequence of panels and of the comic as a whole (cf. Krafft, 1978: 27), as well as providing evidence for Krafft's construal of the comic as an image–text interplay or a text of images (*Bildertext*).

The analysis of reference chains also helps to define and distinguish various sign types which are described according to their respective functions in the meaning-making processes. We give an overview of these sign types in Table 2.1. If an element in a panel is used as a reference to previous or following elements, for example, it is a 'comic sign', which is mostly context-independent, represents characters and objects of the story and is thus a constitutive unit of the comic. If this sign has an individual contour and structure and can be clearly characterized, it is understood as a closed sign whose representation cannot be expanded. Elements which can only be interpreted in contextual dependence, in contrast, are elements hierarchically subordinated to the comic signs and understood as open signs. They represent, for example, smaller parts of characters, such as hands or legs, which can only be

Table 2.1 Overview of different sign types and their definitions in Krafft (1978).

comic signs = elements in a panel used as a reference to other elements		

open signs = no individual contours or structure ⇓	*closed signs* = individual contours and structure ⇓	
space signs = construct a scene	*plot signs* = construct events/processes	⇒ *motivated signs* = unbound comic lexemes
		conventionalized signs = bound comic morphemes

identified as belonging to a specific character due to the context. These elements contribute to the identification and individualization of the superior unit and thus count as indices within a specific interpretation context.

Within these categories of open and closed signs, Krafft distinguishes further between 'space signs' (*Raumzeichen*), which refer to and construct the depicted scene and are generally open signs, and 'plot signs' (*Handlungszeichen*), which are connected to events and processes and are closed signs. They serve as chains of substitutions within the network of reference chains, and thus help to establish cohesive patterns of a character or event in the story. Space signs, in contrast, do not substitute with other elements but instead allocate panels to the same space or setting as shown in previous panels. All of these signs are thus constitutive parts of the network of reference chains which characterize the comic as an image–text interplay of substitution chains and sequences of allocations (cf. Krafft, 1978: 60).

Space signs and plot signs are also described as what Krafft terms *motivated* signs. These are generally iconic and give rise to representations of 'reality' and stand in contrast to *conventionalized* signs which constitute the technical features specific to the comics medium, such as speech bubbles, panels, arrows between panels and so on. Moreover, referring back to the work of Hünig and his use of Koch's generalization of lexical and morphological entities across all levels of semiotic abstraction, Krafft sees the motivated signs as unbound *comics lexemes* and the conventionalized signs as bound *comics morphemes* (Krafft, 1978: 107). This then allows him to consider the role particularly of comics morphemes as control signals for recipients in the communication process signalling internal states, movement and other modifications of the basic events and figures shown, as well as exploring other classes, such as metaphorical usages, of independent, unbound signs.

With regard to descriptions by Pforte (1974c) and Riha (1974) that comics are independent word–image 'unities' and so a synthesis of two sign systems, Krafft furthermore argues that the notion of textuality can help to analyse rules concerning the interplay of these sign systems (cf. Krafft, 1978: 110). However, based on a small analysis of a few examples, he concludes that the described synthesis manifests itself only in the respective comic text, thus on the level of the Saussurean *parole*, and not, as assumed before, on the level of *langue*, that of the sign system, i.e., the comic as a medium. Since image and word or verbal text underlie the respective code regularities, these codes are not consequently directly interwoven, but are put together in a text or passage which can then be analysed as instantial components of the whole comic.

In further analyses, Krafft consequently divides the respective comic texts into 'blocks' of images and texts which each are constituted by reference chains and which then help to construct the overall story on the two different levels. Although Krafft remains within the semiotic tradition of separating the various semiotic codes from each other, he also highlights the inter-dependence of these reference chains in each panel, as is the case, for example, when verbal text blocks in the form of speech bubbles are integrated in visual parts. For Krafft, it is this overlap of two heterogeneous code systems that then constitutes the rather special textuality of comics.

Krafft's discussion offers an important landmark in the systematic analysis of comics, setting out many of the features and mechanisms that any adequate account will need to cover. The many references to Krafft's work that can be found not only in linguistically oriented work on comics, but also in literary or culturally theoretical approaches show a wide reception, albeit not always application of his achievements.

3.1.7. Wienhöfer (1979)

Friederike Wienhöfer's starting point is comics' specificity and the peculiarity of the interdependencies of words and images to which she intends to apply a general semiotic as well as linguistic and aesthetic framework. Based on 'problems of covariation' (cf. Wienhöfer, 1979: II), or the distribution of image–text combinations, her main analytical objects are onomatopoeia and their typographical realizations. Onomatopoeia is considered particularly interesting because of its close intertwining of 'verbal–acoustic' and 'visual–graphical' resources. To support systematic analysis, Wienhöfer works with an impressive corpus of about one thousand, two hundred onomatopoetic examples from various comics in different languages, which also prompts her to include some thoughts about translation problems. Wienhöfer's claim of systematically examining inferences with regard to their role and function for the meaning-making process is an innovative one and, besides the general Peircean idea of again seeing reception as an active process of semiosis similarly to several other works of that time, pursues in addition the aim of developing a media specific and adequate didactics of comics focusing on the material inventory of the medium. Wienhöfer's work thus constitutes a particularly complex and voluminous combination of several parallel traditions for the analysis of fine details of the artefacts studied. In fact, it should be noted that Wienhöfer's use of Peirce here is far more precise and far-reaching than suggestions typically found in English-language articles that Peircean semiotics may be relevant for comics research, even those made relatively recently (cf., e.g., Magnussen, 2000). Many of these latter proposals simplify the Peircean account analogously to the simplifications we noted above for Saussure.

Wienhöfer defines comics as an aesthetic object exhibiting both a visual and a verbal rhetorical force. She then sets out a detailed determination of this object's 'formal aspects' by working out a rich repertoire of visual and verbal signs in comics, introducing so-called discursive signs, namely signs in a serial relation to each other and placed in a syntagmatic combination of elements selected from a set of paradigmatic options. Her main focus is then laid on the taxonomy of word-image interdependencies in order to describe the specific character of their relationships; her overview of image-combinations in comics is summarized in Table 2.2. By distinguishing, for example, visual and verbal 'conductances' as well as (spatio-) temporal hiatuses or so-called split panels (i.e., several panels that together show one image), she organizes the relationships between image and text as these are given, on the one hand, within a panel on a microscale and, on the other hand, within bigger, macroscale sectors of the comic page or above, such as the page sequence or episode sequence (cf. Table 2.2). For each of these, she also offers substantial examples in an extensive appendix. She then closes her introductory discussion with some initial thoughts on visual and verbal rhetorics as a further theoretical approach to the analysis of comics.

In a second part of her book, Wienhöfer offers a comprehensive analysis of her corpus with regard to aspects such as typography, expressivity, phonematic and morphematic structures as well as further sign theoretical discussions, closing with a comparison of translations of these onomatopoeia in various comics examples. Wienhöfer's conclusion is that onomatopoetic elements, for which there is no

Table 2.2 Overview of image–text combinations in comics according to Wienhöfer (1979: 78)

single image	row technique		serial technique
	image sequence	page sequence	episode sequence
image–text relationship	image to image relation	page to page relation	episode to episode relation
microscale	I	II	III
	macroscale		

intrinsically linguistic tool to describe aspects of iconicity or similarity, can best be captured with the help of Peircean semiotics and a discussion of 'icons' and 'super-icons' (Wienhöfer, 1979: 294–299). The idea here essentially is that whereas the use of typography in normal text serves primarily a semiotically 'null' role of easing identification with little contribution to signification, in the case of onomatopoeia in comics there is a doubling of semiotic potential: both language and typography contribute to the meaning-making process, or semiosis, as suggested in Figure 2.5. Each of the two triangles shown in the figure corresponds to a Peircean 'sign' involving an object (referent), a representamen (sign vehicle or medium) and an interpretant (sign interpretation). Wienhöfer therefore suggests that the interpreted verbal sign is brought together with the object of the typographical sign, which then gives rise to a further composed aesthetic interpretation: the comic onomatopoeia, or 'super-icon', appearing on the right of the figure.

Crucially, each of the triangles in the figure draws attention to the distinct contributions of the two distinct repertoires of signs involved, their material bases and individual conventions of use. Wienhöfer sets out, for example, something of the range of properties of the verbal signs that support their use for particular ends, such as rhythm, glides, sharp beginnings or ends, gradual beginnings and ends, and so on (Wienhöfer, 1979: 302). Continuing in this vein, she fills out the meanings added into the interpretative process following a detailed and comprehensive description in terms of Peirce's immediate and dynamic object, the dynamic and final interpretant and the triadic relations between them. The result serves to track processes of semiosis from typography through to aesthetic and emotional effect. The Peircean notions of active semiosis and sign interpretation are therefore predominant on all levels and Wienhöfer joins the ranks of those works that mostly focus on more general description of signs and their dynamic interpretation. Wienhöfer's account therefore contrasts with more dictionary-like treatments such as Havlik's (1981) listing of over two thousand two hundred onomatopoeic forms and their uses in German comics from around the same time, and presents not only examples of onomatopoeia but also attempts to explain just how and why they work semiotically.

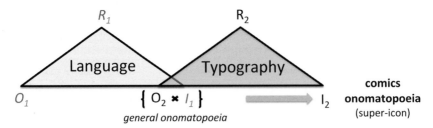

Figure 2.5 Wienhöfer's view of the basic semiotic structure of onomatopoeia in comics as two combined Peircean sign-triangles (Representamen, Object and Interpretant); adapted from Wienhöfer (1979: 295).

3.2. Consolidation and breadth: the 1980s and 1990s

Following this veritable explosion of work that we have selected from in the 1970s, the research appearing in the 1980s builds on the foundations laid, considering other examples for analysis and extending the analysis schemes available. This work can in many senses be said to culminate with the very extensive and closely argued treatment of the comic form by Kai Riedemann, whose analysis draws on most of the preceding positions and sets out a further highly detailed and well-motivated framework within which comics may be classified and analysed. Other work from this period includes, for example: Strobel (1987), Grünewald (1991) and Itälä's (1994) application of the linguistic concept of cohesion (Halliday and Hasan, 1976) to relations between text and images in comics, which is not directly German research although published in German. Common themes that continued were the need to define comics more effectively, particularly as the range of artefacts falling under visual narrative became more established, and more explicit attempts at broad classification in literature and across media (Baur, 1984).

3.2.1. Riedemann (1988)

Kai Riedemann's basic starting point is one that echoes through much of the previous research and which has only grown more important as time goes on. The research challenge is to explain how individual panels may combine in the process of interpretation to form larger coherent units *without* assuming that the meaning of the panels is already fixed out of context. This therefore rejects the idea of visual compositionality and adopts again more of the Peircean dynamism in interpretation insisted on by Kloepfer, Wienhöfer and others. Riedemann's approach is to take up the challenge of providing 'contextual' interpretations of the contributions made by the various components of comics, considered very broadly over individual pictorial elements, textual contributions and larger configurations and combinations of such information. On the basis of this theoretical account, Riedemann then provides one of the most theoretically detailed and empirically broad analyses of Schulz's *Peanuts* attempted to date, drawing on nine collected volumes with strips from 1976 to 1983 to motivate the description followed by a detailed quantitative evaluation of volumes 21 and 22 (1976–1978), each with 188 pages, to articulate fine-grained analyses.

Riedemann begins as do many with the question of definition, drawing on the usual text and image combination as extended by its use for narrative. To this, he adds the basic question of just which levels or facets of context need to be considered in order to characterize precisely the contextual influences on the visual material appearing. Here, he criticizes many previous definitions as mixing issues of form (e.g., 'comics contain speech balloons and panels'), function ('storytelling'), material distribution ('appear in newspapers, in magazines', etc.), and genre ('humorous', 'adventure', etc.) and seeks to provide a more rigorous definition by clearly separating out the contributing factors. To do this, Riedemann makes stronger use of notions of textlinguistics and the kinds of analytic questions that this requires – for example, he argues that important for an account is not the question of *where* a comic strip might appear (e.g., in a newspaper) but rather the issue of what consequences that placement might have on the form and content of the resulting comic strips (e.g., short in length, reoccurring characters, closed stories or explicit seriality, etc.). By these means, Riedemann is able to set out a far more homogenous and focused view of his object of analysis as a kind of text serving particular functions and exhibiting certain structural properties.

Peanuts is selected for the investigation because of the well-established nature of this particular comic strip and its positive critical acclaim. Riedemann then also further refines some of the previous notions of text types (often mixed with publication forms) that had been applied to comics – for example, Fuchs and Reitberger's (1973) division according to comic strip, comic book and comic album. Riedemann introduces a particular subtype of comic strip, the *gag-strip*, to which he allocates *Peanuts*. This is an important step that is still too often paid insufficient attention: as Riedemann makes clear, it is quite possible that different types of comics may well exhibit different kinds of structures, and so one needs to be explicit about just what kind of comic one is investigating. He argues that the 'gag'-like structure of *Peanuts* is going to give rise to short sequences with a build-up and a punchline, which may not at all generalize to other uses of the comics form.

Riedemann then considers just what kinds of facets the notion of 'context' might have, again thoroughly reviewing the different options available. In the end, he chooses to focus on the 'text-internal' context – that which today we might describe more as 'co-text' – since this is the only information that is equally available to both producer *and* receiver. This leads him to a brief discussion of the nature of communication, picking out a broad sender-message-receiver model where the message is to be considered from the perspective of being a carrier of semiotically charged information. Here he argues that, for comics, a methodology must be open to discovering meaning-making elements in any of the physical elements that might be exchanged; this is described in terms of Posner's (1980: 688) extended notion of 'linguistic poetics'. The essential idea is that it is up to the analysis to find which physical traces are serving which kinds of communicative functions and that this discovery is, in the last resort, a necessarily creative component of the work done by an interpreter (which includes the analyst). An approach of this form naturally relates both to quite modern views of textuality, particularly in the context of multimodality and semiotics (cf. Bateman, 2011) and to the critical role of 'codes' as conventionalized sources of interpretative decisions. Finally, Riedemann emphasizes that this is to consider comics, and the gag-strip *Peanuts* in particular, as *texts* – the interpretation of any of the components contributing to the text must be made in the light of this.

Riedemann also draws the lesson from previous approaches – particularly those of Koch and Hünig – that at certain levels of analysis there needs to be a switch from a textual, structural account to a perceptual, cognitive approach. This is motivated in terms of the levels of units introduced by Koch – when moving below the morpheme to consider how these might be recognized, it is necessary to invoke principles of Gestalt perception so that any inappropriate 'bottom-up' composition can be avoided. Then, with morphemes and conventionalized elements – such as the reoccurring figures and characters of the *Peanuts* strip – in place, Riedemann argues that even individual panels are going to have a complex internal organization and be capable of carrying substantial meaning in their own right. This means that they too should rather be considered as 'textemes', in Koch's terms, and are not simply elements to be combined 'syntactically' or, following Krafft, to be given meaning only in combination (Riedemann, 1988: 46).[3] This provides the necessary flexibility in interpretation that Riedemann is aiming for and opens up appropriately the question of how meaningful elements can be combined to produce new meanings – a central question addressed subsequently both in cognitive approaches to discourse interpretation and in formal linguistic accounts of dynamic semantics. Much of what Riedemann discusses is therefore compatible with a broad range of approaches to text and discourse that have been developed since.

With this foundation in place, Riedemann then returns to his starting question of just how, and in what ways, the (text-internal) context of a comic contributes to and constrains a comic's recipient's interpretations of the visual–verbal elements and combinations occurring. Thus, rather than assuming that visual elements may be defined independently of their use in context in some kind of lexicon, as attempted by some earlier work, he opens up the possibility that it is the contribution made to specific texts that is decisive and so sets out to explore this in detail by focusing on the specific forms present in his corpus. The resulting description provided is then substantial. The visual, verbal and typographical means employed for expressing movement, internal mental states, audible events, framing/perspective choices, communicative events, text–image relations and verbovisual rhetoric and many more are subjected to detailed analysis. Taken together, the results argue that Schulz is able in *Peanuts* to move to a quasi-lexicalized communicative form, where paradigmatic conventionalized alternatives are available for pre-structuring interpretations in all of the areas addressed (Riedemann, 1988: 302). This then draws increasingly on the knowledge of the readers of *Peanuts* concerning those conventions, defining in effect a comic-specific 'semiotic mode' that can be employed with considerable flexibility and succinctness.

Riedemann concludes by pointing out that his detailed treatment of *Peanuts* and the descriptive mechanisms uncovered still need to be explored for other comics and types of comics; one more recent application building partly on his framework can be found, for example, in Krichel's (2006) treatment of Bill Watterson's *Calvin and Hobbes*.

3.2.2. Weber (1989)

Heinz Weber's approach explicitly places itself as a component of textlinguistics, asking questions concerning the textlinguistic notions of connection, coherence and cohesion and their possible application to comics (cf. de Beaugrande and Dressler, 1981). Working towards this, he also draws extensively on previous work from film theory, therefore exploring further the transmedial and crossmedial properties of comics as a visual medium. Weber's description is also one of the few that is written in English in any case and so our characterization of it can be quite brief.

Weber divides the descriptive task of analysing comics into three main areas or 'sections': a graphic section, a cinematographic section and a textual section. The graphic section captures the usual resources of pictorial representation, page layout, colouring, etc. The textual section covers the verbal utterances of the participants in the comics and the, in filmic terms, non-diegetic textual material of captions, intertitles and so on. Weber's primary contribution is then in the inclusion of the cinematographic section, which focuses on the constructed *dynamics* of comics – i.e., the succession of panels and accompanying changes or variation in aspects of framing, 'camera' angles, distance and so on. The use of such cinematographic devices when describing comics naturally raises issues of its own, although as long as this is understood as potentially requiring media-specific reinterpretations, it does appear to offer a useful way into examining how comics are being constructed.

After introducing these distinct areas, Weber goes on to characterize several phenomena important for comics in terms of 'combinations' or interactions between them. This is also important in that it enables him to recognize that, for example, text may be being used both in order to express verbal utterances and, due to typographical or other pictorial variation, graphically expressed effects as well. A further example Weber offers is of 'speed lines', which he sees as involving both the graphic and cinematographic sections. Weber also draws some interesting comparisons between the structure of comics and (particularly German) accounts proposed at that time for filmic structure and there is potentially much more here to consider.

Weber concludes by pointing out that he has in his account focused primarily on structural aspects of the comics he has analysed – i.e., on their *syntagmatic* organization. Although this succeeds in at least delineating many techniques at work for establishing connectivity in panel sequences, he argues that future work will need also to address paradigmatic aspects, bringing in attention to 'semantic and pragmatic' relations also.

3.3. Re-emergence: the 2000s and after

As can be seen in our selection above, the number of new theoretical or empirical studies appearing in German on comics in the 1990s was relatively low. This is also somewhat paradoxical in that it was precisely in the 1990s that comics research established itself in Germany, with the formation of several important research groups. However, many of these drew on input from literature and cultural studies and so the main work appearing at that time does not then meet our present selection criteria. For a time, the detailed, but then also complex, semiotic accounts appeared to have secured the foundations and it was considered necessary for other frameworks to address higher levels of abstraction as comics and related forms took their place alongside other forms of literature and cultural aesthetic artefacts. It was then only in the 2000s that substantial publications began again to appear that returned to some of the basic questions concerning how comics can be interpreted by their recipients, drawing on textlinguistic and semiotic foundations in order to state their questions in ways that might be addressed empirically.

Since 2000, there has also been an explosion in German-language introductions to the form and study of comics. There are many textbook and basic introductions, each of which leads readers through the primary technical features assumed for comics – in most respects not differing substantially from the detailed descriptions already given in work in the 1970s and 1980s – as well as setting out basic narratological concerns for describing storytelling transmedially. Examples include Grünewald (2000), Schüwer (2008) and Dittmar (2011). Developments in the aesthetics of comics have also appeared combining formal, cognitive, literary and art history concerns (Hein et al., 2002). The extent to which these can also feed into empirical studies is, however, still unclear as this is often not a goal.

Finally, 2005 also marked the establishment of the *Gesellschaft für Comicforschung* ('ComFor': Society for Comics Research), which now involves a continuously growing group of researchers bringing together research related to comics within several interdisciplinary events and workshops.

3.3.1. Packard (2006)

For our selection from the 2000s, we begin with Stephan Packard's *Anatomie des Comics* (English: 'Anatomy of Comics') since this is one approach that goes significantly beyond repeating previous descriptions of comics' technical features and assumed sign inventories (Packard, 2006). Packard sets out on what he terms an 'experiment' in the analysis of comics in which he combines aspects of Peirce's semiotics and the psychoanalytic approach of Jacques Lacan to build an analytic framework capable, on the one hand, of fine-grained description of comics and, on the other hand, of relating those descriptions to certain psychoanalytic constructs.

His combination of Peirce and Lacan builds on a formal approach to segmenting semiotically charged materials inspired by Peirce's existential graphs – a diagrammatic form of logical representation that has only relatively recently been shown to exhibit important formal properties of logics in general – and Spencer-Brown's (1969) *Laws of Form*. The relation to Lacan is built drawing on Lacan's discussion of metonymy as remaining within boundaries and metaphor as going beyond or transgressing boundaries. Packard sees this 'remaining within' or 'going beyond' as itself metaphorically related to the notions of boundaries inherent in both Peirce's existential graphs and Spencer-Brown's graphical notations. While such a combination may be somewhat contentious and is certainly unusual regarding its technical foundations, it does provide Packard with a systematic way of exploring the signifying practices of comics in a way that itself transcends notions of text and image, not only allowing both pictorial and verbal elements to be combined in analyses but also opening up aspects of how comics might acquire their affective meaning. This latter is an area that is certainly under-addressed in the other more textlinguistic-oriented approaches we have discussed, although more common in literary-style analyses. Consequently, Packard also adopts later in his analyses ideas from Bakhtin, particularly that of the chronotope, which concerns how language and discourse structure space and time (Bakhtin, 1981: 84–258); this then further bridges detailed analysis and well-established literary and aesthetic concerns.

Packard starts with a sustained critique of the idea that the meaning of comics can be built compositionally from meanings already inherent in individual panels, thus echoing several of the arguments we have seen so far voiced against compositionality. Moreover, referring back to Krafft's work, he argues that although a contextualization of panels is necessary for a comprehensive account of interpretation, it is not sufficient to describe comics as similar to verbal language. Comics panels provide more complex structures and also independent content that need further examination from a broader semiotic perspective. To characterize this more complex process of building meaning from sequences of panels, Packard applies both the Peircean tradition of unlimited semiosis and the three kinds of logical inference that Peirce distinguishes: deduction, induction and abduction (Packard, 2006: 99). Packard then offers illustrations of these different kinds of semiotic work necessary for building interpretations. Deduction is the most direct, straightforward manner of finding meaning in the medium, that is, in the concrete panels and sequences of panels – for example: recognizing reoccurring visual elements as repeated instances of a single figure, such as Donald Duck (Packard, 2006: 102). Induction is then the mechanism that Packard suggests is responsible for grouping panels together into larger units or sequences (Packard, 2006: 104): that is, a 'macrostructure' in the sense developed in textlinguistics by, for example, van Dijk (1980). Finally, abduction is intended to capture the process by which a 'rule' can be found explaining why it is that certain material is presented in a comics sequence at all (Packard, 2006: 118) – that is, a general assumption that can *motivate* what is shown, rendering its occurrence intelligible. Packard derives this view drawing on Peirce's descriptions of semiosis and the necessity for augmenting iconic representations with indexical references in the service of achieving fully fledged symbols, which may function as propositions and participate in 'arguments'.

Packard's unusually deep consideration of comics' semiotic foundations leads him to group the phenomena of interest in comics analysis rather differently to most other approaches. Whereas traditionally, in Germany as elsewhere, comics have been considered as primarily hybrid messages combining text and image in sequence, Packard considers this hybridity to be only a secondary phenomenon. As he notes, this also cannot be considered a medium-defining characteristic as it is perfectly possible to have comics without words. In this part of the discussion, he presents interesting considerations of the necessarily distinct contribution of texts – following the requirements of verbal language (syntax, semantics, and so on) – and that of sequences of images – that follow their own principles of combination.

The primary hybridity involved in comics according to Packard is then the medium-intrinsic one of allowing already complex internally structured and meaningful segments, that is, panels, to build into further structured and meaningful units. Packard rejects here any notions of simple connections between, for example, panels and temporal intervals or points and draws attention to cases where panels may involve complex temporal and spatial extents of their own. Combining the information contributions of such complex entities is seen as a major challenge, and it is to help resolve this that he introduces the notion of the sign space (*Zeichenraum*) as a place in which semiotic interpretations can unfold drawing on Bakhtin's chronotope. In Packard's account, a developing space involving the characters, their actions, setting and so on needs to be assumed and individual panels may segment and provide perspectives on this space as the comic creators deem fit with no requirement that 'snapshots' or other temporally restricted realizations occur – that is, the storyworld information given in any panel may overlap or be simultaneous with that in other panels, may share or reveal other aspects of the setting, and so on (Packard, 2006: 83).[4] This position therefore shares many similarities with critiques made elsewhere of a too tight linking of panels and 'moments' (cf., e.g., McCloud, 1993; Cohn, 2010).

The specific descriptive framework offered by Packard then consists primarily of a graphical representation, inspired by those of Peirce and Spencer-Brown, of the constitutive semiotic elements contributing to any panel. These range freely over the material present in any panel reflecting the secondary nature of the text–image distinction as far as Packard is concerned. The identified elements then function as starting points for considerations of the ways in which various selected comics examples construct their meanings and are taken to give rise to particular affects for their readers. Detailed discussions are offered in three short analyses of Gaiman's

Sandman, Ott's single-page comic *Alice im Wunderland* and Marvel's *Captain America*. Here, as elsewhere, however, the analysis is illustrative rather than broadly empirical.

Packard makes several connections between his approach and ideas developed in textlinguistics with respect to the processes of describing and understanding verbal texts and so taking this discussion further would be an interesting direction for future research. Packard's developing definition of comics applies in important respects just as well to verbal discourse as it does to comics (Packard, 2006: 71–84), and we saw above that he explicitly relates aspects of comics interpretation to macrostructures as proposed for verbal discourse. There are, however, further comparisons and similarities yet to be drawn out. For example, Packard sees the main contribution of textlinguistic accounts as lying in the area of the inductive construction of macrostructures although many modern accounts of verbal discourse rely directly on abductive inferences, offering additional mechanisms for characterizing many of the phenomena that Packard is grappling with also; we have described this approach to comics interpretation elsewhere (cf. Bateman and Wildfeuer, 2014). This relation could also therefore be considered more closely. Nevertheless, the issues that Packard raises in his illustrative examples are extremely valuable for all those wishing to push the boundaries of comics analysis.

3.3.2. Frahm (2010)

Ole Frahm's *Die Sprache des Comics* (English: 'The Language of Comics') cannot be understood as a comprehensive and coherent argument for the analysis of the language of comics as its title suggests, but is instead a collection of individual studies on comics and their analysis, mostly focusing on aesthetic and comics-specific aspects of these visual narratives. The author works with almost a hundred examples of panels, sequences or pages from comics from different genres and time periods, ranging from early examples such as *The Yellow Kid* through famous scenes from *The Adventures of Tintin* or *Mickey Mouse* to newer works such as Al Capp's *Shmoo* from 2008.

Moreover, although the title of his book might appear to promise a discussion of the linguistic or semiotic character of comics, Frahm in fact turns away from accounts of the kind described above and argues more for an aesthetic analysis of individual works in their uniqueness. He does not consequently focus on particular units of comics; nor does he offer a detailed description of their specificity. Instead, and based on a question raised in Nietzsche's *The Gay Science* from 1882 concerning the sustainability of laughing, Frahm connects Nietzsche's critical comments with the development of comic strips and their claim of being funny, describing comics as 'small literature', a description going back to the concept of the '*littérature mineure*' first mentioned by Deleuze and Guattari and returning again at the outset of our review above. Comics are, in this sense, seen to be innovative mainly because of their small and parodistic character and not because of inter-relationships between image and text, which, on the contrary, 'chase away' every shine and appearance of characters and signs in the comic (cf. Frahm, 2010: 9).

This apparent rejection of the relevance of the interdependence of image and text plays a significant role in Frahm's work, which then goes further and denies any systematic structure of the signs or semiotic resources used in a comic. This is a natural consequence of Frahm's argument that the language of comics is 'ambiguous' and cannot be described in terms of a system, which Frahm – similarly to Krafft (1978) – equates with *langue*. Instead, every synthesis, if any synthesis is interpretable, takes place on the level of the *parole*, on which individual instances of comics 'begin to talk' (cf. Frahm, 2010: 24). Frahm holds comics to integrate writing and image only at the level of the *parole*, the individual speech act, which he takes as also including the act of drawing images and writing and their material reproduction (cf. Frahm, 2010: 13). These composite speech acts are analysed individually and in detail, drawing a host of ideological critical interpretations which, in their own right, are interesting and possibly valuable, but at the same time deliberately divorce themselves from the possibility of systematic investigation. Frahm then argues more generally that any approach to the analysis of comics should position itself more closely to speech act theory than to semiotics, whose well-known achievements by, for example, McCloud or, in the German context, by Packard as summarized above, are seen as losing their way in 'idealized formalisms' and 'semiotic metaphysics' (cf. Frahm, 2010: 15).

Frahm's analyses then follow in the spirit of this discussion by reflecting on specific 'moments' within comics and their individual, specific materiality. He suggests that it is not the recipient's task to create a unity of the heterogeneous signs, writing and image, but to enjoy their specific uniqueness, tensions, contradictions, which cannot then be summarized in any overarching evaluation or formalization (cf. Frahm, 2010: 32). As an example of the directions this engenders, McCloud's principle of *closure* is considered as a mere phenomenon of mentalism, which is not seen as helping in the recognition of the fragmentary nature of the comic or its distraction. Instead, Frahm considers it necessary to work out elements of the comic's parodistic aesthetics and their politics, which Frahm then performs in individual analyses in the two main parts of his book. These analyses then combine portions of Neo-Marxist, post-structuralist and post-feminist theories to set out, for example, the deconstruction of characters in the famous German *Father and Son* comics or the representation of urban structures and spaces in classical comic strips such as *Yellow Kid, Little Nemo* and *Krazy Kat*.

Unfortunately, particularly for our current goals, Frahm's descriptions and his orientation to the idiosyncrasies of *parole* do not prompt him to analyse the variously assumed 'weird signs' in a comic in further detail. Fine-grained properties and individual features of the comics he discusses, such as the panel or colour, are incorporated in his interpretations when they fit. In general, he in fact avoids systematic description of features or specific characteristics in favour of subjective descriptions and readings of aesthetic effects and parodistic elements. Whether these interpretations succeed or not is then in the eye of the beholder, and it is certainly questionable whether the title of this book is appropriate for its content, despite at first glance appearing compatible with kinds of questions raised by the other accounts that we have described. Indeed, in one helpful, and by and large sympathetic review, Packard (2010) suggests that that title may itself be seen as a deliberate parody – interpretation in this direction undermines the reliability of what is being argued still further, however.

3.3.3. Müller (2012)

Marcus Müller's contribution to a further collection of papers on the language(s) of comics (cf. Pietrini, 2012) returns to a more traditional kind of analysis, dealing with multimodal interaction of semiotic resources in comics and the general relevance of the concept of multimodality for their analysis. By exemplarily analysing several panels from the *Lucky Luke* series, Müller focuses on graphical details such as body posture and facial expressions as indices for stereotyped social interaction. Multimodal discourse analysis as well as questions of contextualization, he explains, can help to work out the dynamic interpretation of these indices. In contrast to traditional accounts of simply decoding signs from a semiotic perspective, he underlines the importance of actual meaning attribution due to the specific context in which these indices are embedded and which contain visually noticeable cues that guide the interpretation and classification. He thereby follows the Peircean idea of unlimited and active semiosis and disagrees with any static description of meaning not taking into consideration the specific context.

Müller distinguishes, on the one hand, a horizontal embedding of cues within so-called 'chains of contextualization'. For this, he uses the example of the visual element of raised eyebrows in the *Lucky Luke* series which can be interpreted differently according to the respective context in which they are each embedded. Their interpretation as an index for fear, for example, is only given for the use in one specific panel where these visual signs are furthermore related to other indices of fear, such as drops of sweat, lightly rouged cheeks, a specific body posture and the use of elliptic verbal language and interjections. In a further example, in contrast, showing a different character having the same eyebrows, they serve a different function and represent consternation, since the character's body posture, his facial expression and the language used in the speech bubbles are also different, constructing a further specific context. By comparing these various contextualizations of one and the same visual element, Müller works out that this varying use causes a constant process of interpretation and re-evaluation of the meaning assigned to these elements. As a consequence, this repetitive use has at the same time the function of constructing cohesion and coherence between the various scenes and characters, helping the recipient to (re-)identify the various characters because of the respective elements used for their characterization.

This second analytical aspect prompts Müller in a further step to think about the so-called multimodal display of group constellations, such as that of the Daltons in his example analysis of the *Lucky Luke* series. He describes this multimodal display as the overall characterization and representation of the group by the use of specific visual or verbal elements throughout the comic book or on several pages. With regard to the Daltons, it is in particular their specific hierarchical representation due to their increasing body height, which leads to a visual recognition of this group in several contexts. The further description of this group is, in contrast, rather monotonous and coherent, mostly realized in strong visual parallels of their body posture, for example. The multimodal analysis of this strong 'grammatical parallelism', as Müller describes it, can help to find out more about the representation of the group and their social status in comparison to other groups or individual characters.

Müller's work represents an example analysis for which no further empirical examination is intended, although definitely showing promising potential for such work. By following the, by this time, finally entrenched trend of considering not only verbal elements but also the interaction of several semiotic resources within texts or discourses, he demonstrates the usefulness of this analysis not only for questions of meaning construction, but also with regard to revealing social practices and the interaction patterns that may be reflected in comics.

3.3.4. Knieja (2013)

Jolanta Knieja's work on the structure of comics returns in many respects to orientations such as those of Weber (1989) described above by drawing explicitly on German textlinguistic accounts from the 1980s and 1990s (cf. de Beaugrande and Dressler, 1981; Brinker, 1997). In particular, she focuses on the identification of the specific text type of comics and their prototypical characteristics. Besides this general text-analytical claim, the author also joins the ranks of those accounts that try to give comprehensive definitions of comics as a scientific object. Her focus thus rather lies on the theoretical description and not on the analytical examination.

As a starting point, Knieja (2013: 132) defines comics as complex textual units with a communicative function that can only be analysed with regard to its constituting and complementarily effecting verbal and visual components. Again following the work by Krafft (1978), these elements must then be examined both from an internal, linguistic and structural perspective as well as from an external, functional and situational level – Knieja argues that in more traditional textlinguistic work these have not yet been considered in combination. As a result, it is then possible to work out a default text pattern for comics which shows basic qualities of the comics' textuality, such as functionality and situationality or specific topics and their structuring (cf. de Beaugrande and Dressler, 1981). Knieja's examination leads to a detailed and partly formal description of several functions of the text type of comics whose dominating role is that of entertaining.

Whereas most of Knieja's text deals with classificational descriptions of individual textual qualities, the only promising remarks with regard to the actual analysis of comics are given in the last part where Knieja lists the comics' specific components of the so-called cluster structure of comics, such as the visual scene or drawing, the speech and thought bubbles, para-verbal expressions (which are, in her opinion, mostly onomatopoeia), block-text as well as label lines or arrows that indicate the reading path (cf. Knieja, 2013: 140). All of these elements interact within a functional network which is, according to the author, set up as a hypertextual system in which each component has its particular function. Unfortunately, Knieja leaves unspecified how these functions can be examined in further detail with regard to their meaning-making qualities. Even though she emphasizes the multimedial specificity of comics (though not describing it as multimodal) and the need to analyse the communicative-functional competition (p. 141) of the two codes (the visual and the verbal), she does not offer any further examination or example description, instead simply concluding that the text-type specific definition helps to differentiate comics from caricatures, cartoons and graffiti as well as related text types such as illustrated recipes or advertisements. This then lies a considerable distance from her original textlinguistic allusions.

3.3.5. Horstkotte (2013), and Horstkotte and Pedri (2011)

Silke Horstkotte's work is primarily situated within narratology and, specifically, transmedial narratology as she takes comics and other forms of visual narrative to raise important challenges for core terms of the theory (Horstkotte, 2009). Her analyses of comics thus attempt both to bring out more of their medium-specific workings and to clarify such classic narratological issues as 'who tells?' (i.e., the question of narrators) and 'who sees?' (the question of *focalization* and subjective 'filtering') – both questions that are hotly debated within the international narratology community. Horstkotte's work is consequently readily accessible within that context with several English language publications.

A reoccurring theme in her work is to consider what happens to traditional narrative terms developed for literature employing visual metaphors (e.g., 'who sees' and 'perspective') when the considered medium is *itself* visual. Here she argues forcefully that any simple reduction of the narrative terms to questions of visual perspective or merely optical representation would miss the explanatory point of the narratological framework. In particular, and relating then to the selection criteria for work on comics we are applying here: 'even though it is premised on the subjective filtering of characters' or narrators' minds, focalization operates at the *discourse* level, since it is here that textual signals cue the reader to reconstruct the storyworld under the aspectuality of a specific fictional mind' (Horstkotte and Pedri 2011: 335; original emphasis).

Thus, Horstkotte emphasizes that narratological focalization must be seen as an active process of interpretation on the part of the reader/viewer and cannot be reduced to a more 'surface' description of the visual properties of a depiction.

Although highly compatible with current linguistic and textlinguistic models of discourse interpretation, many of Horstkotte's conclusions orient instead towards the older view that we classified as 'Saussurean' above. For example, within a collection of English papers edited by German researchers addressing narrative structures in comics and graphic novels with regard to their complexity and diversity, Horstkotte highlights several rather complex examples of how panel size, shape, placement, drawing style and other technical features of comics influence the construction of the storyworld in order to argue that 'there is no universal grammar for this decoding as there is in verbal narrative in a natural language, or in the established narrative format of the Hollywood movie' (Horstkotte, 2013: 32). Further, with the help of examples of narrative beginnings from Gaiman's *Sandman* and Moore's *Watchmen*, she states that existing approaches to the study of comics as a narrative medium are not able to fully cover the 'multiplicity of factors at play' (p. 32), the 'infinite variety of graphic style' (pp. 32–33) or the 'discursive qualities of the narrative representation' (p. 33).

Supporting these pronouncements, Horstkotte draws much on Groensteen's (2013) focus on the non-sequential aspects of comics design, in which connections may be drawn more freely across pages and sequences of pages. In her view, all elements on the page, no matter in which structure they are arranged, are potentially influencing the reading process. With a discussion of a page from Gaiman's *Preludes and Nocturnes*, for example, Horstkotte (cf. 2013: 33) criticizes Eisner's (1992) idea of defining comics as linear, sequential artefacts that can (always) be broken down into small units structured within grids and gutters to be filled by interpretation and within which the recipient's linear reading of the narrative sequence can in some way be controlled. Instead, the *Sandman* example is described as a non-grid like layout without any gaps, which, nevertheless, constructs meaning and atmosphere. This and other examples which might even have a stronger grid-like structure do not then justify any general assumption of a linear sequentiality of panels in a comic page, which Horstkotte describes as a 'too reductive' term (p. 34).

Unfortunately, Horstkotte's argument confuses concepts that it is important to distinguish, merging not only 'sign' with 'grammar' and 'linearity' but also 'reading' with 'eye movements' and 'interpretation'. The discussion of how comics pages and other multimodal documents are perceived and read is already a closely considered topic (Cohn, 2013; Hiippala, 2012; Holsanova et al., 2006), and the essential aspect of non-linearity has been taken up particularly effectively by Bucher (2011). It is thus questionable to what extent Horstkotte's characterization of the field as involving a 'dated and overly strict conception of reading' (p. 38) is accurate, at least when moving beyond the primarily literary or narratological circles within which her work situates itself. Indeed, her own remarks on the chosen examples do not move beyond the descriptive and no specific framework for concrete examination beyond broad narratological readings is provided. Consequently, we can characterize Horstkotte's account as orientating to a certain extent towards the more dynamic interpretative semiotics called for within the Peircean semiotic tradition, taking in the interplay of a richer variety of signs than the strictly verbal, but at the same time as exhibiting a rather overstated rejection of linguistic and textlinguistic methods – methods that could open up access to more recent developments in our understanding of the mechanics of interpretation in which her desired 'dynamic hermeneutic process that combines bottom-up and top-down interpretive schemata' (Horstkotte, 2013: 38) has already received considerable attention.

3.3.6. Uhl (2013)

Benjamin Uhl's short essay from the same collection in which Knieja's work appears deals with a comparison between a novel as a prototype of text-based, that is, verbal, narratives and comics as hybrid forms of visual and verbal narration. Its aim is to work out the differences in the representation of time and space in both text types as well as in the configuration of their fictionality. For this, Uhl uses example pages from *Donald Duck, Batman*, Scott McCloud's *Understanding Comics*, as well as *The Simpsons* and *Fantastic Four*. Each page serves to exemplify differences in the verbal or visual representation of time and space. The descriptions and explicit references to the respective elements, however, are relatively short and not very explicit.

The author focuses on the mostly structuralistically shaped morphological analysis of basic grammatical word classes that are used in novels to express spatial and temporal relations between events, characters and objects in the story. According to Uhl, these relations are mainly constructed by function/synsemantic words (i.e., prepositions, conjunctions, pronouns, articles) that have only little lexical meaning, but especially serve to express grammatical relations within the sentences in which they are used. He argues that these words are obligatory for verbal narratives and their representation of spatial and temporal circumstances (cf. Uhl, 2013: 148), which is already a highly questionable hypothesis. Information about space and time in and of the narrative can of course be represented by other formulations that are, for example, constructed by content words such as verbs, nouns and adjectives. Uhl also counts adverbs as function words, which disagrees with general linguistic classifications (cf. Helbig and Buscha, 1988).

In his comparison, Uhl concludes that comics, in contrast to verbal narratives, do not show this obligatory use of function words for spatial and temporal information since it is mostly the visual level that expresses these qualities. As a consequence, it is 'not necessary', but optional, that spatial markings, for example, are realized verbally (cf. Uhl, 2013: 152). Uhl does not, however, further reflect on the visual construction of time and space – which would be an interesting question to ask. Instead, he describes the visual level as the implicit language of the image (cf. Uhl, 2013: 156), which seems to construe it as less powerful than verbal language. This is unfortunate, since several examples of the comic pages reproduced in the article feature interesting uses of layout and structuring of panels, which are definitely worth being analysed with regard to their representation of time and space. Uhl only summarizes that the narrative mechanisms to establish these narrative categories are completely different, potentially implying that they are, consequently, not further comparable.

A further issue for discussion is Uhl's problematization of the so-called 'narrative authority' or narrator in comics in comparison to that in novels. With this concept, narratological approaches normally refer to the question of who is telling the story, which is, in verbal texts, often an actual narrator, talking from the first- or third-person perspective. For non-verbal texts, the question of who (or what) is telling the story when a narrator in the form of verbal text in captions is not available, for example, is a matter of active debate (cf. Packard, 2014) and several accounts fundamentally question the existence of any such authority. It is thus even more disputable whether its 'explicitly verifiable existence', as Uhl (2013: 158) argues, can be seen as a basic underlying condition for the construction of a narrative as suggested in more traditional structuralist perspectives. The author is aware of the general problem, but does not relate it further to more contemporary approaches and discussions in narratology or literary theory.

4. A brief critical evaluation of the story so far

Our overview of approaches from the early 1970s until the current day has shown a relatively balanced distribution of approaches among the accounts as either orienting towards the structuralist tradition of applying Saussurean dichotomies or focusing more on the Peircean broad definition of the sign and his thoughts on actual processes of semiosis. This allocation does not, however, follow any specific historical background of developments or progressions in the discipline of linguistics – on the contrary, there are both early accounts of comics analysis that already tend to more recent developments, such as the analysis of all types of signs in a multicodal or multimedial environment, as well as more recent accounts that re-orient back towards rather dated textlinguistic work (e.g., Uhl, Knieja).

This latter constitutes a somewhat problematic trend within a German comics research community which is, at the same time, now also aiming at opening up towards the broader international context and the considerable advances made with respect to multimodality, textlinguistics and discourse in recent years. While these accounts recognize, on the one hand, that textlinguistic methods will be necessary to deal appropriately with the complex medium of comics, they fail, on the other hand, to respond to the enormous changes that have occurred in the field of linguistic (and other relevant disciplines') approaches to text in the meantime.

In general, almost all the works we have seen consider comics as a particular text type and thus include general thoughts on a textual analysis of the whole artefact – a fact indeed going back to profound developments made within German linguistics since the 1960s, which finally has also included analyses of larger units. A relatively limited number of these approaches delve deeper into more specific theoretical arguments for such text-based examinations, taking a rather broad definition of text as a coherent unit of (verbal or visual) propositions as a starting point. Most of them avoid moving along explicitly semiotic lines and prefer instead a more generic perspective on comics as complex textual artefacts. Newer accounts from the 2010s (e.g., Müller, Horstkotte) then also include the level of discourse which has, as a linguistic subject, attracted attention in Germany only at a relatively late stage of development (cf. Spitzmüller and Warnke, 2011).

A further growth of interest over time can be observed with regard to the question of a joint analysis of verbal and visual elements, mostly in terms of text–image relations as a central feature of description. As a consequence, analyses of only the verbal details in comics have mostly been replaced by examination of both levels – although in the 1970s the verbal level sometimes still seems to have been the major focus of interest, at least to bring about the often naive application of analytical categories for verbal texts to visual elements. Nevertheless, and since clear frameworks for the analysis of these visual elements were only starting to emerge at the time, most accounts showed promising and innovative ideas for initial consideration. Over time, and particularly from the late 1990s onwards, a general increase of interest in and focus on smaller details of the visual level is observable and can probably be explained as a further consequence of the iconic turn in the humanities generally.

Rather surprisingly, however, none of the accounts, with the clear exception of Müller (2012), explicitly follow the linguistic developments associated with this turn in the context of multimodality, which all tend towards the equal treatment of semiotic resources across the board and which no longer see language as the dominant locus of communication. Although a few accounts, also in the 1970s already, describe the multimedial or multisensory structure of comics, applications of the extensive methods developed for multimodal analysis since the mid-1990s are almost completely absent from our reviewed contributions. Similar to the rather slowly evolving changes in the descriptions of text and discourse, multimodality as a research focus within German linguistics appears to be only a newly arising topic still in need of considerable awareness-building concerning its potential contributions.

The same seems to be true for other currently dominating trends within the international context of research on comics, such as the interest in perception studies or eye-tracking research and, in general, the huge fields of cognitive psychology and neurocognition. Whereas Hünig and Riha indeed include initial (and for that time clearly innovative) thoughts on how the perception of comic pages influences their interpretation, advances in these research areas in the last few years seem to not yet be fully adopted. A few first trends can be observed only in very recent developments that have not yet been published and whose potential we review briefly in the section following.

Besides the diverse changes over time, we can determine particular points of interest that seem to dominate a certain number of the accounts. One of those is, for example, the firmly anchored question of defining the subject matter of comics research, which is still an important goal in many works published today, perhaps as a result of an apparently still felt lack of legitimacy of the research area (cf. Groensteen, 2009). Several of these accounts repeat the critique of comics as a trivial genre that brings about the need for a didactic approach (e.g., Riha, Pforte, Wienhöfer) and a more profound explanation of how to understand their 'simple and pre-literary' handling (in comparison to non-trivial texts). There are also approaches that seem to first ignore the textual complexity of comics, while then focusing subsequently on precise description of all elements of the artefacts, including also peculiarities of their materiality – which is also a central factor for those works that define comics as a specific medium or text type. Their main aim is then to distinguish comics from other verbal–visual texts such as advertisements or caricatures.

As a last topic of organization, we refer to the accounts' manifestations as being either theoretical or empirical. With regard to our specific focus on requirements for empirical research, it must be seen as a rather unsatisfactory result that such a high number of works still offer mainly theoretically oriented discussions. Even the rather large-scale and comprehensive approaches of Hünig, Riha, Krafft, Wienhöfer and Riedemann do not provide specific empirical claims which, in a further step, might allow a more detailed inspection of the practical consequences of their theories. Thus, although all accounts provide relatively well-founded and extensively discussed insights into their methodological suggestions, they are not able to provide a solid basis for further empirical examination and so make it rather difficult for other research projects to follow in their footsteps.

5. Conclusions and future directions

We have attempted above to give a broad overview both of the range of approaches adopting linguistic, textlinguistic and semiotic methods in German research on comics and a sense of the now considerable history of work in the area. Although much research still comes from narratology and literary theory – probably also based on the fact that most research on comics is, if at all, academically anchored within literary or art studies – an increasing openness towards and interest in more linguistically and empirically oriented work can be observed. However, conference and workshop programs of the German Society for Comics Research and of other working groups (such as the specific comics network within the German Society of Media Sciences) still include only a small proportion of talks and discussions explicitly dealing with semiotic or linguistic questions and rather focus on specific genres or narrative topics. Approaches such as that of Müller (2012), for example, are thus rather exceptional and stand apart from the general trend.

It should nevertheless be evident that a considerable body of experience in research on the complex multisemiotic artefacts that are comics has now been gathered in the German context. Although semiotically and linguistically motivated approaches to practical comics analysis have much to offer, for them to be effective it is also necessary to follow up theoretical foundations and technical descriptions with empirical investigations. This demands that appropriate methodologies for such research receive adequate attention. Conversely, we have seen that there is currently somewhat of a gap in approaches that are both theoretically well founded and capable of supporting empirical research on a broader scale. Indeed, given the rich variety of complex and sophisticated accounts of comics given in the German semiotic and textlinguistic traditions in the 1970s and 1980s, it is surprising that one of the most common precursors cited for current research in Germany has become the rather simpler presentation of McCloud (1993). Earlier works are commonly cited in passing as 'reductionist' or 'structuralist', an evaluation that engages sufficiently neither with the details of the semiotic and textlinguistic positions employed nor with more up-to-date developments in those fields that would offer much for current research questions.

This situation is not, however, at all specific to the German comics research situation. Indeed, we share here a general critique also raised by Neil Cohn, for example, that many recent criticisms made of employing linguistically inspired methods for comics analysis as a visual medium 'do not adequately understand what language is or hold an outdated view on language' (Cohn, 2014: 58). Cohn suggests that such critiques rest on structuralist views of language and linguistics that no longer apply and we have now seen this in the German context as well. As a consequence, we, like Cohn, also consider it essential for progress that hypotheses and analyses should be pursued in a manner that is supportive of, or at least works towards, empirical evaluation. A further need to anchor this against a backdrop provided by semiotics arises from the need to achieve frameworks sufficiently strong to apply across the board whenever 'comics', however defined, are to be explored. Without a sufficiently strong theoretical background, methodology alone is not going to be of use.

It is therefore heartening that moves in this direction can be found in initial workshops or similar events now being held or planned at various locations around Germany. Here, we do find attention to contemporary questions of empirical analysis coming both from a cognitive and (neuro-)psychological perspective or from the context of digital humanities and digital image processing, for instance. One promising demonstration of such networking is, for example, the newly founded interdisciplinary research group 'Digital and Cognitive Approaches to Graphic Narrative', while further developments in this vein can also be seen in the meetings of established groups such as the German Society for Comics Research. There is also increasing networking at an international level because of the growing number of researchers in Germany that are active internationally rather than in specifically German contexts – for such cases, the link to a specifically German school or area of research is then correspondingly difficult to maintain. Stommel et al. (2012), for example, present results on the automated segmentation of comics pages, while Schneider (e.g. 2013) situates his work with respect to international developments in both cognitive linguistics and cognitively oriented narratology. Similarly, while our own development of a framework for the dynamic discourse interpretation of comics is part of the broader German research context on comics (Wildfeuer and Bateman, 2014), our work is by no means restricted to that context (cf. Bateman and Wildfeuer, 2014). The effects of this internationalization in the future will be interesting to observe.

To further both these developments and the general aim of opening up German comics research for more extensive empirical investigations, it may be useful to return one last time to the question of the definition of comics. For example, Eckart Sackmann, a figure active in the establishment of comics research in Germany, writes as part of his entry on comics in the important German Brockhaus encyclopaedia that comics are neither genre nor presentation form (*Gattung*), but a literary-artistic form of expression (*Ausdrucksform*) (Sackmann, 2010: 6). Broad definitions of this kind, focusing on what is done with comics rather than particular claims concerning their form or distribution context, have certainly been beneficial in encouraging cross-medial comparisons and actively engaging a variety of disciplinary approaches (see also, for example, recent discussions about the terms *graphic novel* and *comics* in Hochreiter and Klingenböck, 2014). Nevertheless, methodologies that would make stronger connections with empirical investigations still tend to be marginalized. As Sackmann continues:

> Although the image dominates over the text, comics are to be seen primarily as a form of literature because, in contrast to the situation in visual arts, the graphical aspect of comics is never a purpose in its own right but always first a carrier of the drama and action.

(Sackmann, 2010: 6; our translation)

This certainly goes too far. Comics 'belong' to literature just as little as Hollywood films 'belong' to art history, or oil painting 'belongs' to interior decorating. Indeed, Sackmann himself presents an example of a comic serving as a set of instructions (*Gebrauchscomic*), a genre rarely addressed for its literary value. It needs then to be accepted that comics may serve many functions and so can be analysed from many perspectives – including literature, art history, graphic design, critical theory, cultural studies, visual communication, and many more. Each of these disciplinary orientations provides methods and conceptual frameworks beneficial in particular cases.

There is one property of comics that remains across all their various manifestations and purposes, however – and that is their status *as texts*. Thus, had Sackmann written that comics be seen as primarily a form of 'text' (rather than literature), then his claim would have been more appropriate – texts can also be used for many purposes and can draw on a variety of semiotic resources. This emphasizes again that textlinguistic views are going to be relevant for describing comics, no matter what those comics are being used for. Moreover, the existence of methodologies and results for the empirical investigation of language use and texts offers a considerable range of techniques potentially valuable for the study of comics as well. Therefore, reassessing some of the older German research addressing comics from a textlinguistic perspective in the light of more contemporary developments in linguistic discourse processing and discourse semantics may offer significant opportunities for furthering dialogues between literary-artistic, cultural, and other more abstract interpretations of comics, on the one hand, and empirically verifiable issues of reception and processing, on the other.

Acknowledgements

This work was partially funded by a cooperative research mobility grant (PPP HK, Project: 56156404) from the German Academic Exchange Service (DAAD). We furthermore thank Stephan Packard and his students at the University of Freiburg, as well as Andreas Veits from the University of Hamburg, for critical comments and useful additions.

Notes

1. Baumgärtner indeed mentions the 'peculiar syntax of comics episodes' and describes the basic pattern of the two example *Tarzan* pages as not only typical for adventure stories, but also as text-type specific structures (cf. Baumgärtner, 1970: 77). For this, however, he does not deliver any systematic overview or system of rules, which would be a logical consequence of the application.

2. The same process can also operate the other way round, as in the case of Kloepfer's second example, *Les frustés*, in which the verbal code is transformed into an iconic sign by losing the characteristics of arbitrariness and abstractness and becoming more and more concrete.
3. *... dass die Einzelpanel sich gegenseitig Kontext geben, dass sie Elemente eines Textes sind und daher nur vom Text aus und auf den Text hin adäquat gelesen werden können* (Krafft, 1978: 12).
4. *Die Panelgrenzen zerschneiden also erst ein bereits vorausgehendes Ganzes; wir werden daher statt von der Simultaneität der einzelnen Panels von dem Vorgang einer Anatomie sprechen, der jenes Ganze in der Struktur des Panels unterworfen ist* (Packard, 2006: 83).

References

Bakhtin, M. M. (1981). *The Dialogic Imagination: Four Essays*. Translated by C. Emerson and M. Holquist. Austin, TX: University of Texas Press.

Barthes, R. (1973). *Mythology*. London: Paladin.

Barthes, R. (1977). *Image – Music – Text*. Edited and Translated by Stephen Heath. London: Fontana Press.

Bateman, J. A. (2011). The decomposability of semiotic modes. In: K. L. O'Halloran and B. A. Smith (eds), *Multimodal Studies: Multiple Approaches and Domains*, Routledge Studies in Multimodality (pp. 17–38). London: Routledge.

Bateman, J. A. (2014). *Text and Image: A Critical Introduction to the Visual/Verbal Divide*. London and New York: Routledge.

Bateman, J. A. and Wildfeuer, J. (2014). A multimodal discourse theory of visual narrative. *Journal of Pragmatics*, 74: 180–218. http://dx.doi.org/10.1016/j.pragma.2014.10.001.

Baumgärtner, A. C. (1970). Die Welt der Comics als semiologisches System. In: H. D. Zimmermann (ed.), *Vom Geist der Superhelden. Comic Strips. Colloquium zur Theorie der Bildergeschichte in der Akademie der künste Berlin* (pp. 71–78). Gebr: Mann Verlag.

Baur, U. (1984). Für eine Gattungstheorie des Comics. In: Z. Skreb and U. Baur (eds), *Erzählgattungen der Trivialliteratur*, Innsbrucker Beiträge zur Kulturwissenschaft 18 (pp. 263–273). Innsbruck: U. B. Innsbruck.

Brinker, K. (1997). *Linguistische Textanalyse: Eine Einführung in Grundbegriffe und Methoden*. Berlin: Erich Schmidt Verlag, 4th edn.

Bucher, H.-J. (2011). Multimodales Verstehen oder Rezeption als Interaktion. Theoretische und empirische Grundlagen einer systematischen Analyse der Multimodalität. In: H.-J. Diekmannshenke, M. Klemm and H. Stöckl (eds), *Bildlinguistik. Theorien – Methoden – Fallbeispiele* (pp. 123–156). Berlin: Erich Schmidt.

Cohn, N. (2010). The limits of time and transitions: challenges to theories of sequential image comprehension. *Studies in Comics*, 1(1): 127–147.

Cohn, N. (2013). Navigating comics: an empirical and theoretical approach to strategies of reading comic page layouts. *Frontiers in Psychology*, 4(186). doi:10.3389/fpsyg.2013.00186.

Cohn, N. (2014). Building a better 'comic theory': shortcomings of theoretical research on comics and how to overcome them. *Studies in Comics*, 5(1): 57–75.

D'Angelo, M. and Cantoni, L. (2006). Comics: semiotic approaches. In: K. Brown, A. H. Anderson and L. Bauer (eds), *Encyclopedia of Language and Linguistics* (pp. 627–635). Amsterdam, Boston, Heidelberg, London: Elsevier, 2nd edn.

de Beaugrande, R. and Dressler, W. U. (1981). *Introduction to Text Linguistics*. London: Longman.

van Dijk, T. A. (1980). *Macrostructures*. Hillsdale, NJ: Lawrence Erlbaum Associates.

Dittmar, J. F. (2011). *Comic-Analyse*. Konstanz: UVK Verlagsgesellschaft mbH.

Eco, U. (1964). Lettura di Steven Canyon. In: U. Eco (ed.), *Apocalittici e integrati* (pp. 219–263). Milan: Bompiani. English translation in Wagstaff (1987), pp. 20–25.

Eco, U. (1972). *Einführung in die Semiotik*. München: Fink.

Eisner, W. (1992). *Comics and Sequential Art*. Princeton, WI: Kitchen Sink Press.

Fludernik, M. (2009). *Introduction to Narratology*. London: Routledge.

Frahm, O. (2010). *Die Sprache des Comics*. Philo Fine Arts.

Fuchs, W. J. and Reitberger, R. C. (1973). *Comics – Anatomie eines Massenmedium*. Reinbek: Rowohlt.

Greimas, A.-J. (1966). *Structural Semantics: An Attempt at a Method*. Lincoln and London: University of Nebraska Press, 1983. Originally published as *Sémantique structurale: Recherche de mèthode* (Librarie Larousse, 1966), Translated by D. McDowell, R. Schleifer and A. Velie.

Groensteen, T. (2009). Why are comics still in search of cultural legitimization? In: J. Heer and K. Worcester (eds), *A Comics Studies Reader* (pp. 3–12). Jackson, MI: University Press of Mississippi.

Groensteen, T. (2013). *Comics and Narration*. Jackson, MI: University Press of Mississippi. Translated by A. Miller, from the original French *Bande desinée et narration: Système de la bande desinée 2* (2011).

Grünewald, D. (1991). *Vom Umgang mit Comics*. Berlin: Volk und Wissen.

Grünewald, D. (2000). *Comics*. Tübingen: Niemeyer.

Gülich, E., and Raible, W. (eds) (1972). *Textsorten. Differenzierungskriterien aus linguistischer Sicht*. Frankfurt am Main: Athenäum.

Halliday, M. A. K., and Hasan, R. (1976). *Cohesion in English*. London: Longman.

Havlik, E. J. (1981). *Lexikon der Onomatopöien. Die lautmalenden Wörter im Comic*. Frankfurt: Fricke.

Hein, M., Hüners, M., and Michaelsen, T. (eds) (2002). *Ästhetik des Comic*. Berlin: Schmidt.

Helbig, G., and Buscha, J. (1988). *Deutsche Grammatik. Ein Handbuch für den Ausländerunterricht*. Leipzig: VEB Verlag Enzyklopädie.

Hiippala, T. (2012). Reading paths and visual perception in multimodal research, psychology and brain sciences. *Journal of Pragmatics*, 44(3): 315–327. doi:10.1016/j.pragma.2011.12.008.

Hochreiter, S., and Klingenböck, U. (2014). *Bild ist Text ist Bild. Narration und Ästhetik in der Graphic Novel.* Transcript Verlag.

Holsanova, J., Rahm, H., and Holmqvist, K. (2006). Entry points and reading paths on newspaper spreads: comparing a semiotic analysis with eye-tracking measurements. *Visual Communication,* 5(1): 65–93.

Horstkotte, S. (2009). Seeing or speaking: visual narratology and focalization, literature to film. In: S. Heinen and R. Sommer (eds), *Narratology in the Age of Cross-Disciplinary Narrative Research* (pp. 170–192). Berlin: de Gruyter.

Horstkotte, S. (2013). Zooming in and out: panels, frames, sequences, and the building of graphic storyworlds. In: D. Stein and J.-N. Thon (eds), *From Comic Strips to Graphic Novels: Contributions to the Theory and History of Graphic Narrative.* Narratologia / Contributions to Narrative Theory 37 (pp. 27–48). Berlin and New York: de Gruyter.

Horstkotte, S., and Pedri, N. (2011). Focalization in graphic narrative. *Narrative,* 19(3): 330–357.

Hünig, W. K. (1974). *Strukturen des Comic Strips. Ansätze zu einer textlinguistische-semiotischen Analyse narrativer Comics.* Hildesheim: Olms. (Published version of a doctoral dissertation at the University of Trier/Kaiserslautern from 1973.)

Itälä, M.-L. (1994). *Kohäsion im Bildtextverbund Comic.* Turku: Turun Yliopisto.

Jappy, T. (2013). *Introduction to Peircian Visual Semiotics.* Bloomsbury Advances in Semiotics. London and New York: Bloomsbury.

Kagelmann, H. J. (1976). *Comics. Aspekte zu Inhalt und Wirkung.* Bad Heilbrunn: Klinkhardt.

Kloepfer, R. (1977). Komplementarität von Sprache und Bild. Am Beispiel von Comic, Karikatur und Reklame. In: R. Posner and H.-P. Reinecke (eds), *Zeichenprozesse. Semiotische Forschung in den Einzelwissenschaften* (pp. 129–145). Wiesbaden: Athenäum.

Knieja, J. (2013). Die Cluster-Struktur des Comics: ein Weg zur Bestimmung des Textmusters. In: O. Brunken and F. Giesa (eds), *Erzählen in Comic: Beiträge zur Comicforschung* (pp. 131–144). Essen: Christian A. Bachmann Verlag.

Knilli, F., Schwender, C., Gundelsheimer, E., and Weisser, E. (1983). Aspekte der Entwicklung zu einer visuellen Kultur am Beispiel des Comics. Der Stand der Forschung in der Bundesrepublik. *Communications,* 9(2/3): 149–189.

Koch, W. A. (1971). *Varia Semiotica.* Hildesheim: Olms.

Krafft, U. (1978). *Comics lesen: Untersuchungen zur Textualität von Comics.* Stuttgart: Klett-Cotta.

Kress, G. (2000). Multimodality. In: M. Kalantzis and B. Cope (eds), *Multiliteracies: Literacy Learning and the Design of Social Futures* (chapter 9, pp. 182–202). London: Routledge.

Kress, G. (2003). *Literacy in the New Media Age.* London: Routledge.

Krichel, M. (2006). *Erzählerische Vermittlung im Comic am Beispiel des amerikanischen Zeitungscomics* Calvin and Hobbs. Trier: Wissenschaftlicher Verlag Trier.

Magnussen, A. (2000). The semiotics of C. S. Peirce as a theoretical framework for the understanding of comics. In: A. Magnussen and H.-C. Christiansen (eds), *Comics and Culture: Analytical and Theoretical Approaches to Comics* (pp. 193–207). Copenhagen, Denmark: Museum Tusculanum Press, University of Copenhagen.

Martin, J. R. (1995). Text and clause: fractal resonance. *Text*, 15(1): 5–42.

Martinez, M., and Scheffel, M. (1999). *Einführung in die Erzähltheorie*. München: Beck.

McCloud, S. (1993). *Understanding Comics: The Invisible Art*. New York: HarperPerennial.

Morris, C. W. (1938). *Foundations of the Theory of Signs*. Chicago, IL: University of Chicago Press.

Müller, M. (2012). 'Halt's Maul Averell!' – Die Inszenierung multimodaler Interaktion im Comic. In: D. Pietrini (ed.), *Die Sprache(n) der Comics* (pp. 75–90). Meidenbauer.

Norris, S. (2002). The implication of visual research for discourse analysis: transcription beyond language. *Visual Communication*, 1(1): 97–121.

O'Halloran, K. L. (2000). Classroom discourse in mathematics: a multisemiotic analysis. *Linguistics and Education*, 10(3): 359–388.

Oomen, U. (1975). Wort – Bild – Nachricht: semiotische Aspekte des Comics Strip PEANUTS. *Linguistik und Didaktik*, 24: 247–259.

Packard, S. (2006). *Anatomie des Comics. Psychosemiotische Medienanalyse*. Göttingen: Wallstein.

Packard, S. (2010). Rede, nicht Sprache des Comics. Ole Frahms ergiebige Kunstlektüren als fröhliche Comicwissenschaft. Rezension über: Ole Frahm: Die Sprache des Comics. Hamburg: Philo Fine Arts. GmbH Co. KG 2010. *IASLonline* http://www.iaslonline.de/index.php?vorgang_id=3152.

Packard, S. (2014). Wie narrativ sind Comics? Aspekte historischer Transmedialität. In: S. Hochreiter and U. Klingenböck (eds), *Bild ist Text ist Bild. Narration und Ästhetik in der Graphic Novel* (pp. 97–168). Bielefeld: Transcript Verlag.

Peirce, C. S. (1931–1958). *Collected Papers of Charles Sanders Peirce*. Cambridge, MA: The Belknap Press of Harvard University Press.

Pforte, D. (1974a). *Comics im ästhetischen Unterricht*. Frankfurt: Athenäum.

Pforte, D. (1974b). Plädoyer für die Behandlung von Comics im ästhetischen Unterricht. In: D. Pforte (ed.), *Comics im ästhetischen Unterricht* (pp. 9–13). Frankfurt: Athenäum.

Pforte, D. (1974c). Zur Produktion von Comics. In: D. Pforte (ed.), *Comics im ästhetischen Unterricht* (pp. 277–292). Frankfurt: Athenäum.

Pietrini, D. (2012). *Die Sprache(n) der Comics*. München.

Posner, R. (1980). Linguistische Poetik. In: H. P. Althaus, H. Henne and H. Ernst (eds), *Lexikon der Germanistischen Linguistik* (pp. 687–698). Tübingen: Niemeyer, 2nd edn.

Posner, R. (1986). Zur Systematik der Beschreibung verbaler und nonverbaler Kommunikation: Semiotik als Propädeutik der Medienanalyse. In: H.-G. Bosshardt (ed.), *Perspektiven auf Sprache: Interdisziplinäre Beiträge zum Gedenken an Hans Hörmann* (pp. 267–313). Berlin/New York: W. de Gruyter.

Posner, R. (2009). Roland Posner. In: P. Bundgaard and F. Stjernfelt (eds), *Signs and Meanings: Five Questions* (pp. 125–137). Copenhagen: Automatic Press / VIP.

Propp, V. (1968). *The Morphology of the Folktale*. Austin, TX: University of Texas Press. Originally published in Russian in 1928.

Riedemann, K. (1988). *Comic, Kontext, Kommunikation: die Kontextabhängigkeit der visuellen Elemente im Comic Strip – exemplarisch untersucht an der Gag-Strip-Serie*

'*Peanuts*'. Frankfurt am Main: Lang. (Published version of a doctoral dissertation from the University of Hamburg, 1987.)

Riha, K. (1974). Die Technik der Fortsetzung im Comic strip. Zur Semiotik eines Massenmediums. In: D. Pforte (ed.), *Comics im ästhetischen Unterricht* (pp. 151–171). Frankfurt: Athenäum.

Rippl, G. (2004). Text-Bild-Beziehungen zwischen Semiotik und Medientheorie: Ein Verortungsvorschlag. In: R. Brosch (ed.), *Ikono/Philo/Logie: Wechselspeile von Texten und Bildern*. Potsdamer Beiträge zur Kultur- und Sozialgeschichte 2 (pp. 43–60). Berlin: Trafo Verlag.

Sackmann, E. (2010). Comic. Kommentierte Definition. *Deutsche Comicforschung*, 6: 6–9.

Sandig, B. (1972). Zur Differenzierung gebrauchssprachlicher Textsorten im Deutschen. In: E. Gülich and W. Raible (eds), *Textsorten. Differenzierungskriterien aus linguistischer Sicht* (pp. 113–124). Frankfurt am Main: Athenäum.

Sandig, B. (2000). Textmerkmale und Sprache-Bild-Texte. In: U. Fix and H. Wellmann (eds), *Bild im Text – Text und Bild* (pp. 3–30). Heidelberg: Winter.

Saussure, F. de. (1915). *Course in General Linguistics*. New York / Toronto / London: McGraw-Hill and the Philosophical Library, 1959. Edited by C. Bally and A. Sechehaye, in collaboration with A. Riedlinger; Translated by W. Baskin.

Schnackertz, H. J. (1980). *Form und Funktion medialen Erzählens. Narrativität in Bildsequenz und Comicstrip*. München: Fink Verlag.

Schneider, C. W. (2013). The cognitive grammar of 'I': viewing arrangements in graphic autobiographies. *Studies in Comics*, 4(2): 307–332. doi:10.1386/stic.4.2.307_1.

Schüwer, M. (2008). *Wie Comics erzählen. Grundriss einer intermedialen Erzähltheorie der grafischen Literatur*. Trier: WVT Wissenschaftler Verlag.

Scollon, R., and Scollon, S. (2003). *Discourses in Place: Language in the Material World: Reading and Writing in One Community*. London: Routledge.

Spencer-Brown, G. (1969). *Laws of Form*. London: Allen & Unwin.

Spillner, B. (1982). Stilanalyse semiotisch komplexer Texte. Zum Verhältnis von sprachlicher und bildlicher Information in Werbeanzeigen. *Kodikas/Code. Ars Semeiotica*, 4/5(1): 91–106.

Spitzmüller, J. and Warnke. I. H. (2011). *Diskurslinguistik: eine Einführung in Theorien und Methoden der transtextuellen Sprachanalyse*. Berlin: De Gruyter.

Stanzel, F. K. (1979). *Theorie des Erzählens*. Göttingen: Vandenhoek.

Stommel, M., Merhej, L. I., and Müller, M. G. (2012). Segmentation-free detection of comic panels. In: L. Bolc, R. Tadeusiewicz, L. J. Chmielewski and K. Wojciechowski (eds), *International Conference on Computer Vision and Graphics (ICCVG)*, Warsaw, Poland, 24–26 September 2012 (pp. 633–640). Berlin: Springer.

Strobel, R. (1987). *Die 'Peanuts' – Verbreitung und ästhetische Formen. ein comic-bestseller im medienverbund*. Carl Winter.

Todorov, T. (1966). Les catégories du récit littéraire. *Communications*, 8: 125–151. Translation available in Todorov (1972).

Todorov, T. (1972). Die Kategorien der literarischen Erzählung. In: H. Blumensath (ed.), *Strukturalismus in der Literaturwissenschaft* (pp. 263–294). Köln: Kiepenheuer and Witsch, übersetzt von Irmela Rehbein.

Uhl, B. J. (2013). Raum- und Zeitlinguistik des Comics. In: O. Brunken and F. Giesa (eds), *Erzählen im Comic. Beiträge zur Comicforschung* (pp. 145–162). Bachmann Verlag.

Van Leeuwen, T. (1999). *Speech, Music, Sound.* London: Macmillan.

Wagstaff, S. (ed.) (1987). *Comic Iconoclasm.* London: Institute of Contemporary Arts.

Weber, H. J. (1989). Elements of text-based and image-based connectedness in comic stories, and some analogies to cinema and written text. In: M.-E. Conte, J. S. Petöfi and E. Sözer (eds), *Text and Connectedness: Proceedings of the Conference on Connexity and Coherence.* Studies in Language Companion Series 16 (pp. 337–360). Amsterdam: John Benjamins.

Weinrich, H. (1976). *Sprache in Texten.* Klett.

Welke, M. (1974). *Die Sprache der Comics. 4. Auflage.* Dipa-Verlag.

Wienhöfer, F. (1979). *Untersuchungen zur semiotischen Ästhetik des Comic Strip unter der besonderen Berücksichtigung von Onomatopoese und Typographie. Zur Grundlage einer Comic-Didaktik.* Pädagogische Hochschule Bonn dissertation.

Wildfeuer, J., and Bateman, J. A. (2014). Zwischen *gutter* und *closure*. Zur Interpretation der Leerstelle im Comic durch Inferenzen und dynamische Diskursinterpretation. *Closure. Kieler e-Journal für Comicforschung*, 1: 3–24. http://www.closure.uni-kiel.de/data/closure1/closure1_wildfeuer_bateman.pdf.

Zimmermann, H. D. (1970). *Vom Geist der Superhelden. Comic Strips. Colloquium zur Theorie der Bildergeschichte in der Akademie der Künste Berlin. Schriftenreihe der Akademie der Künste, Band 8.* Berlin: Gebr. Mann Verlag.

3

No Content without Form:

Graphic Style as the Primary Entrance to a Story

Pascal Lefèvre

1. Introduction

Line drawing plays a crucial role in the visual narratives of comics for both an artist's creative process and a reader's experience. The underlying story has to be told, at least partially, in a purely visual way by these marks on paper (or screen), and the reader has to construct the diegetic world and events on the basis of these marks (Lefèvre, 2011). Line drawings may go a long time back in human history, but the visual system of the human species evolved to deal with natural scenes. Nevertheless, the perception of man-made pictures (some with black contour lines and flat colours) seems quite effortless and usually quite accurate. How this might be possible is a crucial question in this text, but we also ask how individual strokes can form a graphic style and how can we analyse this formal aspect that plays a crucial role in creation of meaning. Style is important as philosopher Nelson Goodman (1978: 40) stated, because the 'discernment of style is an integral aspect of the understanding of works of art and the worlds they present'.

The few theorists of the art of drawing (like Petherbridge, 2010) have largely neglected drawing in the sphere of entertainment. There is, however, no fundamental reason not to include illustrators like Dick Bruna, animators like Tex Avery, and comics artists such as André Franquin in a general contemporary history of the art of drawing. In all these fields, predominantly related to entertainment, it is foremost line drawing, in many varieties, that has played a crucial role. Obviously, the drawings made by these artists were usually just a phase in the production for works reproduced on a massive scale and foremost aimed at children, which may have contributed to a non-recognition or rejection by the art world. While high art neglected drawings for entertainment, there are, however, many drawing guides for comics artists, usually of a specific genre like superheroes or *shojo manga* (for example, Lee and Buscema, 1984; Graphic-Sha, 2001; Coope, 2002; Nichols, 2011), and a specialized magazine *Comic Art* (2002–2007) and many monographs providing references about comics artists. A more theoretical or systematic approach of graphic style in comics theory is, by contrast, rather exceptional.

Here, the topic of line drawing will be approached from an interdisciplinary perspective, connecting comic theory to research in fields like empirical perception studies and theoretical aesthetics. On the whole, this contribution will less be concerned by what lines stand for, than their formal expressive qualities,[1] and will focus on examples from various comics traditions (foremost North America, Western Europe and Japan).

2. The nature of drawings

Before going into drawing for comics, we will consider some common characteristics of drawings in general. Artists, critics and philosophers have proposed different definitions of drawing (Van Alphen, 2008), but let us take, for starters, the prototypical definition by the *The New Encyclopædia Britannica* (1995: 460):

> Drawing as formal artistic creation might be defined as the primarily linear rendition of objects in the visible world, as well as of concepts, thoughts, attitudes, emotions, and fantasies given visual form, of symbols and even of abstract forms. This definition, however, applies to all graphic arts and techniques that are characterized by an emphasis on form or shape rather than mass and colour, as in painting. (. . .) Drawing,

in short, is the end product of a successive effort applied directly to the carrier, which is usually paper.

Like all other pictures, figurative drawings consist of marks (which are the result of a selection process by an artist) that might stand for something else. Line drawing can be seen as a specific form of communication, different, for example, from depictions in paintings or photography. Unlike the optical denotation system of a photograph or painting, where marks stand for different colours and intensities in the optic array, in the figurative line drawing denotation system, explains Willats (1990), marks stand for permanent features of the scene, like true edges. In drawings, lines can represent the edges of objects, the objects themselves, the cracks in the objects, or the texture on the objects (Cutting and Massironi, 1998). In nature, by contrast, there are not black contour lines around people or objects; so the technique of black contours is, in fact, quite remarkable – though we seldom pay conscious attention to it. Drawings, like other pictures, are different from natural scenes in various aspects (Cutting and Massironi, 1998), because they consist of the following components:

a The representing medium (comics are typically represented on a planar and two-dimensional medium, like paper or a screen),

b the depicting array (particular arrangement of lines, brush strokes and so on),

c the depicted array (the scene that is represented),

d the depicted world (the larger world to which the depicted scene belongs),

e the mapping or the correspondence between the b) and c).

In addition, it is widely accepted that figurative pictures have a dual nature: they are, on the one hand, a somewhat analogous representation and, on the other hand, an expression (e.g. Rawson, 1979; Peters, 1981; Arnheim, 1983; Aumont, 1990; Massironi, 2002; Jolley, 2008; Groensteen, 2009; Augustin et al., 2011; Ostromoukhov, 2013). Moreover, one can consider this dual nature both from the perspective of the creation and from the perspective of the perception. The creator of a hand made picture not only represents a scene by means of visual cues, but also imposes a visual interpretation of that particular scene. Each drawing delivers by its graphic style a specific view on reality, implying a visual ontology, 'the definition of the real in visual terms' (Rawson, 1987: 19). Whatever causes the final result of drawing, it is through this picture that the viewer perceives a created world and is thus confronted with the object-in-the-picture from the point of view (including graphic choices, framing, type of colouring . . .) that the picture / artist offers.[2] The viewer thus must also deal with this dual nature, since he or she will both recognize a somewhat analogous representation of something and experience a particular sensation related to the formal properties of this picture. Thanks to this style-specific information, art perception differs from natural perception (Augustin et al., 2011), but the process happens as unconsciously; usually the interpretation of figurative pictures do not cost us, at least at a conscious level, a lot of energy.

Moreover, a fascinating byproduct of this process is that, generally, the viewer implicitly comes to believe or accept that the way the scene is represented in this picture is a correct expression of this (fictive) scene. A successful artistic solution, argues Arnheim (1971: 144), is so compelling that it looks like the only possible realization of the subject. Another possible explanation is the fact that most viewers, except trained spectators (like critics), do not make much effort to differentiate the expression-part from the representation-part, because both are intricately intertwined. One has to mentally imagine that a scene could have been drawn in another manner (different kinds of strokes, hatching, depth cues, point of view ....). Only in rare circumstances another interpretation of the same scene is realized in practice (there are only a few 'remakes' in the field of comics).

Furthermore, there is probably a kind of primacy-effect (Lefèvre, 2007), in the sense that people usually prefer the first version of something they encounter and they accept the first visual interpretation as the ideal one. Readers who are familiar with the latest editions of the *Tintin* comics may well be surprised to read the 'same' stories in an earlier version of the 1930s (in black and white, other graphic style, other page layouts). While people may complain about the quality of the drawing before they start reading, on a basic level, once they 'get into the story' (Busselle and Bilandzic, 2008; Van Laer et al., 2014), the style becomes seemingly 'neutral'.

3. Biological foundations of the efficiency of line drawing for human visual perception

While line drawing plays only a small role in contemporary art (though there seems recently some kind of a revival of line drawings), this particular type of expression has played a prominent role in the field of the visual narratives. Though some comics rendered with painterly styles were published in the last decades (Richard Corben, Alex Barbier, Jon Muth, Kent Williams), line drawing, in many varieties, has remained the overall dominant technique among comics artists. This devotion to contour lines may be quite surprising, because they are almost absent in our vision of natural scenes (there are, for instance, no black lines around people). Our human visual system was shaped in the past in response to a natural environment, not to line drawings (Sayim and Cavanagh, 2011: 1). How can we explain then that contour lines are so ubiquitous and so effective in depiction? Even if many conventions in line drawings are culturally based, the suggestion that they are purely a convention, which is passed down through learning (Gombrich, 1987; Goodman, 1976), turns out to be unsatisfying. A more plausible explanation is that contour lines trigger reactions of our visual system. Hubel and Wiesel (1962) demonstrated that the very first stages of the visual processing involved finding discontinuities in brightness, colour, and depth. Melcher and Cavanagh (2011: 362) explain the relevance of this finding for the perception of line drawings:

> Some of these discontinuities capture important information about the objects and surfaces in a scene, but many are accidental and uninformative. Artists making a line drawing usually focus on the most important of these transitions in brightness, colour, and depth, leaving out the edges of cast shadows and transitions in colours. (...) When an artist is able to depict the form of an object, this signifies an understanding (implicit or explicit) of the key contours that must be extracted by the visual system in the brain in order to recognize the three-dimensional structure of a particular object. The process of drawing is essentially a process of selection.

So, the orientation-tuned units of our visual system, originally evolved to respond to natural scenes, seems to work as good with artificial lines.[3] Also in perception of natural scenes, there is thus a system of edge enhancement at work that helps the visual system to construct a 'sketch' of objects in view, which is sufficient to assign a percept to a specific category of objects (Bruce and Young, 2000: 57).

In addition to contour lines, there are other aspects to line drawings – as they are used in visual narratives – that efficiently take advantage of our visual system: for instance, the fact that such drawings offer a simplified representation, leaving out many details, selecting particular parts.[4] Furthermore, drawings can interpret and stress certain features in a more pronounced way. Gestalt psychologist Rudolf Arnheim (1971: 149) claims that the better picture is one that chooses telling characteristics, and that those must be unambiguously conveyed to the eye. This outcome can be obtained by picture elements such as simplicity of shape, orderly grouping, distinction figure and ground, use of lighting and perspective and distortions.

Subjectively, we believe that we experience a richly detailed visual world, which is complete and accurate, but, as empirical research (such as 'change blindness' studies like Rensink, 2002) has convincingly demonstrated, we see very little of it in any detail (Mather, 2014: 53–54). We should not confound an image with a percept in our brain. One of the hypotheses of visual perception, namely the coarse-to-fine processing (Vuilleumier and Pourtois, 2007; Hegdé, 2008; Goffaux et al., 2010; Campana and Tallon-Baudry, 2013), may explain why simplified line drawings already do partly the work that our visual system, in the first phases, is meant to do. Namely, they form immediate coarse percepts.[5] Another cognitive advantage of line drawings is that they facilitate a mapping of graphics and meaning that can be easily stored in memory (a graphic schema) that can then be re-used over and over again in production (Cohn, 2013, 2014). This observation of schematic forms led Wilson (1988) to state that drawing involves transmission of culture-specific schemas instead of the representation of perception. Hochberg and Brooks (1996: 383) even suggest that comics approximate the ways in which people think of the visual world, which would be an explanation for their popularity. The efficiency of such simplified and expressive line drawings may also be one of the reasons why photo-novels (visual narratives using photos) never could develop as a real competitor for comics. Marion (1993: 101) explains that photographic panels tell more than the narrative needs.

4. From strokes to style

While the efficiency of the line drawings can be rooted on a biological evolutionary foundation, the matter of 'graphic style', I would argue, is rather a matter of cultural choices and personal idiosyncrasies. Line drawings can be realized with many different techniques and with many different formal aspects. Though one must not confound drawing instruments and graphic styles, some techniques offer only limited choices of formal options (Danto, 1981; Martin and Rude, 1997). For instance, a line made by an inflexible instrument (ballpoint pen) has only two characteristics: direction and trace. Barbieri (1991: 21) calls such a uniform line '*linea piatta*' (flat line). In the field of comics, artists like Altan, Hergé or Schulz tend towards use such uniform inking, while others (like Baudoin), using brushes, prefer lines with varying thicknesses and structures. By contrast, a flexible instrument as the brush offers many other qualities: jagged, dry, thick, thin … Such irregular lines, which immediately suggest texture, are called 'modulated lines' (Barbieri, 1991: 29). An artist has not only the choice of how to render the contour lines, he or she can also suggest volume and texture by various devices such as hatchings, screen tones, etc. However, adding texture can also impede the quick visualizability of an image (Barbieri, 1991: 28). The representation in pictures of changes in light intensity that give information about the shape of a viewed surface ('shape from shading') is called 'tonal modelling'. Willats (1997: 128) explains further:

> In pictures based on optical denotation systems the picture primitives denote features of the array of light reaching the eye or the camera, rather than physical features of the scene such as edges and contours.

At what point does a collection of strokes become a graphic style? If we define a 'style' in the manner of music scholar Meyer (1989: 3) as 'a replication of patterning, whether in human behaviour or in the artefacts produced by human behaviour, that results from a series of choices made within some set of constraints', we can look for replications of patterning in drawings (for a more detailed philosophical discussion of the complex concept of style, see Ross, 2003). A visual narrative can even more than a single drawing make the particularity of its style prominent, since the graphic style is, in principle, repeated from panel to panel in all its appearances and variations (including deviations, as we will see). There can be various systematics at play in a drawing, like the way the lines are drawn, or the way lines are closely combined (hatching). The systematics may not always be the result of a conscious choice by the artist (Genova, 1979: 324; Ross, 2003), but for describing the systematics of a style it does not matter much whether style is the result of conscious choices or not.

While few art historians have tried to differentiate the various components or parameters of a drawing style (a notable exception is Rawson, 1987), more recent computational studies have made the first steps in inventorying the components of an individual style. Kalogerakis and his colleagues (2012) and Ostromoukhov (2013) are trying to create algorithms to account for artists' style of hatching, but the most interesting experiment so far has been conducted by Berger et al. (2013), who invited seven artists to use a digital (Wacom) pen to draw portrait sketches on the basis of a reference photograph. The researchers captured each stroke as a parameterized curve along with the pen parameters (tilt, pressure, location) and stored each stroke as a transparent bitmap for later use in the synthesis of new sketches. More specifically, they focused the stroke analysis on four aspects (Berger et al., 2013: 3):

The spatial distribution – *where* do artists draw strokes?
The temporal distribution – *when* do artists draw strokes?
Stroke statistics (length, amount, overlap etc.) – *how* do artists draw strokes?
Stroke classification (contour strokes, shading strokes) – *what* types of strokes are used?

In addition, they measured also the variations of the artists' interpretation of a face by using the correspondence between the portrait sketches and the photograph face shape created by a mesh fitted on both. By quantifying the strokes and the shapes of the seven artists, they were able to define the style of each artist algorithmically, so that they could generate new sketches on the basis of new portrait photographs in the style of each individual artist. While these kinds of studies suggest that it is possible to make a checklist of style features, some scholars (Douven, 1999; Wollheim, 1995; Walton, 1979) are resisting such 'localistic views', arguing that style features do not inhere in works in any straightforward way (for a discussion, see Ross, 2003: 241–242).

Now, we are trying to understand the components of graphic style in general, and thus it is crucial to remember that graphic style is only one component of style in comics, because also the formal appearance of verbal elements, the *mise en scène* and framing (Lefèvre, 2012, 2014), and the page layout will influence the look of a work. And in addition to the choice of lines, there are also other aspects that define a graphic style, like the way people and objects are represented (respecting the natural proportions or not?). Though all these aspects interact dynamically, for the purpose of this contribution, we will limit ourselves to the issue of graphic style (and only briefly mention aspects such as colouring and *mise en scène* – see for this last issue Lefèvre, 2012). A coloured version of a comic offers a quite different visual experience than a black and white edition (compare, for instance, the black and white editions of Hugo Pratt's *Corto Maltese* or Otomo's *Akira* with their coloured ones). But even more than the colouring, it is the graphic style of Hugo Pratt or Katsuhiro Otomo that primarily differentiates these works on a formal level. It is arguably more important for the visual experience if, for instance, an artist deforms the normal proportions or renders the world in round style (Disney, Tezuka, Franquin). Just as we assume the realism of black and white photos, the reader can easily accept the visualization of a fictive world purely in black and white. In a study of audience evaluations of reality of media texts, Hall (2003: 639) found that the participants tended to use different realism conceptualizations for different media genres and that their conceptualizations tended to focus on different features of the evaluated text:

> Materials that are purported to represent historical or nonscripted events seemed to prime audiences' evaluation of the materials in terms of factuality, whereas fantasy or science fiction texts seemed more likely to bring issues of emotional involvement or narrative coherence to the foreground.

As Buselle and Bilandzic (2008) have shown, fictionality does not affect narrative processing, but that 'the narrative must achieve or maintain coherence among different schemas and mental models, such as the story world and the genre'. The concept of coherence is thus crucial and we will use it in our model for the study of graphic style.

5. A model to study graphic style

As reception studies (Buselle and Bilandzic, 2008) have suggested, the concept of coherency comes forward as quite crucial in the interpretation of a represented fictional world. Moreover we cannot speak of style without formal features that are governed by some internal coherence. Coherency can come into play, in the case of a comic, at various levels (page design, lettering, etc.), including graphic style. In addition to coherency, the functionality of drawings in a visual narrative is also crucial (Groensteen, 2009: 163), because an individual panel is not designed to be taken separately. Rather, it is meant to be read in a sequence of panels that show an event.

5.1. Coherency

According to Rawson (1987: 78), speaking of the art of drawing, master artists use a variety of strokes and forms within an ordered whole:

> Without precision in formulating the elements there can be no true variety. For it is only possible to recognize variety and variation if distinctions between the forms are made quite clear. And there can only be variety within an ordered structure, or else differences are simply chaos and not variation. Variation implies a substratum of norm-units which are varied.

The Chinese artist Shitao (1984: 85–86) wrote in 1710 that when a painter tries to decipher and decompose the world into parts, the result will be dead, because the eye can immediately see the sterile and soulless fabrication. The coherency of a graphic style in a visual narrative can consist of various factors, but every single drawing will not necessarily use them all.

Detail   The amount of details versus the degree of simplification (Baetens and Lefèvre, 1993: 37), or the spectrum between specific and generic (stand for a class of people, objects . . .). For instance, does the artist draw every leaf (including the nerves) of a tree or does he just suggest foliage of a tree as a whole in one, simple outline? Or does the artist (like Blanquet in *La Nouvelle aux Pis*, 2001), use only silhouettes to tell a complete story?

Deformation   The amount and degree of deformation versus respecting normal proportions.

Line   What kind of lines dominate the image (rectangular or rather rounded lines; clear, crisp lines or rather vague, 'hesitant' lines).

Distribution   The amount and type of traces and the way they are distributed (Baetens and Lefèvre, 1993: 40). Some drawings, like those of Calpurnio or Copi, are made of a few lines, while others (as in Pascal Doury's *Théo, tête de mort*, 1983) are completely covered with strokes. By contrast, the Chinese artist He Youzhi often leaves two or three corners of his drawings blank (Gorridge, 2010: 243).

Depth   Planimetric versus regressional (Wölfflin, 1950). In a planimetric approach, the background is perpendicular to the spectator, the figures stand fully frontal, in profile or with their backs towards us (for instance, Osvaldo Cavandoli's animation films of *La Linea*), by contrast, in recession 'figures and architectural spaces present diagonals that shoot from foreground to background' (Bordwell, 2005: 167). One can delve also further in 'projection system', the way the supposed three-dimensional world of the diegesis is translated onto the two-dimensional plane of the page (Willats, 1997). Every projection system has its possibilities and limitations: objects that appear on a flat surface can never show the complete reality of that three-dimensional object. In the course of history, visual artists have developed several means or tricks to suggest a voluminous space on a flat surface: interposition or overlapping, convergence, relative size, density gradient, etc. Spatial relations between figures or objects in a picture can be described by projection systems.

Light   To what extent is tonal modelling used to suggest various light conditions? In real life, direct light produces both shadows and shading, which gives the viewer an idea about the form and texture of the object and the direction of the light source. Artists may suggest shadows and shading by simple drawing techniques, like grouping a lot of lines that produces a darker effect (as in the work of Crumb).

Colour   Degree of coherency in black and white or in colouring. Flat colours or colours that suggest the three-dimensional effects (by varying the brightness of the colours). Colours can be analysed from various perspectives: choice of technique, naturalistic colouring or not, flat colouring or not, the relation with line drawing, types of colours, functions, etc. To describe colours, one can use the three-dimensional system of Munsell, who defined in 1905 colours on the basis of three parameters: hue, saturation and brightness (these are related to physical properties of wavelength, purity and intensity).

To test our concepts, we will apply them to a small sample from an experienced comics artist Elzie Segar, a daily strip from his *Popeye*-series (1932), see Figure 3.1:

Figure 3.1 Elzie Crisler Segar (1932), *Popeye*, daily strip, originally published 12 December 1932. This image is from *The Complete E. C. Segar Popeye,* Volume 8, dailies 1932–1934, Fantagraphics, 1988, p. 6.

Detail   Very simplified renderings both of characters and objects. The finest details appear in the facial expressions of the characters, but even those are rendered with a few dots and simplified lines.

Line   Quite rounded lines that shape the rounded anatomy of Popeye (especially head, under arms and legs), but even the slender, breastless Olive Oyl is not drawn in completely straight lines, but with some waving lines. Most lines are somewhat modulated, meaning that they have some varying thickness – contributing to lively expression of the characters.

Deformation   While Olive Oyl and Popeye are in the cartoon mode, thus characterized by many explicit deformations (like the striking double chin of Popeye) in comparison to an average adult, the other woman (Dina Mow) in the fifth panel is remarkably less deformed (and thus more titled to the naturalistic mode), which is quite unusual, but sometimes recurring in the *Popeye*-series. The difference in graphic style is probably motivated by the purpose to make a beauty distinction between Olive and Dina even more pronounced, Popeye is clearly touched by Dina's beauty.

Distribution   If we make abstraction of lettering and the balloons, most visual marks are to be found rather in the central zone of each panel. This is the place where the heads of the characters and their hands are usually located, the predominated means of body language. In addition to the lines that are used to indicate contours or shading, there is another kind of lines in the drawing, non-mimetic graphic elements that contribute narratively salient information (Kennedy, 1982), for example in the last panel the bodily shaking of Popeye. Since these marks are not present in each panel, the only coherency in their use is that they are just used when they are needed to confer some bodily/mental expression.

Depth   While the characters (and some elements of the location like the windows) are rather positioned rather in planimetric way, some of the marks that indicate the few items of the location (like the carpet) suggest a recessive composition. So, the visualization of the space is not totally coherent, because visual devices are giving contrasting information (in the fourth panel, the border of the carpet and the plinth of the wall are slanting somewhat, but the windowsill is horizontal).

Light   On the characters, there is no tonal modelling, only in the background (e.g., under the windowsill, beyond the open doorway) shading is suggested by a group of parallel lines. So the use of light in this tier is rather coherent regarding the characters, but different concerning some objects in the background.

Colour   This daily comic of the early 1930s, like most dailies of that period, does not use colour, only three quite differentiated 'colours': black, white and greys. Considering the original publication in the newspaper white should be understood as the usual colour of the paper of such publications. Furthermore, the same deep black is used both for contour lines as for colouring parts of the cloths (and for the hair of Olive). It is precisely thanks to these uniform black zones in each panel that the visual attention remains focused on the characters, and not, for instance, on elements of the location. There is finally only one tone of grey, which is produced by regular distribution of fine dots (those are produced by a screen tone and not hand drawn). Thanks to their uniformity and limited brightness, the large grey zones, can give a little gravitation to the scene (so that characters don't float in the air) without attracting attention on their presence (they are narratively not important for the scene). By contrast, the upper zone of the panels, and of the upper diegetic space, that is left blank (though dominantly filled with the balloons, it has also some free space). Except for the verbal messages, in this zone we see no visual interesting elements presented. The use of blacks, whites and greys is therefore quite coherent.

So, in a daily strip like *Popeye / The Thimble Theatre*, which was running already several years (so the artist had already time to 'perfect' his way of drawing), the graphic style is quite coherent. Deviations within the 'Popeye system' (of 1932) were, however, still possible, mostly they were motivated by narrative needs (different rendering of two competing women for Popeye).[6] But there remain also inconsistencies in the way elements of the background are presented, which is probably less striking for an ordinary reader, because this zone of the drawing attracts less attention than the characters. As I noted earlier (Lefèvre, 2009), inconsistencies in the representation of the diegetic space in comics are quite common, the decor is often volatile. Even a strongly codified style as Hergé's so-called Clear Line is not a hundred percent consequent in its application: while in principle only flat colouring is used in the coloured *Tintin* albums (Tintin's shirt is in the same hue, saturation and brightness all around his body), there appears usually a soft red blush on the characters' cheeks. There is a good reason for this slight deviation: imagine the Tintin face without that soft red blush on the cheeks – it would certainly be less lively and natural. In addition to this conventionalized deviation from the colour norm in *Tintin* (one might say that exceptions confirm the rule), there are also more incidental deviations.[7]

So, all these visual cues can be applied to serve quite different goals. Because a comic usually consists of a large body of individual panels, a reader not only must consider the coherency within a panel, but also the coherency within a sequence (or the complete work). It may be interesting to see if there is a systematic approach by the artist and to what degree every element responds to the system, and, if there are deviations from the system, to wonder what could be their motivation. There can be several reasons for this phenomenon: for instance, not all artists have worked out a consistent way of drawing, or they just like to deviate because confining themselves to a system can become quite a boring activity. On the other hand, some styles have become recognized as typical for a particular author of group of works (like *shojo manga*). Both critics and readers will notice particular graphic styles, be they individual or group styles. Solely on the basis of single drawing, one can distinguish a Hergé from a Franquin, a Tezuka from an Otomo, an Eisner from a Kirby. Of course, there are artists that are able to draw in very different graphic styles and can imitate another artist's style. In fact, the studio system, which we find in various comics industries, is based on the assumption that assistants learn to imitate the graphic style of the master, so that a reader won't notice the difference between a page realized by the master and another realized by his studio member. A famous example is the 'fake' *Tintin* page that Hergé's assistants, Bob de Moor and Jacques Martin, realized in 1965 (Lecigne, 1983: 40–41). Artists can use graphic style also in ironic and self-conscious adoption of someone else's style to make personal statements (Ross, 2003: 234). An example is the innocent looking graphic style of Nekojiru that refers to the simple but cute drawings for children, as in the case of Dick Bruna (*Nifty*) or his imitator Yuko Shimizu (*Hello Kitty*). Nekojiru, by contrast, often placed her characters in cruel situations.

A complicating factor to speak of an individual style is the empirical fact that almost every artist has evolved his graphic style over a longer period. While the systematic style may not always be an explicit, rational choice, it may well be a practice acquired over time. Personal limitations may, moreover, influence the coherency of a graphic style. If someone wants to speak about an individual style of a certain artist, he or she has to indicate more precisely for which period, or even which individual work, the established norms are valid. There are also works that are composed of alternations between various graphic styles like Nicolas Devils's *Saga de Xam* (1967), or Daniel Clowes's *Wilson* (2010). However, within every short story Devil and Clowes use a coherent style. Furthermore, in many of comics and animated films, two different styles are used: one for the characters and another one for the backgrounds. For example, in the later *Corto Maltese* stories, the cars are rendered with many details, while the characters are strongly stylized with a few lines. In exceptional cases, such as the *Dirty Laundry Comics* (1974) by Robert Crumb and his companion Aline Kominsky, or Mazzucchelli's *Asterios Polyp*, two explicitly different graphic styles are contrasted within the borders of one panel to express the divergence between two characters (for a more extended analysis, see Duncan, 2012). But the general norm remains, nevertheless, that within a visual narrative one coherent graphic style is applied (artists often specialize in a particular style).

A further, complicating issue is to determine how an individual style relates to a group style. Unfortunately, no comics scholar has yet conducted a large-scale research like Bordwell et al. (1988) did for determining the typical classical Hollywood style. In that study, they selected a hundred films in an unbiased fashion to analyse them formally (and tested their conclusions on almost two hundred other Hollywood films of the 1915–1960 period). Only in such a way can one soundly determine historical norms of a group style and prove assumptions that a critic may have.

5.2. Narrative functionality

In general, states Genova (1979: 324), style features are functionally defined: 'any recurrent feature which expresses meaning is a style feature'. As we have seen, drawings in a visual narrative are not made to stand on their own as autonomous works of art, but have, by definition, a principal narrative purpose: various panels of a sequence have to show the evolution of an event to the reader. The classic ideal in comics are clear, easy interpretable panels (Krafft, 1978: 73). So, the possible norms one may use to evaluate autonomous drawings do not necessarily function in the same way for drawings that serve to narrate. There is a link between certain graphic styles and certain genres. Witek (2012: 30–32) explains that the cartoon mode often assumes

> a fundamentally unstable and infinitely mutable physical reality, where characters and even objects can move and be transformed according to an associative or emotive logic rather than the laws of physics', while the naturalistic mode 'makes the implicit claim that

its depicted worlds are like our own, or like our own world would be if specific elements, such as magic or superpowers, were to be added or removed. However cursory the attempts to support its truth claim might be, that claim supplies the metaphysical structure underlying the visual and narrative strategies of the naturalistic tradition of comics.

A humoristic story will traditionally be rendered in a cartoony way, to make the characters and their expressions look funnier – almost like a clown uses explicit make-up to underscore his facial features and expressions.

While an artist generally continues to work in a similar graphic style, there are also artists who try to explore quite different graphic styles, someone like Alberto Breccia often had been trying to find the right style for the stories he wanted to tell or that he adapted (Imperato, 1992: 26): 'Every short story, every story, has its own ambiance. My fundamental problem consists in trying at most to suggest this ambiance so that the reader can be submerged in this sphere. I'm therefore obliged to change every time my instruments and my ways to adapt a text.'[8]

Also, comics that are 'poorly drawn', from a classic point of view, can be popular and thus quite functional. For instance, the arguably limited drawing capacity of Scott Adams did not hinder his comic strip *Dilbert* from becoming a worldwide success. One could even argue that this quite sterile and static style is well suited to represent the dull corporate world of Dilbert.

The fact that drawings have a narrative purpose in comics refers to the first aspect of the previously discussed dual nature of a picture: to represent something. As I argued elsewhere (Lefèvre, 2011: 17):

Traditionally comics are designed to be read quickly, which explains the preference for stereotypical elements that are easily recognized. Thus the main characters are usually dressed in a typical, familiar outfit, and are rendered with typified body and facial features: think of Superman and Batman in superhero comics, Mickey Mouse in animal comics, Tintin in classic *bande dessinée*, and Astro Boy in *shonen manga*. The ease of identification is not limited to the main characters, for the complete design of a canonical comic must be clear and accessible, especially those for young children. Only in a minority of comics – for example, in graphic novels – do artists deviate from these strict standards.

When we study a graphic style we can consider to which extent the graphic style is fit to represent the fictive world and to show events in this diegetic world. For example, it is no wonder that in the emotional Japanese girls' *manga* exaggerated big eyes play an important role, as we know that a lot of emotions pass via the eyes.[9] In our case study of the *Popeye* strip (of 1932), it was evident that the dominant cartoon mode was applied to suggest a humoristic intent and context. By this graphic style, the reader understands that he or she does not have to expect a world completely comparative to reality, but rather a humoristic fiction.

Regarding colouring, most comics combine some realism with a functionalist approach; the colours are to a certain extent analogous to reality (e.g., the grass is green, the sky is blue), but on the other hand, the colours have to achieve a good legibility for the panel: by respecting the contour lines and the use of contrasting colours, crucial parts of the image are stressed. Similar to the way that line drawings offer us a simplification of how nature looks to us, the choice of a particular type of colouring can also present such a simplification. While we see colours in nature having all kinds of different tonalities (due to the way light is reflected), in fact, we know that a shirt has the same colour all the way round. So, the use of flat colouring builds on this knowledge. Again, for a coarse view of a scene, all the small colour or light variations are not needed. A group of visual narratives (like *Tintin, Niffy, Jimmy Corrigan*) therefore use only flat colouring (the same saturation and brightness of a hue). In more contemporary graphic novels, colours are also used in a more symbolic way, such as in *Asterios Polyp*, where the two main characters are associated with quite contrasting colours.

While we have been focusing on the function of drawings for the narrative, we have to consider also features within drawings that escape such a functioning. Not all traces are in fact meaningful from a purely narrative point of view, but they may form their own parametric organization. As Bordwell (1986: 275) affirms, the stylistic system of a particular work may create patterns distinct from the demand of the plot and thus make the style and the plot equal in importance, or even give style the dominance over the plot. Often, such a parametric mode involves a limited range of stylistic options, otherwise it would become too difficult for the spectator of a film or reader of a comic to recognize stylistic repetition and staying alert for more or less distinct variations (Bordwell, 1986: 287). An example of parametric use of graphic style in comics is the constantly changing colours of the same background in Régis Franc's short comic *Hong Kong, terre de contrastes* (1982): for instance, the same tree trunk jumps on the first page from orange to green and to pink, and keeps changing the following four pages (without any atmospheric cause for this changing). In a way, this parametric use of aleatoric colour underscores visually the meaning of the title *Hong Kong, land of contrasts*.

6. Conclusion

Graphic style, as part of the larger style of a visual narrative, plays an important role because it is through its components (marks on paper or screen) that the reader has to form a percept of the diegetic world of the story. Though the concept of graphic style is used in quite different ways, it is important to try to define it as a particular way of drawing, of a rather conventionalized way of grasping of the (fictive) world by visual means. Line drawings are particularly efficient, thanks to their simplification and expressive qualities. Though line drawings with their black contour lines may seem quite artificial and quite different from natural scenes, there is growing empirical evidence that the line drawings are processed by the same visual system. The development of particular graphic styles is, on the other hand, rather a matter of cultural preferences at a particular period of time (but probably also unconscious choices may play a role). So we can assume that there is an interaction between the way biological evolution has shaped our visual perception and the way particular cultural or personal conditions play a role in the way an artist draws and in the appreciation by an individual perceiver (Deregowski, 1984; Bullot and Reber, 2012; Cohn, 2013). If we are to construe a model to analyse graphic style in visual narratives like comics specifically, we should take into account aspects like the internal coherency and the functionality of drawings for the narration.

Notes

1. For semiotic approaches like the linguistically informed ones, see Gauthier (1976) and Cohn (2013). Furthermore, Meesters (2010) is arguing for using cognitive linguistics in the analysis of graphic styles.
2. Deregowski (1984: 1) emphasizes: 'Although grammatically a concrete noun, a picture is in fact a perceived attribute of a pattern which remains undetected by an observer as long as he fails to perceive that the pattern at which he is looking conveys to him a visual image of some other object than itself.'
3. Sayim and Cavanagh (2011: 1) explain this further: 'These orientation-tuned units evolved to efficiently detect the contours in the natural world (Olshausen and Field, 1996), but even though the edges in the world are typically marked by a discrete change in surface attributes – lighter on one side that the other, for example – these units respond as well to lines – lighter in the middle and dark on both sides, for example, or even illusory contours that are suggested by context but not physically present (. . .). In other words, the receptive field structure that efficiently recovers edges, also works well for lines even though it was not designed to do so.'
4. Comics artists understood this quite rapidly. The Swiss educator and nineteenth-century creator of visual narratives Rodolphe Töpffer wrote about graphic style that *'suffit, et au-delà, à toutes les exigences de l'expression comme à toutes celles de la clarté. (. . .) Cela vient de ce qu'il ne donne de l'objet que les caractères essentiels . . .'* (quoted by Groensteen, 2009: 346). Some decades later Lederer (1923: 69) advised, in his guide for aspiring comic strip artists, not to use too much detail: 'In a general way very little detail is requisite for a strip cartoon. I might almost say the less the better. Unless the story told depends to a certain definite extent on some object outside of the characters themselves the background should be very much subordinated. This is especially so because too much detail is confusing to the eye and is apt to dull the entire effect. The human figures should, with few exceptions, dominate the picture – take up the greater space. The lines outlining the figures, human or otherwise, and the minor accessories in direct connection with them should contain heavier lines, more pronounced than those indicating the background and minor accessories.'

5. Melcher and Cavanagh (2011: 366–368) offer various reasons why artists may have taken advantage of this coarse processing system: like artists can provide an incomplete image and leave to the perceiver to fill in the details. A typical example is the so-called 'clear line' style we find among artists such as Émile-Joseph Pinchon, George McManus, Kabashima Katsuichi and Hergé. The clear line aims at maximum legibility, as Groensteen (2009: 346) explains: 'The Clear Line, it's drawing at service of reason; she assures us that the world decipherable. Hergé spoke of "illuminating" line' (my translation of the French text: *'La ligne claire, c'est le dessin au service de la raison; elle nous assure que le monde est tout entier déchiffrable. Hergé parlera d'une ligne « éclairante ».'*).

6. Nofuentes (2011) speaks of 'composite style', Smolderen (2014) of 'polygraphy', and Groensteen (2013) of 'graphic polyphony'.

7. For example, when a car is dredged out the murky water of the port of Saint-Nazaire (*Le Temple du Soleil*, 1946), the car is covered by mud that is slowly sliding off. The suggestion of the body of the car covered by different hues of mud could not have been done effectively in the flat colouring mode. Furthermore, the cobbled street is suggested by different soft stains of brown.

8. My translation of the French text: *'Chaque nouvelle, chaque récit, a son ambiance propre. Mon problème fondamental consiste à essayer de rendre le plus possible cette ambiance pour permettre au lecteur de la saisir de la façon la plus complète possible. Je suis donc obligé de changer chaque fois mes instruments et ma façon d'interpréter le texte.'*

9. Yuki et al. (2006) link this practice to the Japanese culture where emotional refrainment is the norm.

References

Arnheim, R. (1971). *Art and Visual Perception: A Psychology of the Creative Eye*. Berkeley, CA: University of California Press.

Arnheim, R. (1983). The rationale of deformation. *Art Journal* (*The Issue of Caricature*), 43(4): 319–324.

Augustin, M. D., Defranceschi, B., Fuchs, H. K., and Carbon, C.-C. (2011). The neural time course of art perception: an ERP study on the processing of style versus content in art. *Neuropsychologia*, 49: 2071–2081.

Aumont, J. (1990). *L'image*. Paris: Nathan.

Baetens, J., and Lefèvre, P. (1993). *Pour une lecture modern de la bande dessinée*. Bruxelles: Centre Belge de la Bande Dessinée.

Barbieri, D. (1991). *I linguaggi del fumetto*. Milano: Strumenti Bompiani.

Berger, I., Shamir, A., Mahler, M., Carter, E., and Hodgins, J. (2013) Style and abstraction in portrait sketching. *ACM Transactions on Graphics*, 32(4), Article 55: 1–12.

Bordwell, D. (1986). *Narration in Fiction Film*. London: Methuen.

Bordwell, D. (2005). *Figures Traced in Light: On Cinematic Staging*. Berkeley, CA: University of California Press.

Bordwell, D., Staiger, J., and Thompson, K. (1998). *The Classical Hollywood Cinema: Film Style and Mode of Production to 1960*. London: Routledge.

Bruce, V., and Young, A. (2000). *In the Eye of the Beholder: The Science of Face Perception*. Oxford: Oxford University Press.

Bullot, N. J., and Reber, R. (2013). The artful mind meets art history: toward a psycho-historical framework for the science of art appreciation. *Behavioral and Brain Sciences*, 36(2): 123–137.

Buselle, R., and Bilandzic, H. (2008). Fictionality and perceived realism in experiencing stories: a model of narrative comprehension and engagement. *Communication Theory*, 18: 255–280.

Campana, F., and Tallon-Baudry, C. (2013). Anchoring visual subjective experience in a neural model: the coarse vividness hypothesis. *Neuropsychologia*, 51: 1050–1060.

Cohn, N. (2013). *The Visual Language of Comics: Introduction to the Structure and Cognition of Sequential Images*. London: Bloomsbury.

Cohn, N. (2014). Framing 'I can't draw': the influence of cultural frames on the development of drawing. *Culture and Psychology*, 20(1): 102–117.

Coope, K. (2002). *How To Draw Manga*. London: Tangerine Press.

Cutting, J. E., and Massironi, M. (1998). Pictures and their special status in perceptual and cognitive inquiry. In: J. Hochberg (ed.), *Perception and Cognition at Century's End* (pp. 137–168). London: Academic Press.

Danto, A. C. (1981). *The Transfiguration of the Commonplace: A Philosophy of Art*. Cambridge, MA: Harvard University Press.

Deregowski, J. B. (1984). *Distortion in Art: The Eye and the Mind*. London: Routledge & Kegan Paul.

Douven, I. (1999). Style and supervenience. *The British Journal of Aesthetics*, 39(3): 255–262.

Duncan, R. (2012). Image functions: shape and color as hermeneutic images in *Asterios Polyp*. In: M. J. Smith and R. Duncan (eds), *Critical Approaches to Comics, Theories and Methods* (pp. 43–54). New York: Routledge.

Gauthier, G. (1976). Les *Peanuts*: un graphisme idiomatique. *Communications*, 24: 108–139.

Genova, J. (1979). The significance of style. *Journal of Aesthetics and Art Criticism*, 37(3): 315–324.

Goffaux, V., Peters, J., Haubrechts, J., Schiltz, C., Jansma, B., and Goebel, R. (2010). From coarse to fine? Spatial and temporal dynamics of cortical face processing. *Cerebral Cortex*, 21(2): 467–476.

Gombrich, E. H. (1987). *Art and Illusion: A Study in the Psychology of Pictorial Representation*. Oxford: Phaidon Press.

Goodman, N. (1976). *Languages of Art: An Approach to a Theory of Symbols*, 2nd edn Indianapolis, IN: Hackett.

Goodman, N. (1978). *Ways of Worldmaking*. Indianapolis, IN: Hackett.

Gorridge, G. (2010). *Créer une BD pour les Nuls*. Paris: Éditions First.

Graphic-Sha (2001). *How to Draw Manga: Getting Started*. Graphic-Sha Publishing.

Grennan, S. (2011) *Comic Strips and the Making of Meaning: Emotion, Intersubjectivity and Narrative Drawing*. PhD Thesis, CCW, University of the Arts, London.

Groensteen, T. (2009). *La bande dessinée, son histoire et ses maîtres*. Paris/Angoulême: Skira Flammarion/La cite international de la bande dessinée et de l'image.

Groensteen, T. (2012). Style. *9e Art*. Retrieved from http://neuviemeart.citebd.org/spip. php?article464, consulted 10 July 2014.

Groensteen, T. (2013). *Comics and Narration*. Jackson: University Press of Mississippi.

Hall, A. (2003). Reading realism: audiences' evaluations of the reality of media texts. *Journal of Communication,* 53(4): 624–641.

Hegdé, J. (2008). Time course of visual perception: coarse-to-fine processing and beyond. *Progress in Neurobiology*, 84: 405–439.

Hochberg, J., and Brooks, V. (1996). Movies in the mind's eye. In: D. Bordwell and N. Carroll (eds), *Post-Theory: Reconstructing Film Studies* (pp. 368–387). Madison, WI: The University of Wisconsin Press.

Hubel, D. H., and Wiesel, T. N. (1962). Receptive fields, binocular interaction and functional architecture in cat's visual cortex. *The Journal of Physiology*, 160(1): 106–154.

Imperato, L. (1992). *Alberto Breccia: Ombres et lumières*. Paris: Vertige Graphic.

Jolley, R. P. (2008). Children's understanding of the dual nature of pictures. In: C. Lange-Küttner and A. Vinter (eds), *Drawing and Non-Verbal Intelligence: A Life Span Perspective* (pp. 86–103). Cambridge: Cambridge University Press.

Kalogerakis, E., Nowrouzezahrai, D, Breslav, S., and Hertzmann, A. (2012). Learning hatching for pen-and-ink illustration of surfaces. *ACM Transactions on Graphics*, 31(1), Article 1: 1–17.

Kennedy, J. M. (1982). Metaphor in pictures. *Perception*, 11(5): 589–605.

Krafft, U. (1978). *Comics lesen*. Stuttgart: Kiett-Cotta.

Lecigne, B. (1983). *Les héritiers d'Hergé*. Bruxelles: Magic Strip.

Lederer, C. (1923). *Cartooning Made Easy: A Course of Instruction in Thirty Up-to-the-Minute Lessons in Four Books*. Chicago, IL: Judy Publishing.

Lee, S., and Buscema, J. (1984). *How To Draw Comics the Marvel Way*. New York: Touchstone.

Lefèvre, P. (1999). Recovering sensuality in comic theory. *International Journal of Comic Art*, 1(1): 140–149.

Lefèvre, P. (2007). Incompatible visual ontologies? The problematic adaptation of drawn images. In: I. Gordon, M. Jancovich, and M. P. McAllister (eds), *Film and Comic Books* (pp. 1–12). Jackson, MI: University Press of Mississippi.

Lefèvre, P. (2009). The construction of space in comics. In: J. Heer and K. Worcester (eds), *A Comics Studies Reader* (pp. 157–162). Jackson, MI: University Press of Mississippi.

Lefèvre, P. (2011). Medium-specific qualities of graphic narratives. *SubStance*, 40(1): 14–33.

Lefèvre, P. (2012). *Mise en scène* and framing: visual storytelling in *Lone Wolf and Cub*. In: M. Smith and R. Duncan (eds), *Critical Approaches to Comics: Theories and Methods* (pp. 71–83). New York: Routledge.

Lefèvre, P. (2014). *Tools for Analyzing Graphic Narratives and Case Studies*. Retrieved from: <https://sites.google.com/site/analyzingcomics/home>.

Madden, M. (2006). *Ninety-Nine Ways to Tell a Story: Exercises in Style*. London: Penguin.

Marion, P. (1993). *Traces en cases. Travail graphique, figuration narrative et participation du lecteur. Essai sur la bande dessinée.* Louvain-la-Neuve: Academia.

Martin, G., and Rude, S. (1997). *The Art of Comic Book Inking.* Milwaukee, WI: Dark Horse Comics.

Mather, G. (2014). *The Psychology of Visual Art: Eye, Brain and Art.* Cambridge: Cambridge University Press.

Massironi, M. (2002). *The Psychology of Graphic Images: Seeing, Drawing, Communicating.* Mahwah, NJ: Lawrence Erlbaum Associates.

Meesters, G. (2010). Les significations du style graphique: *Mon Fiston* d'Olivier Schrauwen et *Faire semblant, c'est mentir* de Dominique Goblet. *Textyles, Revue de lettres belges de langue française*: 36–37, 215–233.

Melcher, D., and Cavanagh, P. (2011). Pictorial cues in art and in visual perception. In: F. Bacci and D. Melcher (eds), *Art and the Senses* (pp. 359–394). Oxford: Oxford University Press.

Meyer, L. B. (1989). *Style and Music: Theory, History, and Ideology.* Chicago, IL: University of Chicago Press.

Nichols, K. (2011). *Draw DC Universe: Learn to Draw the Heroes and the Villains.* New York: Klutz.

Nofuentes, A. (2011). *Le style graphique composite dans la bande dessinée: histoire, théorie et applications narratives.* Master paper, Université de Poitiers, École Européenne Supérieure de l'Image.

Ostromoukhov, V. (2013). Non-photorealistic shading and hatching. In: P. Rosin and J. Collomosse (eds), *Image and Video-Based Artistic Stylisation* (pp. 63–76). London: Springer.

Peters, J. M. (1981). *Pictorial Signs and the Language of Film.* Amsterdam: Rodolpi.

Petherbridge, D. (2010). *The Primacy of Drawing.* New Haven, CT: Yale University Press.

Rawson, P. (1979). *Seeing through Drawing.* London: British Broadcasting Corporation.

Rawson, P. (1987). *Drawing.* Philadelphia, PA: University of Pennsylvania Press.

Rensink, R. A. (2002). Change detection. *Annual Review of Psychology*, 53: 254–277.

Ross, S. (2003). Style in art. In: J. Levinson (ed.), *The Oxford Handbook of Aesthetics* (pp. 228–244). Oxford: Oxford University Press.

Sayim, B., and Cavanagh, P. (2011). What line drawings reveal about the visual brain. *Frontiers in Human Neuroscience*, 5, article 118: 1–4.

Shitao (1984). *Les Propos sur la peinture du moine Citrouille-amère.* Paris: Hermann Paris.

Smolderen (2014). *The Origins of Comics: From William Hogarth to Winsor McCay.* Jackson, MI: University Press of Mississippi.

Van Alphen, E. J. (2008). Looking at drawing: theoretical distinctions and their usefulness. In: S. Garner (ed.), *Writing on Drawing: Essays on Drawing Practice and Research* (pp. 59–70). London: Intellect Books.

Van Laer, T., De Ruyter, K., Visconti, L. M., and Wetzels, M. (2014). The extended transportation-imagery model: a meta-analysis of the antecedents and consequences of consumers' narrative transportation. *Journal of Consumer Research*, 40(5): 797–817.

Vuilleumier, P., and Pourtois, G. (2007). Distributed and interactive brain mechanisms during emotion face perception: evidence from functional neuroimaging. *Neuropsychologia*, 45(1): 174–194.

Walton, K. L. (1979). Style and the products and processes of art. In: B. Lang (ed.), *The Concept of Style* (pp. 72–103). Ithaca, NY: Cornell University Press, 1987.

Willats, J. (1990). The draughtsman's contract: how an artist creates an image. In: H. Barlow, C. Blakemore, and M. Weston-Smith (eds), *Images and Understanding*. Cambridge: Cambridge University Press.

Willats, J. (1997). *Art and Representation: New Principles in the Analysis of Pictures*. Princeton, NJ: Princeton University Press.

Wilson, B. (1988). The artistic Tower of Babel: inextricable links between culture and graphic development. In: G.W. Hardiman and T. Zernich (eds), *Discerning Art: Concepts and Issues* (pp. 488–506). Champaign, IL: Stipes Publishing.

Witek, J. (2012). Comics modes: caricature and illustration in the *Crumb Family's Dirty Laundry*. In: M. J. Smith and R. Duncan (eds), *Critical Approaches to Comics, Theories and Methods* (pp. 27–34). New York: Routledge.

Wölfflin, H. (1950). *Principles of Art History: The Problem of the Development of Style in Later Art*. New York: Dover Publications.

Wollheim, R. (1995). Style in painting. In: S. Kemal and I. Gaskell (eds), *The Question of Style in Philosophy and the Arts* (pp. 37–49). Cambridge: Cambridge University Press.

Yuki, M., Maddux, W. W., and Masuda, T. (2006). Are the windows to the soul the same in the East and the West? Cultural differences in using the eyes and mouth as cues to recognize emotions in Japan and the United States. *Journal of Experimental Social Psychology*, 43(2): 303–311.

4

Conceptual Metaphor Theory, Blending Theory and Other Cognitivist Perspectives on Comics

Charles Forceville

Chapter Outline

1. Introduction

In this chapter, I will discuss how conceptual metaphor theory and blending theory provide useful scholarly perspectives on the study of comics. Before going into detail, however, I want to very briefly sketch the broader framework of cognitive science within which these theories can be positioned. The adjective 'cognitive' or 'cognitivist' labels an increasingly influential strand in contemporary humanities disciplines. A great bonus of this development is that it facilitates building bridges with the kind of empirical research that has hitherto primarily been the field of the social sciences. 'Cognitivism' covers a variety of models, which have in common that they focus on how interpretations of discourses, irrespective of the medium in which they occur, can be explained by the workings of the mind. Furthermore cognitivism prizes systematicity and pattern-finding, and is usually contrasted with ideologically oriented approaches. The linguist George Lakoff and the philosopher Mark Johnson succinctly state that 'cognitive science is the scientific discipline that studies conceptual systems' (Lakoff and Johnson, 1999: 10), adding that 'the term *cognitive* is used for any kind of mental operation or structure that can be studied in precise terms. [...] Memory and attention fall under the *cognitive*. All aspects of thought and language, conscious or unconscious are thus *cognitive*' (ibidem: 11, emphasis in original). The film scholars David Bordwell and Noël Carroll propose that 'a cognitivist analysis or explanation seeks to understand human thought, emotion, and action by appeal to processes of mental representation, naturalistic process, and (some sense of) rational agency' (Bordwell and Carroll, 1996: xvi). The narratologist David Herman argues that 'both narrative theory and language theory should [...] be viewed as resources for – elements of – the broader endeavour of cognitive science. The result: a jointly narratological and linguistic approach to stories construed as strategies for building mental models of the world' (2002: 2). Mark Johnson 'attempts to articulate a naturalistic approach to values and moral deliberation that seems [...] compatible with the account of embodied, situated meaning and understanding that has emerged in the cognitive sciences over the past three decades' (2014: 2).

While cognitivists are fully aware of the importance of culture and ideology in the production and reception of discourse, they begin by focusing on how understanding can be explained by mechanisms that are rooted in biological, Darwinian survival (e.g., Boyd et al., 2010). Key elements of this are that we attribute intentionality to our fellow human beings and that, other things being equal, we are likely to help our fellow human beings achieve their goals (e.g., De Waal, 2009); that optimal communication presupposes that we are good at 'reading each other's minds' (e.g., Sperber and Wilson, 1995); that human communication does not only entail transmitting information, but also sharing *attitudes* about that information with others, probably as a way of expanding common ground to aid social identification and bonding (Tomasello, 2008: 282); and that we make sense of our lives by storytelling (Johnson, 2003: chapter 7). Finally, since what unites human beings is having a specific body, much cognitivist research deploys the term 'embodied cognition': knowledge structures are ultimately rooted in humans' motor skills and sensory perception.

Film scholars such as Bordwell and Carroll can be credited with having been the first to apply cognitivist principles to non-verbal and partly verbal discourses.

Researchers working in other media than film are now following suit. It is encouraging that comics and political cartoons are beginning to be examined from cognitivist angles as well. After all, as McLuhan emphasized long ago, 'the medium is the message' (McLuhan, 1964: 14); and the medium of comics differs fundamentally from that of both verbal language (for instance in typically drawing on both the verbal and the visual mode) and from that of film (for instance, in presenting information in sequences of static images, not moving ones; and in not drawing on the sonic mode). Comics and cartoons therefore have their own, medium-specific affordances and constraints. Accepting cognitivist tenets such as those briefly sketched above provides a robust base for patterned strategies to interpret comics. This type of research can in turn feed into insights into visual and multimodal communication more generally. Finally, it can offer new perspectives on cognition, particularly if theoretical findings are formulated as hypotheses to be tested in experimental research.

In this chapter, I will report on cognitivist-oriented work done in the area of comics and cartoons – the latter here considered as standalone varieties of comics that humorously criticize people (often politicians) and events in the world. No claim to exhaustiveness can be made; I will simply discuss a number of publications I am aware of that analyse comics and cartoons from a perspective inspired by cognitive linguistics (CL), specifically by conceptual metaphor theory (CMT) and blending theory (BT).

The chapter has the following structure. In section 2, the bare bones of conceptual metaphor theory and blending theory will be sketched in what, for reasons of space, cannot be more than mere sound bites – just enough to help understand the use that cartoon and comics scholars in the ensuing sections (3 and 4) make of these theories. Section 5 briefly suggests how other cognitive approaches may benefit cartoons and comics research and vice versa, and in the final section some concluding remarks are made.

2. Conceptual metaphor theory, blending theory, image schemas and the embodied mind

Lakoff and Johnson (1980) introduced CMT, although several contributions in Ortony (1979) anticipate some of its dimensions. Defining metaphor as 'understanding and experiencing one kind of thing in terms of another' (1980: 5), they claim that 'metaphor is primarily a matter of thought and action, and only derivatively a matter of language' (ibidem: 153). We are only able to conceptualize abstract and complex phenomena by *systematically* understanding them in terms of concrete phenomena. Concrete phenomena are things that we can perceive with our sensory organs and experience via our bodies' motor functions. Because of this systematic metaphorizing of the abstract in terms of the concrete, Lakoff and Johnson's theory is also referred to as the 'embodied' theory of metaphor. We thus metaphorize all the time, although we are usually not aware of this. For instance, we conceptualize TIME in terms of SPACE[1] ('your holiday is *approaching* fast', 'in the *coming* weeks', 'the *following* month'), and we often use BUILDINGS – alongside other concrete domains – to structure THEORIES ('the *foundations* of your plan are weak'; 'his argument *fell apart*', '*support/ shore up* a theory'). According to CMT, most apparently creative metaphors can be traced back to conceptual ones (Lakoff and Turner, 1989), although this latter idea is not uncontroversial (for some discussion, see Forceville, 2013a). Johnson (1987) explores the 'embodied mind' in greater detail, and among many other things illuminates how our awareness of physical forces structures our understanding of causation itself. Each metaphor has an underlying TARGET A IS SOURCE B structure (see Table 4.1). In fact, since what matters for a metaphor's interpretation is primarily what can be done with/to B, and the valuations and emotions adhering to B, it would be better to capture this dynamic nature (Cameron et al., 2009) in the formulation 'A-ING IS B-ING'.

While a fundamental hybridity thus characterizes each metaphor, there are many other forms of hybridizing that cannot be captured by CMT. This awareness gave rise to blending theory (also known as 'conceptual integration theory'), pioneered by Fauconnier and Turner (e.g., Fauconnier and Turner, 2002). Like CMT, BT postulates

Table 4.1 In a metaphor, some features are literally true of both target and source; others are mapped, or projected, from source to target, thereby changing the target; and yet others are not mappable from source to target

Target		Source
MAN	IS	A WOLF (Thomas Hobbes)
Living creature	↔	Living creature
	↔	. . .
	←	Being aggressive, cruel, bloodthirsty
	←	. . .
	X	Having four legs, a tail
	X	. . .
MARRIAGE	IS	A SEESAW (Hans Dorrestijn)
Phenomenon in the world	↔	Living creature
	↔	. . .
	←	When one spouse goes up/is happy, the other necessarily goes down/is unhappy
	←	. . .
	X	Being made of non-animate material
	X	. . .

Adapted from Forceville, 1996: 11, after Black, 1979.

that different semantic domains (in BT called 'input spaces') merge to create a new 'blended space', or 'blend', which combines selected elements from the input spaces and as a result yields new, emergent meaning that was not present in either of the input spaces. For instance, one could say that 'half-way through this year's football competition, Ajax is three places ahead of itself compared to last year.' The two input spaces here are 'Ajax's position in the football competition after X matches *this year*' and 'Ajax's position in the football competition after X matches *last year*', where the

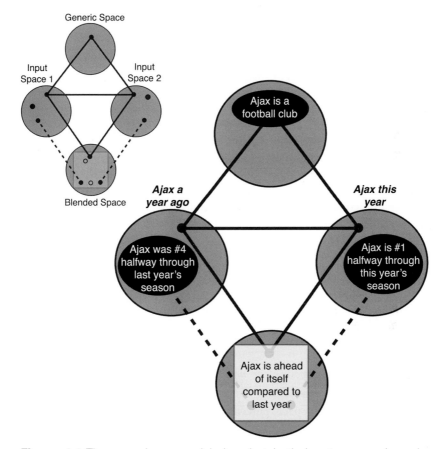

Figure 4.1 The generic space labels what both input spaces have by definition in common; this is also retained in the blend. The uninterrupted lines indicate these stable features. In the Ajax example, for instance, 'being Ajax football club' is such a feature. Input space 1 labels 'Ajax a year ago'; input space 2 labels 'Ajax this year'. Each of the input spaces bestows some unique features to the blend (indicated as black dots connected by interrupted lines). Input space 1 yields 'Ajax takes the number four place half-way through the competition in last year's season'; Input space 2 yields 'Ajax takes the number one place half-way through the competition in this year'. In the blended space, new features arise that do not occur in any of the other spaces (indicated by open dots), notably, 'Ajax is *ahead* of itself compared to last year'.

blended space yields the emergent meaning of Ajax this year 'winning' in a virtual race against itself.

As such, this emergent meaning is not different from what happens in creative varieties of metaphor as discussed by Black (1979; see Forceville, 2004), but BT can accommodate elements that Black's theory of creative metaphor or, for that matter, CMT, cannot. In the first place, a blend can 'democratically' merge two input spaces, whereas a metaphor always makes a statement about a target in terms of a source, never the other way round. Secondly, BT can model non-metaphorical hybrids, such as the virtual match that Ajax plays against itself, and counterfactuals (for instance, 'If I were you . . .', or the conceptualization of aliens in science fiction combining human and non-human characteristics). Thirdly, blended spaces, unlike metaphors, can be the result of more than two input spaces.

Problems with BT are that every hybrid can, retrospectively, be modelled as a blend, which as such is not very illuminating, and that it is not quite clear what qualifies as an input space. Moreover, the role of pragmatics in the theory deserves to be discussed more elaborately. That is, the theory requires more constraints and construction principles. A promising principle is that blends allow 'compression' of events that in reality take place sequentially into a single representation – and this latter is something that happens in many cartoons and comics panels.

To conclude this section: both CMT and BT rely on mental structures known as 'image schemas'. 'An *image schema* . . . is a dynamic pattern that functions somewhat like the abstract structure of an image, and thereby connects up a vast range of different experiences that manifest this same recurring structure' (Johnson, 1987: 2, emphasis in original). Examples of image schemas are CONTAINMENT, SOURCE-PATH-GOAL, LINK, PART-WHOLE, CENTRE-PERIPHERY, BALANCE, MOTION, and FORCE. Beate Hampe elaborates:

- Image schemas are *directly meaningful* ('experiential'/'embodied'), *preconceptual* structures, which arise from, or are grounded in, human recurrent bodily movements through space, perceptual interaction, and ways of manipulating objects.
- Image schemas are highly *schematic* gestalts which capture the structural *contours* of sensory-motor experience, integrating information from multiple modalities.
- Image schemas exist as *continuous* and *analogue* patterns *beneath* conscious awareness, prior to and independently of other concepts.
- As gestalts, image schemas are both *internally structured*, i.e., made up of very few related parts, and highly *flexible*. This flexibility becomes manifest in the numerous transformations they undergo in various experiential contexts, all of which are closely related to perceptual (gestalt) principles (Hampe, 2005: 1–2, emphases in original).

Image schemas are basic mental scaffolds for meaning-making that are necessarily incomplete and open-ended; they always need to be complemented by specific, detailed information before they can give rise to contextually relevant meaning. They are thus essential components of the knowledge repertoire that human beings can recruit in their understanding of cartoons and comics (and of all other potentially meaningful information).

3. Studies on cartoons drawing on CL, CMT and BT

Several scholars have used CMT and BT to help explain how it is that we understand political newspaper cartoons.

3.1. Metaphors in political cartoons

El Refaie (2003) was probably the first to extend the applications of metaphor theory to standalone political cartoons. Drawing on CMT, El Refaie makes the important observation that paying attention to the conceptual level of visual metaphors (that is: identifying their underlying A-IS-B structure) should not lead to neglecting the specific *formal* stylistic rendering of target and source. This is already often ignored in CMT scholarship focusing on *verbal* manifestations of conceptual metaphors; the analyst of its *pictorial* varieties should moreover be sensitive to the specific affordances of the visual mode. El Refaie points out that 'while language is perhaps more precise in expressing some areas of meaning, other meanings may be shown more easily and more effectively in images rather than in words' (2003: 84). She repeats this warning a bit later: 'visual metaphors are not always simply translations into the visual mode of verbal metaphors [...]. Provided that the viewer is familiar with the context, a cartoon is thus sometimes able to convey a complex message in a much more immediate and condensed fashion than language' (2003: 87). Moreover, El Refaie states, visuals may more easily give rise to affective responses than language does. She also emphasizes how indispensable socio-political background knowledge is for interpreting political cartoons. Even though she analyses only four cartoons, she hints at the possibility that certain target domains are metaphorized *systematically* in terms of the same source domains (e.g., IMMIGRATION in terms of INVASION). Indeed, this point is shown to be correct in Reehorst's (2014) extensive and detailed analysis of the metaphors used in cartoons published during two presidential election campaigns.

El Refaie (2009) further pursues the analysis of visual/pictorial and multimodal metaphor (in cartoons, multimodal metaphors draw on combinations on visuals and

Figure 4.2 Nicholas Garland, *Daily Telegraph*, 2
November 2004 (discussed in El Refaie, 2009).

language). She discusses a cartoon by Nicholas Garland in the *Daily Telegraph* (see
Figure 4.2) that shows a baby with the face of George Bush Jr crawling away from a
big fire toward a box of matches with the text '4 more years', suggesting that re-election
of the president will cause more trouble of the kind he already caused up till that
moment. Comprehension of the cartoon depends on the metaphors GEORGE BUSH
IS A TODDLER and TIME IS SPACE – the latter because the baby 'crawls toward the
future'. Using this and other cartoons as stimulus material in an experiment with
twenty-five sixteen- to nineteen-year-olds in Bradford, UK, El Refaie found
that these young people – often from British-Asian backgrounds – lacked the basic
socio-political background knowledge to understand the metaphors. The experiment
is a healthy reminder that analysing cartoons and other visuals, whether or not
accompanied by language, should take into account the knowledge and beliefs (what
Sperber and Wilson, 1995, call 'cognitive environment') of their recipients.

Teng (2009), expanding on Teng and Sun (2002), joins El Refaie (2003) in pointing
out that the visual surface structure of cartoons needs to be taken into account no less
than the conceptual meaning of the elements they contain. He points out that the
design of cartoons can alert viewers to similarity between visual elements by depicting
them as belonging to the same 'group'. This can be captured in the metaphor
SIMILARITY IS ALIGNMENT. For example, a cartoon by Clay Bennett from 2002,
labelled 'endangered species', shows three animals in a row: a rhinoceros (heading:
'Southern Africa'), a panda ('Western China') and a (symbolical peace) dove ('Middle
East') (Figure 4.3). In this case, the captions, together with the image alignment
(which has a family resemblance to Forceville's [1996] 'pictorial simile') cue a
metaphorical interpretation; but the concept of image alignment seems a useful tool
for the analysis of elements in cartoons and comics panels more generally.

Schilperoord and Maes (2009), investigating a corpus of one hundred and
seventeen Dutch and twenty-seven international editorial cartoons, rightly emphasize
one important generic dimension of such political cartoons, namely that they are

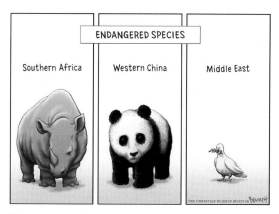

Figure 4.3 Cartoon by Clay Bennett, *The Christian Science Monitor*, 24 May 2002, page 10 (discussed in Teng, 2009).

always *critical* of a person or state of affairs in the world (as opposed, for instance, to advertisements, which typically convey *positive* features of a product; see Forceville, 1996: 104), and this is a central factor in the interpretation of the metaphor. (Arguably, another genre-specific element is that a political cartoon is supposed to be at least mildly humorous.) The authors' findings reveal that certain source domains (such as MARRIAGE, FUNERALS, BOXING, SHIPS and ANIMALS) recur in their corpus, which yet again confirms the CMT idea that we conceptualize certain targets *systematically* in terms of certain sources – but it also shows that such sources are not necessarily embodied (e.g., 'marriage').

Although acknowledging that 'the interpretation of cartoon metaphors is to a certain extent driven by genre-related, pragmatic considerations' (Schilperoord and Maes, 2009: 219), the authors 'intend to account for the metaphoric conceptualization and critical stance of editorial cartoons *in terms of what is actually shown in the image*, rather than in terms of the cultural and general discourse context' (ibid., emphasis in original). While I agree that there are often text-internal verbo-visual cues that alert the viewer to activate negative mappings (one can think here of hyperbolic elements), surely these are always subservient to the judgment that all these appear in a picture belonging to the genre of the 'political cartoon' – and this is indispensable *pragmatic* knowledge. For instance, one of the cartoons discussed was published at the time of the world champion soccer tournament in Japan and South Korea. We see the pictorial metaphor FOOTBALL IS SUN, in which the earth revolves around a 'football'-sun. But there is nothing *intrinsically* critical about the mapping from SUN to FOOTBALL. Any critical mappings ('these days, everything revolves around football; ridiculously, it has become more important than the sun itself!') depend on the genre-attribution: this is a political cartoon, which has 'critical stance' as one of its genre-conventions. But in a football fanzine, the same picture would presumably evoke the same mappings from source to target – but with a positive slant. The broader point here is that the meaning of *all* text/internal information can as it were be overruled by considerations of genre. I therefore propose that genre is the primary cue for channeling interpretation and constitutes the single most important pragmatic element steering viewers' interpretations of discourse.

Bounegru and Forceville (2011) examine a corpus of thirty cartoons from the first two weeks in October 2008 about a single topic: the suddenly exploding financial crisis. We postulate that twenty-five of the cartoons contain metaphors that have FINANCIAL CRISIS or a concept closely related to it as target domain. Our brief was to examine whether we could cluster the source domains under general labels. Indeed we could: the most often recurring source is NATURAL DISASTER; other recurring source domains are ILLNESS/DEATH and BEGGING. The relevance of being able to find recurring source domains in non-verbal and not-just-verbal cartoons is that this supports Lakoff and Johnson's central idea that we *think* metaphorically. If correct, this means that we should be able to identify many non-verbal and multimodal manifestations of conceptual metaphors. We pay considerable attention to explaining on what grounds we categorize a metaphor as a 'monomodal visual metaphor' (which requires that target and source should be identifiable without any aid of verbal captions or 'spoken' texts) or as 'multimodal metaphors' (which requires that eliminating either visuals or text would result in the disappearance of either target or source). One of the complex issues in this assessment is that whereas *at the time of accessing* a specific political cartoon, much essential information can be easily retrieved from the socio-political context (at the time of publication concepts such as '9/11', 'exploding financial crisis', 'Christmas', 'Olympic Games', etc. are clearly foremost in most newspaper readers' minds), this is no longer the case at a later moment. Davies (1995), for instance, discusses many old political cartoons whose meaning is baffling for the reader of his paper. This rapid process of becoming incomprehensible can mean that the republished version of cartoons (as in the online versions of the cartoons we used as data in our paper) require verbal captions that were not necessary at the original time of publication. In turn, this has the consequence that categorizing a given metaphor as monomodally visual ('both target and source can be retrieved from the visual information') or as multimodal of the verbo-pictorial variety ('the target is only given visually, and the source is only given verbally, or vice versa') may depend on the background knowledge of the viewer of analyst *at the moment of accessing the cartoon*. Finally, Bounegru and Forceville (2011) show that the source domains all have a strongly embodied dimension, but that this embodied dimension is usually to be complemented by cultural knowledge. Worth mentioning is that even within the NATURAL DISASTER domain, although undoubtedly inspired by embodied experience, there are cultural differences: a Thai cartoon chooses the source domain TSUNAMI, and a Swiss one AVALANCHE.

3.2. Beyond metaphor in political cartoons: blends and cultural models

Bergen (2003) examines a corpus of two hundred and nineteen cartoons that all appeared in the week following 9/11, demonstrating how their interpretation depends on mechanisms explained by a combination of CMT, BT, and cultural models (Holland and Quinn, 1987). He finds many instances of the 'personification' variety of metaphor, such as NATION IS PERSON (specifically the familiar USA IS UNCLE SAM). Some visual hybrids cannot be theorized in terms of a simple metaphorical TARGET A IS SOURCE B format. For instance, a cartoon showing Uncle Sam with smoke coming from his hat (Figure 4.4), accompanied by the text 'A day of infamy' requires the awareness of at least four 'input spaces': the USA-IS-UNCLE-SAM metaphor; the smoking Twin Towers; the ANGER IS SMOKE-FROM-THE-HEAD metaphor; and the attack on Pearl Harbor in 1941 (via the 'a day of infamy' text).

Here, a BT approach works better than a metaphorical analysis because it can handle more than two input spaces (although an input space can itself consist of a metaphor, as in this case: USA IS UNCLE SAM). Unfortunately, Bergen's analysis of another cartoon which shows a hybrid of the collapsing Twin Towers and the attack on Pearl Harbor in terms of a blend ignores that *metaphors are subtypes of blends*. This is not very clear from Fauconnier and Turner's work, but Grady et al. repeatedly discuss 'metaphoric blends' (1999: 114, *et passim*), thereby acknowledging that there are other types of blends as well. Spelling out the consequences of this mistaken view is beyond the remit of this chapter (for some discussion, see Forceville, 2004). Bergen ends with briefly discussing the importance of cultural models for the understanding of political cartoons. In his corpus, he specifically identifies the NEED-TO-EXTERMINE-VERMIN model (invariably used in the TERRORISTS ARE VERMIN metaphor) and the fairytale model, in which an innocent victim is morally wronged by a villain. Although Bergen acknowledges the importance of captions and 'spoken' texts, he does not systematically address the issue what is their precise role in the cartoons' metaphors and blends.

Figure 4.4 Post-9/11 cartoon by Mit Priggee (discussed in Bergen, 2003).

Marín-Arrese (2008) extends the work by Bergen (2003), investigating a number of political cartoons in France, Britain and Spain following the French 'no' in the referendum of 29 May 2005, held to decide on acceptance/rejection of the European Constitution. Marín-Arrese, too, shows how viewers need to draw on conceptual metaphors, blends, and cultural models, to make sense of the cartoons. Moreover, she insists on the importance of metonymy. Metonymy – the trope that until Barcelona (2000) and Dirven and Pörings (2002) was seen as metaphor's plainer, less sexy sister – can be defined as the trope in which one concept *stands for* another concept from the same domain. In 'all *hands* on deck', 'hands' refers to the sailors in possession of those hands; in '*the first violin* is ill today', 'the first violin' refers to the player of the violin. Marín-Arrese's insistence on the pertinence of metonymy makes sense: after all, abstract concepts ('democracy', 'referendum', 'rejection') cannot themselves be depicted, and thus must be somehow cued by symbols (e.g., 'Marianne' for France), stock situations, and sociocultural scenarios (e.g., Spanish bullfighting, British foxhunting, the assassination of Caesar, the sinking of the Titanic, Zeus' abduction of Europa) – many of which can be understood as drawing on metonymy.

Political cartoons are supposed to be funny, and different theorists concur in pointing out that humour always depends on an unexpected integration of two incompatible scenarios (e.g., Attardo, 1997). Consequently, it is no surprise that Marín-Arrese finds BT – which after all always draws on minimally two input spaces – useful in modelling how cartoons are interpreted. Her analyses point up several pertinent issues: often, blends depend themselves on other (metaphoric or non-metaphoric) blends; an 'input space' can be rendered visually, verbally, or in both modalities (which shows that BT can help model multimodal discourse). One of the paper's most fruitful and promising findings is the pertinence of the notion of 'condensing time' by showing causes, events, and consequences in a single picture, discussed as 'compression' in BT.

Although not explicitly mentioned by the author, the cartoons she discusses all draw on highly embodied source domains/input spaces, which further supports a central CMT tenet. Of course, awareness of these always needs to be complemented by cultural background knowledge, as is now commonly accepted within CMT (Gibbs and Steen, 1999; Kövecses, 2005).

4. Studies on comics drawing on CL, CMT and BT

In Cohn (2013a), the author (who earlier demonstrated the pertinence of metaphor, metonymy and blends in a discussion of three-panel promotional strips, in Cohn, 2010) provides an overall framework for analysis informed by insights by cognitive linguists such as Ray Jackendoff and Len Talmy. Other cognitivist work zooms in on specific elements within comics. Specifically, studies on comics expanding on CMT have hitherto focused on the representation of movement, time, and emotions.

4.1. Cognitive linguistics as inspirational model for analysing comics

Neil Cohn's monograph *The Visual Language of Comics: Introduction to the Structure and Cognition of Sequential Images* constitutes undoubtedly the most complete and ambitious CL-inspired analysis of comics – understood as a medium allowing for the combination of sequential images and verbal language in all kinds of permutations – hitherto published. As its title suggests, Cohn pushes the analogy between comics and (verbal) language as far as he can, while simultaneously making clear that '*comics are **not** a language*, but they are written in a visual language of sequential images' (Cohn 2013a: 2, emphases in original). While I have problems accepting Cohn's use of the words 'grammar' and 'vocabulary' in this context, this is mainly a matter of terminology. I would say that visuals do not have a grammar or a vocabulary, but that they have *structure* (Forceville, 1999) and, in my terminology, it is such structure that Cohn systematically investigates. In Chapter 2, he discusses the distinction between 'open class' items in panels (elements that can be drawn in endlessly varying ways) and 'closed class items' (recurring elements such as balloons and movement lines that have a more or less fixed form). Chapter 3 focuses on 'panel templates', conventionalized panels and panel sequences, which the artist and the reader can retrieve from memory, for production and reception purposes, respectively. Next, the various functions that panels can fulfil are illuminated. For instance, a panel can set the scene, show prolonged action, or depict a climactic action. Awareness of typical events and of narrative scenarios helps the reader understand panels and relations between panels. Cohn continues with analysing how page layout can facilitate or block the reader's path from one panel to another, presenting a number of 'rules' that are typically observed in this navigating process. Chapter 6 summarizes earlier research, some of it experimental, on motion lines and balloons. Cohn here also presents his own experimental research testing the relative contribution to understanding of the variables identified and explained in his theory in preceding chapters. Although far more internationally accessible than verbal languages, visuals are not universally comprehensible, and thus their meaning must to some extent be *learned*. To illustrate this point, the second part of the book comprises chapters on three types of 'visual language': American Visual Language (and its various 'dialects'), Japanese Visual Language (*manga*), and Central Australian Visual Language (Aboriginal sand drawing). Throughout the book, the author emphasizes that comprehension of comics (as of anything else) results from bringing to bear cognitive schemas upon the word and image comics 'texts'.

Cohn's monograph has several strengths. In the first place, it provides an all-encompassing framework for the analysis of sequential art that thanks to its systematic nature enables and invites application, expansion and refinement by other scholars. For the same reason, it functions as a treasure trove for experimental research, some of which he has already conducted himself. Furthermore, while obviously seeking to contribute substantially to comics scholarship, the author is right to consider his study to feed into visual studies theory more generally. A self-imposed limitation of the study is that the focus on how the visual part of comics convey meaning means that little is said about its verbal accompaniment, let alone about their interaction (but see Cohn, 2013b). Finally, Cohn introduces a substantial number of new terms for the many variables discussed in the book. However, most of these terms do not correspond with any that earlier theorists deployed. It depends on whether this precise but idiosyncratic terminology will catch on whether it should be considered a strength or weakness of this monograph.

4.2. Image schemas and conceptual metaphors in comics

Drawing on Johnson (1987) and Talmy (2000), Potsch and Williams (2012) discuss image schemas and conceptual metaphors as sources of embodied understanding that are useful in the analysis of comics. The TIME IS SPACE metaphor (Lakoff and Johnson, 1980) is a very important one in the American action comics the authors analyse. Time and space, in turn, are crucial building blocks in the image schema of CAUSE–EFFECT. After all, only an event A that has preceded an event B could have caused that event B, whereas the reverse is not true. Potsch and Williams argue that awareness of these two schemas helps comics readers understand sequences of events, and their causal relationships – even if these events are depicted in a single panel.

With respect to the TIME/SPACE/CAUSATION schemas, the authors distinguish three 'stylized symbols commonly used in action comics to represent the dynamics of events: ribbon paths, motion lines, and impact flashes'. They explain:

> *Ribbon paths* indicate movement within a comic panel from one location to another, emphasizing the path traveled by the character or object that moves; [. . .] *Motion lines* emphasize motion without regard to path (to starting and ending locations) and are used to place the reader in the center of action as if moving with the characters, providing a participant's perspective to heighten the drama. *Impact flashes* represent the application or exchange of forces: sites where movements are initiated or terminated and, in particular, collisions between characters or objects in motion.
>
> (Potsch and Williams, 2012: 15, emphases in original)

a)    b)

Figure 4.5 a) From: *Michel Vaillant: De Dwangarbeider* (Jean Graton, 1984) (original in colour), b) From: *Guust: Van Flaters Gesproken* (Franquin, 1977) (original in colour).

They discuss several comics panels to show what they mean. Figures 4.5a and 4.5b exemplify the three elements in two panels I chose myself.

In Figure 4.5a, the straight lines on the road are motion lines; the curved white bands above the wheels would be ribbons paths. Perhaps the circular configurations behind the exhaust pipes count as impact flashes (note that other terms are in use; and arguably ribbon paths are a subtype of motion lines). In Figure 4.5b, the eponymous Guust Flater (in French: Gaston Lagaffe) has just hit a screwdriver with a hammer in order to open a tin of sardines. We see ribbon paths showing the trajectory of the hammer, the screwdriver, and the sardine tin, while the star-like configuration below Guust's left hand is an impact flash (supported by the onomatopoeic 'Tsjak' – as is the tin's trajectory by 'ZZZ'). As in the superhero comics panel that Potsch and Williams analyse as the last one in their paper, we draw on our knowledge of the SOURCE-PATH-GOAL schema to determine the order of events in this panel: Guust first lets the raised hammer come down on the screwdriver, which subsequently causes the screwdriver to jump away to his right, and the tin to start a fateful journey to his left.

Potsch and Williams argue that ribbon paths, motion lines, and impact flashes are not *arbitrary* signals, but motivated, embodied ones, as we draw on schemata developed from our experiences in real life to make sense of them.

4.3. Emotion metaphors in comics

A complex concept that is typically structured and understood by means of metaphors is that of emotions. Kövecses (1986) specifically discusses ANGER, PRIDE and LOVE. The predominant metaphor for ANGER that Kövecses identifies is ANGER IS HOT FLUID IN A PRESSURIZED CONTAINER. The idea here is that an angry person feels the anger 'boiling' in his body-container; this causes pressure that needs somehow to escape or be released; and this in turn gives rise to expressions such as 'the *steam* was coming out of his ears', 'she almost *hit the ceiling*', 'they *burst out* against me'. My own work on comics started because of an interest in trying to see whether, and if so, how, this conceptual metaphor also manifests itself visually in the comics medium. In Forceville (2005a), I choose the album *Asterix and the Roman Agent* (Goscinny and

Uderzo, 1972), featuring many angry people, and inventory all the visual signals that help communicate to the viewer: 'this character is angry'. A distinction is made between facial expressions, arm positions, the flourishes around emotionally affected characters' heads (labelled 'pictorial runes', after Kennedy, 1982, but also known under other names), and contours of text balloons and their tails. On the basis of a systematic analysis of 103 angry characters in the 398 panels in the album, I provisionally conclude that the anger manifestations in this album are at least *commensurate* with the pressurized container metaphor. But it needs to be acknowledged that some of the manifestations of anger are also compatible with other metaphors, such as ANGRY BEHAVIOUR IS AGGRESSIVE ANIMAL BEHAVIOUR or ANGER IS INSANITY. However, these, and others, arguably all fit a more encompassing metaphor: EMOTIONS ARE PHYSICAL FORCES (Kövecses, 2008). Acceptance of the above reasoning is important for CMT since, as with Potsch and Williams' findings, it would confirm the embodied status of the source domain in emotion metaphors. But even if the reasoning is not accepted – a sceptic might argue that the various anger cues are conventionalized but arbitrary signals rather than conventionalized but motivated ones – this line of research still encourages systematic study of recurrent signals of emotion (and of anything else, for that matter) in comics.

Shinohara and Matsunaka (2009) take Kövecses' and Forceville's work as a starting point to examine signs of anger and other emotions in Japanese *manga*. By and large, they find the same runes that Forceville (2005a) found in *Asterix and the Roman Agent*, but identify two additional signals for emotions: the 'popped-up' vein rune (see Figure 4.6) cues anger, while sometimes non-realistic backgrounds in panels symbolically convey characters' moods (e.g., a black, but non-literal, 'cloud' behind a character suggests that she is angry).

Abbott and Forceville (2011) point up a non-literal emotion-related element in the *manga* series *Azumanga Daioh* that is not mentioned by Shinohara and Matsunaka

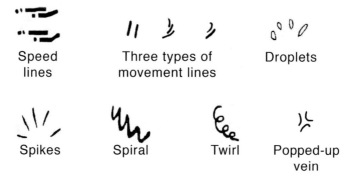

Figure 4.6 Stylized examples of pictorial runes used in *Tintin and the Picaros* (adapted from Forceville, 2011a: 877); the popped-up vein appears in *manga*, as identified by Shinohara and Matsunaka (2009).

(2009) and that does not belong to the standard 'super-deformed style' in *manga* (in which emotionally affected characters temporarily sport, for instance, unrealistically big square mouths and eyes substituted by stars): the temporary (literal!) disappearance of characters' hands. In a systematic investigation of all 1,257 panels in volume four of the series, in which one or more of the six heroines are recognizably present, we found that they are without hands in one of the following situations: (1) they make an involuntary movement (e.g., when tripping over); (2) they are very angry; (3) they fantasize or daydream. We see as common element in these three situations the loss of control, formulating the metaphor LOSS OF HANDS IS LOSS OF CONTROL. Correlating the three reasons for hand-loss with each of the six heroines, we claim that the (in)frequency of hand-loss and its specific reason helps characterize the heroines, and thus functions as a narratological tool.

Although not analysing comics, Díaz Vera (2013) deserves to be mentioned here. This author draws, among others, on Forceville (2005a) to discuss patterns in body postures and facial expressions in a medieval 'predecessor' of the comics medium: the famous Bayeux tapestry, which depicts, in thirty-two scenes, the events leading to the 1066 Norman Conquest of England. Díaz Vera inventories all visual manifestations of the emotions GRIEF, FEAR, and ANGER in the tapestry. In order to be correctly understood by viewers, these depictions need to conform to certain stereotypes that, while rooted in real-life behaviour, indexically cue these emotions in a stylized manner. The author distinguishes nineteen different signals. Seven of these pertain to facial expressions (involving the eyes, eyebrows and mouth); ten pertain to bodily gestures (involving head, neck, shoulders, trunk, arms, hands and legs); and two pertain to body size. Díaz Vera concludes that the pictorial signals analysed in the Bayeux tapestry 'are commensurate with the results of research on the linguistic expression of emotions' (2013: 282). As does Forceville (2011a) for the comics album he analyses, the author points out that none of the signals identified can singlehandedly cue an emotion, while conversely a given signal can be used, in combination with other signals, to cue different emotions.

In Forceville (2011a), I investigate all panels of Hergé's *Tintin and the Picaros* (1976), providing a 'catalogue' of the pictorial runes used in this album (see Figure 4.6). My provisional conclusion is that (a) a limited number of runes are recurrently used; (b) each of the runes has a basic meaning, which depends on its form, its orientation, and its location. From a CMT point of view, the most interesting finding is that the 'twirl' rune is used both (literally) to help cue physical movement and (figuratively) to help cue 'drunkenness' and 'confusion'. If we understand the latter as 'movement-in-the-head', we can postulate a motivated similarity between the 'literal' and the 'metaphorical' use of the twirl; a visual version of EMOTION IS MOTION.

Even if my hypothesis that pictorial runes have a basic, embodied meaning should be correct, this does not mean that their meaning is necessarily always self-evident. Usually additional visual and verbal information is required to assess their precise meaning, and in any case the meanings have become conventionalized. But from the point of view of theorizing the relation between visual communication and cognition, it is worthwhile to further investigate the idea that the manifestations of runes, pictograms and other non-realistic signs are rooted in embodied meaning, and therefore constitute non-arbitrary signs.

Forceville et al. (2010) investigate another stock element in mainstream comics: the text balloon. Analysing a corpus of six albums (European comics as well as American ones), we present six visual variables of comics balloons that have narrative significance: (1) contour of the balloon; (2) inclusion of pictograms; (3) inclusion of standalone punctuation marks; (4) use of colour; (5) deployment of more than one type font; (6) behaviour of tails. A corpus of some four thousand balloons from six comics albums is examined with reference to these variables. The counting part of the project enables us to say something about the balloon-strategies of each artist, but our primary goal is to formulate a 'blueprint' of the typical text balloon and its most common variations. Such a blueprint enriches the stylistic toolkit of the comics analyst and can be used for comparing balloon use across artists, periods, movements, and cultures.

Forceville (2013b) expands on these findings, using BT to inventory how balloon variables can be creatively used to convey narrative information. The leading idea is to consider the narrative information the artist presumably wanted to convey in an original manner in terms of a blend. This blend has as two input spaces (1) the concept of the text balloon as vehicle for carrying a character's speech or thought; and (2) an unusual *formal* element in the balloon that somehow confers a specific meaning to the saying or thinking. The examples analysed thus differ from the norms and standard-deviations-from-the-norm identified in Forceville et al. (2010). The various creative balloon uses all present information about one of the following: manner of speaking, topic of speaking, or identity of speaker.

4.4. Emotions in comics: unpublished work

Several students of mine have written on pictorial runes, mostly in unpublished essays and MA theses. I report on this work in Forceville (2011b). I here highlight some findings from of this summary. Eerden (2004, 2009), expanding on Forceville (2005a), considers various visual markers signalling emotions both in several *Asterix* comics and *Asterix* animation films. Probably because animation films have movement as well as sound, they have less need to draw on pictorial runes than comics do. Eerden finds some pertinent postures for anger not identified by Forceville (2005a), and some animation-specific runes. In his thesis, Eerden (2004) also analyses another emotion in an *Asterix* comic, 'romantic love', theorized on the basis of verbal manifestations in Kövecses (1986). One of Eerden's conclusions is that anger and love usually deploy the same set of runes, while the facial and postural information tends to differ. Interestingly, Eerden finds that handbooks for budding comics and animation artists make suggestions for how to express emotions that are very similar to those he and Forceville have found.

Thijs van Eunen (2007), in his MA thesis, expands emotions in comics research by focusing on two hitherto unexamined emotions, fear and pride. He also takes into account insights by McCloud (2006). For 'fear', the droplets-rune is the most commonly occurring marker (present in over eighty per cent of sixty-two cases). Other markers are 'white face' and salient arm/hand positions. Pride has no really unique runes, but does feature specific bodily signals: a protruded chest, an upward head, and a mouth that curls downwards. Van Eunen compares his findings for anger and love in *Asterix* with those in another comics series, Carl Barks's *Donald Duck*. He finds considerable overlap between the markers used for both series, but *Asterix* makes a much richer use of the emotion-marker repertoire than *Donald Duck*. Finally, the author discusses some differences arising from the fact that *Asterix* features humans and *Donald Duck* animals.

Having compiled a corpus of more than 5,500 messages containing the word 'disgust' or any of a series of synonyms on Twitter, Jasper Moes (Moes, 2010) develops a prototype scenario of disgust in the spirit of Kövecses (1986, 2000), which he subsequently applies to a substantial sample of *Calvin and Hobbes* cartoons (Bill Watterson). Like Forceville, Eerden, and van Eunen, Moes finds that several pictorial markers are used both for anger and for disgust (the latter emotion much more rare than the former in the Watterson sample), although a tongue hanging out of a mouth and a hand held on a stomach are reliable markers for disgust. Moes finds a hitherto unmentioned marker for anger: an angry Calvin may have his hands on his hips.

Alaina Schempp (2011), finally, implicitly corroborates van Eunen's earlier findings about pride: she analyses this emotion in a Scott Pilgrim comic, and finds as key feature 'expansion of the body'. In addition, she proposes that the symmetric arrangement of characters in the composition of a frame for 'romantic love' could be seen as a rendering of Kövecses' (1986) LOVE IS UNITY metaphor.

The systematic study of pictorial runes, balloons, pictograms, facial expressions, and body postures has only just begun: clearly many more analyses – in different albums by the same artist, comics by different artists, different periods, different traditions etc. – need to be conducted to confirm, or disconfirm, the patterns and tendencies hitherto found.

5. Other pertinent cognitivist approaches

As indicated in the introduction, other cognitivist oriented approaches besides CL/CMT/BT provide fruitful perspectives on the further development of comics scholarship, and of visual studies more generally. I would like to mention very briefly two that are particularly pertinent.

5.1. Cognitivism in film studies

Cognitivist film scholars (united in the SCSMI – Society of Cognitive Studies of the Moving Image, with its journal *Projections*) have much to contribute to theorizing narration in comics and other non-verbal and multimodal media. Bordwell and Carroll (1996) is a collection of cognitivist studies opening with polemical chapters by the two editors. The 'grand theory' they criticize is psychoanalysis, the dominant paradigm of the day, and its 'successor' culturalism. Both authors emphasize the importance of ideologically unaligned scholarship; the need to fit models to data rather than the other way round; the value of explicit, corpus-driven research; the difference between the honourable scholarly pursuit of identifying patterns and the equally honourable, but very different, scholarly pursuit of 'criticism'. (Kukkonen, 2013, argues along very compatible lines for the medium of comics – although in much less harsh tones.) Murray Smith's (1995) proposal to replace the vague concept of viewers' 'identifying' with film characters by a 'structure of engagement' that distinguishes between recognition of characters, alignment with characters, and allegiance with characters allows for easy adaptation to comics and cartoons. Tan (2001) provides a cognitive psychologist's take on the central role of emotion in film (see also Plantinga, 2009). Grodal (2009) develops the PECMA model (perception, emotion, cognition, and motor action) to explain how we understand film. Scholars specifically interested in metaphor and 'embodied cognition' in film will find Coëgnarts and Kravanja (2014) and Fahlenbrach (in preparation) of interest. A further step is taken in Shimamura (2013), which shows how the central tenets of cognitivist film scholarship are at the basis of empirical research involving viewers' understanding of film fragments (in the form of experiments drawing on verbalized responses, eye-tracking, reaction times, brain scans, etc.). Again, much of this provides ideas for comics and cartoons research.

5.2. Relevance theory

Although Sperber and Wilson's (1995) views on metaphor differ substantially from those of CMT, their relevance theory is clearly cognitivist in character. Taking their cue from Gricean pragmatics, these authors build their theory of communication and cognition on the fundamental assumption that human beings (probably *all* species) are biologically hardwired to pay attention to relevant data in their environment. In their communication, human beings usually try to help each other achieve their goals, and that is why communication is governed by the principle of optimal relevance: a given communicator tries to formulate her message to a given addressee in such a way that the message will have the best possible effect at the least possible mental effort for that specific addressee. A positive effect is any information that helps the addressee achieve his goals – which range from exceedingly short-lived ones such as wanting to know the time or where the station is, to very broad and vague ones such as wishing to be free of pain, having enough to eat, or being happy. For present purposes, it is pertinent to note that while Sperber and Wilson claim that their theory holds for all communication, they have hitherto mainly focused on face-to-face communication. Attempts to extend the model to other modalities such as the visual, and to mass-communication, are still rare (see Forceville, 1996, chapter 5, 2005b, 2014; Yus, 2008, 2009; Forceville and Clark, 2014).

6. Concluding remarks and further research

This chapter has discussed a number of CL/CMT/BT-inspired studies that propose fruitful angles for analysing comics and cartoons. For one thing, these studies contribute models for systematically analysing comics' medium-specific repertoire (pictorial runes, balloons, ribbons, facial expressions and body postures, etc.) to create meaning. Conversely, they help analyse how abstract concepts such as 'emotion' and 'time' can be visually conveyed. Some scholars have gone beyond theorizing pertinent variables, and have started to test their occurrence and significance in corpora and in experimental research. This latter work is in its infancy, and deserves to be expanded: the variables discussed, and others (see Forceville et al., 2014) need to be examined for instance cross-culturally, diachronically, and in different subgenres of comics. Such investigations are not just of interest to comics scholars, but will benefit both visual studies more generally and cognitive science. It is important that CL, CMT and BT are further explored for their usefulness in analysing comics and cartoons, but are considered as complementing, not replacing, other approaches. Given that comics and cartoons draw on the two modalities of visuals and written language, they also provide an excellent medium for furthering the budding discipline of multimodality (Jewitt, 2013). However, this requires that scholars pay more structural attention not only to patterns in comics' visuals, but also to their verbal language, and the interaction between both. Bateman (2014) offers good leads for this line of research.

Cognitivist approaches are indispensable for developing the study of comics into a serious humanities discipline, while in turn such cognitivist-oriented comics scholarship is a *sine qua non* for theorizing visual communication and, indeed, cognition itself.

Acknowledgement

I thank Neil Cohn for critical comments on earlier versions of this chapter, and for drafting Figure 4.1 for me.

Note

1. It is customary in CMT to refer to concepts by SMALL CAPITALS, and to refer to the verbal manifestations of such concepts and conceptual metaphors in *italics*.

References

Abbott, M., and Forceville, C. (2011). Loss of control is loss of hands in *Azumanga Daioh* volume 4. *Language and Literature*, 20(2): 91–112.

Attardo, S. (1997). The semantic foundations of cognitive theories of humor. *Humor*, 10: 395–420.

Barcelona, A. (ed.) (2000). *Metaphor and Metonymy at the Crossroads: A Cognitive Perspective*. Berlin: Mouton de Gruyter.

Bateman, J. (2014). *Text and Image: A Critical Introduction to the Visual/Verbal Divide*. London: Routledge.

Bergen, B. (2003). To awaken a sleeping giant cognition and culture in September 11 political cartoons. In: M. Achard and S. Kemmer (eds), *Language, Culture, and Mind* (pp. 23–35). Stanford, CA: CSLI Publications.

Black, M. (1979). More about metaphor. In: A. Ortony (ed.), *Metaphor and Thought* (pp. 19–43). Cambridge, MA: Cambridge University Press.

Bordwell, D., and Carroll, N. (1996). Introduction. In: Bordwell and Carroll (eds), *Post-Theory: Reconstructing Film Studies* (pp. xiii–xvii). Madison, WI: University of Wisconsin Press.

Bounegru, L., and Forceville, C. (2011). Metaphors in editorial cartoons representing the global financial crisis. *Journal of Visual Communication*, 10: 209–229.

Boyd, B., Carroll, J., and Gottschall, J. (eds) (2010). *Evolution, Literature and Film*. New York: Columbia University Press.

Cameron, L., Maslen, R., Todd, Z., Maule, J., Stratton, P., and Stanley, N. (2009). The discourse dynamics approach to metaphor and metaphor-led discourse analysis. *Metaphor and Symbol*, 24: 63–89.

Coëgnarts, M., and Kravanja, P. (eds) (2014). *Image [&] Narrative*, 15(1) at http://www.imageandnarrative.be/index.php/imagenarrative (special issue on embodied cognition).

Cohn, N. (2010). Extra! Extra! Semantics in comics!: the conceptual structure of *Chicago Tribune* advertisements. *Journal of Pragmatics*, 42: 3138–3146.

Cohn, N. (2013a). *The Visual Language of Comics: Introduction to the Structure and Cognition of Sequential Images*. London: Bloomsbury.

Cohn, N. (2013b). Beyond word balloons and thought bubbles: the integration of text and image. *Semiotica*, 197: 35–63.

De Waal, F. (2009). *The Age of Empathy: Nature's Lessons for a Kinder Society*. New York: Harmony.

Davies, L. J. (1995). The multidimensional language of the cartoon: a study in aesthetics, popular culture, and symbolic interaction. *Semiotica*, 104: 165–211.

Díaz Vera, J. E. (2013). Woven emotions: visual representations of emotions in medieval English textiles. *Review of Cognitive Linguistics*, 11: 269–284.

Dirven, R., and Pörings, R. (eds) (2002). *Metaphor and Metonymy in Comparison and Contrast*. Berlin: Mouton de Gruyter.

Eerden, B. (2004). *Liefde en Woede: De Metaforische Verbeelding van Emoties in* Asterix [Love and anger: the metaphorical representation of emotions in *Asterix*]. MA thesis, Media Studies, Universiteit van Amsterdam, NL.

Eerden, B. (2009). Anger in *Asterix*: the metaphorical representation of anger in comics and animated films. In: C. Forceville and E. Urios-Aparisi (eds), *Multimodal Metaphor* (pp. 243–264). Berlin: Mouton de Gruyter.

El Refaie, E. (2003). Understanding visual metaphors: the example of newspaper cartoons. *Visual Communication*, 2: 75–95.

El Refaie, E. (2009). Metaphor in political cartoons: exploring audience responses. In: C. Forceville and E. Urios-Aparisi (eds), *Multimodal Metaphor* (pp. 173–196). Berlin: Mouton de Gruyter.

Eunen, T. van (2007). *Angst, Woede, Liefde en Trots: De Visuele Representatie van Emoties in* Asterix *en* Donald Duck [Fear, anger, love, and pride: the visual representation of emotios in *Asterix* and *Donald Duck*]. MA thesis, Media Studies, Universiteit van Amsterdam, NL.

Fahlenbrach, K. (ed.) (in prep.). *Embodied Metaphors in Film, Television, and Video Games: Cognitive Approaches*. London: Routledge.

Fauconnier, G., and Turner, M. (2002). *The Way We Think: Conceptual Blending and the Mind's Hidden Complexities*. New York: Basic Books.

Forceville, C. (1996). *Pictorial Metaphor in Advertising*. London: Routledge.

Forceville, C. (1999). Educating the eye? Kress and Van Leeuwen's *Reading Images: The Grammar of Visual Design* (1996). *Language and Literature*, 8: 163–178.

Forceville, C. (2004). Review of Fauconnier and Turner (2002). *Metaphor and Symbol*, 19: 83–89.

Forceville, C. (2005a). Visual representations of the Idealized Cognitive Model of anger in the Asterix album *La Zizanie. Journal of Pragmatics*, 37: 69–88.

Forceville, C. (2005b). Addressing an audience: time, place, and genre in Peter van Straaten's calendar cartoons. *Humor*, 18: 247–278.

Forceville, C. (2011a). Pictorial runes in *Tintin and the Picaros. Journal of Pragmatics*, 43: 875–890.

Forceville, C. (2011b). Structural pictorial and multimodal metaphor. (*A Course in Pictorial and Multimodal Metaphor*, Lecture 7/8 http://semioticon.com/sio/courses/pictorial-multimodal-metaphor/).

Forceville, C. (2013a). Concluding observations and further research. (*A Course in Pictorial and Multimodal Metaphor*, Lecture 8/8 http://semioticon.com/sio/courses/pictorial-multimodal-metaphor/).

Forceville, C. (2013b). Creative visual duality in comics balloons. In: T. Veale, K. Feyaerts, and C. Forceville (eds), *Creativity and the Agile Mind: A Multi-Disciplinary Study of a Multi-Faceted Phenomenon* (pp. 253–273). Berlin: Mouton de Gruyter.

Forceville, C. (2014). Relevance Theory as model for analysing visual and multimodal communication. In: D. Machin (ed.), *Visual Communication* (pp. 51–70). Berlin: Mouton de Gruyter.

Forceville, C., Veale, T., and Feyaerts, K. (2010). Balloonics: the visuals of balloons in comics. In: J. Goggin and D. Hassler-Forest (eds), *The Rise and Reason of Comics and Graphic Literature: Critical Essays on the Form* (pp. 56–73). Jefferson, NC: McFarland.

Forceville, C., El Refaie, L., and Meesters, G. (2014). Stylistics and comics. In: M. Burke (ed.), *The Routledge Handbook of Stylistics* (pp. 485–499). London: Routledge.

Forceville, C., and Clark, B. (2014). Can pictures have explicatures? *Linguagem em (Dis) curso*, 14(3), special issue on Relevance Theory edited by Francisco Yus.

Gibbs, R. W., Jr, and Steen, G. J. (eds) (1999). *Metaphor in Cognitive Linguistics*. Amsterdam: Benjamins.

Grady, J., Oakley, T., and Coulson, S. (1999). Blending and metaphor. In: R. W. Gibbs Jr and G. J. Steen (eds), *Metaphor in Cognitive Linguistics* (pp. 101–124). Amsterdam: Benjamins.

Grodal, T. (2009). *Embodied Visions: Evolution, Emotion, Culture, and Film*. Oxford: Oxford University Press.

Hampe, B. (2005). Image schemas in cognitive linguistics: introduction. In: B. Hampe (ed.), *From Perception to Meaning: Image Schemas in Cognitive Linguistics* (pp. 1–12). Berlin: Mouton de Gruyter.

Herman, David (2002). *Story Logic: Problems and Possibilities of Narrative*. Lincoln: University of Nebraska Press.

Holland, D., and Quinn, N. (eds) (1987). *Cultural Models in Language and Thought*. Cambridge: Cambridge University Press.

Jewitt, C. (ed.) (2013). *The Routledge Handbook of Multimodal Analysis* (2nd edn). London: Routledge.

Johnson, M. (1987). *The Body in the Mind*. Chicago: University of Chicago Press.

Johnson, M. (2003). *Moral Imagination: Implications of Cognitive Science for Ethics*. Chicago: University of Chicago Press.

Johnson, M. (2014). *Morality for Humans: Ethical Understanding from the Perspective of Cognitive Science*. Chicago: University of Chicago Press.

Kennedy, J. (1982). Metaphor in pictures. *Perception*, 11: 589–605.

Kövecses, Z. (1986). *Metaphors of Anger, Pride and Love*. Amsterdam: Benjamins.

Kövecses, Z. (2000). *Metaphor and Emotion*. Cambridge, MA: Cambridge University Press.

Kövecses, Z. (2005). *Metaphor in Culture: Universality and Variation*. Cambridge: Cambridge University Press.

Kövecses, Z. (2008). Metaphor and emotion. In: R. W. Gibbs (ed.), *The Cambridge Handbook of Metaphor and Thought* (pp. 380–396). Cambridge: Cambridge University Press.

Kukkonen, K. (2013). *Contemporary Comics Storytelling*. Nebraska: University of Nebraska Press.

Lakoff, G., and Johnson, M. (1980). *Metaphors We Live By*. Chicago: University of Chicago Press.

Lakoff, G., and Johnson, M. (1999). *Philosophy in the Flesh: The Embodied Mind and its Challenge to Western Thought*. New York: Basic Books.

Lakoff, G., and Turner, M. (1989). *More than Cool Reason.* Chicago: University of Chicago Press.

Marín-Arrese, J. I. (2008). Cognition and culture in political cartoons. *Intercultural Pragmatics,* 5: 1–18.

McCloud, S. (2006). *Making Comics: Storytelling Secrets of Comics, Manga and Graphic Novels.* New York: HarperCollins.

McLuhan, M. (1964). *Understanding Media: The Extensions of Man* (2nd edn). New York: McGraw-Hill.

Moes, J. (2010). *Metaphors of Anger and Disgust: Visual Representations of the Idealized Cognitive Models of the Emotions* anger *and* disgust *in* The Complete Calvin and Hobbes. Research MA thesis, Media Studies, Universiteit van Amsterdam, NL.

Ortony, A. (ed.) (1979). *Metaphor and Thought.* Cambridge: Cambridge University Press.

Plantinga, C. (2009). *Moving Viewers: American Film and the Spectator's Experience.* Berkeley: University of California Press.

Potsch, E., and Williams, R. F. (2012). Image schemas and conceptual metaphor in action comics. In: F. Bramlett (ed.), *Linguistics and the Study of Comics* (pp. 13–36). New York: Palgrave Macmillan.

Reehorst, L. (2014). *Metaphor in American Editorial Cartoons about the Presidential Elections of 1936 and 2012.* Unpublished research MA thesis, University of Amsterdam, Dept. of Film Studies. [dare.uva.nl/document/544278]

Schempp, A. P. (2011). Pictorial signs of *pride* and *romantic love* in the comic book series *Scott Pilgrim* volumes one and six. Paper for Pictorial and Multimodal Metaphor Course, Media Studies, Universiteit van Amsterdam, NL.

Schilperoord, J., and Maes, A. (2009). Visual metaphoric conceptualization in editorial cartoons. In: C. Forceville and E. Urios-Aparisi (eds), *Multimodal Metaphor* (pp. 213–240). Berlin: Mouton de Gruyter.

Shinohara, K., and Matsunaka, Y. (2009). Pictorial metaphors of emotion in Japanese comics. In: C. Forceville and E. Urios-Aparisi (eds), *Multimodal Metaphor* (pp. 265–293). Berlin: Mouton de Gruyter.

Smith, M. (1995). *Engaging Characters: Fiction, Emotion, and the Cinema.* Oxford: Clarendon Press.

Sperber, D., and Wilson, D. (1995). *Relevance: Communication & Cognition* (2nd edition). Oxford: Blackwell.

Talmy, L. (2000). *Toward a Cognitive Semantics. Vol. 1: Concept Structuring Systems.* Cambridge, MA: MIT Press.

Tan, E. S. (2001). The telling face in comic strip and graphic novel. In: J. Baetens (ed.), *The Graphic Novel* (pp. 31–46). Leuven: University Press Leuven.

Teng, N. Y. (2009). Image alignment in multimodal metaphor. In: C. Forceville and E. Urios-Aparisi (eds), *Multimodal Metaphor* (pp. 197–211). Berlin: Mouton de Gruyter.

Teng, N. Y., and Sun, S. (2002). Grouping, simile, and oxymoron in pictures: a design-based cognitive approach. *Metaphor and Symbol,* 17: 295–316.

Tomasello, M. (2008). *Origins of Human Communication.* Cambridge: MIT Press.

Wilson, D., and Sperber, D. (2012). *Meaning and Relevance.* Cambridge: Cambridge University Press.

Yus, F. (2008). Inferring from comics: a multi-stage account. In: P. S. Cremades, C. Gregori Signes, and S. Renard (eds), *El Discurs del Comic* (pp. 223–249). Valencia: University of Valencia.

Yus, F. (2009). Visual metaphor versus verbal metaphor: a unified account. In: C. Forceville and E. Urios-Aparisi (eds), *Multimodal Metaphor* (pp. 147–172). Berlin: Mouton de Gruyter.

5

Relatedness:

Aspects of Textual Connectivity in Comics[*]

Mario Saraceni

---

1. Aims of the chapter

This chapter proposes some reflections on the way in which the various panels that compose a comics text are related to one another so as to form, and be perceived as, a unified whole. The theoretical underpinnings will be primarily grounded in the field of linguistic studies. The reason for this is twofold. First, the fact that language has been studied and analysed for a much longer time, better, and infinitely more thoroughly than comics, means that there exist well-established analytical frameworks, models

---

[*] Another version of this chapter originally appeared in the *The Graphic Novel*, edited by Jan Baetens, 167–179. Leuven: Leuven University Press.

and terminology that can be 'borrowed' to provide a solid basis for an understanding of comics too. Second, and more importantly, I am convinced that the application to comics of linguistic analytical tools can produce results which reflect back to the study of language-based texts and, ultimately, to the study of texts in general.

2. Theoretical background

In this chapter, the term 'language' is used in a broader sense than usual, essentially equivalent to the semiotic concept of *code*, or system of signs. Besides, for the purposes of this chapter, it will specifically designate two types of signs: *verbal* signs and *visual* signs. Therefore, 'language' will be considered as a superordinate of 'verbal language' and 'visual language':

LANGUAGE

verbal language (words)   visual language (pictures)

Although it is not an extraneous notion in semiotics, 'visual language'[1] is still struggling to enter the field of linguistics. One very important exception has been provided by Gunther Kress and Theo van Leeuwen (1996), who have developed a model whereby existing linguistic notions are applied to the analysis of images. They have formalized such a model into what they call a 'grammar of visual design', the importance of which lies in the fact that it demonstrates that syntactic and semantic rules apply to images too.

Kress and van Leeuwen express the originality of their work in linguistic terms: while previous studies have sought to analyse 'lexis' i.e. the individual elements of images, their own concentrates on the 'grammar', that is on how these elements are interrelated to form meaning. The argument is that this approach is more complete than the previous one, which, although a valid one, does not 'tell the whole story' (Kress and van Leeuwen, 1996: 1).

However, although a move from the word level to the sentence level certainly represents a much needed step forward in the study of images as conveyors of meaning, the whole story is still not told. Since communication, be it visual or linguistic, normally occurs in *texts* rather than in individual sentences. Hence, in order to fully understand the capabilities of visual language, more study is needed beyond the sentence level, into the domain of the 'text'.

As regards verbal language, the domain of text has been the main interest of text-linguistics. More specifically, text-linguistics has been concerned with one fundamental question: what is it that makes a collection of sentences a text? Accordingly, a great many of this type of studies have sought to find criteria for 'textness' (see, especially, Halliday and Hasan, 1976 and 1985; van Dijk, 1977; de Beaugrande and Dressler, 1981; Lyons, 1981; Cha, 1985; Hoey, 1991; Martin, 1992; Sinclair, 1993).

The main notion that has been developed in these studies is that of *cohesion*, which has been regarded as the main property that a string of sentences should possess in order to be considered a text. As Rosamund Moon extremely succinctly puts it: 'Cohesion makes texts into texts' (Moon, 1998: 278). Essentially, cohesion has been described as a set of lexico-grammatical features which tie sentences together. From this perspective, therefore, the way in which the various sentences are bound together has been seen as a property of the text itself: 'If a passage of English containing more than one sentence is perceived as a text, there will be certain linguistic features present in that passage which can be identified as contributing to its total unity and giving it texture' (Halliday and Hasan, 1976: 2).

While this has been the predominant view, other scholars have proposed different ideas. Most notably, Brown and Yule (1983) rejected the idea that the theoretical concept of *text* should meet precise criteria of 'textness'. In particular, they argued that cohesion is not at all a necessary property of texts and stressed the importance of the *reader's perception* of text as such: 'We do not see an advantage in trying to determine constitutive formal features which a text must possess to qualify as a "text". Texts are what hearers and readers treat as texts' (Brown and Yule, 1983: 199).

Despite its being so radically different from the notion of cohesion, the validity of this idea has been recognized in virtually all studies which have dealt with text connectivity, and has been given the general name of *coherence*. However, while it is accepted that cohesion is not a sufficient condition for a text to be coherent, the notion of coherence has been given comparatively much less emphasis. Besides, cohesion and coherence have been described as separate entities, with the latter being given a kind of ineffable status. As Michael Hoey summarizes, '... cohesion is a property of the text, and ... coherence is a facet of the reader's evaluation of a text. In other words, cohesion is objective, capable in principle of automatic recognition, while coherence is subjective and judgements concerning it may vary from reader to reader ...' (Hoey, 1991: 12).

In my view, cohesion and coherence are interacting parts of the same phenomenon, which I prefer to call *relatedness*. I believe that the ways in which texts hang together are the result of both aspects: the textual and the cognitive. As far as the unity of text is concerned, the fundamental question that the reader has to answer at each point in the text is: how does this passage *relate* to the rest of the text? In order to find an answer to this question, he or she will have to look both in the text and in their mind.

2.1. Sentences and panels as fundamental text units

The idea itself of text unity implies the corollary idea that texts are formed of smaller units and, indeed, in text-linguistics it is a common assumption that 'a text is formed out of a sequence of sentences' (Cha, 1985: 6). In the case of comics, such text units are immediately identified as the panels, and the above statement can be accompanied by an equivalent one: 'a comics text is formed out of a sequence of panels'. This clarifies the analogous functions that sentences and panels have as text-forming units.

Thus, sentences and panels represent the most identifiable units into which language-based texts and comics texts are respectively arranged. However, their equivalent text-forming function is not the only feature that makes it possible to propose a parallel between the sentence and the panel. First of all, an obvious element of comparison between sentence and panel is of a graphical nature, in that in an extremely simple definition, the sentence could be regarded as a portion of text delimited by two full stops, whose function is then similar to that of panel borders in comics: they represent a graphical boundary for the unit. Although there exist other linguistic units such as the phrase and the clause, neither of them is as easily identifiable as the sentence.

The reasons why the sentence is the linguistic element closest to the panel could be summarized in Table 5.1. So, if a text is a collection of identifiable units, the question is: 'how are these units related to each other?' Relatedness has to do with the ways in which these smaller units are related to each other.

Table 5.1 Linguistic elements

Linguistic element	In favour	Against
paragraph	It is a graphical unit easily identified and isolated It can contain variable amounts of information	Unlike the panel, it is not a necessary component
sentence	It is an easily identified and isolated unit (thanks to punctuation) It can contain variable amounts of information	
clause	It is a formal element that can be isolated	Unlike the panel, the information is limited to one subject and one process It is not as easily recognizable as the panel
phrase	It is a formal element that can be isolated	The amount of information never equates with that of the panel It is not as easily recognizable as the panel.

3. Towards a linguistic-visual and textual-cognitive model of relatedness

I see textual and cognitive components of relatedness as existing on a graded cline rather than representing opposite poles. Along this cline, three broad categories can be placed: repetition, collocation, and closure (inference); which, graphically, can be represented as:

RELATEDNESS

repetition　　　　collocation　　　　closure (inference)

3.1. Repetition

By *repetition*, I mean textual elements that are recognisably and objectively repeated within a text. In its simplest from, it is equivalent to what Hasan calls 'exact repetition of lexical item' (Halliday and Hasan, 1985: 81). The extract from Peter Kuper's *The System* (Figure 5.1) illustrates this type of repetition.

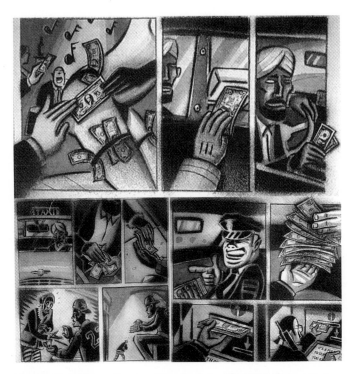

Figure 5.1 Peter Kuper, *The System* (© 1997 Peter Kuper. Reproduced by permission of PM Press: www.pmpress.org).

Here 'money' is a recognisably and objectively repeated element that guarantees connectivity between one panel and the next throughout the sequence. Similarly, the continuous and prominent presence of the characters' hands constitutes the other principal element of repetition that binds the panels together, thereby conveying the meaning of 'money being passed from hands to hands'.

In linguistic terms, repetition can be subdivided into *exact repetition* (the element is repeated exactly as it is) and *relexicalization* (the element is repeated but undergone a slight (semantic) change) (e.g. synonymy, hyponymy, meronymy, etc.). In this second case, the importance of the cognitive component already begins to emerge. Figure 5.2 shows an example of what could be called 'visual relexicalization'.

Here between the second and the third panel there occurs a relexicalization whereby a cash-machine is replaced by a video-game. Repetition is still very evident (the item 'screen' is present in all four panels) but, compared to the sequence in Figure 5.1, the cognitive aspect has relatively more importance, since the connection between the cash-machine and the video-game depends not only on the repeated presence of the screen, but also on the reader's perception of the two.

Figure 5.2 Peter Kuper, *The System*. (© 1997 Peter Kuper. Reproduced by permission of PM Press: www.pmpress.org).

Thus, this already represents a move towards the cognitive end of the cline. If relexicalization can still be considered as a form of repetition, other lexical relations become gradually more dependent on the reader's cognition. This is precisely the case in relations of collocation.

3.2. Collocation

The concept of collocation is based on the assumption that words tend to keep the same company, which entails that the occurrence of a particular word generates in the reader/hearer a certain expectancy for the occurrence of other words that belong to the same company (see Firth, 1957; Sinclair, 1987).

In relations of collocation, 'lexical items enter into patterns which are not predicted by grammar and are to some extent independent of both grammatical structure and a lexical item's formal scatter' (Martin, 1992: 276). Such 'independence' clearly entails that the reader plays a determining part in the recognition of this type of relations. In the passage shown in Figure 5.3 from Seth's *It's a Good Life If You Don't Weaken*, collocation is crucial for the relatedness across the panels.

Figure 5.3 Seth, *It's a Good Life If You Don't Weaken*. (© 1996 Seth).

Here elements of repetition are still present, but collocation plays a very important role, so much so that without the reader's input the relatedness of the passage would be very feeble. Relations like

snow	-	winter
lightning/rain	-	end of winter
birds in the sky	-	spring
heat	-	summer
roadwork	-	summer
falling leaves	-	autumn
Halloween pumpkin	-	autumn

can only be established by each individual reader, since they are by no means objective. The connection between the Halloween pumpkin and autumn, for example, can only be made by someone familiar with Anglo-American culture. And, in general, the whole sequence makes sense only for people who live in parts of the world where there are seasonal phenomena like those depicted in the panels.

Significantly, according to van Dijk, '. . . the connection between propositions is determined by the *relatedness of the facts* denoted by them . . .' (van Dijk, 1977: 47), and such relatedness relies on a common *frame*, i.e. 'a subsystem of knowledge about some phenomenon of the world' (*ibid.*: 135). This suggests that for van Dijk the 'relatedness of facts' is fundamentally a matter of world knowledge.

A further move towards the cognitive side of the cline occurs if we consider the issue of relevance. Winter (1994) sees relevance as the main factor that guarantees successful communication in spite of the fact that communication itself is inevitably imperfect:

(. . .) communication is imperfect if only because *we cannot say everything about anything at any time.* Quite apart from the physical fact that neither we nor our listeners have unlimited energy, time and patience, very powerful forces prevent this perfection. We are forced to settle for saying less than everything by the need to produce *unique sentences* whose selected content has been in some way *predetermined* by that of its immediately preceding sentences or by the previous history of its larger message structure. The central discipline acting upon our production of sentences in a discourse structure is the need for relevance.

(Winter, 1994: 47)

For Winter, relevance forms the foundation for Clause Relation, which he defines as 'the shared cognitive process whereby we interpret the meaning of a Clause or group of clauses in the light of their adjoining clauses or groups of clauses' (Winter, 1994: 49).

3.3. Closure or inference

As seen, Winter claims that communication is imperfect because of the inevitable incompleteness of information that can be conveyed at one time. This introduces the third aspect of relatedness, that which relies not on what is overtly present in the text, but on what the text does *not* say.

Closure is a term that belongs to the field of visual cognition. Arthur Asa Berger defines it as 'the way our minds "complete" incomplete visual material that is given to us. We fill in the blanks, so to speak. We also form a gestalt or "whole" out of bits and pieces of information that we have – unifying them into something that is more than the sum of the parts' (Berger, 1989: 54).

Although this definition refers to visual material, I think that the fundamental concept can be applied to language-based texts too, and to narrative texts in particular. In fact, Brown and Yule (1983) express what is effectively the same idea when they state that '... although there may be no formal linguistic links connecting contiguous linguistic strings, the fact of their contiguity leads us to interpret them as connected. We readily fill in any connections which are required' (Brown and Yule, 1983: 224).

What such a claim implies is that relatedness is not exclusively a property of the text, but also something that the reader *assumes* to be there. The importance of closure/inference for my textual/cognitive cline lies in the fact that with closure/ inference relatedness becomes totally a matter of cognition, since it relies on absent pieces of information.

If, in its simplest definition, a text is a sequence of discrete units, it follows that between every unit and the next, there occurs an interruption, of variable dimensions and significance, during which something is left out. The act of 'filling in any connections which are required' is precisely what closure (or inference) can be thought of. As Umberto Eco observes, a text 'is intertwined with white spaces, with interstices to be filled' (Eco, 1979: 52, my translation).

In comics, these white spaces are not only metaphorical but also physical, represented by the gap, called *gutter*, between one panel and the next.[2] So, the mental process of filling in missing pieces of information is constantly active in the reader of comics. Of course this is not always necessarily a particularly complex operation. In fact, most of the times *closure* can be described as an unconscious process on the part of the reader.

However, although perhaps in the majority of cases *closure* can be said to be an unconscious and almost instinctive psychological phenomenon, at some other times little or complete absence of textual clues can cause the need for the reader to actively contribute to the logical sequence of what would otherwise seem to be only a spatial left-to-right sequence.

The passage in Figure 5.4 calls the reader for this type of contribution.

Figure 5.4 Tom Hart, *The Sands* (© 1998 Tom Hart).

Closure in comics has been investigated by Scott McCloud, whose discussion of the topic is based on what he calls 'panel-to-panel transitions'. He distinguishes six types of transitions (McCloud, 1993: 70–72):

1 moment-to-moment: a small change in time;
2 action-to-action: a progression of actions;
3 subject-to-subject: a change between characters;
4 scene-to-scene: a change between locations or scenes;
5 aspect-to-aspect: glimpses of a place, idea or mood;
6 non-sequitur: no logical connections between images.

What I find particularly valuable about McCloud's taxonomy is that it allows one to relate each category to a greater degree of reader's involvement. In fact, the six types of transitions fundamentally reflect my textual/cognitive cline, with the moment-to-moment and action-to-action types involving more repetition and the scene-to-scene and aspect-to-aspect types relying more on collocation and common semantic fields. McCloud's categories can thus be seen as a reflection of the explicit/implicit scale of relatedness, here reorganized to reflect this scale of reader involvement (scene-to-scene collapses together with subject-to-subject):

1 moment-to-moment: complete repetition (all the elements of one panel are repeated in the next);

2 action-to-action: high degree of repetition (most elements of one panel are repeated in the next);

3 aspect-to-aspect: collocation and/or semantic space (the elements of the two panels tend to co-occur or are items of the same semantic field);

4 subject-to-subject: few elements of explicit relatedness, usually based on common semantic field;

5 non-sequitur: no explicit markers of relatedness at all.

I do not agree, however, with the theorization of non-sequitur transitions, which McCloud defines as ones which offer 'no logical relationship between panels *whatsoever!*' (McCloud, 1993: 72). Rather, I think that in this type of transition relatedness still obtains, if anything, because of the mere adjacency of the panels. As Quirk et al. (1985) assert, 'connection may be covert as well as overt ... Mere juxtaposition ... is an icon of connectedness, even where the juxtaposed parts have no grammatical or lexical feature in common' Quirk et al., 1985: 1425).

In the absence of textual clues, the relatedness between text units relies entirely on the reader's input, but there is nothing to justify *un*-relatedness. Significantly, the examples that McCloud uses to illustrate 'non-sequitur' transitions (Figure 5.5) are not part of authentic texts.

This argument leads to another observation: many text-linguistics studies insist on the fact that cohesion is a phenomenon whereby one sentence is connected to its immediate predecessor or, in the case of cataphora, to its immediate successor. This idea that sentences are connected to those in their near neighbourhood is expressed in a particular explicit way in, for example, Halliday and Hasan (1976), Lyons (1981) and Sinclair (1993). The concept of *cohesive chain*, developed by Hasan in Halliday and Hasan (1985: 83–96), represents a move further, in that it considers connections across the whole length of a text. However, because of their linear nature, even in cohesive chains 'distant' connections are only indirect ones, since they obtain only via a series of direct connections with neighbouring items.

Figure 5.5 Scott McCloud, *Understanding Comics* (© 1993 Scott McCloud).

An important step forward is represented by the model developed by Michael Hoey (1991), who sees the connections between different parts of a text as a network rather than as a set of chains. In Hoey's model, different items are directly connected with others regardless of the distance that exists between them. In order to make sense of the sequence in Figure 5.4, for example, the reader needs to refer to other, more or less distant, parts of the novel.

4. Conclusion

In this chapter, I have argued that what makes a text be perceived as such is a combination of textual and cognitive factors. The interaction of these two forces produces relatedness between text units, and this relatedness is based on three broad phenomena: repetition (with all its different shades and degrees of exactness), collocation, and closure (or inference). While one of them may have more prominence in certain instances, these phenomena are not separate entities, but normally act concurrently. By using wordless passages from comics texts, I aimed to show that much of what can be said about verbal language also applies to visual texts, in the personal conviction that the visual elements of comics constitute – and are analysable as – a proper language in its own right.

Notes

1. For a very interesting contribution to the development of the concept of visual language, see Horn (1998).
2. Sometimes the panels of a comics text are not separated by a gutter but only by the borders of the panels. However, even in these cases the division between panels retains its importance, since it does not depend on the actual amount of physical space but on the narrative hiatus between the panels.

References

De Beaugrande, R., and Dressler, W. (1981). *Introduction to Text Linguistics*. London: Longman.

Berger, A. A. (1989). *Seeing Is Believing: An Introduction to Visual Communication*. Mountain View, CA: Mayfield Publishing.

Brown, G., and Yule, G. (1983). *Discourse Analysis*. Cambridge: Cambridge University Press.

Cha, J. S. (1985). *Linguistic Cohesion in Texts Theory and Description*. Seoul: Daehan Textbook Printing.

van Dijk, T. A. (1977). *Text and Context*. London: Longman.

Eco, U. (1979). *Lector in fabula*. Milan: Bompiani.

Firth, J. R. (1957). *Papers in Linguistics: 1934–1951*. London: Oxford University Press.

Halliday, M. A. K., and Hasan, R. (1976). *Cohesion in English*. London: Longman.

Halliday, M. A. K., and Hasan, R. (1985). *Language, Context and Text: Aspects of Language in a Social-Semiotic Perspective*. Victoria: Deakin University Press.

Hoey, M. (1991). *Patterns of Lexis in Text*. Oxford: Oxford University Press.

Horn, R. (1998). *Visual Language: Global Communication for the 21st Century*. Bainbridge Island, WA: MacroVU.

Kress, G., and van Leeuwen, T. (1996). *Reading Images: The Grammar of Visual Design*. London: Routledge.

Lyons, J. (1981). *Language, Meaning and Context*. London: Fontana.

Martin, J. R. (1992). *English Text*. Amsterdam: Benjamins.

McCloud, S. (1993). *Understanding Comics*. New York: HarperCollins.

Moon, R. (1998). *Fixed Expressions and Idioms in English*. Oxford: Clarendon Press.

Quirk, R., Greenbaum, S., Leech, G., and Svartvik, J. (1985). *A Comprehensive Grammar of the English Language*. London: Longman.

Sinclair, J. (1987). Collocation: a progress report. In: R. Steele and T. Threadgold (eds), *Language Topics: Essays in Honour of Michael Halliday* (pp. 319–331). Amsterdam: Benjamins.

Sinclair, J. (1993). Written text structure. In: J. Sinclair, M. Hoey and G. Fox (eds), *Techniques of Description: Spoken and Written Discourse* (pp. 6–31). London: Routledge.

Winter, E. (1994). Clause relations as information structure: two basic text structures in English. In: M. Coulthard (ed.), *Advances in Written Text Analysis* (pp. 46–68). London: Routledge.

6

A Little Cohesion between Friends; Or, We're Just Exploring Our Textuality:

Reconciling Cohesion in Written Language and Visual Language

Eric Stainbrook

1. Introduction

An understanding of the cohesive principles of the visual language used in comics has to be prefaced by stating or establishing a set of terms or concepts upon which to build that understanding. First, I begin with the belief that works in visual language do constitute discrete texts and are indeed 'read', and that the reading of these texts occurs via consistent and predictable cognitive standards. As noted by Cohn (2013), a reading of visual language ultimately occurs on a global level, i.e., taking a 'macro' view of the larger textual sequence. This chapter, however, will limit itself to the connective properties perceivable on the micro-level, that is, on the level of discrete images and linguistic utterances.

Text, according to De Beaugrande and Dressler (1983), must meet seven standards: cohesion, coherence, intentionality, acceptability, informativity, situationality, and intertextuality. The first two standards deal with perceptible surface features of the text. Intentionality and acceptability deal with the needs and motivations of the creator and of the receiver of the text, respectively; whereas the final three standards are concerned with 'higher-order' content and context of the text. Because issues relating to authorial intention and to a reader's acceptance are pragmatic concerns best applicable only to individual, discrete reading events, intentionality and acceptability cannot be addressed adequately in a general discussion of the entire comics medium. This particular chapter seeks to address only one of these areas of textuality, specifically the surface of the text and how the visual narrative meets textual standards of cohesion and coherence.

The examination of cohesion in visual language sequences begins with a structured study of the various surface elements of the visual language text. In earlier work (Stainbrook, 2003), I described three primary classifications of surface textual elements in visual language: *graphical representation, icons,* and *linguistic utterances.* (For those already familiar with Cohn's (2013) system of classification, these may roughly equate to open-class lexical items, closed-class lexical items, and written language, though I will not suggest they are entirely equivalent.)

Specifically, in regards to visual language, aside from the useful though as yet undefined ability to recognize visual language as visual language from prior experience, one of the primary elements helping to form connectivity in such texts is the predictable replication of visual style displayed from panel to panel in the visual sequence. A reader's ability to recognize that the disparate panels of artwork fall into a common vision of representation likely enhances the reader's acceptance of the panels as part of the same overall unit of meaning.

Through a number of artistic choices, the artist typically aids in textual receptivity by repeating key stylistic elements, providing the reader a framework to cognitively link the panels. It may be concluded that the artist's drawing style factors into the internal connectivity of visual texts, but also that artistic constancy is not a prescriptive factor in the creation of cohesive texts.

Style, however, is not the only obvious connective factor in the artwork of a visual text. Within the artwork of visual language, the pictorial content may be interpreted as connective by the reader. A reader must be able to connect images from one panel to others in the sequence. For example, in a *Peanuts* comic strip, a multi-panel sequence may feature three panels in which Snoopy is depicted in various positions or with various attributes. A reader must first identify each figure as representing the same character of Snoopy, despite variances in line quality, perspective or figure size. Subsequently, the reader must have at his or her disposal a schema to allow the representations of Snoopy to be connected according to predictable rules. The reader's ability to properly identify the three different images in the sequence as representative of the character or actor Snoopy is essential to meaning-making in a visual text. The reader must perceive each iteration not as a drawing of a dog, but as a sign that refers to a shared concept. This suggests a decision to treat the images as signifiers in a text. Once the reader has agreed to identify each drawing as a sign representing the same character, that reader must be able to link those drawn signs in predictable ways.

In addition, as will be explored later in this chapter, the visual language reader must not only cognitively link panels of artwork, but must also manage connections between instances of written text (i.e., between caption and caption, between caption and dialogue balloon, between dialogue balloon and dialogue balloon, etc.), and between word and image. It is possible that each of these connective varieties, and the cognitive acts they demand, functions via a separate and unique conceptual principle. However, the number of such connections in a typical comic, and the ease with which most readers can navigate these varying word–word, word–image, and image–image connections, suggests that a single theoretical principle is more likely at work in the cohesion of visual texts. At the very least, a single theoretical principle for all cohesive elements in visual narratives offers a more convenient and consistent set of classifications and terminology for discussion of visual narrative connexity.

First, it is necessary to discuss the basic theory of cohesion and connection in the surface elements of standard written language. Then, we will look at McCloud's (1993) popular model for connectivity in visual texts. Finally, we will explore how these models can be reconciled into a consistent, over-arching model for textual cohesion that can successfully incorporate both the reading of words and of image into a single textual flow.

2. Cohesion in written language

To fully develop a concept of cohesion in visual language, the connexity of graphical elements must be construed in terms that do not run counter to the connexity of the written elements. If a reader must process contrasting cohesive principles simultaneously in visual language reading, that reader's ability to comprehend the combined text might well be compromised too. It is necessary, therefore, to determine whether principles of linguistic connexity could be at work in the reading of graphical content in visual language. Specifically, it will benefit us to explore the applicability of accepted categories of cohesion in standard written English to the artistic content of the visual text.

Halliday and Hasan (1976) describe several basic forms of textual *cohesive* ties in written English: *reference, substitution* (and its subcategory, *ellipsis*), *conjunction* and *lexical cohesion*. Reference, substitution, ellipsis and conjunction are primarily grammatical in nature, the first three of these relying on syntactic transformations to link segments of a text, and the fourth relying on the addition of an explicit grammatical marker to indicate a semantic link. The first of these cohesive ties, reference, works by directing the reader's attention to a matching referent elsewhere in a given text. Reference usually functions using demonstrative pronouns or the adjectives 'this', 'that', 'these' or 'those' in conjunction with a repeated noun or noun phrase. These references can direct the reader's attention forward to a future use of the same term later in the text (*cataphora*) or backward to a past use of the same term in the text (*anaphora*). For example, in the passage, *John held the winning lottery ticket in his trembling hands; this ticket would change his whole life*, the use of the word 'this' in the second phrase directs the reader to link the ticket in the second phrase ('This ticket would change his life') with the word ticket in the first phrase ('John held the winning lottery ticket …'). Such references force a reader to look forward and backward through a text to link ideas, creating connections in the reader's mind between different segments of a text. However, the ideas of anaphora and cataphora, as abstract concepts that point a reader to specific past or future textual references, cannot be represented in non-linguistic form in the artistic content of comic panels. Expressed more succinctly, there is no representational image that depicts demonstrative adjectives or pronouns (the connexity provided by the repetition of the word 'ticket' is an example of lexical repetitive cohesion, an entirely different kind of cohesive tie). It is unlikely, therefore, that referential ties are at work between two panels of artwork.

Similar problems exist with both substitution and ellipsis as cohesive ties in visual narrative artwork. Substitution functions as a cohesive tie in written English primarily through the use of pronouns as substitutes for nouns, noun phrases or verb phrases used elsewhere in the text. Ellipsis functions as a cohesive tie in written English by presenting the reader with a null value for some required syntactic element, forcing the reader to scan through surrounding text to find a matching phrase to satisfy the null value. Because neither artistic representation nor the flow of panels appears to function based on principles of formal transformational syntax, the application of substitution and ellipsis to a visual narrative text would be difficult, even though we could imagine a null representation in visual narrative artwork. The drawing of a figure or object in outline or silhouette might be perceived as presenting a null value, leading the visual narrative reader to look through the artistic representations in other panels for an image that would satisfy the missing value presented by the outline or silhouette. This would indeed help to create connection between panels in the reader's mind. It is unclear, however, whether this 'ellipsis' would be processed by the reader using the same connective principle found in syntactic ellipsis in written English. Once again, though, the concept of pronoun does not appear to have an equivalent in artistic representation.

Conjunction, as a cohesive tie in written English, is typically signalled by the use of a simple conjunction (including 'and', 'but' and 'or'), a variety of adverbs, or certain prepositional phrases (Halliday and Hasan, 1976). In contrast to reference, substitution and ellipsis, conjunction helps to form textual connections not by directing the reader to other points in the text, but by linking various segments of the text in a number of prescribed manners. A conjunction not only tells a reader that a connection should be interpreted, but it tells the reader the nature of that connection, that is, temporal, causal, additive or adversative (Halliday and Hasan, 1976).

Temporal ties link semantic units in a linear sequencing based on chronology. Causal ties link two semantic units in a specific logical relationship; the action indicated or implied in one unit is the logical cause of the action indicated or implied in the other semantic unit. Additive ties occur when one semantic item adds to, enhances, modifies, or otherwise agrees with the conjoined semantic unit; additive conjunctions may include words and phrases like 'and', 'also', 'in addition', 'furthermore' and 'moreover'. Adversative ties set up opposition or qualification between two semantic units; adversative conjunctions may include words or phrases like 'but', 'however', 'even so', 'despite this', 'elsewhere' and 'meanwhile'.

Like the cohesive ties discussed above, conjunction is grammatical in nature, but unlike the first three ties listed above, conjunction is not dependent upon syntactic transformations. Though conjunctions cannot be directly represented in the visual surface of visual narrative artwork, the types of cognitive connections created with grammatical conjunctions are manageably comparable to the types of inter-panel connections described by McCloud (1993); we do link semantic units in visual narratives according to predictable rules. A reader of visual narratives, then, may be using many of the same concepts of conjunctions as a reader of standard written texts; however, there are differences between the manner in which these concepts are activated by standard written texts and the manner in which they are activated by panels of visual language. While grammatical conjunction is explicitly designated by particular signs in the text, conjunction between panels occurs outside of the specific visible signs of visual language art, in the void of the gutter. Additionally, the gutter does not reveal the nature of the conjunction. Addition, causation, etc., are still interpretable between panels, but the reader must interpret the nature of the conjunction from other clues or signs in the text. Conjunctive cohesion in visual language and in standard English texts may be functioning similarly on a conceptual level, but there do not seem to be any correlative signs or markers. Ultimately, it is difficult to translate the three wholly syntactical cohesive ties (reference, substitution and ellipsis) directly to the reading of panel-to-panel connections. In other words, there is no apparent quid pro quo between those three syntactic connective strategies in written English and the connective strategies between the artwork in a sequence of panels. However, the types of cognitive connections suggested by conjunction do indeed occur between panels.

The fifth variety of cohesive tie, as outlined by Halliday and Hasan, is lexical rather than grammatical. Lexical cohesion is based on reiteration of a lexical element. In standard written texts, such lexical reiteration manifests as simple repetition of a word, the use of synonyms, the use of subordinate or superordinate terms, or the use of general nouns that reference a class to which a given word belongs. These four levels of reiteration present a kind of scale of cognitive separation between an instance of a word and its co-referent. Reiteration in the level of direct repetition of a word offers a one to one relationship between two words with the exact same referent (*Tom bought two new ballcaps. Tom loved buying ballcaps*). When one word in the word pair is replaced by a synonym, the two words still connect to the same or nearly same cognitive referent, though the visible sign is different (*Tom bought two new ballcaps. Tom loved buying hats*). In the next level of reiteration, one of the paired items is subordinated to the other within a common set or class of cognitively connected referents (*Tom bought two new ballcaps. Tom loved buying clothes*). Here, ballcaps is subordinate to clothes in that a ballcap is a type or variety of item understood by the reader to belong to the category of clothes. The last level of reiteration occurs when a word is paired with a general noun, a word that is broad enough to include an indeterminate number of items (*Tom bought two new ballcaps. Tom loved buying things*).

Throughout a text, such repetitions can occur repeatedly at any or all of these levels. Each repetition recalls for the reader a set of concepts that reinforce the shared meaning and unity of a text. The power of this repetition does not occur within a conceptual vacuum, of course. Each of the iterations occurs within a context that functions to reinforce the shared reference of the word-pairs.

Along with reiteration, another variety of lexical cohesion generally occurs in written texts: collocation. Collocation occurs when lexical pairings, rather than evoking the same referent, evoke a contrasting but related referent. Take, for example, the sentence pairing, *Helen had always liked cats. Dogs were too messy and needy for her tastes*. In this pairing, 'cats' and 'dogs' are collocates. They are neither synonyms nor subordinates, neither one being subordinate to the other. However, both terms belong equally to a common class or set of referents, in this example, 'pets' or 'animals'. Collocation still creates textual cohesion, however, because the shared class links the two lexical items; moreover, a meaningful interpretation of the text requires a reader to understand that these two items are being contrasted and that each item must be processed with respect to the other. The cohesion is not occurring at the level of the sign but at a level of ideation beyond the sign. This distinction will prove to be important to an understanding of the reading of visual narratives.

The question remains, of course, how these linguistic connective devices relate to the reading of a series of panels in a visual sequence, if, in fact, they are relevant at all.

3. Cohesion in visual language art

As stated previously, a reader of visual text must link panels of the text, including their graphical contents, in order to create meaning; the reader knows that each panel is connected to its neighbouring panels. Some cognitive process occurs which allows the reader to link panels (and their contents) into some larger idea.

McCloud (1993) defines this process as one of 'closure'. He argues that 'in the limbo of the [comics] gutter, human imagination takes two separate images and transforms them into a single idea. Nothing is seen between the two panels, but experience tells [the reader] something must be there' (pp. 66–67). The panels must be reconciled by the reader through a cognitive event of closure that allows the reader 'to connect these moments and mentally construct a continuous, unified reality' (p. 67). McCloud proposes six categories of closure, reflecting various cognitive transitions between panels: moment-to-moment, action-to-action, subject-to-subject, scene-to-scene, aspect-to-aspect, and non-sequiturs. However, we must question the notion that panels are the true units of meaning in visual language. In addition, we must question whether the idea of closure can be described in purely visual terms; a reader reconciles not only panels of artwork but a variety of verbal manifestations as well.

The first of McCloud's transitions is based upon temporal closure. In McCloud's moment-by-moment transition, the reader perceives the latter of any two sequential panels as representing content that immediately follows the first panel in time. In such a sequence, McCloud argues, the reader is able to apply some cognizance of time to the images in the panels. Somewhere in the gutter between panels, a lapse of time has occurred, or rather, a reader is able to extrapolate a missing moment of time. The reader's ability to conceive of 'missing time' between the panels, and to conceptually 'fill in' this time, allows the reader to achieve closure in the sequence.

McCloud's second category of closure is action-to-action, where we again have a form or variance of temporal closure. In addition, a causative element is argued. A reader might, using action-to-action closure, perceive that the action depicted in the first panel must lead to the action or event depicted in the second. The missing element between the panels is again temporal; however, in this form of closure, the reader must also apply some form of logic to arrive at a reading that says the action implied in panel one caused the action implied in panel two. A distinction between moment-to-moment and action-to-action closures must depend therefore on a reader's ability to perceive a causative element that is not, or not always, depicted directly in the visual medium.

The third variety of closure posited by McCloud is subject-to-subject. Here, the missing element between the images may be either spatial or temporal, though McCloud makes the argument that the panels joined by subject-to-subject closure must exist within the same scene or idea. In essence, it must be presumed by the reader that an over-arching connection already exists throughout the panel sequence before the reader may correctly interpret subject-to-subject closure. McCloud alludes to this problem with subject-to-subject closure by noting that a 'degree of reader involvement [is] necessary to render these transitions meaningful' (p. 71), though McCloud leaves the nature and extent of this involvement, and how this involvement differs from reader involvement in other forms of closure, to be explained by others.

In order for subject-to-subject closure to work, the reader must be able to frame the sequence within a common scene, an understanding of a shared space and time. However, if the shared reference of scene is removed, then the reader is free to interpret the images as referring to alternate places or times. In this situation, the reader would need to apply scene-to-scene closure to link the panels meaningfully. In this type of closure, the reader must apply external logic, using clues in the panel images or texts, to determine the nature and degree of the scene shift. Frequently, this type of closure is indicated by, or accompanied by, a text caption explaining the transition, that is, 'Meanwhile . . .' or 'Fifteen minutes later . . .' or 'Tokyo, Japan'. As with subject-to-subject closure, a reader must come with an over-arching schema in order to properly interpret the scene change and to situate the multiple scenes within a single cohesive text.

McCloud's fifth type of closure is aspect-to-aspect, in which the panels in a sequence are interpreted as representing 'different aspects of a place, idea or mood' (p. 72). This type of closure would be at work in a panel sequence wherein one panel shows a leaf at the end of a branch, a second panel shows a tree, and a third panel shows a group of trees in a park. To correctly interpret these panels as a sequence, a reader must have a concept that the leaf is related to the tree, which in turn is related to the grouping of trees in the park. There may be a temporal element to the sequence, *à la* moment-to-moment closure wherein the reader is meant to interpret motion away from the leaf to a larger view of the park; however, a temporal connection is not strictly mandated. In the described example, the relationship is spatial in nature, though if McCloud's postulate is correct and aspect-to-aspect closure may link aspects of an idea or mood, then the heart of the relationship may be conceptual or logical rather than strictly spatial. These categories of closure reveal themselves as dependent on conceptual factors at least as much as on visual factors in the panels.

The final type of panel-to-panel relationship as described by McCloud is the non-sequitur, which is simply a catch-all term for panel sequences with no apparently meaningful connection. Such non-sequiturs would most likely be found in experimental works, whose design may often include the disruption of a reader's standard connective practices.

McCloud's categories work for most practical purposes. Each panel-to-panel relationship is indeed distinct from the others, and between them, they appear to account for most of the possibilities for inter-panel narrative closure. Several limitations to his categories do exist, however. First, McCloud's varieties of closure are based on the notion of visual language as a strictly narrative form. But it quickly becomes clear that visual language is not strictly narrative in development and structure; therefore, a range of non-narrative relationships must also be accounted for in any classification of panel-to-panel closure. Secondly, McCloud's categorization of panel-to-panel relationships is based on descriptions of the visual content of the panels, on the outward appearance or manifestation of the inter-panel relationships. What is lacking is a theoretical principle upon which to base these particular classifications. McCloud invokes 'reader involvement' as a fundamental element in closure but does not offer further clarification into the matter. In the construction of a theory of visual language reading, it is preferable to identify varieties of connexity that are based on how the textual features relate to each other rather than on what those textual features depict.

4. Cohesion in visual language revisited

Despite these differences and concerns, or perhaps because of them, we can see the possibility of reconciling McCloud's categories of panel-to-panel narrative closure and the cohesive principles of standard written English. Of the linguistic cohesive ties, the ones that may be applied to images (i.e., the ties that are non-syntactic) are conjunction and lexical cohesion. Conjunction is itself subdivided by Halliday and Hasan into four major categories: *temporal, causal, additive* and *adversative*. Lexical cohesion can be split into *lexical repetition* (at a number of levels of abstraction) and *collocation*.

The issue then becomes one of discerning the ways in which we can reconcile conjunction and lexical cohesion with McCloud's closure categories. To a surprising extent, this reconciliation is readily achieved. Moment-to-Moment closure corresponds fairly clearly to temporal conjunctive ties in English. Action-to-Action closure corresponds with strong correlation to causal conjunctive ties in English. Subject-to-Subject closure, however, can be seen as an additive conjunctive tie or as adversative, depending on the relationship implied between the subjects. Similarly, Scene-to-Scene closure can be seen as an adversative conjunctive tie or as additive, depending on the relationship implied between the scenes. McCloud's Subject-to-Subject and Scene-to-Scene closures overlap with the additive and adversative conjunctive ties in English, but do so on different principles of classification. McCloud's classification of closure is based on the content of the panels, whereas the conjunctive tie favoured in this theory of visual language reading is based on the nature or quality of the tie. Finally, McCloud's Aspect-to-Aspect closure is a clear correlate of lexical cohesion. If we take these comparisons at face value, it is easy to reconcile McCloud's descriptive categories to a broader, more inclusive set of cohesive ties that work not only between panels of artwork but that do not contradict the cohesive ties between the written features of visual language. This classification of ties offers us a single set of cognitive principles (if we conceive of linguistic ties as a single set) that can apply to a reading of both words and images in visual narratives.

There are, of course, some problems with this attempt to directly correlate McCloud's categories of closure with the linguistic ties laid out by Halliday and Hasan. One of the limitations with McCloud's descriptive categories is that they only account for classes of narrative closure. Visual texts are not necessarily narrative in form. In fact, panels can be sequenced according to a number of logical principles, including spatial sequencing, numerical sequencing, and other logical sequencing. A classification of panel-to-panel closure needs to account for cohesive ties that would link the images in, for example, a visual text of the semaphore flag signals (Zeek, 2001) or a visual text depicting items in the food pyramid. The surface of a comic page offers a somewhat less rigorous lineation of the text; panels may sometimes be laid out in sequential arrangements that are atypical to standard written texts. For example, Carel Moiseiwitsch (1991), in her comic 'Priapic Alphabet', arranges her panels alphabetically by the first letter of whatever is pictured or implied in each panel; ergo, the panel featuring a prisoner (P) precedes a panel for quadriplegic (Q), which precedes a panel depicting refugees (R), and so on. Temporal sequencing, therefore, is only one of several types of sequencing a reader must process. Halliday and Hasan's category of temporal conjunction is too narrow to accurately manage the sequential conjunctions in visual language. I have therefore proposed a broader category of sequential conjunctive tie that includes the temporal sequential cohesion of both standard written texts and visual texts as well as the spatial, numerical and logical sequencing found in non-narrative visual language sequences. This theory of visual language cohesion then seeks to re-conceive Halliday and Hasan's temporal, causal, additive and adversative conjunctions as sequential, causal, additive and adversative. In essence, temporal sequencing is inadequate to describe the possibilities of panel sequencing in visual language. A broader category of sequential tie can successfully incorporate the chronological sequencing of the temporal tie along with a range of non-chronological sequencing necessary to a theory of visual language reading.

Another problem with reconciling connexity of image with connexity of word lies in the descriptive term 'lexical cohesion'. In visual texts, a reader is dealing with ties not only between lexical items, but between images and between lexical items and images. Can images be connected by 'lexical cohesion?' A lexical item and an image do not always mean the same thing, nor mean it in the same way. If we consider the difference between the lexical item 'dog' and an image of a dog, the differences are readily apparent. The word 'dog' is always an abstraction, and relies heavily on context to be interpreted. The image of a dog, however, can often tell us the breed, posture, expression, and general appearance of a specific dog, even what the dog is doing. Moreover, the word 'dog' can be transformed, become the plural 'dogs', or the adjective 'doggy', or even a verb. The image cannot be similarly transformed to serve different grammatical roles. This problem may be merely semantic. The nature of lexical cohesion allows for not only strict repetition of a lexical sign, but for synonyms, subordinate and superordinate terms, general class terms, and collocates. The repetition, then, is not of lexical items, but repetition of the idea or concepts signified by the lexical items. If this is the more accurate principle behind lexical cohesion, we can certainly apply it to the repetition of concepts in visual language, including both words and images. However, 'conceptual repetition' might be a more accurate term for the connective principle, both in regards to visual language and to standard written texts.

5. Cohesion through writing in visual language: framed and graphic text

The complexity of visual narrative cohesion, however, does not lie solely in the visual language artwork nor in icons. The complexity of reading visual language is found in the dual reading of image and word, two disparate encoding systems. A necessary focus of our inquiry, therefore, must be the use of linguistic signs as meaningful components of visual language.

Within the visual text, written words typically appear in four distinct manners: framed text, graphic text, balloon text and caption text. The first two of these manners are related to visual narrative artwork and icons, respectively. Framed text refers to linguistic signs that appear as part of the representational artwork. For example, in Kuper's (1996) *The System*, a comic book written entirely without dialogue balloons or captions, a number of panels still contain linguistic signs. One panel on the third page of Issue One shows a character purchasing a newspaper at a newsstand. Displayed around the newsstand are several posters, magazine covers and newspapers with visible headlines reading, 'Muir Fights Big Business', 'President Muir?', 'Why America Doesn't Trust Rex', 'Last Weeks of Race: A Report', and 'City News: Muir Rips Rex in Debate'. Later in the same issue, another character is reading a newspaper clipping and portions of the news article are visibly represented in the artwork. Other types of framed text in this particular comic include graffiti on subway cars, marquees outside of businesses, writing on T-shirts and other clothing, and traffic signs. Some of these instances of framed text are not specifically relevant to a coherent reading of the comic. A stop sign at an intersection in the background of the picture, for example, does not contribute meaningfully to the cohesion of that panel to other panels. Other examples of framed text like the newspaper headlines mentioned above are in fact important to the overall plot of the comic. Of the varieties of text in visual narratives, framed text comes closest to the kind of word-art interaction focused on in the word-art studies of Vos (1998) and others, who examined words in art and as art. The reader must perceive the framed text as both representational image and linguistic sign: these are images drawn to represent linguistic signs. A reader does not always know, when viewing panels containing framed text, which instances of framed text are important and which are not, which instances are intended merely to be image and which are meant to be read (see Figure 6.1). It is therefore incumbent on the reader to process each instance of framed text and to hold the information at the ready until other clues let the reader know whether this information is vital to the reading.

Graphic text represents elements of visual language that are iconographic in nature. The terms icon and iconography, of course, bear the baggage of being used in many different contexts to mean different things. Here, I draw broadly on semiotics and aesthetic philosophy, primarily Mitchell (1986), to describe a classification of image that is neither linguistic nor obviously representational, but rather a class of image that through cultural acceptance has come to mean itself. For example, the panel borders or gutters of the visual text are surface features of the text that are neither linguistic nor representational. This category of semiotic sign is often seen as

Figure 6.1 An example of a panel with framed text. There are multiple samples of writing in the image, including the words 'Men', 'Team', 'Daily News', and 'Third Victim Identified'. The reader must recognize the writing as part of the representational art and must also hold the written information in readiness to be used later or to be connected to other elements in the visual narrative.

Figure 6.2 The panel sequence features a variety of common visual text elements that function as visual icons, being neither writing nor representational image. The elements are understood contextually by the comic reader.

synonymous with visual language itself. Certain textual elements in visual language are presented in ways that take on features of iconological function, that is, they have become identifiable as something other than mere text or representational image (see Figure 6.2). The *Batman* TV series made fun of this particular kind of text with its bold-lettered 'POW', 'SOCK', and 'BAM' animation. Whereas icons can represent sound or impact with conventional lines, graphic text often attempts to represent the same concepts of sound or impact with onomatopoeic text. Each instance of graphic text must be interpreted within the context of its immediate (or adjacent) panel; the reader must identify the source and 'meaning' of the graphic text from the related visual language artwork. For example, if a panel shows the image of a series of pipes with steam venting from those pipes, and this image is accompanied by a graphically presented 'word', 'hisssssssssssss', the successful reader determines that the written text 'hisssssssssssss' should be associated with the escaping steam and that it represents the sound of the steam. This successful reading depends upon the reader's external knowledge of steam, that it does make a sound when escaping from pressurized pipes and that 'hisssssssssssss' can be reasonably attributed to the sound of that steam escaping. In addition, graphic text must be interpreted as a visual device, not merely as linguistic sign. The colour and size, as well as aesthetic features of the graphic text, must be considered by the comics reader. Very large, brightly coloured graphic text, for example, might imply greater volume than smaller, less bold graphic text. Such an interpretation is a convention, of course, and can only occur if the reader is applying meta-linguistic or non-linguistic meaning to the graphic text.

6. Cohesion through writing in visual language: dialogue balloons

The greater portion of linguistic signs in visual language, however, is found in dialogue balloons and in captions. On the surface, the difference between these two presentations of linguistic signs appears obvious. Dialogue balloons appear visibly within the panel and, via visual language icons, the writing within the balloons is directly attributable to specific characters in that panel. In contrast, captions are not visually linked to any particular character and are not necessarily tied to the interior of the panel. Captions, and the utterances contained in those captions, may occur outside the borders of panels, and may connect not to an individual panel but to an entire panel sequence. These surface differences, however, are stereotypes and do not account for all possibilities of balloons and captions. Lobdell and Pollina (1999), for example, in *Hellhole*, issue one, present all dialogue in captions, preceding each line of dialogue with a name to indicate the identity of the speaker. In other instances, a dialogue balloon may visually be presented above a multi-panel sequence, ostensibly tying the sequence together as a cohesive element in the manner of a caption. Therefore, the distinctions between dialogue balloons and text captions must be considered traditions or standards, rather than rules of the medium. Even so, we can speak of general differences in how these linguistic elements cohere to each other and to the content of panels.

Dialogue balloons are most commonly seen in two varieties, as indicated by visual narrative icons: the speech balloon and the thought balloon. A number of other varieties are possible, however, as have been discussed earlier. Each of these varieties of dialogue balloon offers similar types of cohesion in the visual narrative text.

Standard written text exhibits several types of cohesive principles that have been discussed previously: reference, substitution, ellipsis, conjunction and lexical cohesion. An investigation of visual language cohesion must examine whether these cohesive principles are at work between two dialogue balloons and/or between dialogue balloons and artwork. Reference, for example, refers to a range of syntactically cohesive elements that include demonstrative adjectives and pronouns, e.g., *I have completed an assessment report. This report will revolutionize our business*, wherein the demonstrative adjective 'this' causes the reader to connect the report in the second sentence to the report mentioned previously in the text. It should come as little surprise that this cohesive principle can function between two dialogue boxes within a panel, thus linking the balloons in the presentation of a coherent dialogue. However, an investigation of cohesion in visual language needs to consider inter-panel reference more than intra-panel reference. Reference can more effectively work as a cohesive element when it functions between dialogue boxes in different panels. If the first panel in a sequence features dialogue reading, 'I found a strange device in his office', and a subsequent panel features dialogue reading, 'Let me see that device you found', a reader is being asked to make a textual connection between the two dialogue balloons, and, by extension, between the two panels that contain the respective dialogue balloons.

Substitution, as a cohesive element, can occur between dialogue balloons in a visual text when a noun, verb, or clause stated explicitly in one point in the text is replaced by an alternate noun, verb, or clause elsewhere in the text. Ellipsis, a specialized variety of substitution, functions by removing a syntactic element from an utterance, or replacing the original syntactic element with a null value, forcing the reader to scan through the nearby text to find the missing element. As cohesive elements in visual language, substitution and ellipsis can readily occur between dialogue balloons in different panels. For example, if a dialogue balloon in one panel contains the following text: 'Will you marry me?' and a dialogue balloon in the following panel contains the text, 'I don't think so', a reader is able to use the cohesive elements she would normally use in standard written text to link the word 'so' to the clause in the previous panel's dialogue balloon. Likewise, the cohesive principle of conjunction can be easily transferred from standard written text to the text found in dialogue balloons, e.g., dialogue balloons containing the utterances 'It's time to go to bed', and 'But I'm not tired'. Conceptually repetitive elements (i.e., lexically cohesive elements) are also decidedly straightforward when applied to the writing in selected pairs of dialogue balloons. A specific term or phrase uttered in one dialogue balloon may be repeated in a later balloon or may be implied through the use of a collocate term (an item belonging to the same class of items as the original item).

That we can apply these cohesive principles to the written texts contained in visual language is not surprising. As a concept, applying these principles to linguistic utterances in visual language is no different from applying them to dialogue in standard written texts. But the visual language reader is being asked to do more than find coherence between written utterances. A visual language reader must perform the less expected task of finding coherence between word and image.

A look again at reference can illustrate the word–image cohesion at work in a visual text. In the example of reference given above, in one panel, a dialogue balloon may contain the text, 'I found a strange device in his office', and a subsequent panel may feature a dialogue balloon containing the text, 'Let me see that device you found'. However, visual language often presents the reader with a situation in which one of these linguistic utterances is elided entirely. The reader may be presented with a panel of artwork showing a character picking up a strange object in an office. Later in the comic, another panel features a different character drawn with a dialogue balloon containing the utterance, 'Let me see that device you found'. In this instance, the demonstrative adjective 'that' is used as a reference to a previous iteration of 'device'. However, no written iteration of 'device' occurs previously. What occurs previously is a non-linguistic image. The reader must match the demonstrative reference to an earlier element in the text, and in this instance, that element is not a word at all; the reference is to an image – which may or may not have been understood by the reader to be a 'device'. The earlier discussion of the differences between the word 'dog' and the image of a dog also applies to this example of reference. When the reader sees the panel showing a character picking up a strange object, the precise sign 'device' is not indicated. How therefore can the demonstrative 'that device' connect to the earlier image of the strange object? The reference must not be to the specific word 'device'

Figure 6.3 a) Panel sequence showing demonstrative reference between words. In this sequence, the demonstrative 'that' points the reader to the word 'device' in the first panel. b) Panel sequence showing demonstrative references between image and word. In this sequence, the demonstrative 'that' points to the image of the device in the first panel.

but to a range of concepts implied by the image and that may include the same idea evoked by the word 'device' (Figure 6.3).

There are some instances in standard written texts where the referenced item does not appear anywhere in the written text. Instead, the reference would be to some item external to the text and understood by the reader to be the object of the reference: *exophora*. It is not clear, however, that exophoric reference applies to this example of reference in visual language; the object of reference, though outside of the written dialogue, is not outside of the visual surface of the text, nor can it be perceived as an element outside of the textual structure of the text. At question here for future study is whether exophora can properly be applied to any and all references not explicitly present in the written text, or whether it should be applied only to references outside the conceptual framework of the text.

As with reference, word–image cohesion is also possible using the principles of substitution and/or ellipsis. In the example of substitution given above, one panel in a sequence might feature a passage of dialogue reading, 'Will you marry me?' and a subsequent panel might contain the passage, 'I don't think so'. Once again, in the comic, a writer can elide the first written utterance, opting instead to show a character kneeling and extending a ring to another character, with no accompanying text. If the next panel were to feature the dialogue, 'I don't think so', the reader could still derive the meaning of 'so' without the presence of any original clause for which to substitute 'so' (Figure 6.4). As with reference, the idea of exophora can be invoked here. In spoken English, speakers can use nominal, verbal or clausal substitution to replace non-uttered concepts. Imagine if the current example of one character extending a diamond ring to another were not describing a series of visual narrative panels but was instead describing an actual event in the physical world. If two people were in such a situation, one could say to the other, 'I don't think so', and she would be understood by the other person or by a third-party observer. Language rules must be allowing a language user to substitute for the idea behind a linguistic utterance, even if the utterance is not made explicit. The primary condition for such a substitution would be the shared context of the producer and receiver of the utterance. In the visual narrative example described above, the visual artwork presents such a context, and – via the reader's search for sufficient contextual clues by which to properly interpret the substitution – textual cohesion between picture and word and between panels can be achieved.

Figure 6.4 a) A panel sequence showing cohesion through substitution. In this sequence, the word 'so' in the second panel substitutes for the idea of marriage with the question, 'Will you marry me?' from the first panel. b) A panel sequences showing cohesion through substitution. In this sequence, the word 'so' substitutes for the idea of marriage expressed through an image.

The same kind of contextual clues can help a reader interpret word-image conjunction. In the dialogue pairing, 'It's time to go to bed', and 'But I'm not tired', the conjunction 'but' forces a connection between the utterances by articulating a relationship between the two lines of text. Furthermore, the conjunction indicates the nature or value of that relationship; the conjunction 'but' in 'But I'm not tired' indicates to the reader that this utterance is being presented in opposition to an earlier utterance (see Figure 6.5a). Unlike reference and substitution (including its subcategory of ellipsis), which fashion cohesion by transformation of syntactic elements, conjunction fashions cohesion by the addition of a connective device. A consideration of whether such a connective device could work between word and image leads to an affirmative conclusion. If the first line of dialogue is removed from a panel showing a woman pointing towards a child's bed (or perhaps a two panel sequence showing a woman pointing at a clock, then at a child's bed), the child's dialogue, 'But I'm not tired', in the subsequent panel can be clearly interpreted (see Figure 6.5b). The conjunction 'but' can successfully be read to place the phrase 'I'm not tired' in opposition to the image of the woman pointing to the bed. Not only are the picture and the dialogue coherent

Figure 6.5 a) In this example of conjunction between words, the girl's utterance, 'But I'm not tired', is connected to the woman's line, 'It's time to go to bed' through the use of the conjunction 'but', b) In this example of conjunctive cohesion between image and word, the girl's utterance, 'But I'm not tired', is cohesively tied not to other words, but to an image within the visual text.

with each other, but the nature of their connection is just as plain as the connection would have been between two lines of written text.

Conceptual repetition and collocation between visual narrative artwork and the written text in dialogue balloons is less surprising if only because of its ubiquity. Even so, the importance of word–image repetition and collocation should not be overlooked. For example, if two dialogue balloons in separate panels of a text refer to the action hero 'Leopard-Man', the simple repetition of the name forces a connection between the two utterances. Both utterances share a common referent. However, in visual language we often find instances where the appearance of a lexical term, like 'Leopard-Man', might be followed or preceded by a panel showing an image understood by the reader to represent Leopard-Man. As described earlier, the image and the sign are not necessarily equal in their meaning or interpretation. It is difficult to conclude that one refers specifically to the other. If, instead, the *idea* of the action-hero Leopard-Man is the referent for both, then the lexical name and the image refer to the same character. Such a shared reference would qualify as conceptual repetition. But to call this shared reference 'lexical cohesion' or 'lexical repetition' would be a misnomer, as one part of the connective link is not lexical at all. The question is reinforced, then, as to whether the nature of this cohesive device is indeed lexical or if it is not better described as ideal or conceptual repetition.

However, despite the apparent ability of the visual language reader to substitute word–image cohesion for word–word cohesion, it is important to be aware of specific limitations on how the word–image substitution may occur. Note that in the examples given above for reference and for substitution, the most obviously syntactic of the textual cohesive ties, the first line of dialogue has been replaced by an image, and the written text in the subsequent dialogue balloon either refers back to the image or presents a substitute for the concept presented in the image. If this process were reversed and the first line of dialogue were to be preserved and the second utterance replaced by an image without linguistic features, the cohesive principles of reference and substitution would no longer function as clearly. If, for example, a comic presented a panel showing a man on his knees extending a diamond ring, accompanied by the text, 'Would you marry me?' and then presented a second panel showing a woman with a look of disdain or disgust but without dialogue, the reader could still draw cohesive ties but those ties would no longer be formed by substitution. Ironically, the most obvious cohesive tie would be the cataphoric reference 'you' in the utterance 'Will you marry me?' Without an earlier referent, the reader would need to look to the later panel for the most likely referent for 'you', the image of a woman with a look of disdain. But the image itself cannot supply the pronoun necessary to make a reference, nor can it provide a demonstrative adjective, nor can it provide syntactic substitution. The image cannot be transformed the way linguistic utterances can; the image can replace only the referent not the reference. The image can only take the place of the original noun or clause in the cohesive tie of substitution; it cannot replicate the syntactic substitution found in the second grammatical element (the 'so' in 'I don't think so'). In essence, these cohesive ties between word and image are one-way streets, as least as far as reference and substitution are concerned.

With conjunction, the issue is somewhat obscured. Just as an image cannot replicate the grammatical roles of pronouns or demonstrative adjectives, that image also cannot reproduce specific conjunctions. However, as described earlier in this chapter, panel-to-panel connective ties have certain described qualities, even without the presence of any words. If the panel sequence showing the mother directing her child to bed is presented with the line of text, 'It's time for you to go to bed' in the first panel, and the image of a screaming or unhappy child in the next panel (without the utterance, 'But I'm not tired'), the reader can clearly interpret not only that a connection exists between the dialogue and the artwork, but something of the adversative nature or quality of that connection. Despite the fact that the general nature of the conjunction 'but' can be interpreted in this panel sequence, it is not clear that the image itself contains any feature comparable to the conjunction that would indicate that the picture of the child is in opposition to anything. The interpretation of opposition is contextual rather than dependent on any explicit sign or marking in the representational artwork.

7. Cohesion through writing in visual language: captions

The other major classification of written text in visual language is the caption. Captions, in general terms, have a different relationship to the panels than do dialogue balloons. Though there is, as stated previously, blurring between balloons and captions, balloons may typically be perceived as part of the content of the panel images. The balloons are tied to specific actors within the image and, in the ideation of the text, represent specific communicative acts being performed by those actors. In contrast, the caption is further removed from the content of the artwork both visually and conceptually. Because the caption presents content that is essentially external to the action of the artwork, the caption interacts with the artwork in slightly different ways from the manner in which balloons interact with the same images, though the basic cohesive principles at work remain the same.

The text in captions can interact with the content of other captions, with the content of dialogue balloons, and with the images in the panels (including framed text, graphic text and certain icons). In addition, captions interact with other word-image combinations in a hierarchy of connexity. In terms of textual cohesion, the same principles of word–word interactions that apply to dialogue balloons apply to captions. Syntactically cohesive ties, including reference, substitution and ellipsis, normally function between instances of written text in visual narratives in the same manner in which they function in standard written texts. Likewise, conjunction and lexical cohesion function normally as cohesive elements between written elements in visual language, whether caption-to-caption or caption-to-balloon.

It is within caption-to-image cohesion that we see some difference from balloon-to-image cohesion, though the difference is not dramatic. Reference, substitution and ellipsis function as cohesive ties between captions and images in the same manner as they do between balloons and images. Caption text can refer to images and can syntactically substitute for the content of images, though the images cannot refer to the caption text nor syntactically substitute for the caption text. Also, conjunctive ties can exist between caption text and image, that is, the caption may relate to the image in an additive manner, or in a causal manner, and so on. The caption, however, can offer a unique variation by presenting the explicit conjunction that connects two panels.

As discussed earlier, panel-to-panel connections can function in manners similar to conjunctive ties in written English. However, the exact nature of the conjunctive tie is not explicit in panel-to-panel connexity; addition, causality, etc. must be inferred contextually. Captions have the ability to present the explicit conjunction, not necessarily providing traditional content but providing a conjunctive sign or phrase, for example, 'Then ...', or 'Later'. It is possible, then, to conceptualize two panels or panel sequences as the equivalents of clauses being connected by a conjunctive caption (this conceptualization is metaphorical; it would be a mistake to consider panels as actual equivalents of linguistic clauses). This conjunctive function is not typically provided by the other varieties of written text in visual language.

One other important consideration to make with regards to the cohesive function of captions relates to the ability of captions to cohere not merely to individual instances of linguistic utterances or to individual panels of artwork, but, in fact, to connect to larger units of meaning or signification. A caption can connect conceptually to the combined whole of word-and-image in a panel or to a combined sequence of such panels. The text in such a caption would refer to all of the visual content in the combined panels on that page.

Corollary to the notion of hierarchical captions, it is also important to note that captions are not necessarily arranged in direct, sequential order; a given caption does not necessarily link directly to the preceding nor to the following caption. A caption may sometimes represent only one of several narrative voices in a text. Therefore, if three captions appear within a panel, those three captions may or may not represent three utterances in a single narrative thread; they may instead represent three unique narrative or conceptual threads, linking not to each other directly, but instead linking to related captions elsewhere in the text.

Structurally, the ability of comics to create hierarchies of captions and overlapping textual lines gives readers a type of cognitive task not generally demanded by standard written texts. The reader must be able to parse various conceptual units subordinate to other conceptual units, link them cohesively, and build a continuous flow of meaning. For instance, captions may be linked to the text in some of the following ways:

- a caption within a panel of artwork may cohere conjunctively or via conceptual repetition with the elements depicted in the artwork of that panel;
- a caption external to that panel may cohere conjunctively or via conceptual repetition with the internal caption, the artwork of the panel, and/or the merged concept of the internal caption and the artwork;
- or, an even higher level of caption juxtaposed to a panel sequence may cohere conjunctively or via conceptual repetition with captions in the panels and captions connected externally to individual panels, with the elements depicted in the artwork of individual panels, and with the entire overarching panel sequence.

In order to accomplish this task, the reader must hold key conceptual elements at the ready until they may be called upon. At heart, this cognitive process is not unlike the process of linking elements in standard written texts; however, the degree of this process can be magnified in visual narratives in large part because the textual elements may be broken up into visual chunks and into overlaps rather than ordered in a continuously linear expression of words.

This hierarchical chunking and layering of textual elements is an essential feature in the reading of visual language; the visual layout of textual elements creates a reading event that is not always strictly linear in its progression. Even so, the elements remain cohesive according to a common set of textual principles. The connections between these myriad elements appear more manageable when properly conceived as conceptual connections rather than as connections between contrary sets of surface signifiers. Mitchell's (1986) insistence that drawings and written words are, at their most basic, simply representations of the idea provides a basis for readers to connect all of the disparate visual elements and layers of those elements in the visual text. However, finer details of cognition in the processing of non-linear texts fall outside the strict bounds of this current exploration of cohesion, which focuses primarily on those surface signifiers.

8. Discussion

So we have now seen how principles of cohesion in written language can be reconciled to McCloud's description of closure in visual texts. We can then map these connections and crossovers (see Table 6.1) to see that while there are some cohesive rules that apply only to the written word, the visual text can achieve cohesion through many of the same principles, and moreover, that word and image can cohere to each other via a common set of cohesive principles. Having a single set of cohesive rules that can apply simultaneously to the verbal and visual elements of the text allows us to

Table 6.1 Standard word/image cohesion in visual language

	Syntactic cohesion (reference, substitution and ellipsis)	Non-syntactic grammatical cohesion (conjunction)	Conceptual cohesion (repetition and collocation)
Image-to-image cohesion	None	Yes, but the conjunction is implied, not explicit.	Yes
Image-to-word cohesion	Yes, but the cohesion works only in one direction.	Yes	Yes
Word-to-word cohesion	Yes	Yes	Yes

In addition to word/image cohesion, visual narrative connexity is supplied through artistic style and through visual language icons, including panels and balloons.

integrate all the surface elements of the visual text within a single set of cognitive functions.

Looking at the varieties of textual connections involving word and image in visual language, several patterns should be evident that must guide us in a shaping of a theory of visual language textuality and the reading of visual language. Firstly, written utterances can cohere to other written utterances via any of the cohesive ties normally found in written language. The utterances are not meant to be placed into a linear order, so a reader must learn to link utterances properly to the images in the panels as dialogue or captions, and they must determine which utterances connect to others. Secondly, word and image can cohere using the same connective principles as word-to-word cohesion; however, the syntactic cohesive ties can only work in one direction (the word referring to, or substituting for, the image). Thirdly, images can connect to each other via ties comparable to the non-syntactic cohesive ties of standard written English (specifically, conjunction and conceptual repetition). Moreover, a reading of visual language forces us to challenge the commonly used cohesive categories of temporal conjunction and lexical cohesion in favour of sequential conjunction and conceptual repetition.

A brief look at one two-panel sequence can demonstrate how some of these cohesive features work to fashion a coherent visual narrative text (Figure 6.6).

The two panels in this sample are linked sequentially; the images are linked spatially by both the ski-slope and by the two halves of one character's head and are linked temporally by the repetition of the image of the skier and by the dialogue balloons. The reader must make the successful connection between the two images of the skier to determine that they refer to the same actor. The connection is more complicated than McCloud's simple moment-to-moment theory of closure would suggest because the connection is based on several sequential notions. Still, the

Figure 6.6 An original two-panel visual narrative sequence.

connection is manageable, despite the illusion of a single foreground image to contrast the multiple background images. The panels are sequentially conjunctive, and a successful reading depends on the reader being able to understand the images as representing agents and events in a conceptual schema. Once again, the discussion of a visual narrative reading event evokes the need for conceptualization and for a conceptual framework by which to fashion meaning. This conceptual evocation is at the heart of how visual narratives are read.

The visual language icons also help to create cohesion in the form of the linked speech balloons connected to the image of the character Robert. The balloon lines cutting across the gutter force the two panels to be joined visually and conceptually through the speech attributed to Robert. The utterances attributed to Robert and Paul also serve to create cohesion through the use of pronouns and substitution. Robert's utterance, 'Look at him, Paul', offers reference to 'John' from the caption (and, by extension, to the image of the skier, which is in turn a form of lexical or conceptual repetition). The use of the pronouns 'you' and 'I' by Robert and Paul also serve to link their dialogue balloons; as does the syntactic substitution in Paul's dialogue. Just as cohesive is the use of the syntactic substitute 'that' in Robert's question to Paul, 'Would you ever do that?' The most probable meaning or antecedent for 'that' is contained within the image of the skier flying off the ski jump. The interpretable meaning is dependent on reading the image and the writing together as signs of a shared conceptual framework of actors and events.

The two captions are also connective in this sequence, but in different ways. The caption within the first panel, by virtue of its visual location, can be interpreted as connecting specifically to the first panel in the sequence. This caption, 'John shot into the air', coheres in part by repetition; the word 'John' and the image of the skier each refer to the same conceptual character or agent. The general relationship corresponds to the cohesive repetitive tie in standard written English. This particular caption and the image in the corresponding panel repeat or restate much of the same information. The caption is supplying neither cause nor effect; it is not supplying information regarding preceding events; it is not supplying modification or evaluation; it is not providing contrasting nor adversative information.

The larger caption, however, applies not only to the first image in the sequence, but to the entirety of the sequence, to the sum of the images and words of both panels. The reader can make a number of connective ties between the text in the caption and the panel sequence, including repetitions of character names and the conceptual repetition of 'his skill' with the images of the successful ski jump. Even so, the larger caption's primary relationship to the sequence is additive, offering description and modification that elaborates on the characters and events presented in the panel sequence. Note that nothing in the images provides information regarding the location of action nor the relationship between the characters; the reader relies on the content in the captions for this information. In contrast, none of the written material mentions skiing or ski-jumping, which is the core action or event in this narrative sequence. The two images can be linked together without the written text, but the larger narrative as it is presented depends on information supplied by the writing; in the same vein, the writing is loosely coherent at best and depends on the image to complete the meaning for the reader. Two disparate sign systems work together in visual narratives, according to common connective principles, to create a shared representation of conceptual schemas.

None of this is to say that the categorizations of connective ties described in this chapter represent the fullness of reading visual language and its combination with written language. This chapter has focused on the surface elements of a visual narrative text and how the contrasting elements of images, icons and words can be pulled together into a single text. The reading of a visual text, that is, that actual making of unified meaning, occurs on the level of conception, not in the surface features of a comic. There are certain shared connective features of both word and image that can allow a reader to link the two. Moreover, a successful reading of a comic depends on a reader's ability to translate both image and word into ideas. And it is at this level of ideation, at a level that treats character, agent, action, event and situation, and so on, apart from whatever surface signification, that a singular reading can manifest.

References

Cohn, N. (2013). *The Visual Language of Comics: Introduction to the Structure and Cognition of Sequential Images*. London: Bloomsbury.

De Beaugrande, R., and Dressler, W. (1983). *Introduction to Text Linguistics*. Boston, MA: Longman.

Halliday, M. A. K., and Hasan, R. (1976). *Cohesion in English*. New York: Longman.

Kuper, P. (1996). *The System* (vol. 1). New York: DC Comics.

Lobdell, S., and Pollina, A. (1999). *Hellhole* (vol. 1). Berkely, CA: Image Comics.

McCloud, S. (1993). *Understanding Comics: The Invisible Art*. New York: Harper Collins.

Mitchell, W. J. T. (1986). *Iconology: Image, Text, Ideology*. Chicago, IL: University of Chicago Press.

Moiseiwitsch, C. (1991). Priapic alphabet. In: D. Noomin (ed.), *Twister Sisters: A Collection of Bad Girl Art* (pp. 198–199). New York: Penguin Books.

Stainbrook, E. J. (2003). *Reading Comics: A Theoretical Analysis of Textuality and Discourse in the Comics Medium*. Doctoral Dissertation, Indiana University of Pennsylvania, Indiana, PA.

Vos, E. (1998). Visual literature and semiotic conventions. In: M. Heusser, C. Cluver, L Hoek, and L. Weingarden (eds), *The Pictured Word: Word and Image Interactions 2* (pp. 135–148). Atlanta, GA: Rodopi.

Zeek (2001). *The Art of Shen-ku: The Ultimate Traveler's Guide of This Planet: The First Intergalactic Artform of the Entire Universe*. New York: Perigree.

Part II

Psychology and Development of Visual Narrative

7

Manga Literacy and *Manga* Comprehension in Japanese Children*

Jun Nakazawa

Chapter Outline

---

* This chapter is an updated and expanded version of 'Development of *manga* (comic book) literacy in children'. In: D. W. Shwalb, J. Nakazawa and B. J. Shwalb (eds), *Applied Developmental Psychology: Theory, Practice, and Research from Japan* (pp. 23–42). Greenwich, CT: Information Age Publishing.

1. Introduction

1.1. Japanese cultural setting of *manga*

Manga are Japanese comics, defined as 'media expressing humor, irony, and a story by one or many successive abbreviated, exaggerated or deformed pictures, with words, sound-effects, or notations in panels' (Nakazawa, 2000a: 316). The Chinese characters (*kanji*) to spell out *manga* are '漫画.' '漫 (*man*)' means funny, comical and varied, and '画 (*ga*)' means picture. Thus, *manga* signifies something that is not only funny but also a variety of stories based on a succession of pictures.

Manga are read by adults as well as children in Japan. Popular *manga* are commonly remade into animations or video games, and Japanese animation and video games are dubbed and exported around the world. *Manga* are indeed among the main forms of children's popular culture worldwide. *Manga* is also one aspect of Japanese popular culture, and it is at the root of such currently worldwide popular social phenomena as 'Cool Japan' (the Japanese government's campaign for the international influence of Japanese pop culture), 'Otaku culture' (devoted fans of specific pop culture phenomena such as *manga* and animation characters), and 'Kawaii' (expression for cute and feminine expressions of pop culture) (Ingulsrud and Allen, 2009).

Manga are usually published as anthology magazines or books. Magazines are published weekly or bi-weekly, and include about twenty serialized *manga* works. *Manga* books are published every three or four months, compiling the serialized episodes from one serial *manga* together into one volume. In 2013, more than 440 million *manga* magazines and more than 438 million *manga* books were sold in Japan, representing thirty-six per cent of 879 million total publication sales (Shuppan Kagaku Kenkyusho, 2014). The number of copies printed of *One-Piece* (Volume 74, June 2014), which is the most popular comic book in Japan, was 4 million (one book per thirty Japanese people) (Shuppan Kagaku Kenkyusho, 2014). Since the 1990s, *manga* has been exported to many countries outside Japan. For example, *One-Piece* is published more than thirty countries, and its animated TV programme is now broadcast in more than forty countries.

Why was *manga* first developed and accepted in Japan? There are several reasons. First, Japan has a long history of pictorial media (Schodt, 1983). For instance, satirical cartoons date back to the 'Choju Giga (Frolicking Animals)' picture scrolls (*Emaki*) depicted by Toba in the twelfth century. Picture scrolls presented pictures and letters concurrently, and the readers integrated these two types of information in order to understand the story. *Manga* reading also requires one to integrate both the picture and word information. In addition, the simplified pictures were influenced by Zen philosophy and the development of wood-block prints such as Ukiyoe in the Edo era. Western-style comics and cartoons such as the panel frame system from the Meiji era (1808–1912) and Disney's animation techniques after the Second World War have also influenced today's style of *manga*.

The second reason for *manga*'s proliferation was economic. In the era of poverty following the Second World War, *manga* were a low-cost form of entertainment. It was inexpensive to print *manga* in large quantity, and cartoonists could present dynamic cinematic stories without the costs of producing a film, using only paper and pens (Natsume, 1996).

The third reason was the attractiveness of *manga* expression techniques that differ from Western comics. *Manga* used movie-like techniques (panning, zooming, montage and slow motion) (McCloud, 1993), which made *manga* easy to convert into animation. The most important feature of *manga* is that the size, arrangement, and form of panels are flexible, unlike Western comics that consist of almost same-size and square panel arrangements. This gives a depth and rhythm to *manga*, which now have begun to appear in Western comics (McCloud, 1993). Another feature of *manga* is that emotions are expressed in characters' eyes; in contrast the mouth is the most expressive part of the face in the Western comics (Wagner and Turlington, 2002). *Manga* characters' eyes are drawn extremely large while the nose and mouth are drawn comparatively small. Such a child-like face has ethological attractiveness for human as a 'Kindechenschema: baby schema' (Lorentz, 1943). *Manga*'s baby schema comprises the basis of the '*kawaii* (sweet and cute)' feeling.

1.2. The purpose of this chapter

In 2001, the Japan Society for Studies in Cartoon and Comics was founded. In 2006, Kyoto Seika University founded a Faculty of *Manga*, and now there are twenty-one universities that have a *Manga* Studies course. In 2008, Gakushuin University started a graduate programme in *manga* studies, called a 'graduate course in cultural studies on corporeal and visual representation'. As such, systematic research about *manga* has gradually become organized in Japan. However, psychological research about *manga* is not common. In particular, the cognitive mechanisms of *manga* reading and *manga* story comprehension are important subjects in this research field (Cohn, 2013; Cohn and Paczynski, 2013; Cohn, Paczynski, Jackendoff, Holcomb and Kuperberg, 2012). On the subject of psychological studies of *manga*, Nakazawa (2005a) described his *manga* literacy research. This chapter adds other new Japanese *manga* research to further explain the effects of *manga* reading on children's cognitive functions.

1.3. Early research on *manga*

Psychological research on *manga* by the early 1990s focused mainly on classification of *manga* and their expressive style using multidimensional scaling (Kawaura, 1977), image ratings of *manga* characters (Oshiro and Fukuhara, 1990), quantitative content analysis (Mori, 1990), and qualitative analysis from a clinical psychological viewpoint (Suga, 1990). During the 1990s, however, research on *manga* reading gradually progressed. For example, in 1996 a symposium on *manga* research was held at an annual convention of the Japanese Association of Educational Psychology (Kogo, Nakazawa, Muramoto, Murata and Kogo, 1996). Recently, *manga* research symposia at Japanese psychological conferences are held almost every year (Table 7.1), while some researchers have written review articles about psychological studies of *manga* (Ieshima, 2007; Tamada, 2010).

Research on *manga* reading started in the 1990s by Nakazawa (1994, 1996, 1997, 2002a; Nakazawa and Nakazawa, 1993a, 1993b) during an era that saw the growth of cognitive psychology in Japan. These research studies examined the following research questions: how is *manga* read, how do *manga* expressive techniques affect *manga* story understanding, how does *manga* story comprehension develop, and what kind of *manga* literacy is needed to comprehend *manga*? At the same time, cartoonists such as Natsume (1992, 1996, 1999) in Japan and McCloud (1993) in the United States expressed hypotheses as practitioners about relationships between *manga* expression and comprehension, which in turn influenced psychological researchers.

2. Literacy for *manga* drawing and reading

2.1. *Manga* drawing literacy

Wilson (1997, 1999, this volume; Wilson and Wilson, 1987) has discussed the influence of *manga* on Japanese children's art. He claimed that children's pictures reflected both development and culture, and believed that *manga* affect Japanese children's cognitive functions related to drawing. Wilson and Wilson (1987) asked children to create visual narratives by drawing pictures in six empty frames, both in Japan, where children are surrounded by *manga*, and in Egypt, where children do not see or draw icons, for religious reasons. They found that Japanese children's drawings were superior to Egyptians' in expressive technique, space processing, and story composition. Wilson (1997, 1999) also reported a strong influence of *manga* characters on Japanese drawings by preschoolers. For example, one preschool girl drew a human figure with a heart-shaped face, razor-cut hair, and eyes the shape and nearly the size of saucers, which are all traits characteristic of figures in *manga*. Toku (2001) compared the drawings of US and Japanese elementary school children. She found that spatial treatments such as horizons were more developed in Japanese children, and that their figure drawings were unrealistic, *manga*-like expressions. Specifically, girls drew the face with big eyes and a small nose and slender body, and boys drew muscular forms and emphasized motions.

Table 7.1 *Manga* research symposia at Japanese psychological conferences

Year	Title	Speaker and discussant	Annual Conference
1996	Latent cognitive *manga* research	Kogo, C., Nakazawa, J., Marumoto, T., Murata, N., & Kogo, T.	JAEP38th Annual Conference
2004	Psychology and *manga* research	Amamiya, T., Nakazawa, J., Yamaguchi,Y., Inoue, T., Sumiyama, S., & Masuda, N.	JPA68th Annual Conference
2005	*Manga* as media	Ohomori, T., Kurata, K. Murao, M., Kumada, M., Ishii,T., & Nakazawa, J.	JPA69th Annual Conference
2006	*Manga* and self: what we learn by *manga*?	Ieshima, A., Sugamura, G., & Urata, Y.	JSDP17th Annual Conference.
2006	Collaboration between *manga* and psychology	Ieshina, A., Sugamura, G., Nakazawa, J. Mutho, T., & Kure, T.	JPA70th Annual Conference
2007	Direction of *manga* psychology	Ieshima, A., Nakazawa, J., Saika, T., Natsume, F., Sugamura, G., & Mutho, T.	JPA71st Annual Conference
2009	Development of *manga* psychology, (1) cognitive psychology, educational psychology	Ieshima, A., Sugamura, G., Sugaya, M., Tamada, K., Amamiya, T., Nakazawa, J., & Ichikawa, S.	JPA73rd Annual Conference
2010	Development of *manga* psychology, (2) clinical psychology and medical science	Ieshima, A., Nakazawa, J., Saito, S., Iwamiya, K. Yokota, M., & Sugamura, G.	JPA74th Annual Conference
2010	Visual narrative research: examination of story structure of *manga*	Ieshima, A. , Sugaya, M., Yamada, Y., & Saito, K.	JSDP21st Annual Conference.
2011	Development of *manga* psychology, (3) social psychology, sociology	Nakazawa, J., Sugamura, G., Kosugi, K., Kitamura, H. Ieshoima, A., & Ohgino, M.	JPA75th Annual Conference
2012	Apply *manga* for education	Ieshima, A, & Matsumoto, K.	JSDP23rd Annual Conference.
2013	Development of the research about *manga* for education.	Matsumoto, K., Ieshima, A., Tamada, K., Yamada, T., Sugaya, M., & Machida, M.	JAEP55th Annual Conference

JAEP: Japanese Association of Educational Psychology, JPA: Japanese Psychological Association. JSDP: Japanese Society of Developmental Psychology

Toku attributed these forms to the strong influence of *manga* on Japanese children's human drawing.

Similarly, Cox, Koyasu, Hiranuma and Perara (2001) asked seven- and eleven-year-old children in the UK and Japan to draw human figures. Japanese children's pictures consistently received higher ratings for expressiveness than the UK children's. Cox et al. (2001) also discussed this result in terms of both greater exposure to graphic images in Japanese school art curriculum and the widespread influence of *manga* in daily Japanese life.

2.2. Cartoonists' practical hypotheses of *manga* reading

In the 1990s, *manga* cartoonists made practical hypotheses about the construction of *manga*, and *manga* reading. What kinds of component construct *manga*, and how do these components contribute to a reader's *manga* understanding? Let us consider a practical hypothesis about *manga* expression and understanding presented by a cartoonist. Natsume (1996) claimed that *manga* are made of three elements: pictures, letters, and panels. Pictures are of two types: normal pictorial depictions such as humans and objects, and also abstracted metaphorical marks. The latter type of picture expresses motions and mental/emotional responses by adding marks, symbols, icons, or notations. Natsume calls this abstracted picture the *kei yu* (形喩) or 'metaphoric form'. Takekuma (1995) categorized *kei yu* into two categories: 'manpu (漫符: *manga* mark which has its own meaning to some extent)', and 'kouka (効果: effect, which adds to the pictures and makes some sense of the physical or psychological effects)'. *Manpu* are often marks that are incorporated into images, such as action lines to depict motion or bloody noses to depict lust. *Kouka* are often background patterns, such as flowers to convey emotions related to love, or vertical lines to imply gloom.

Letters, words and sentences appear in word balloons mainly to indicate the speech of characters, and explanatory texts are also stated in panels. In *manga*, we find another element with the middle-character of word and pictures. For example, although word balloons show letters of speech, the form of the word balloon itself adds more meaning to the speech, e.g., indicating as *kei yu* the strength of speech (Shirahata, 1995). Moreover, onomatopoeia expresses not only sound but also a state of mind, metaphoric of psychological/emotional response (mental sound) that is peculiar to Japanese (Wagner and Turlington, 2002). Natsume (1995a) calls this metaphoric expression of sound *on yu* (音喩). *On yu* are hand-written onomatopoeia, drawn as pictures with the function of a picture. It looks like Japanese calligraphy – the fusion of letter and picture.

Panels separate *manga* in both time and space by guiding the reader's eye movement sequentially. Natsume (1996) suggested three functions of panels: (1) time sequence telling the reader the order to read, (2) compression and release which guides readers' psychological sensation and emotion, and (3) special expressions to define the frame of pictures and support the meaning of pictures. The space between each panel, called the 'gutter' in English, is called '*mahaku* (間白) (Natsume, 1995b). *Mahaku* do not only separate panels but also are actively used to express passage of time and psychological distance (McCloud, 1993).

2.3. Development of literacy for reading *manga* pictures

What kind of basic skills are needed in the process of reading and understanding *manga*? How do these skills develop? The first step in understanding *manga* is to understand of the pictures themselves (Willow and Houghton, 1987). *Manga* pictures are simplified, deformed, semiotic expressions ('semiotics' are the expression of meaning through signs and symbols). The reading of these semiotic pictures requires ample exposure to a pictorial environment including picture books in early childhood, and a knowledge base about drawing things and events (Levie, 1987). For example, Liddell (1996) showed pictures to children of England (which had a rich pictorial environment) and South Africa (in a poorer pictorial environment) and asked children to describe the pictures. Misunderstanding of pictures by South African third-grade children were twice as frequent, compared to their English counterparts (e.g., thinking that the tree behind the house grew on the roof of the house; or mistaking a green caterpillar for a snake or watermelon).

Nakazawa (2005b) examined *manga* picture understanding by kindergartners (n = 19), first- (n = 61), fourth- (n = 59), sixth- (n = 69), and eighth-graders (n = 70) (see Figure 7.1). The thief drawn in the stereotypical Japanese picture wears a striped t-shirt, hides his face with a cloth, and shoulders something in wrapping cloth of arabesque pattern. Even among preschool children, 50% of participants understood this picture to be that of a thief. Another picture presented a man wearing a suit and necktie and standing in front of a blackboard, and the interpretation that this was a teacher increased with age. To recognize him as a teacher, children need to combine the man's image with the blackboard image, and to infer from them both. Another picture was of a junior high school student in Meiji Era (about a hundred and fifty years ago) wearing a Japanese kimono and a Western-style cap. No kindergartners could correctly interpret this picture and correct interpretations again increased with age, but even among eighth-graders, accuracy was only 67.1%. To answer correctly, children needed historical knowledge about student fashions of Japan starting to interact with Western cultures. Thus, both cognitive ability and background knowledge were required to understand *manga* pictures.

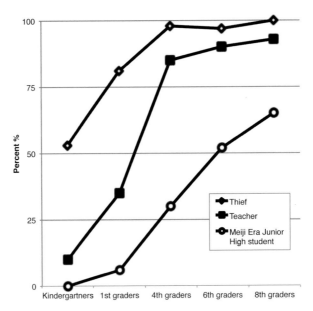

Figure 7.1 Picture understanding (from Nakazawa, 2005b).

2.4. Development of literacy in reading marks/ notation (*kei yu*)

Marks added to pictures are used to express physical movement and a psychological response, and these marks (*kei yu: manpu* and *kouka*) contribute to *manga* understanding. Muto and Toyama (unpublished) presented two *manga* pictures to second-, fourth-, and sixth-graders. One was a *manga* picture with marks, and another did not include the marks. When asked the meaning of the pictures, children's correct responses increased with age. In addition, even second-graders had better scores on pictures with the mark than without the mark, showing that second-graders already understood the function of *kei yu*.

As noted earlier, *manga* depict motions (Friedman and Stevenson, 1980) and mental/emotional states by using various marks and notations. Cultural learning experiences are required to understanding these marks. For example, adults of Botswana interpreted a sweat mark used in Western comics as blood, rain and tears (Byram and Garforth, 1980). The understanding of *manga* marks is also influenced by differences in experiences with *manga* in the course of development, and may be influenced by different types of *manga* marks, such as *manpu* and *kouka*.

Nakazawa (2005b) asked the meaning of the twelve *manga* marks to a sample of kindergartners, first-, fourth-, sixth-, and eighth-graders. Understanding of *manga* marks progressed along with grade level (Figure 7.2), and the marks were divided into

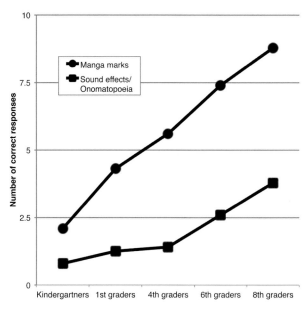

Figure 7.2 Understanding *manga* marks and sound effects/onomatopoeia (from Nakazawa, 2005b).

three types based on the increasing percentage of correct answers. The first type (e.g., running, surprise) was relatively easy to understand for about half of kindergartners and more than 90% of eighth graders. These marks were related to movement (action lines) and change in facial expression. The second type of mark was of moderate difficulty and expressed psychological/emotional responses such as conflict, confusion, discovery, or applause. Most kindergartners could not understand these, and correct interpretations increased with age to maximum of about 60% of eighth-graders. These are '*manpu*' (Takekuma, 1995) which express human psychological responses. The development of understanding of '*manpu*' suggests that it relates to children's development of understanding of other's thinking as part of the development of 'theory of mind'. This kind of semiotic expression is learned as a function of contact with *manga*. The third type of mark was more difficult to understand. No kindergartners and only half of eighth-graders could understand these marks. These marks expressed the psychological atmosphere of the situation and were abstract and symbolic in nature, for example, background patterns, such as '*kouka*' (Takekuma, 1995). Abstract expression of these marks makes them difficult to understand.

Nakazawa (2004) also asked about the meaning of *manga* marks to fourth-graders (nine to ten years old), university students (nineteen to twenty-one years old), and older adults (thirty to seventy years old). University students understood the *manga* marks best, and there were no differences between fourth-graders and adults. Although the understanding of *manga* marks appears to develop gradually, adults who grew up in an era when *manga* was only for children had relatively fewer *manga*-reading experiences, and thus may have poor *manga*-reading literacy.

Nakazawa (2005b) reported the ease of understanding marks depicting motion, like action lines. These representations are primitive and basic expressions, as seen in the Japanese Emaki 'Choju Giga (Frolicking Animals) in the twelfth century. (Choju Giga is one of the roots of *manga*.)' Thus, they may be understandable even in early childhood. Friedman and Stevenson (1975, 1980) showed that action lines with human stick-figures were understood by 30% of preschool children and first-graders, and this rate increased to 70% of sixth-graders. Mori (1989) presented object motion animation to four- to five-year-old preschool children and asked them to choose the pictures that most conveyed motion among pictures of objects with action lines, pictures of skewed objects, and the pictures of objects with an after-image. Preschool children chose the pictures of objects with action lines as best. Similarly, Mori (1995) found that preschool children perceived a car with action lines as moving faster than a car without action lines. In addition, preliminary research has suggested that these marks may be understood in animals outside of humans. Tomonaga (2011) found that a chimpanzee perceived the direction of motion of objects (a picture of an apple and a chimpanzee) with action lines. These research studies suggested that action line is a relatively primitive *manga* mark, and that even preschool children and primates could understood its meaning.

Nakazawa (2005b) reported further on difficulties in reading 'kouka' marks. Because the 'kouka' is an abstract pattern symbolizing the psychological state of the character or the situation, often in the background of a panel, it is difficult to comprehend. Kikuchi, Yoshida, and Yagi (2005) examined the psychological effects of 'kouka' marks by asking university students to rate their impression and emotions for 5 abstract patterns added to the back of a female character (vertical line, horizontal line, concentrated line, dotted line and skewed line). They reported that a vertical line shows a calm impression but indicates negative (helplessness and loneliness) emotions, horizontal lines and concentrated lines show active impression and denote surprise or impatience, dotted lines show a positive impression and express joy and hope, and skewed lines give an impression of dark and anxiety, and arouse the emotion of anger or malice.

Murata (1994) also examined university students' understanding of 'kouka'. She asked 'expert' *manga*-reading students (those who often read *manga*, in the top 25% for the amount of contact with *manga*) and 'non-expert' students (those who seldom read *manga*, in the lower 25%) for their impressions of the background patterns. Expert students attributed meaning to the background patterns more than did the non-expert students. They also interpreted the patterns' psychological meanings more correctly than did non-experts. Moreover, when students were presented with background patterns that were changed to be different from the original text, expert students gave richer interpretations. Apparently skill and experience in *manga* reading were needed to comprehend the abstract mental expressions given in the background of a scene.

Additional research has studied the understanding of the shape of word balloons. A rounded balloon expresses a normal voice, and jagged balloons express a loud voice or screaming. Rounded balloons with a small babble pattern indicate thinking (inner speech). Nakazawa (2005b) reported that preschool children did not understand the meaning of such shapes of word balloons, and children gradually come to understand them better. Thought balloons, which present picture in the balloons and show what the character is thinking, are depicted differently than word balloons. Takashima (2002) reported that three-year-old children start to understand the meaning of thought balloons and that by age five they fully understand them.

2.5. Development of literacy for reading sound effects and onomatopoeia (*on yu*)

As mentioned earlier, one special feature of *manga* is the use of sound effects and onomatopoeic expressions (*on yu*) in the form of graphical letters. Even the same sound effects and onomatopoeias give different impressions depending on context and graphical features of style and letter size (Miyamoto, 1990). When Japanese university students are asked to make the sounds around them, they often use *on yu* – sound effects and onomatopoeic expressions (Komatsu and Yoshimura, 2005).

Nakazawa (2005b) asked kindergartners, first-, fourth-, sixth- and eighth-graders the meanings of seven kinds of sound effects and onomatopoeic expressions (*on yu*), and found that comprehension increased with grade level (Figure 7.2). For example, the percentage of correct answers to the sound effects of *katakata* (the sound of wooden clogs) was 5% of kindergartners, 31% of first-graders, 25% of the fourth-graders, 33% of sixth-graders, and 54% of eighth-graders. In Nakazawa's (2004) research on fourth-graders, university students, and adults, the understanding of *on yu* by both university students and adults was greater than that of fourth-graders. There were no statistical differences between university students and adults. Because onomatopoeic expressions not only appear in *manga* but also in novels, adults who had less *manga*-reading experience could still understand them.

2.6. Development of literacy for context: reading through a sequence of panels

In order to understand *manga*, a reader needs to not only understand the expression of each panel, but also the story conveyed through connecting each panel and the context. In research outside of Japan, even three-year-old children can begin to understand the causal relations in sequential panels (Gelman, Bullock and Meck, 1980). In a culture with rich pictorial stimulation, like picture books and comic books, children tend to read stories by connecting pictures. For example, Liddell (1996, 1997) compared UK and South African children (second- and third-graders) and reported that UK children interpreted a story by connecting pictures more than did the South African children. Elsewhere, Byram, and Garforth (1980) reported that adults in Botswana did not understand that the characters repeated across three-panel comics were the same character, and could not integrate the panels into one story. The same results were reported in Nepal by Fussell and Haaland (1978).

Nakazawa and Nakazawa (1993a) gave children four panels of a *manga* comic strip and asked them to arrange the panels in order. The percentage of correct answers was low for kindergartners (5.2%) and first-graders (6.6%) but high among fourth- (80.0%), sixth- (81.2%), and eighth-graders (92.9% correct). It appeared that during the second and third grades, this contextual understanding greatly developed. In another task, Nakazawa and Nakazawa (1993a) showed children a four-panel cartoon with one panel blank, and asked what kind of picture should go in the blank. No kindergartners or first-graders could answer correctly, while 14% of fourth-graders, 45% of sixth-graders, and 54% of eighth-graders answered correctly. On the other hand, Nakazawa (2004) college students (n = 75; nineteen- to twenty-one-year-olds) were superior in their ability to both understand panel sequences and fill in blank panels, compared with equal results for fourth-graders (n = 60) and adult students (n = 18; thirty- to seventy-year-olds). Fourth-graders were still acquiring this literacy through daily *manga* reading, whereas the adult student cohort grew up in an era when *manga* was only for children. Most of these adults do not read *manga* now, and their only *manga* experience was back in childhood. These results suggested the importance of having story schema for *manga* narrative understanding.

In another study, Enokizu (1997) examined the role of schema in *manga* understanding by using a priming procedure. He asked to students to read two four-panel comics one panel at a time and to press a key immediately after they understood the meaning of the second story. The two comics were either the same or different depending on the micro or macro story structure. If the micro story structure of paired comics were the same, comprehension time was faster. Reading the first comic activated the micro story structure, and it primed and facilitated understanding of the second comic.

2.7. Cultural comparison of *manga* literacy

In the first ever cross-cultural study of *manga* literacy, Nakazawa and Shwalb (2012) administered a *Manga* Literacy Test to university students in the United States and Japan, and found that Japanese students had higher scores on every test item. As this test used Japanese *manga* materials, it was advantageous for Japanese students who were accustomed to Japanese *manga* expression rules. A *manga* literacy score was computed by standardizing the raw score of each item, and then calculating the sum of each standardized score. The correlation (*r value*) between the *manga* literacy score and reading and viewing experience of *manga* and animation was significant but low: the correlation between the literacy score and the frequency of watching animation ($r = .177$) and reading *manga* ($r = .149$) were significant in Japan, and frequency of watching Japanese animation ($r = .160$) was significant in the US.

2.8. Development of *manga* story comprehension

2.8.1. Story comprehension test

Next we shall examine the research question of 'How does *manga* story comprehension develop?' Nakazawa and Nakazawa (1993a, 1993b) developed a *manga* story comprehension test called the CCCT (Chiba University Comic Comprehension Test). For five minutes, participants read a ten-page *manga* story excerpted from the forty-five-volume series of *Doraemon manga* books by F. F. Fujiko, the most popular children's *manga* in Japan and Asia. *Doraemon* uses almost all the basic *manga* expressions, and reading *Doraemon* does not require expertise in reading literacy skills. In addition to its popularity, most Japanese children have a shared knowledge base about the story-world of *Doraemon*. Thus, we can compare *manga* reading comprehension ability for the *Doraemon manga* with a common knowledge base. After doing a filler task for one minute, children were asked to recall the story and write it down (for kindergartners and 1st graders the interviewer wrote their recall down individually), and they then answered questions to assess understanding of the story contents. The results of the CCCT are presented in Figure 7.3. Although first-graders understood *manga* better than kindergartners, a bigger gain in comprehension was found between first and fourth graders (story recall: maximum = 12, K 0.3, first 1.5, fourth 4.4, sixth 7.0, eighth 7.2; understanding: maximum = 23 K 1.1, first 2.9, fourth 8.5, sixth 11.2, eighth 12.1). *Manga* story comprehension improved throughout elementary school, suggesting that children become able to understand *manga* as stories as they progress in age (Nakazawa and Nakazawa, 1993b).

Nakazawa's (1997) first study divided university students into cohorts based on their ages of twenties, thirties, forties, fifties, and sixties, and examined their exposure to *manga* and reading comprehension with the CCCT. Contact with *manga* was most frequent in the twenties, and a difference was found between cohorts in their twenties, forties and fifties. In both recall and understanding of *manga* stories, students in the twenties and thirties had higher scores than did students in their fifties and sixties. It is difficult to determine whether the cause of age differences was based on differences in *manga*-reading experience between generations or based on declining cognitive and/

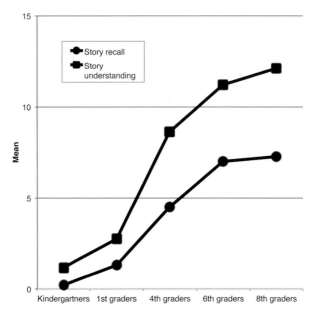

Figure 7.3 *Manga* story comprehension (from Nakazawa and Nakazawa, 1993b).

or attentional abilities with age. However, in Nakazawa's (1997) second study, nineteen-to twenty-year-old university students who read *manga* once or more weekly were compared with a group who did not read them at all. *Manga* readers had higher recall scores on the CCCT than non-readers. This result suggested that reading experiences may account for the above cohort differences.

What kinds of correlations are found between *manga* reading comprehension and other measures? We also examined the connection between *manga* reading comprehension and academic achievement and preferences for school subjects. Nakazawa and Nakazawa (1993a) found significant correlations between *manga* reading comprehension and achievement in Japanese language arts (reading and writing) in all fourth, sixth and eighth grade (fourth: $r =. 587, p <. 01$; sixth: $r =. 634$, $p <. 01$; eighth: $r =. 471, p<. 01$). This suggested that textbook reading and *manga* reading share common mechanisms of comprehension.

3. Relation between *manga* reading literacy and story comprehension

Do *manga* reading literacy skills contribute to *manga* story comprehension? Nakazawa (2000b) examined this among fourth-, sixth-, and eighth-graders using a multiple regression analysis. According to these analyses, *manga* story comprehension was predicted by *manga* literacy skills, in the following order: literacy for sound effects/onomatopoeia (*on yu*), pictures, panel order, blank panels, blank word balloons (filling in conversations in open word balloons of a four-panel cartoon), and *manga* marks (*kei yu*). This suggests that having the literacy skills for reading panels and the literacy skills of reading for context through a sequence of panels are a basis of story comprehension in the *manga* format.

Nakazawa (2004) classified several *manga* literacy skills into two groups using factor analysis: (1) literacy skill for reading panel contents, e.g., understanding pictures, word balloon expressions, and emotional expressions, and (2) literacy skill for read panel contexts (contextual reading), e.g., arranging panels in order, filling in panel contents, and filling in words in word balloons. Multiple regression analysis showed that *manga* comprehension of fourth-graders was determined by both of the literacy factors, yet only the contextual reading literacy factor determined *manga* comprehension among university students. Elementary school children need both panel-reading and context-reading literacy skills. Among university students who may already have acquired panel-reading skills, context-reading skills became important to read *manga*. As older participants were small in number, we were unable to conduct multiple regression analysis of their data. However, older subjects who had lower CCCT scores made these comments: 'I could not follow the story context' (a seventy-year-old), and 'Even if I read the *manga* story, I could not concentrate on it. I really think my generation cannot read *manga*' (a sixty-one-year-old). As such, difficulties with *manga* context reading were related to low *manga* comprehension ability.

4. Eye-tracking behaviour with *manga* reading

4.1. Panel configuration and eye tracking

Ishii, Ikaki, Kurata, Omori and Masuda (2004) examined panel configuration as a determinant factor of *manga* reading eye movement. They found that participants' eye movements skipped over panels (i.e., non-fixated panel) of the following two types: one was a panel following a panel in which the word balloon had many words, and the other was the upper panel in which two panels were displayed in a vertical stack. Because words have rich informative values, our eyes are guided to such an informative panel and we may skip the former panel. As Japanese *manga* are read from right to left, and from top to bottom, the typical eye-tracking pattern of *manga* reading is a reversed-Z pattern. Two vertically stacked panels disturb this reading pattern, and cause one to skip the upper panel. This means that *manga* panels may be read by using peripheral vision. The researchers thus changed the position of word balloons, and rearranged the two panels from vertical to horizontal, and found panel skipping decreased. Ikaki, Ishii, Omori, Kurata and Masuda (2005) examined another cause of panel skips: the position of the human figure and an open cut panel with no border. These two features are effective at catching the eye and panels following them are often skipped. Therefore, when they changed the position of the human face and changed the borderless panel to a usual closed panel, they found a decrease in panel skipping. In addition, Omori, Ikaki, Ishii, Kurata and Masuda (2005) reported that such a modification of panel configuration increased participants' recall of panels, but it had no effect on their story comprehension.

4.2. Differences in processing related to *manga* comprehension ability

What kinds of information processing accounts for individual differences in *manga* reading comprehension? Nakazawa (2002b) compared the eye movements made during *manga* reading by two seventh-grade girls, one of whom read *manga* every day ('A') while the other read *manga* about one day per week ('B'). I then administered a story recall test and comprehension test from the CCCT. Subject A outscored Subject B on both the recall test and the comprehension test. According to the analysis, both girls made random eye movements that did not follow the sequence of panels. This kind of random eye movement seems to be characteristic of *manga* reading, whereas in text reading eye movements are fixed on a line of letters. These eye movements may reflect free information gathering from pictorial stimuli and rechecking as a metacognitive function. Subject A repeated a visual sequence of 'leftward, downward, left, down' movement patterns (reversed-Z pattern) much more often than did Subject B. In addition, Subject A skipped more panels and word balloons and made fewer useless eye movements, compared with Subject B who fixated on word balloons more often. This suggested that the girl who read *manga* less often tried to understand the story by reading sentences in word balloons, as reflected in her longer reading times (39.8 seconds/page, as compared with 19.5 seconds/page for Subject A). Subject B concentrated on sentences in word balloons and accumulating this information may have overloaded her working memory. As a result, she forgot the first half of the story and only replied correctly to comprehension questions about the second half of the story. Meanwhile, Subject A had more *manga* reading experience and knew the typical 'script' of a *Doraemon* story. Using her prior knowledge she read and interpreted the story easily and without any information overload, as evidenced by her smooth eye movements.

5. A cognitive processing model of *manga* reading comprehension

What kinds of processes are at work in *manga* understanding? Nakazawa (1996) proposed a cognitive processing model for *manga* reading comprehension on the basis of earlier models of discourse understanding (e.g., van Dijk, 1987) and our own research findings, depicted in Figure 7.4. The left side of Figure 7.4 represents *manga* as a stimulus. *Manga* is composed of pictures (also *kei yu* types of word balloons, and pictorial aspects of *on yu*), letters (texts in word balloons as conversations, explanatory text outside of word balloons and textual aspects of *yu*), and panels (form and arrangements). These panel components depicted a variety of expressive styles, and the information, aroused emotion, and excitement of *manga* varied depending on the expressive styles.

The middle and right side of Figure 7.4 depicts the process of *manga* understanding. It consists of short-term memory (STM) or working memory, long-term memory (LTM), and the regulation process of these aspects of information processing. First, *manga* information is put into STM. Here, information in *manga* panels are coded and identified as pictures (object, human, facial expressions, posture, *kei yu*, pictorial aspects of *on yu*, and types of word balloons, etc.) letters (in and outside of word balloons as conversation and explanatory notes, *on yu* as letters etc.) and forms and arrangement of panels. Literacy for reading panel contents (pictures, *kei yu*, letters and *on yu*) has an important role in this step, as information in a panel is integrated and identified to create the meaning of each panel. The second step is a formation of short propositions. The information in each panel is connected and the *manga* reader works to understand contexts from the panel sequence. Comparatively short episodes are made into a unit, and the content of each unit is understood as a short proposition. The third step is the integration of short propositions. Short propositions are now integrated into the whole context as a story. Literacy for reading panel sequences has an important role in Steps 2 and 3. Here, schemas and scripts help the reader to understand a storyline. The fourth step is the formation of macro propositions, and the theme of the whole story is understood at this point. These working memory process interact with the LTM (right upper part of the Figure 7.4), which include declarative knowledge of *manga* expressions/*manga* grammar (pictures, *kei yu*, types of word balloons, panel arrangements. etc.), declarative knowledge about letters and sentence grammar, knowledge of panel reading sequence, and story schemas (story grammar) and scripts. In addition, episodic memory is also important for comprehension of *manga* panel and story in light of one's personal experiences. Cognitive regulatory process regulate the preceding activities. For example, while reading a *manga*, metacognitive monitoring check the children's understanding of a line, and if something is difficult to understand, the child may know to invoke the strategy of rereading a previous page.

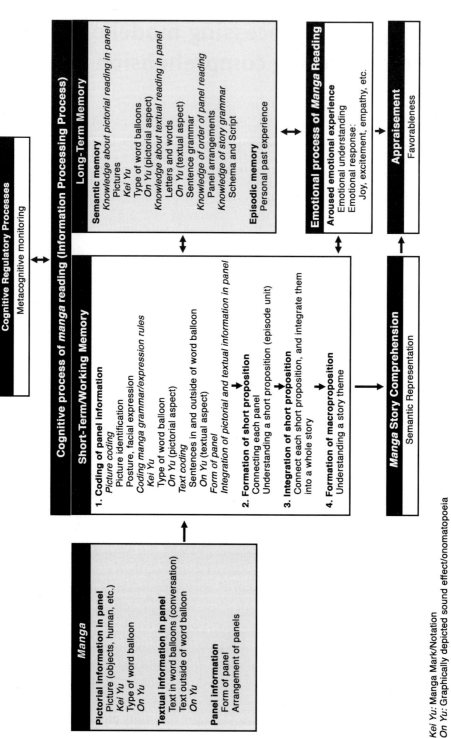

Figure 7.4 Process model of *manga* reading comprehension and appraisement (based on Nakazawa, 1996).

Kei Yu: Manga Mark/Notation
On Yu: Graphically depicted sound effect/onomatopoeia

Parallel with these congnitive process, and emotional process works during *manga* reading. Emotional processes (joy, sad, fear, excitement, empathy, etc.) aroused by *manga* reading interacts with STM and LTM, and works to facilitate the understanding of emotional aspects of a *manga* story. It also works as an appraisement of favourableness of *manga* works.

From a developmental point of view, improvements in attention skills enable a child to code information from panel contents (pictures, letters, *kei yu*, *on yu*) and panel arrangements. Memory development (growing capacity of working memory) is the foundation for context reading from many panels. General semantic knowledge, *manga*-specific literal knowledge, and context reading based on LTM schemas all combine to help children read *manga* as stories. With cognitive development based on both maturation and cultural experiences, children become able to compose propositions. Understanding of *manga* stories may differ depending on the expression styles of *manga*. Simple and basic expressive styles, like that used in *Doraemon*, may be easily understood by preschool children, but if *manga* use complex, subtle, and symbolic expressive styles, as in many *manga* for girls, it may difficult even for adults who lack *manga* reading experiences to comprehend.

6. Applications of *manga*

6.1. *Manga* as learning material

Manga is useful both for amusement and as media for transferring substantive information both in pictures and words. For example, a *manga* book explaining the Japanese economy became a bestseller and even the government white papers are now published in *manga* format. Many popular *manga* characters also appear in the formal elementary school textbooks. There are at least four benefits in using *manga* for learning/instructional materials. First, contents that are difficult to express in text-only format can be easily presented as pictures. Second, by presenting a story with a concrete context and background, abstract concepts are easier to understand. Third, using familiar *manga* characters and *manga* expressions enhances interest and motivation. Finally, when the instructor and learner are depicted in *manga*, readers tend to take the perspective of the learner and easily connect with the learning process via the dialogue depicted between instructor and learner.

Research has demonstrated each of these benefits on learning and instruction. For example, Murata (1993) compared three media for how to choose real estate agents: *manga* that contained only the essential portion of target knowledge (*manga* group), *manga* that depicted only non-essential contents with the essential portion in conversation words (non-essential *manga* group), and a text with all conversations between characters written like a play script (script group). Analysis showed that the *manga* group had the best comprehension, followed in order by the non-essential *manga* group and text group. In addition, this study compared various text versions: the script (all conversations written like a play script), the story text (full story written in prose), and the manual (itemized according to main points), and participants in the manual group had the best comprehension as along with the *manga* group.

Muramoto (1993) did a similar study, and presented students with either a normal *manga* version (though it was not learning *manga*), a word-deleted *manga* version (all the words in word balloons were deleted), or a text script version (scripts were made from words in word balloons). He compared the reading time, story understanding, and story summarization of participants. The text script group had the longest reading times, and the word-deleted *manga* group had the lowest scores for story understanding and story summarization. This indicated that normal *manga* were the most effective media. The pictures in *manga* provided an external situational mental model, and the words in the word balloons helped participants to construct an inner psychological mental model. Thus, both pictures and words together are important for *manga* understanding.

In a related study, Kogo and Kogo (1998) assigned university students to four groups according to whether the learning contents (about alkaline foods) were presented in *manga* or sentence text format, and whether or not a *manga* formatted cover story was added to the materials. Memory of the learning contents was assessed a week later, showing that presentation by *manga* was more effective than by text for retained comprehension, and that the addition of a *manga* cover story enhanced learning. The *manga* cover story made it easier for readers to build a situational model, enabling readers to apply what they learned to new situations.

Sato (1998a) presented materials about classical Japanese literature consisting of either text sentences with *manga* material added, or only as text material. The *manga*-added group performed better than the text-only group in scores for understanding story characters' thoughts and emotions, and in scores for content comprehension immediately and two weeks later. Sato (1998b) compared *manga* material and novelized text material, looking at university students' memory of story contents. She found that the *manga* material group had higher scores after a three-week delay, compared with the text material group. In these studies, learning from *manga* material was more effective than learning from text material. Text materials were somewhat longer because they had to explain many things expressed easily in *manga*. In addition, to understand text materials people need imaging capabilities to compensate for the lack of pictures.

Considering the effectiveness of *manga* materials, learning efficiency is one of its important components. *Manga* presents a situational schema easily, and also presents contents visually, which are difficult to present in words and text. This aspect of *manga* understanding also has an impact on learning time. Kogo (1993) and Sato (1997) reported that, although there was no difference in comprehension scores between *manga* and text material groups, time to learn *manga* material was shorter than that for text material. *Manga* therefore provided an effective learning format. In addition, as described before, the *manga* materials have novelty and fun, which increases the learning motivation (Kogo, 1993; Kogo and Kogo, 1998; Murata, 1993).

Tamada (2012) examined the eye tracking of *manga* learning materials. He presented university students with either word-descriptive *manga* (many descriptive words were presented in the word balloons and panels), or picture-descriptive *manga* (fewer words in the word balloons and panels). He instructed half of the participants that they would be given a comprehension test after reading the materials, and instructed the non-learning group to read *manga* as usual. Tamada analysed the reading time, eye-tracking data (picture-centred fixation or word-reading fixation; global eye-tracking vs. one-by-one panel-focused pattern), and participants' self-evaluation of content understanding. For the word-descriptive *manga* (compared with picture-descriptive *manga*), there were many words that required increased reading fixation and one-by-one panel-focused pattern. Under the instructions to learn the material, word-reading fixation and one-by-one panel-fixated patterns were more frequent than in the non-learning group. This research revealed some of the metacognitive processes of the *manga*-reading process model (Figure 7.4), as university students regulated their *manga* reading to fit the learning objective of *manga* reading.

6.2. *Manga* reading comprehension ability and effectiveness of *manga* learning material

Nakazawa and Mochizuki (1995) and Nakazawa (2002c) examined the effects of *manga* comprehension on the CCCT on the effectiveness of children's learning from *manga* materials. In this study, students learned mathematics ('addition of the different denominator fraction by reduction of fractions to a common denominator'). Most research on *manga* learning material has focused on memory of knowledge presented in the *manga*. However, another important effect of learning is generalization of learning. In mathematics materials, acquiring the math rule is important, because if participants acquire the rule they can generalize it. Fifth-graders (n = 66) who could not solve the relevant arithmetic problems on a pre-test were divided into three groups and presented one of the following learning materials: (1) *manga* materials (*manga* group), (2) novelized text of the contents of *manga* material (novelized text group), and (3) a school textbook-like explanation (school textbook group).

There were no group differences in mathematical achievement scores, sentence text reading comprehension ability, *manga* reading comprehension ability, or fraction calculations skills on a pretest. Comparing gain scores from pretest to posttest, gains by the school textbook group were the highest, followed by the *manga* group and novelized text group (see Figure 7.5). The school textbook-like material presented the main point clearly and was effective. Novelized text material required more time to read and was not efficient. Though the *manga* group did not perform as well as the school textbook group, it outperformed the novelized text group. This result was the same as in other studies: *manga* materials were more effective than text materials (Kogo and Kogo, 1998; Murata, 1993; Sato, 1998a).

Participants were then divided into two groups based on *manga* reading comprehension ability on the CCCT. Gain scores with the *manga* material for the high *manga* comprehension group was larger than for the low-*manga* comprehension ability group. However, there were no such differences between high- and low-*manga* comprehension, for the novelized text group or school textbook groups. This suggests the need to take account of the *manga* comprehension abilities when using *manga* materials. When children asked 'Which is the best material?' and 'Which material is easiest to understand?' most children wanted to use the *manga* material and thought it was easiest to understand. Although the school textbook was objectively the most effective, children's subjective evaluations indicated greater motivational effects of *manga* materials, which suggests usefulness as learning material.

The effects of *manga* literacy on the learning via *manga* material was also examined by Sato (1997). Using the *manga* literacy test of Nakazawa and Nakazawa (1993a), she compared the *manga* learning materials about the usefulness of a dam plant and text materials for the same contents, among fifth-grade children. Children who read *manga* on a daily basis had higher *manga* literacy scores. High *manga* literacy children read faster and understood both the *manga* materials and text materials. Tamada (2009) also examined the effects of *manga* literacy based on Nakazawa and Nakazawa's study (1993a) of *manga* material learning by university students, and found no effects

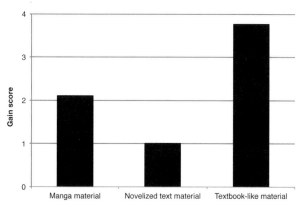

Figure 7.5 Gain score of learning materials (from Nakazawa, 2002a).

of *manga* literacy. He discussed this result in terms of the likelihood that Japanese adolescents have high *manga* reading literacy.

7. Conclusion

What are developmental implications of *manga* and *manga* reading for children? The first point we can make based on the preceding review is that *manga* are easy to understand. If the pictures depart from realism and become simplified as in *manga*, they can be acquired with generality through *manga* reading experience (McCloud, 1993). Pictures in *manga* are simple and can be remembered easily by dual coding of images and verbal codes (Paivio, 1971), even by a young child who cannot read letters well. In addition, not only pictures but also words support children's construction of situational schema. Many *manga* marks and word balloon expressions are learned by children easily through regular *manga* reading. If children acquire the meanings of *manga* marks and expression, *manga* reading becomes easier.

The second point is that various *manga* provide many types of enjoyment depending on the reader's developmental level. For example, preschoolers enjoy *manga* mainly for the attractiveness of pictures. In the middle grades of elementary school, children begin to enjoy the stories in *manga* because they are acquiring *manga* literacy that lead to *manga* story comprehension. Children's cognitive functions such as STM (working memory) capacity, scripts, and inferential ability all affect *manga* comprehension. Thus, children's enjoyment of *manga* depends on their cognitive abilities.

The third point concerns children's daily life in Japan. In Japan, academic achievement is highly valued and competitive entrance examinations for secondary school and university require children to begin intense study from fifth and sixth grade. Children study hard at school and many attend *Juku* (private supplemental academies) until late at night. *Manga* relieves their stress and gives them temporary pleasure during their limited free time. Thus, their difficulties in aspects of daily life may be seen as one reason for the widespread acceptance and popularity of *manga*.

Manga have become influential as media for children throughout the world. Natsume (2006) even claims that *manga* influence some people's way of life. For example, many superstar soccer players in the world say that they were influenced by the Japanese *manga* titled *Captain Tsubasa*. Beyond the cognitive psychological influences documented in this chapter, *manga* may have many other psychological influences on children. This will require further research.

Acknowledgement

The author expresses special thanks to Dr David W. Shwalb, Southern Utah University, for his careful reading and editing of this chapter.

References

Byram, M., and Garforth, C. (1980). Research and testing nonformal education materials: a multi-media extension project in Botswana. *Educational Broadcasting International,* 13: 190–194.

Cohn, N. (2013). Navigating comics: an empirical and theoretical approach to strategies of reading comic page layouts. *Frontiers in Psychology*, 4: 1–15.

Cohn, N., and Paczynski, M. (2013). Prediction, events, and the advantage of Agents: the processing of semantic roles in visual narrative. *Cognitive Psychology,* 67: 73–97.

Cohn, N., Paczynski, M., Jackendoff, R., Holcomb, P. H., and Kuperberg, G. R. (2012). (Pea)nut and bolts of visual narrative: structure and meaning in sequential image comprehension. *Cognitive Psychology*, 65: 1–38.

Cox, M., Koyasu, M., Hiranuma, H., and Perara, J. (2001). Children's human figure drawings in the UK and Japan: the effects of age, sex, and culture. *British Journal of Developmental Psychology*, 19: 275–292.

Enokizu, H. (1997). The effects of priming of story schema on comic strip story understanding. *Proceedings of Annual Conference of 61st Japanese Psychological Association,* 649 (in Japanese).

Friedman, A. L., and Stevenson, M. B. (1975). Developmental changes in the understanding of implied motion in two-dimensional pictures. *Child Development*, 46: 773–778.

Friedman, S. L., and Stevenson, M. B. (1980). Perception of movement in pictures. In: M. A. Hagen (ed.), *The Perception of Pictures* (Vol. 1) (pp. 225–255). New York: Academic Press.

Fussell, D., and Haaland, A. (1978). Communicating with pictures in Nepal: results of practical study used in visual education. *Educational Broadcasting International,* 11: 25–31.

Gelman, R., Bullock, M., and Meck, E. (1980). Preschoolers' understanding of simple object transformations. *Child Development*, 51: 691–699.

Ieshima, A. (2007). The review and perspective of the study on *manga* in psychology. *Kyoto University Research Studies in Education*, 53: 166–180 (in Japanese with English abstract).

Ikaki, T., Ishii, T., Omori, T., Kurata, K., and Masuda, N. (2005). The determinant factors of eye movement in Manga reading. Construction of integrated methodology for clarification of mind. Report of 2004 of Center for Integrated Research on the Mind, Keio University, pp. 207–210 (in Japanese).

Ingulsrud, J. E., and Allen, K. (2009). *Reading Japan Cool: Patterns of Manga Literacy and Discourse.* Lanham, MD: Lexington Books.

Ishii, T., Ikaki, T., Kurata, K., Omori, T., and Masuda, N. (2004). The determinant factors of guide and control of eye movement in Manga reading. Construction of integrated methodology for clarification of mind. Report of 2003 of Center for Integrated Research on the Mind, Keio University, pp. 107–113 (in Japanese).

Kawaura, K. (1977). The style of comics as a mass medium in Japan. *The Japanese Annals of Social Psychology*, 18: 171–185 (in Japanese).

Kikuchi, T., Yoshida, F., and Yagi, Y. (2005). Effects of pattern and color of back lines on mood expression in Manga. *Proceedings of Annual Conference of 69th Japanese Psychological Association*: 60. (in Japanese).

Komatsu, M., and Yosimura, K. (2005). Visually recording aural information through sound expressions in Manga. *Manga Studies*, 8: 26–30 (in Japanese).

Kogo, C. (1993). Memory of learning contents and story of manga learning material. *Proceedings of the 35th Annual Conference of the Japanese Association of Educational Psychology*, 38 (in Japanese).

Kogo, T., and Kogo, C. (1998). The effects of comic-based presentation of instructional materials on comprehension and retention. *Japanese Journal of Educational Technology*, 22: 87–94 (in Japanese with English abstract).

Kogo, C., Nakazawa, J., Muramoto, T., Murata, N., and Kogo, T. (1996). Frontier of Manga research. *Proceedings of Annual Conference of 38th Japanese Association of Educational Psychology*, S. 94–95 (in Japanese).

Levie, W. H. (1987). Research on pictures: a guide to the literature. In: D. M. Willows and H. A. Houghton (eds), *The Psychology of Illustration*. Vol. 1: *Basic Research* (pp. 1–50). New York: Springer-Verlag.

Liddell, C. (1996). Every picture tells a story: South African and British children interpreting pictures. *British Journal of Developmental Psychology*, 14: 355–363.

Liddell, C. (1997). Every picture tells a story – Or does it? Young South African children interpreting pictures. *Journal of Cross-Cultural Psychology*, 28: 266–283.

Lorenz, K. (1943). Die angeborennen Formen möglicher Erfahrung. (Innate form of potential experience), 13. *Zeitschrift für Tierpsychologie*, 5: 235–409.

McCloud, S. (1993). *Understanding Comics*. New York: Harper Collins.

Miyamoto, T. (1990). The effects of graphic properties of 'pictorial letters' in Japanese comic books. *The Science of Reading*, 34: 68–75 (in Japanese with English abstract).

Mori, K. (1989). Perception of movement by action line. *Proceedings of Annual Conference of 53rd Japanese Psychological Association*, 616 (in Japanese).

Mori, K. (1995) The influence of action lines on pictorial movement perception in pre-school children. *Japanese Psychological Research*, 37: 183–187.

Mori, S. (1990). Story analysis of lady's comics. *Seinen Shinri (Adolescent Psychology)*, 82: 136–142 (in Japanese).

Muramoto, T. (1993) Understanding and memory of Manga story. *Proceedings of Annual Conference of 35th Japanese Association of Educational Psychology*, 392 (in Japanese).

Murata, N. (1993). The effects of comic strips as a teaching strategy. *The Science of Reading*, 37: 127–136 (in Japanese with English abstract).

Murata, N. (1994). The effects of expertization reading manga notations. *The Science of Reading*, 38: 48–57 (in Japanese with English abstract).

Muto, T., and Toyama, N. (unpublished). Understanding of manga notations in elementary school children. (Cited in Muto, T. (1992). *Development and Learning in Children's Daily Life* (p. 183). Kyoto: Minerva Shobo) (in Japanese).

Nakazawa, J. (1994). The determinant components of manga reading comprehension. *Proceedings of the 5th Annual Conference of the Japanese Society of Developmental Psychology*, 251 (in Japanese).

Nakazawa, J. (1996). Examination of manga reading comprehension. *Proceedings of the 38th Annual Conference of the Japanese Association of Educational Psychology,* S.94 (in Japanese).

Nakazawa, J. (1997). Development of manga reading comprehension: developmental and experimental differences in adults. *Proceedings of the 8th Annual Conference of Japan Society of Developmental Psychology,* 309 (in Japanese).

Nakazawa, J. (2000a). Comics. In: T. Kuze, and K. Saitho (eds), *Dictionary of Adolescent Psychology* (p. 316). Tokyo: Fukumuta Shuppan (in Japanese).

Nakazawa, J. (2000b). How do children understand comics?: analysis of comic reading comprehension and its development. *International Journal of Psychology,* 35(3/4): 153.

Nakazawa, J. (2002a). How we do read comics? Analysis of comic reading comprehension: the cognitive and cultural implication of manga reading. *The Report of Grants-in-Aid for Scientific Research 1998–2001. (#10610098)* (pp. 5–17) (in Japanese).

Nakazawa, J. (2002b) Analysis of Manga (comic) reading processes: Manga literacy and eye movement during Manga reading. *Manga Studies,* 2: 39–49 (in Japanese with English abstract).

Nakazawa, J. (2002c). Effects of manga reading comprehension ability on children's learning by manga materials. *Research on Teaching Strategies and Learning Activities,* 9: 13–23 (in Japanese).

Nakazawa, J. (2004). Manga (comic) literacy skills as determinants factors of manga story comprehension. *Manga Studies,* 5: 6–25 (in Japanese with English abstract).

Nakazawa, J. (2005a). Development of Manga (comic book) literacy in children. In: D. W. Shwalb, J. Nakazawa, and B. J. Shwalb (eds), *Applied Developmental Psychology: Theory, Practice, and Research from Japan* (pp. 23–42). Greenwich, CT: IAP.

Nakazawa, J. (2005b). The development of manga panel reading literacy. *Manga Studies,* 7: 6–21. (in Japanese with English abstract).

Nakazawa, J., and Mochizuki, C. (1995). Effects of manga reading comprehension ability on children's learning by manga materials. *Proceedings of Annual Conference of 37th Japanese Association of Educational Psychology,* 369 (in Japanese).

Nakazawa, J., and Nakazawa, S. (1993a). Development of manga reading comprehension: how do children understand manga. In: Y. Akashi (ed.), *Manga and Child: How Do Children Understand Manga?* Research report of Gendai Jidobunka Kenkyukai (pp. 85–189) (in Japanese).

Nakazawa, J., and Nakazawa, S. (1993b). How do children understand comics? Analysis of comic reading comprehension. *Annual of Research in Early Childhood,* 15: 35–39 (in Japanese with English abstract).

Nakazawa, J., and Shwalb, D. (2012). Japan and the US comparison of university students' Manga reading literacy. *Proceedings of Annual Conference of 54th Japanese Association of Educational Psychology,* 319 (in Japanese).

Natsume, F. (1992). *Where is Osamu Tezuka?* Tokyo: Chikuma Shobou.

Natsume, F. (1995a). From onomatopoeia to *on yu.* In: *How to Read Manga* (special issue *Taharajima EX*) (pp. 126–137). Tokyo: Takarajimasha (in Japanese).

Natsume, F. (1995b). Mahaku: an active empty. In: *How to Read Manga* (special issue *Taharajima EX*) (pp. 184–195). Tokyo: Takarajimasha (in Japanese).

Natsume, F. (1996). *Why Manga Is Fascinating: Manga Expression and Grammar*. Tokyo: NHK (in Japanese).

Natsume, F. (1999). *Power of Manga*. Tokyo: Shobunsha (in Japanese).

Natsume, F. (2006). *What's Wrong to Learn a Life in Comics?* Tokyo: Random House Kodansha (in Japanese).

Omori, T., Ikaki, T., Ishii, T., Kurata, K., and Masuda, N. (2005). Eye catchers in comics: controlling eye movements in reading pictorial and textual media. Construction of integrated methodology for clarification of mind. Report of 2004 of Center for Integrated Research on the Mind, Keio University, pp. 211–219.

Oshiro, Y, and Fukuhara, M. (1990). Impressions of comic strips and heroes: multidimensional scaling of comic strip perceptions. *The Science of Reading*, 34: 147–154 (in Japanese with English abstract).

Paivio, A. (1971). *Imagery and Verbal Processes*. New York: Holt, Rinehart and Winston.

Sato, K. (1997). Effects of comic expression on comic strip comprehension. *Annual Report of Faculty of Education, Ehime University*, 43(2): 85–95 (in Japanese).

Sato, K. (1998a). Effects of comics on comprehension and memory in classical learning. *Annual Report of Faculty of Education, Ehime University*, 44(2): 45–48 (in Japanese).

Sato, K. (1998b). Effects of comic comprehension and memory. *Annual Report of Faculty of Education, Ehime University*, 45(1): 53–58 (in Japanese).

Schodt, F. L. (1983). *Manga! Manga! The World of Japanese Comics*. Tokyo: Kodansha.

Shirahata, N. (1995). What do the word balloon inform? In: *How to Read Manga* (special issue *Takarajima EX*) (pp. 138–145). Tokyo: Takarajimasha (in Japanese).

Shuppan Kagaku Kenkyusho (Institute of Publication Science) (2014). The latest trend of publication of comics. *Syuppan Geppo (Monthly Report of Japanese Publishing)*, 56(2): 4–13 (in Japanese).

Suga, S. (1990). Development and encounter with manga. *Senen Shinri* (Adolescent Psychology), 82: 34–39 (in Japanese).

Takashima, M. (2002). The development of young children's understanding of representation using thought-bubbles. *Japanese Journal of Developmental Psychology*, 13: 136–146 (in Japanese with English abstract).

Takekuma, K. (1995). Visual guide of 'kei yu.' In: *How to Read Manga*. (special issue *Takarajima EX*) (pp. 78–105). Tokyo: Takarajimasha (in Japanese).

Tamada, K. (2009). The effect of comic reading literacy and spatial ability in learning by comics for adults. *The Society for Applied Research in Memory and Cognition*, VIII.

Tamada, K. (2010). The framework of studies about education and manga through past studies and recent movements. *Philosophy: Mita Philosophy Society, Keio University*, 123: 207–228 (in Japanese with English abstract).

Tamada, K. (2012). The effect of contexts and expression styles of Manga on strategies use when reading manga. *Inquiries into Humans and Societies; Studies in Sociology, Psychology, and Education, Graduate School of Keio University*, 73: 15–28 (in Japanese with English abstract).

Toku, M. (2001). Cross-cultural analysis of artistic development: drawing by Japanese and US children. *Visual Arts Research*, 27: 46–59.

Tomonaga, M. (2011). Chimpanzees perceive 'motion lines'. *Proceedings of Japanese Psychological Association 75th Annual Conference*, 684 (in Japanese).

Van Dijk, T. (1987). Episodic models in discourse processing. In: R. Horowitz and S. Samuels (eds), *Comprehending Oral and Written Language* (pp. 161–196). New York: Academic Press.

Wagner, A., and Turlington, S. (2002). *The Complete Idiot's Guide to Cartooning*. Indianapolis, IN: Alpha.

Willows, D. M., and Houghton, H. A. (eds) (1987). *The Psychology of Illustration*. Vol. 1: *Basic Research*. New York: Springer-Verlag.

Wilson, B. (1997). Types of child art and alternative developmental accounts: interpreting the interpreters. *Human Development*, 40: 155–168.

Wilson, B. (1999). Becoming Japanese: Manga, children's drawings, and the construction of national character. *Visual Art Research*, 25: 48–60.

Wilson, B., and Wilson, M. (1987). Pictorial composition and narrative structure: themes and the creation on meaning in the drawings of Egyptian and Japanese children. *Visual Art Research*, 13: 10–21.

8

What Happened and What Happened Next:

Kids' Visual Narratives across Cultures

Brent Wilson

1. Child art versus visual narrative

Twenty-first-century children live in worlds pervaded by comic strips, comic books, *manga*, and graphic novels. They create them too. Indeed, kids' creation of visual narratives, or at least the drawing of characters possessing the potential to enter into stories, is a nearly global childhood preoccupation. How did it come to be? This is a story yet to be sufficiently well told; nevertheless, it is safe to assume that for as long as adults have created visual narratives, children have too. This is the story I wish to tell – well, it's the story I have been trying to tell for four decades.

For most of the twentieth century, influential educators and psychologists believed that children were natural artists and that their artistic development should unfold with minimal guidance from adults. Art teachers discouraged children from copying images because they believed that imitating others interfered with natural unfolding processes and that it destroyed innate creativity (Arnheim, 1978, 1997; Lowenfeld, 1957). The child art that was noticed, written about, and encouraged in schools consisted mainly of tempera paintings and crayon drawings. These art-like things children made when adults provided them with coloured crayons, juicy tempera paint, big brushes, large sheets of paper, and encouraged them to express their feelings (Cole, 1966) had an affinity to the paintings of the early-twentieth-century German Expressionists and the mid-century Abstract Expressionists (Gardner, 1980). Children's efforts were likened to the seeming naiveté, the flatness, simplicity, exuberance, and abstraction of 'modern art' (Wilson, 1992, 2004). There was, however, an underground visual narrative culture of childhood that went largely unnoticed by educators – or if noticed, then disdained and discouraged, because it disrupted the modernist narrative based on their belief in the necessity of a culturally unmediated artistic development.[1] If children's drawing resembled comic strips and comic books, then they were copying; they were not being creative, they were not behaving naturally. Or were they?

Kids were not always aware of the modernist dictums of their elders, nor did they refrain from copying images. In 1972, while conducting an ethnographic-like study of the indigenous arts in an Iowa community (interviewing the makers of quilts, decorators of mailboxes, designers of family room heritage walls, and painters of watercolours) and simultaneously, conducting a study of the community children's conceptions of art, I encountered the visual narratives of J. C. Holz. Calling himself the 'Phantom Cartoonist', J. C. had posted his handmade comics on a school hallway bulletin board with the invitation 'if you want to see more, write a note'. The cartoonist's classmates clamored to see more, with good reason. J. C.'s comics, initially influenced by Marvel and DC (see Figure 8.1), soon featured the adventures of an original character Birdman, his girlfriend Brenda Rex, and a motley gang of superheroes. J. C.'s comics were as exciting for his schoolmates as they were revealing to a researcher interested in the visual culture of childhood and children's growing conceptions of

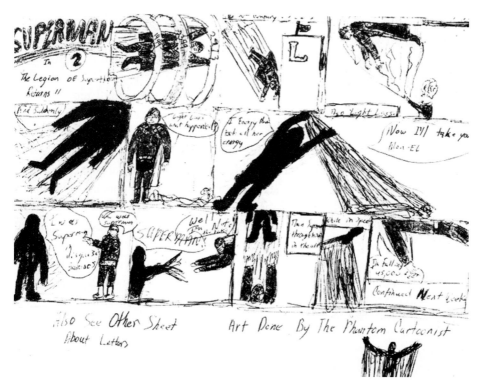

Figure 8.1 The 'Phantom Cartoonist'. J. C. Holz, the self-designated 'Phantom Cartoonist', posted his works on the bulletin board of a rural Iowa elementary school. Even in his usual frantic rush to complete a story and get on to the next, J. C. displayed a mastery of the rudiments of visual storytelling. He cropped images, changed implied distances, used a variety of expressive lines to show actions, and integrated text with images. Soon after he drew this cartoon, he replaced Superman with his own superhero Birdman – and then went on to create a much more sophisticated multi-volume *Birdman* series, which was subsequently exhibited at the University of Iowa (Ulbricht, 2005).

what constituted art. This was the beginning of my exploration of kids' self-initiated visual narratives.

When I published a case study of J. C. Holz's superheroes (Wilson, 1974), I observed that, by age ten, J. C. had mastered most of the Marvel and DC comic book conventions. His narratives had beginnings, tension-filled middles, and cliffhanger endings. The striking characters in his stories developed and transformed themselves as they were placed in moral and ethical dilemmas that called for resolution. In J. C.'s conventional narrative grammar, scenes shifted easily from long shots to medium views and from close-ups to tight shots. Expressive lines exaggerated human actions and facial expressions. Images and text were integrated. Words varied in size, text styles were expressive, and conveyed sounds. J. C.'s handmade comics were at once conventional and creative. How could this be?

J. C. created a sizable stack of comics, but he was also a collector and connoisseur of Marvel and DC comics. He knew the artists and their styles. He told me what was good and not so good about their work. This boy living in a small Iowa town had placed himself squarely within the American tradition of superhero comics. His astonishing production was not the child art that art educators prized and promoted. My J. C. Holz study and studies of how children's drawings were influenced by popular media (Wilson and Wilson, 1977) were greeted with negative reactions from believers and shapers of the modernist creative child artist narrative (Arnheim, 1978). Nevertheless, other artists and art educators recognized a familiar but unacknowledged pattern. I received letters from artists telling me that drawing comics provided the initial skills that had put them on paths leading to careers as artists, designers, and art teachers. Although, as several of them explained, they had shifted from making visual narratives to making paintings and other forms of 'high' art. The J. C. Holz case study revealed a hidden-in-plain-sight form of child art that appeared to provide a child with the means for escaping from his childhood – and for confronting the vicissitudes of adulthood. What else did it portend (Ulbricht, 2005; Wilson, 2005)?

2. Why do kids make visual narratives?

I wanted to explore all sorts of questions, and the more I looked into kids' visual narratives the more questions I formulated: Why did kids create their own comics? Was it to please themselves? Was it to gain recognition from others? Were there deeper and more profound reasons of which kids were unaware? How did kids learn to produce visual narratives? Were they taught, and if so, by whom? Did kids use conventional visual grammars, styles, compositions, and narrative plots for their own purposes? Were there social networks in which kids made and consumed comics? How did different visual cultural traditions shape kids' visual storytelling? Did kids in different parts of the world make different kinds of visual narratives and did they employ different themes and topics? There were larger issues such as whether kids created visual narratives to construct ideas about themselves and their worlds, their future lives, and their conceptions of ethical and moral behaviour – good and evil. Perhaps the largest question was what does making and consuming their own visual narratives contribute to kids' lives – to their cognitive development and cognitive orientation to the worlds in which they now live and to the worlds they might some day construct (Kreitler and Kreitler, 1972: 325–358; Wilson and Wilson, 1983: 19–37)? Of course, I didn't see all these questions initially. I'm still formulating questions and my answers are incomplete.

What follows is a partial account of the visual narrative adventure that has carried me into the lives of some brilliant kids like J. C. and has permitted me to interact with thousands of other kids who drew stories because I asked them to. It is an adventure that has taken me literally around the globe in search of answers to these questions.

3. Case studies of visual narrative and artistic giftedness

J. C. Holz was an exceptional kid, but how exceptional? Were there other kids with similar gifts? As it turns out there were and are.[2] My colleague Marjorie Wilson joined with me in the search. Our criterion was simple; we looked for kids who produced lots of drawings because they wanted to, not because teachers assigned them to. We discovered that almost all of these high producers were creating visual narratives in one form or another (Wilson and Wilson, 1976). Anthony had filled dozens of sketchpads and notebooks with an estimated ten thousand beautifully drawn superhero figures in every conceivable position from every conceivable point of view. The cosmic adventures of these characters extended from one notebook to the next. Kelly created elaborately filigreed Medieval towns and castles and composed stories about the characters who lived in them – characters who were based on her actual friends. When Michael was a small child he created elaborate underground worlds and later, during his teenage years, specialized in designing elaborate costumes for his characters. Lois drew hundreds of horses that lived, talked, and played like humans. Andy filled both sides of nearly four hundred sheets of paper with rock bands, explosions, and factories for manufacturing almost anything one could desire. Tami drew stories of girl detectives in the Nancy Drew tradition. Dirk drew the saga of 'Mister And', 'The Dubser' and the 'Change Bugs'. 'Mr. And' was a crook who shocked bugs with electric waves that changed and controlled them so that they would steal all the money in the world. The Cyclops-like 'Dubser' was born from the nose of a 'changed-person' (Wilson and Wilson, 1983: 19–37; Wilson and Wilson, 2009: 3–41).

In one way or another, these kids drew visual stories that involved creating characters and placing them in tension-filled situations of villainy or deprivation that called for resolution. Whether their visual narratives unfolded conventionally in comic strip frames, were scattered in unframed images that occasionally became massive sagas, or were presented in single frames with complex narrative interactions – the kids were drawing stories. We wanted to know why creating visual narratives was such a powerful motivating force that some kids would spend hours creating them almost every day.

During the 1970s and 1980s, we added dozens of kids to our case studies (Wilson and Wilson, 1983: 3–37; Wilson and Wilson, 2009: 3–41). All we had to do was walk into classrooms and ask, 'Who are the artists in here?' The kids knew, usually pointing in unison to the high producers who were inevitably visual narrators. We analysed the kids' stacks of narratives, visited them in their homes, and questioned the kids and their parents about the kids' motives for producing visual narratives. And since we wondered where their visual narratives would take them as they grew older, we also began to relate their young lives to the childhoods of writers and artists such as C. S. Lewis, Maurice Sendak, Julian Green, Paul Klee, and David Levine (Wilson and Wilson, 1976), all of whom had been childhood visual narrators.[3] As our case studies accumulated, we began to detect patterns and to formulate hypotheses. The young visual narrators were inquisitive; they wanted to know about everything: about themselves now – their minds, bodies, thoughts, emotions, relationships, challenges, problems, triumphs, failures, everything one might want to know about herself or himself – and to speculate about their future selves. Through their drawings they explored the ordinary worlds in which they lived, investigated the past worlds of history and fiction, created possible and seemingly impossible future worlds, and explored the boundaries of moral and ethical behaviour. Although they were voracious consumers of information, they were also creators of knowledge. We saw the kids of our case studies through the lenses provided by Kreitler and Keitler (1972: 325–358). In their *Psychology of the Arts*, the Kreitlers explored the role of artworks in cognitively orienting individuals and societies to beliefs about at least four types of reality: *general beliefs* about the world and anything in it ranging from people and objects to various interrelations and causal effects (pp. 335–339); *beliefs about self –* referring to a person's temporary and constant feelings, abilities, past events and present engagements (pp. 339–344). The Kreitler's third reality, *beliefs about rules and norms*, which reflect the various should-dos and should-not-dos with regard to any act of behaviour (pp. 344–349), and the fourth reality referring to *beliefs about one's wishes and goals for the future* (pp. 349–354). The Kreitlers captured the enormous range of range ideas; actions, interactions and transactions; relationships and causalities that we saw kids exploring in the visual narratives that they were so intent on creating – often for an audience of one, the young maker himself or herself. The Kreitlers saw the cognitive orientating function of art in terms of the consumer, whereas we had come to see kids' creating of visual narratives as fulfilling the very same functions (Wilson, 1976; Wilson and Wilson, 1982: 3–37).[4]

Our case studies convinced us that these prolific young visual narrators were motivated by a variety of interwoven factors. That the kids drew narratives to excite and amuse themselves was obvious, as was the fact that their visual stories gained them the attention and admiration of their peers. More importantly, however, we saw that the kids' visual narratives were experiments in making and remaking personal symbolic world models (Wilson and Wilson, 1979a: 8). It was certainly not just *the world*; it was the countless worlds about which Nelson Goodman wrote, made from nothing but symbols (Goodman, 1978: 1). Piaget also influenced our thinking about the narratives as well, when he wrote 'In order for the child to understand something, he must construct it himself, he must reinvent it' (M. W. Piers, 1972: 27).

The kids in our case studies were exceptional. But what of all the other kids for whom creating self-initiated visual narratives was not a driving passion? Were they also visual narrators – or at least potential visual narrators?

4. Elicited sequential narratives: within and across cultural studies

Once we saw the powerful attraction that the creation of visual narratives held for a few unusual kids, our next undertaking was to investigate the visual narrating abilities of groups of children, most of whom, we assumed, unlike the children in our case studies, had not demonstrated any special interests in creating their own story drawings. We prepared eleven- × seventeen-inch sheets of white paper on which we had printed six frames (approximately four-and-one-half inches square), took them into classrooms, and invited children to draw stories. Our instructions were simple: 'Tell a story through the pictures you draw.' We suggested that children might begin by drawing one or more persons, animals, insects, or imaginary characters, then 'show what happens, what happens next, and how things finally turn out'.

We were astonished by the first story drawings we collected from elementary and middle schools in a Boston suburb. Even six- and seven-year-old children, most of whom we assumed had never drawn a visual narrative within a set of sequential frames, demonstrated that they could depict amazing visual stories that were coherent in both form and content the first time they were invited to do so. Within a few seconds children decided upon a theme or topic, in the first frame or so proceeded to draw a protagonist encountering some sort of problem, and then they depicted clearly through a sequence of carefully framed acts, events, actions, encounters, and expressions how the difficulty was overcome – or not (Wilson and Wilson, 1979a).[5] Moreover, their visual narratives revealed that the children often possessed a complex understanding of human relationships and symbolism far beyond the expectations of most art teachers. Primary-grade children explored important human themes such as birth, growth and death, love and hate, good and evil, crime and punishment, creation and destruction, trial and error, and much more (Wilson and Wilson, 1979b). Six-year-old Tony's Rocket Villain in Figure 8.2 is one of the most amazing examples from Brookline.

5. Cross-cultural studies, visual narrative themes and compositional modes in Australia, Egypt, Finland and the United States

As we showed our first collections of sequential visual narratives to art educator colleagues, they suggested we should collect samples from other countries. In our first cross-cultural study, we analysed differences and similarities in the themes of elicited

Figure 8.2 'The Rocket Villain'. In the first frame, six-year-old Tony drew an evil-looking man approaching a rocket. In frame 2, the man lights the rocket; in frame 3, in a long shot seen through binoculars, the villain is about to be apprehended; alas, the rocket explodes in frame 4; frame 5 shows the consequences: a crashed rocket, a blasted villain and a toppled policeman; and in the final frame, the policemen load the villain's body parts into an ambulance and congratulate themselves. Crime does not pay. Tony, who lived in Boston, liked to read the comic books that his parents imported from Hong Kong and sold in their shop.

visual narratives drawn by middle-class urban and suburban nine- and twelve-year-old children in Australia, Egypt, Finland and the United States[6] (Wilson and Wilson, 1984a: 31–38; 1984b). Employing over two hundred thematic, sub-thematic and plot classifications we found intriguing differences. American and Australian children drew stories containing over twice the number of disequilibrating instances of lack/excess and villainy[7] than the Egyptian and Finnish children. And the American and Australian children were far more likely than the other two groups to resolve the disequilibrium in their stories. There were other striking differences. American children drew combat and contests 40% more frequently than Australian and Finnish children and 72% more frequently than Egyptian children. American and Australian children depicted stories featuring destruction 60% more frequently than Finnish children and 80% more frequently than Egyptian children. Australian children drew stories of triumph and success more frequently than the other three groups. Although some of the thematic differences could be attributed to the small and unrepresentative samples, among the four groups the Egyptian children were obvious outliers. Not only did they depict fewer tension-filled themes, but the style of their drawings and their modes of graphic narrating were very different from those of the other three groups. These enormous differences in content and graphic narrating patterns called for explanations; I undertook a series of studies in order to understand the cultural factors affecting children's visual narrations.

6. Story-drawing themes, compositions, and styles in a Giza village and Cairo moderate-income and wealthy neighbourhoods[8]

In and around Cairo in the early 1980s, Egyptian children of differing social and economic classes, living only a few kilometres apart, shared some aspects of a common visual culture. All were able to view folk renderings commemorating pilgrimages to Mecca, painted on the walls of buildings, and they could see other walls covered with drawings made by Egyptians of all ages, especially children – although many more wall drawings were found in poorer neighbourhoods. Virtually all of the children in the Cairo area also had access to television showing American animated cartoons.[9] Interestingly however, upper middle class children had access to one form of visual culture largely unavailable to children in Cairo's poorer neighbourhoods and villages beyond the pyramids in Giza. The children from wealthy families had access to illustrated books and comics. It was almost as if, by driving a mere thirty kilometres, one traversed the distance between ancient and modern times. The time and the place offered a unique opportunity to investigate how the presence or absence of printed graphic narrative models affected the stories we invited children to draw.

In the early 1980s, Nahia, located in Giza, beyond the pyramids and about twenty kilometres from Cairo, was a village of subsistence farmers and rope-makers. The textbooks used in the village schools were bereft of images – except for a few line drawings. The village walls displayed calligraphic graffiti but few images. Children were occasionally invited to draw in school but no adult models were presented and children learned mainly from observing other children's drawings.

The visual culture of the Embabba area of greater Cairo appeared not to be greatly different from the village of Nahia. A few steps from the school, women were doing laundry and cooking outdoors – as though village life had been transported to the city. Income levels of the parents were modest – they worked in small factories and engaged in other forms of low- and modest-paying employment. The school walls were largely undecorated and the textbooks with three or four illustrations were the same as those in Nahia. Few magazines and other forms of popular visual culture were present in the neighbourhood, although, if the children ventured beyond their neighbourhood, they would encounter various forms of printed visual culture such as billboards and wall posters. The neighbourhood was much like a halfway point between the village and the area of the city where the children of Cairo's wealthy elite attended school.

The Zamalek neighbourhood was located on Gezira Island in the Nile and was home to exclusive shops, embassies, private clubs, and hotels. Zamalek's shops contained illustrated magazines and comic books in Arabic and European languages. In the exclusive private school where we collected story drawings, all the children spoke English and they were taught from illustrated schoolbooks from England and America. Their schoolrooms were decorated with commercially produced and teacher-made illustrations – much as one might see in schoolrooms in North America, Europe, Japan or Korea.

6.1. Draw a story

Third- and sixth-grade students in the three groups – mainly nine- and twelve-year-old children[10] – were asked to draw stories, showing in six frames what happened, what happened next, and how things finally turned out. We wanted to know whether or not the children in the three groups would demonstrate similar visual narration skills, or if the children of wealthy parents with greater access to printed visual narratives would draw stories influenced by cartoons and comics. The children in the three groups drew stories using a variety of narrative means.

6.2. Sequential stories

Drawing a story where the action in one frame is continued in the next frame is one of the distinctive features of the sequential visual narrative. There were enormous differences in the ways in which sequences were depicted among the three groups. Only 4% of nine-year-old Nahia village and 8% of Embabba neighbourhood children drew sequential narratives, while 87% of Zamalak nine-year-old children drew them. Forty-five percent of the Nahia and 60% of the Embabba sixth-graders drew sequential narratives, while all of the Zamalak sixth-grade children drew them ($p < .001$). It is in these data that the consequences of living either within or outside of a visual narrative environment are most fully revealed. The reasons for these enormous differences merit exploration.

6.3. Non-sequential graphic narrations

When the Nahia village and Embabba neighbourhood children were invited to draw stories they almost gleefully filled the six frames. Since few of the nine-year-old and only about half of the Nahia and Embabba twelve-year-old children produced sequential narratives, it is informative to look at just what they drew in the individual

Figure 8.3 Six frames, each with a single image. When children in the Egyptian village of Nahia were invited to draw a story showing what happened and what happened next, they almost gleefully set about filling the frames. However, many of the children drew only single isolated objects such as palm trees, flowerpots, pyramids, and in this series, a television set. The village children used only a few configurations – and used them very economically. For example, they might turn a pyramid upside down to make a flowerpot.

frames (Figure 8.3). Their non-sequential responses generally took one of three forms: (1) they drew a single isolated object such as a person, a donkey, a pyramid; (2) they drew two or more (often related) objects such as three pyramids and the sun, two dolls, a tree and a house; (3) they drew a vignette depicting people or animals engaged in some type of event such as people playing football, visiting the pyramids, picking dates, a butcher cutting meat, or a person feeding chickens. While each of these three responses might count as rudimentary forms of visual narration, isolated single objects showed only the existence of something, two or more objects showed both existence and relationships, and event vignettes showed relationships and implied temporality but they did not show how the events unfolded in time from one frame to the next (see Figures 8.4, 8.5 and 8.6).

Why didn't the village children draw narrative sequences? Surely they knew what stories were; like sixth-grade children in wealthy Zamalak who all drew sequences and like children everywhere, they had heard verbal stories and most of the children would probably have told stories or narrated sequential events had we asked them to – and

Figure 8.4 A frame with two or more related objects.
The frames in the village children's narratives
sometimes looked as if something quite complex
might be happening. Frequently, however, this was not
the case. This frame shows only a doll, candy, and a
pot with a plant – objects with no necessary
relationship to one another.

now I wish I had. Nevertheless, almost none of the third-grade and fewer than half of the sixth-grade village children transferred their experiences with verbal narrations to the unfamiliar task of drawing a story. Apparently, they did not apprehend and apply the narrative structural relationship between the telling and the drawing of what happened and what happened next. It seems that in order to draw a sequential story the children needed access to specific visual narrative models that were not available in the village. Or perhaps the narrative models present in the village were not similar enough to the task of drawing a story – because there were visual narrative models in the village; over ninety-five per cent of the children in each of the groups indicated that they had television in their homes and the daily programming from the Cairo stations included American animated cartoons. I assumed, however, that the cartoon characters, their actions, and the simple plot structures moved so quickly that the children were unable to fix them in their minds and employ them as useful models for their story drawings. Apparently, the printed visual narratives such as those found in illustrated books and comics, not oral stories, and not animated cartoon narratives, provide the most effective models for drawing visual narratives.

Figure 8.5 'Picking Dates'. This vignette by a Nahia village child depicts a person picking dates – a relationship between two things, one acting upon the other, and an event unfolding in time. The style of the figure is fascinating. The profile head with a moon-face is formed from what appears to be a 3 drawn backwards – it's the way Egyptians write the numeral 4 and a formula that the village children used for drawing heads in profile. The profile has the two eyes of the full face – a feature that was common in European and American children's drawings in the nineteenth century (Ricci, 1887; Sully, 1896) but which disappeared in the early part of the twentieth century when children gained access to illustrated books, Sunday funnies, and comic strips (Wilson and Wilson, 1982a).

6.4. Themes

How did producing or not producing a narrative sequence affect the themes embedded within the children's visual narrations? If sequential visual narratives provide children with ways of depicting dynamic models of actual and possible worlds and for experimenting symbolically with how individuals might and should act within those worlds, then can this function be seen in the data? I analysed the themes and plot devices in the sequential narratives of the three groups of children. When narratives of the Zamalak wealthy children were compared to the other two groups, I found that they produced significantly higher percentages ($p < .001$) of narratives relating to: (1) slice of life – the depiction of a sequence of everyday events, (2) development – how something grows or changes, (3) process – a sequence of events occurring in nature, (4) trial – a test of strength or endurance, (5) success – overcoming a trial or test, (6) crime – violation of a law or rule, (7) punishment – paying for misdeeds, (8) combat and contest – competition of various sorts ranging from wars to sports, (9) assistance and giving – extending gifts and providing aid, and (10) destruction – obliteration.

Figure 8.6 Six frames, each with a related vignette. These six vignettes each show an event commonly seen in the village of Nahia – reading from the upper right: a chicken under a tree, a four-legged duck near a pond, preparing vegetables for market, gathering eggs, feeding a mother hen and her chicks, and at the meat market. There is no implied sequence between the events.

Additionally, I examined the plot device (11) disequilibrium – instances of villainy or the lack of something that upset the normal state of affairs.

Disequilibrium provides a way to illuminate the differences between the more static and dynamic worlds depicted. If a protagonist is thrown off-balance – something as benign as falling, hurting oneself, needing help, or as threatening as being accosted by a robber or attacked by a snake – then the threat or lack of something provides an opportunity to depict various ways in which the situation might be returned to a state of equilibrium. At age twelve, nearly half of the Zamalak children depicted stories with disequilibrium, while only a quarter of the same age children in the other two groups did so. The sequential stories drawn by upper-middle-class children even permitted them to depict mutual aid and assistance – if you help me, perhaps later I will have the opportunity to help you (see Figure 8.11) – a theme that is virtually unique to Egyptian children's visual narratives when contrasted with children's narratives from other countries. Thirty-five percent of the Zamalak children drew aspects of this theme, while only 14% of Embabba and 5% of Nahia children did so. The few remaining followers of Rousseau's romantic notion that there is a natural

Figure 8.7 'The Party'. Each of these six vignettes by a Nahia girl is about a party. Nevertheless, one episode does not necessarily follow another – the vignettes could be shuffled and the meaning would remain essentially the same. What is most fascinating about the vignettes is how one child has mastered virtually all the human figure and composition types found in the village children's drawings. She draws square heads and horizontal oval heads common in Egyptian children's drawings but seldom found in other parts of the world – and there are two vertical oval heads – more often used by the children in Zamalak. Other heads are formed with either the Arabic word for 'salt' or 'promise'. Some of the bodies are rectangles with fused neck – a feature so common in the entire Middle East that I have labelled it the 'Islamic Torso'. Several of the bodies have an angular hourglass shape that can be traced back to ancient Egypt. Some of the figures are arranged on implied base lines, and at least three, and perhaps all six, of the frames are composed partially or wholly with a central image and two flanking images – an arrangement used by many of the village children and seldom used by Zamalak children.

child and that sophisticated society diminishes children's natural inclination toward goodness should perhaps be unsettled by these data. Ironically, the Egyptian children who were more likely to encounter popular visual culture from outside Egypt used their resulting visual narrative skills to depict the reciprocal-aid/assisting-others themes deeply embedded within Egyptian culture. In other words, it is as if the imported visual narrative models helped middle-class children to appear more Egyptian rather than less Egyptian (see Figures 8.10 and 8.11).

Figure 8.8 'The Garden'. A twelve-year-old Nahia girl drew a sequential 'growth' theme involving planting (beginning in the upper right frame), nurturing, and finally harvesting dates, in the final frame at the lower left. I have found this slice-of-life/ growth theme – an aspect of what Kreitler and Kreitler (1972) term the 'common reality' – in every country in which I have collected children's story drawings.

The differences between the sequential visual narratives and simpler forms of visual narration are astonishing; the symbolic worlds drawn by the middle-class children were vastly more dynamic, varied and unsettling than the benign and ordinary and everyday worlds of the village children.

6.5. The composition of narrative frames

The reliance on conventional graphic patterns extended to the way children composed the frames of their narratives. I examined ten placement and arrangement patterns and the use of perspective among the village and Zamalak children. The classifications included compositional patterns such as (1) the location of a single central image, (2) the use of implied baselines, (3) the vertical non-overlapping stacking of objects (usually people and animals), (4) receding planes, and (5) the employment of a central image with two flanking images. The village and Zamalak sixth-graders' production of placement patterns was significantly different.[11]

One of the most fascinating differences involved symmetry – a central image balanced by images on either side (see Figure 8.12). Thirty-nine percent of the sixth-

Figure 8.9 'Catching the Fish'. An Embabba boy drew a sequential story in which a moon-faced character catches a fish (reading from right to left beginning in the upper right frame). The narrative theme was classified as both 'trial/test of strength' and 'success/triumph' – two themes that seldom appeared in Nahia village and Embabba narratives but were present in significantly higher numbers in the Zamalak children's stories. This step-by-step approach to sequential visual storytelling appears 'commonsensical' rather than based on encounters with commercially produced visual narratives.

grade village children used this static but satisfyingly balanced configuration, while only 7% of the Zamalak children produced it (p < .001). That is to say, the village children's narrations were something like 'there is this thing in the middle and next to it on either side there are two other things'. There were other fascinating compositional differences; only 10% of the village children drew frames showing planes that gave the illusion of three-dimensional space. Half of the Zamalak children drew planes giving the illusion of three-dimensional space. Half of the village children stacked objects vertically (a way of implying that one object is behind another); only 19% of the Zamalak children did so. More frequently, the Zamalak children drew one object occluding another. These findings reveal how intrinsic biases towards simplicity and balance (Wilson and Wilson, 2009: 44–51), reinforced through models available to village children, led them to produce charming pictures. This simple form of visual narration did not, however, contribute to showing cause and effect – what happened and what happened next.

Figure 8.10 'Giving and Giving'. Egyptian children drew stories about 'mutual assistance/giving' much more frequently than children in other countries. Here (beginning in the upper right frame), a girl picks a flower and in the third frame gives it to her mother; a boy sees this act of kindness, picks a flower, and gives it to his mother. In the final frame, we see two happy gift-givers and a happy mother – in a common Egyptian compositional pattern – a central image and two flanking images.

6.6. What do the differences mean?

Three groups of children separated geographically by only a few kilometres are separated almost as if by centuries when viewed in light of the very different visual narrative environments in which they lived. The Zamalak children's visual narrative environment seemed enormously complex and rich when compared to that of the Nahia and Embabba children (although it would seem quite ordinary when compared to the visual culture of North American children). It was even somewhat impoverished when contrasted with the visual culture of children in Japan, Taiwan, Hong Kong and South Korea. Nevertheless, the Egyptian study permits us to view an emerging visual narrative culture in which one group – the children with access to visual narrative models – drew action-filled and psychologically pervaded sequences where disequilibrium was a common feature, while the village and modest-income children did not. The Zamalak

Figure 8.11 'The Boy Helps the Dog/The Dog Helps the Boy'. Mutual assistance and giving is a theme that appears deeply embedded in Egyptian culture – and this narrative provides a paradigm example. In the sequence (beginning in the upper right frame), a boy sees a dog being hit by a car; in the second frame, he carries the dog to an animal hospital, and in the third frame the boy feeds the recovered dog. In the fourth frame, the boy and the dog are playing on a hill; in the fifth frame, the boy has fallen and broken his foot and the dog runs for help; in the final frame, equilibrium has been re-established. The Zamalak children (who drew the 'I'll-help-you/-you-help-me' theme significantly more frequently than the children in Nahia and Embabba) had encountered visual narrative models from other countries.

children possessed means for visualizing a broad range of human interactions and ways to practise symbolically overcoming difficulties that the village and moderate-income neighbourhood children did not have (see Figures 8.10 and 8.11, and 8.13 and 8.14).

But does it matter that one group of Egyptian children could draw, among other things, the dynamic processes involved in overcoming threatening situations that two other groups of children could not? Many of the Zamalak children imaginatively anticipated the future in their narratives; they considered the consequences of good and bad behaviour; they practised getting out of difficulty, their protagonists assisted others who were in difficulty. The Nahia and Embabba children did not. But is there actually any relationship between what the children anticipated might befall them, what they practised overcoming symbolically, and how they would actually behave in their later

Figure 8.12 Symmetrical compositions with a central image and flanking images.

The village children, more than children in the other two groups, composed their frames with a central image and two flanking images. The symmetry – which satisfies an inborn bias for balance and the avoidance of overlapping shapes – is pleasing, but it impedes complex interactive visual storytelling. I have found this composition in children's drawings in other countries – but not with the frequency found in the Egyptian village.

lives? These are questions that my study cannot answer and yet they are questions that get to the very essence of the cognitive and adaptive benefits of children's visual narrating capabilities. There are other possibilities: did the Nahia and Embabba children have ideas similar to the Zamalak children regarding their futures? Had they perhaps

Figure 8.13 'The Girl and the Snake'. The Zamalak children of wealthy parents drew stories filled with threat and disequilibrium; the village and poor Cairo children seldom did. In this Zamalak sequential story, a girl (in the upper right frame) is sleeping in her bedroom; in the second frame, a snake slithers through an open widow; in the third frame, the girl sits up and screams; in the fourth frame, her father calls a doctor, the doctor arrives and attracts the snake to a bowl of eggs; and in the final frame, the father thanks the doctor. I will refrain from providing a psychoanalytic interpretation.

anticipated using comparable ways of dealing with their possible futures, but simply lacked the visual narrating skills to show them? This question drives us even deeper into the unknown: was it the Zamalak children's visual narrative environment and their possession of visual narrating skills that made it even possible for them to imagine things such as threat-filled futures? And I even wondered if the static single frame vignettes of village life were all the children needed to draw? Wasn't it possible that once the village children became adults, they would continue to live much as their parents, grandparents, and great grandparents had for hundreds of years? In 1982, I doubted that this would be the case. I wrote, 'But can we be so certain that the village child's world will remain so certain, or is it, for that matter, so certain now? It could be that the forces that have the potential to disrupt an individual's or a society's stable structure are just as imminent for the village as for the city' (Wilson, 1982: 271; Wilson and Wilson, 1984b). I believed then, and I believe even more strongly now, that the Zamalak children who symbolically anticipated and conquered trials in their visual narratives were at least in some small measure preparing themselves for the political and religious conflicts of Egypt in the twenty-first century.

Figure 8.14 'Space Wars'. In this narrative, a Zamalak boy shows space battles using long-shots, medium-shots and close-ups – with cropping, occlusions, and the illusion of three-dimensional space. Because their visual culture did not present them as options, the Nahia village and Embabba children did not use these features.

7. Visual narrative worlds without end: tales from Japan

The marked differences in the Zamalak and Nahia village story drawings provided evidence that the mere presence of visual narrative models had an enormous influence on children's production of narrative sequences leading to plot-driven and disequilibrating thematic stories. I characterized the Zamalak children's access to comics, book illustrations, and other printed graphic imagery as being somewhat comparable to that of kids living in North America or Europe. But what of the prowess of kids who have access to visual narrative models many times greater than that of the typical kid living in the West? I'm thinking of Japan (and Taiwan, Korea and Hong Kong).

I acquired my first set of Japanese children's elicited six-frame visual narratives at the time I was studying Egyptian children's story drawings. A casual comparison of a sample of drawings from Osaka revealed how enormously different they were from the stylistic and narrative approaches employed by the Nahia village children. A detailed analysis of Osaka and Nahia children's story drawings revealed just how different (Wilson and Wilson, 1987).[12] On every narrative dimension studied – things such as:

(1) fifteen measures of frame composition such as floating objects, baselines, three-dimensional planes, cropping, and changes in implied distance; (2) ten measures involving narrative sequences and devices, plot structures, disruptions and conclusions; and (3) thirteen themes – classifications such as slice of life, creation, quest/odyssey, assistance, giving, war, contest, trial, death, destruction, failure, success, and misfortune – the Japanese and Egyptian produced significantly different narratives.

To state that the differences were significant reveals only a slice of the visual distinctions between the Japanese and Egyptian samples. The forms of the worlds depicted by the Japanese children had the appearance of inviting three-dimensional planes in which actors appeared to advance and recede from frame to frame. Actors and objects in those spaces revealed their relationships by variations in their sizes, the distances between them, the way they occluded one another and were cropped by the edges of frames. Close things were shown larger and distant objects smaller. The Japanese characters acted, they gestured and jumped, they laughed and cried in the spaces the young visual narrators created for them. The worlds created by the Egyptian children were mostly static and stiff in form. Each actor and object was provided with its own space; occlusions and cropping were rare. Distances implied between viewer and action remained the same from frame to frame. Characters seldom appeared to move and almost never displayed emotions. But what do these enormous formal differences mean to the children, to how they perceive the worlds in which they live? One of our conclusions summarizes a possibility.

The only realities humans know are the realities they themselves construct. As Goodman (1978: 6) claims, 'world-making as we know it always starts from worlds already at hand; the making is a remaking'. To two outsiders viewing the worlds of the Egyptian and the Japanese children through the windows provided by their graphic narratives, the world created by the Egyptian children is an under-approximation of the realities of the world in which they will probably have to live, while the realities created by the Japanese children are over-approximations (Wilson and Wilson, 1987: 20).

Visual narratives in which possible worlds are under-approximated diminish possibilities for exploration and experimentation for how things might be in actual worlds. Visual narratives, such as those created by Japanese children in which possible worlds are over-approximated, provide possibilities for exploration and anticipation of almost any actual world eventuality.

8. *Manga* characters and how to be Japanese

Why were Japanese kids' story drawings so different from those of other children? When I saw my first set of Japanese children's six-frame story drawings, collected for

Doll-like Characters

Cute Animals

Cyborg Characters

Comic, Monster, & Other Types

Mixed Types

Non-manga Types

Figure 8.15 Japanese kids' *manga*-derived characters. These characters were lifted from narratives drawn by Japanese children aged five to twelve. The doll-like figures in the first row (drawn primarily by girls) reveal their *manga* 'genes' in their large highlighted eyes. The cute large-eared animals in the second row were borrowed directly from the *manga* directed to audiences of preschoolers and primary-grade children. The cyborg characters in the third row (drawn primarily by boys) are mostly about power and enhanced physical strength. The fourth row presents monsters – most of them cute – and other *manga*-derived comic types. The fifth row shows characters that have *manga*-derived features as well as features associated with the ways Japanese children draw when influenced primarily by other children. The figures in the final row have virtually no influence from *manga*; they are simply drawn the way in which children draw when they teach themselves or learn from the drawings of other children.

me by a colleague in the early 1980s, I had two thoughts: first, I must acquaint myself with Japanese comic books, and second, I must go to Japan to collect story drawings. The Japanese children's drawings were like no others I had seen anywhere in the world – I knew they were influenced by comics, but at that time I knew nothing of *manga*. Japanese comics had not yet become a worldwide phenomenon. When the large package of *manga* I had requested arrived from Japan, they confirmed my belief that even young Japanese children's story drawings were highly influenced by their comic books. It was obvious that many kids had acquired the rudiments of visual narration from their comics – especially the look of the characters, their expressions and actions. I was fascinated by the patterns of *manga*-style acquisition – especially *manga*-like characters, and how these characters might shape Japanese kids' conceptions of themselves and the realities of their worlds.

In 1989, with permission of Japan's Ministry of Education, I travelled from the bottom of Kyushu, through Honshu, and to the top of Hokkaido visiting schools and eliciting thousands of six-frame story drawings. I discovered that virtually no Japanese child had escaped the influence of *manga*. The six pupils in an isolated elementary school in Hokkaido's northern mountains were as likely to draw characters in the *manga* style as kids in Osaka. I also began to realize that Japanese kids acquired at least two visual languages simultaneously: one was the language of school art – as Efland (1974) termed it 'The School Art Style', and the other was the language of *manga* – with its many dialects. In Japan, both languages were 'taught': in the last quarter of the twentieth century, through the nation-wide use of carefully prepared textbooks, I believe school art instruction was presented more systematically and more effectively in Japan than in any nation in the West. Exemplary school art programmes notwithstanding, I became convinced that *manga*'s influence on children's lives was far greater than school art. Perhaps *manga* was 'taught' more effectively too – but not in the ways we usually think about education.

I was especially interested in which of the two visual languages – the language of school art or the language of *manga* – Japanese children would use when asked to draw stories in school. Would they see the narrative task as a school art project? Or would they use the invitation to draw a story as an opportunity to engage in a *manga*-like drawing activity that was not generally encouraged in schools? At that time, anything having to do with *manga* was absent in the art curriculum. Many educators, including art teachers, saw the influence of *manga* as an unfortunate impediment to true childhood creativity.

In a sample of 1,151 six-frame story drawings by kindergarten, second-, fourth-, and sixth-grade children from locations throughout Japan, I classified:

1 doll-like characters, usually female and often with heart-shaped faces, huge sparkly eyes, and razor-cut bangs,
2 cute animals – rabbits and sometimes bears, foxes, cats, usually with huge ears,

3 cyborg and superhero types including robots, spacemen, and the ubiquitous atomic-powered robot-cat Doraemon,

4 monsters cast in a variety of Godzilla moulds,

5 comical characters in a wide assortment of styles,

6 hybrid characters combining children's imagery and generalized *manga* influences, and

7 non-*manga* characters from the visual culture of Japanese childhood and school art – figures that young children learn to draw primarily from other young children inside and outside school (Wilson, 1999; Wilson, 2000: 162–168; Wilson, 2002).

Table 8.1 shows fascinating patterns. As I expected, kindergarten children produced the greatest number of non-*manga* characters (46%) and they also produced the greatest number of hybrid or mixed types (33%) – characters that were beginning to reveal their *manga* 'genes'. As they grew older, Japanese kids included greater percentages of *manga*-like characters in their drawings. The *manga*-influenced characters of the older children also became more complex and capable of showing a larger range of emotions and actions than those of the younger children. The greater capabilities of the older children's characters made possible narratives of greater complexity and depth of meaning.

8.1. Cute animals

Most of the kindergarten children's *manga*-influenced characters were cute animals (12%). The percentage of these creatures increased to 18% in second- and then declined to 14% in fourth- and 6% in sixth-grade. These data probably reflect both the youngest kids' attraction to simple stylized animals (that are easy to draw) and the profusion of these character types in the *manga* marketed to them. It is fascinating to see how the production of cute animals declines as the children developed interests in other *manga* character types – and as they developed the skills needed to draw more complex characters.

Table 8.1 Japanese children's *manga* and non-*manga* type characters

Grade	Dolls	Animals and birds	Cyborgs	Monsters	Comic types	Other *manga*	Mixed types	Non-*manga*
	%	%	%	%	%	%	%	%
Kindergarten (94)	02	12	05	00	01	01	33	46
Second (351)	12	18	09	03	01	04	18	34
Fourth (409)	14	14	08	02	04	11	16	30
Sixth (297)	19	06	05	01	05	25	14	34
Total (1151)	*11*	*13*	*07*	*02*	*03*	*10*	*20*	*34*

8.2. Doll-like female types

Females with heart-shaped faces, sparkling saucer-sized eyes, and razor-cut bangs are one of the most distinctive and pervasive of all the *manga* character types. It is fascinating to observe the increasing frequency with which Japanese kids – mostly females – drew versions of this alluring character type. Only 2% of the kindergarten children produced the type. In second-grade, 12% drew the character type, and by sixth-grade 19% of the kids were including versions in their stories. I have speculated about how these beautiful female types provide little Japanese girls with templates both for how they could see themselves presently and how they might wish to look as they mature (Wilson, 2000: 167).

8.3. Doraemon

Each of the character types Japanese kids appropriate and adapt from *manga* models has the potential to act out a variety of possible ways of being and behaving within the imaginary worlds of the kids' visual narratives. Sometimes, however, kids went beyond borrowing a type; they appropriated a specific cyborg character; his name was Doraemon. Fujiko-Fujio created the enormously clever and diminutive atomic-powered cat Doraemon in 1969 (see Figure 8.16). The little character emerged from the top drawer of his friend Norbita's desk (and the gateway to the fourth dimension) (Schodt, 1983: 14). Doraemon fulfils Norbita's wishes by taking him on fantastic adventures, and when the companions face trials of any sort Doraemon miraculously rescues them by reaching into his magic kangaroo-like pouch to obtain whatever thing is needed to overcome any difficulty.

In some ways, Doraemon looks somewhat like the little Japanese kids who, for over four decades, have eagerly devoured *Shogakukan* magazine in which he first appeared and then the animated television version that began in 1979. Doraemon's head is as large as his body and his face is a slate for the display of a never-ending array of emotions. His little body and stubby arms and legs make it possible for him to assume almost any position and perform almost any action. Doraemon's features, emotions and actions are easy for kids to draw – consequently, they can make him appear to do almost anything.

This tiny, cute and clever character has nearly complete control over the fantastic worlds in which he and Norbita find themselves. It's the kind of power that Japanese kids can only dream of, and yet the Doraemon they consume has something important to teach them. Between his clever mind and his magic pouch, he has all the inner resources needed to solve any problem. I came to see Doraemon as a stand-in for all Japanese kids – for how they should be. After all, they live in a nation whose children are its most precious natural resource. I wondered if, subconsciously, Doraemon taught Japanese kids that they must be inventive and resourceful and that they must add to the nation's continuous flow of technological miracles. The nation's

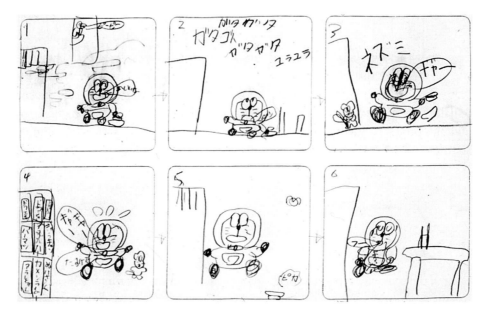

Figure 8.16 *Doraemon and the Mouse.* The diminutive atomic-powered cat Doraemon is a favourite of Japanese kids. When I asked them to draw stories, he was appropriated more than any other character from *manga*. And, like this seven-year-old boy, kids adapted him for their own purposes. In this story, Doraemon is frightened by a mouse and is relieved when the rodent is no longer a threat. The narrative is comically ironic in as much as the Doraemon that kids follow in *manga* is fearless and can solve whatever problem he's presented with; here, he is weak and frightened. It's fascinating to observe how the child changes Doraemon's facial expressions in each frame.

standing in the world rests on the shoulders of a cyborg atomic-powered cat – well, partly perhaps (Wilson, 2000: 170–177).

Big-eyed beauties, cute little animals, superheroes, cyborgs and monsters comprise a collection of signs sending a variety of contradictory signals. They seem to tell Japanese kids simultaneously to be cute and clever, to keep their noses clean but not too clean, to be meek and to be powerful too, to test boundaries but not rock the boat too much, to follow rules and to sometimes break rules. It is no wonder that in their six-frame elicited stories Japanese children so eagerly recreated these characters, imagined new adventures for them, and consequently elaborated upon the possible ways that they – the kids and the characters – might exist within both ordinary and extraordinary worlds.

8.4. *Dōjinshi* comic markets and more characters

While my Japanese research assistant and I were analysing the Japanese children's six-frame story drawings she took a short trip home and returned with a gift. 'Have

Figure 8.17 'Bon Voyage'. In the late 1980s, most Japanese educators with whom I talked dismissed *manga* as crass, of no educational value, and as seducers of children who ought to pursue more wholesome leisure-time activities. Such was not the case with one elementary school headmaster in Sapporo. He helped the children organize an after-school *manga* club and gave them use of the school printer so they could publish their magazine. There were twenty-seven volumes by the time I visited the school. This is paradigm third-site pedagogy. I was continually amazed at the skill with which Japanese elementary school kids drew their *manga* characters. To my Western eye, their characters appeared, nearly, to come from the same mould. To a kid, however, each character was a personal invention with features distinguishing it from all other characters.

you seen these?' she asked, and handed me a catalogue from a medium-sized Japanese comic market and a small collection of, to my eyes, elegant amateur fanzine *manga* (*dōjinshi*) she had purchased at the market. This introduction to *dōjinshi* was sufficient for me to determine that I must make another visit to Japan to study comic markets and the *dōjinshi* phenomenon. (The term '*dōjinshi*' refers to circles or groups of kids who organize themselves to collaboratively produce their own versions of *manga*; it also refers to the fanzine-like *manga* they make.) Without realizing it, I had already encountered *dōjinshi* in its most rudimentary form.

In 1989, an elementary school headmaster in Sapporo surprised me with his interest in my visual narrative project – most of the Japanese educators, including art teachers, had told me in one way or another that *manga* had no educational value and that they wanted nothing to do with it in their schools. The headmaster obviously thought differently; he presented me with a stapled copy of volume 27 of *Bon Voyage* – the school's *manga*-like publication. He told me that years earlier when he had seen some of his pupils drawing their own versions of *manga*, he asked them if they would like to have an after-school *manga* club. He supervised the club's activities and permitted the kids to print their magazine on the school copy machine. I didn't know it at the time, but this was an instance where kids, with the assistance of an adult, were replicating the entire *manga* industry. Eventually, I came to see the various dimensions of group-oriented amateur *manga*-making and presentation as a powerful form of informal pedagogy. I have labelled it third-site pedagogy – where kids and adults voluntarily become colleagues and collaborate on projects that are important to both (Wilson,

Figure 8.18 *Tin Stone*. When a research assistant presented me with this *dōjinshi* made by a Japanese teenager, I decided instantly that I must return to Japan to learn about teenage kids who made their own *manga* and about the comic markets in which they sold their creations to other kids. The effeminate male protagonists in *Tin Stone* reveal how Japanese girls use males and romantic love stories to explore their own sexuality. In this 1988 ten-page *dōjinshi*, two male lovers revel in their own brilliance, which is such that one is moved to exclaim that by comparison 'the real moon is hidden in the dark'. This meandering story is typical of both boys' love and *yaoi*. (*Yaoi* means 'no climax', 'no point', and 'no meaning'.) But it is pretty tame compared to most *yaoi* that feature lots of graphic sex.

2003a; Wilson, 2008).[13] Amateur *manga*-making is a pedagogical enterprise of enormous proportions in Japan – and a phenomenon that is still not well understood.

8.5. *Dōjinshi* comic markets

In 2000, my colleague Masami Toku and I travelled to Japan to attend COMICMARKET (also called Comiket). It's the largest of the approximately two thousand annual and semi-annual markets in Japan that provide venues where amateur makers of *dōjinshi manga* present and sell their works to fans. We wanted to interview the COMICMARKET organizers, and the kids and young adults who produced the *dōjinshi manga* sold in the market. We made a second visit to Japan in 2002 where we continued to interview professional and semi-professional *mangaka* (*manga*-artists), *manga* publishers and editors, directors of *manga* schools, and *manga* critics. I continued to interview members of *dōjinshi* groups and individual *dōjinshi* artists, and visit a variety of *dōjinshi* comic markets in Taipei in 2002, Hong Kong in 2003, and COMICMARKET again in Tokyo in 2008.

Visual culture critic and novelist Yoshihiro Yonezawa was the president of COMICMARKET when Masami Toku and I interviewed him in Tokyo 2000. He told us of his lifelong interest in *manga*, beginning with his boyhood story drawings based on his favourite ninja and robot *manga* characters. By 1975, he had become a *dōjinshi* fan and had seen the need for a venue where amateur visual narrators could show and sell their works to what was then small audience of fans. Yonezawa explained how he and a few colleagues organized a small comic market in December 1975. It consisted of thirty-five *dōjinshi* groups and was attended by about six hundred fans (Wilson and Toku, 2004: 95). Now COMICMARKET is held semi-annually in Tokyo Harbor at the Tokyo International Trade Center, also known as Tokyo Big Sight. The centre houses six enormous halls, eighty thousand square metres of space devoted to the exhibition and sale of *dōjinshi manga* created by amateurs (Wilson and Toku, 2004: 94). At Comiket 84 in August 2013, an estimated five hundred and ninety thousand fans purchased the *dōjinshi manga* produced by members in thirty-five thousand *dōjinshi* clubs. I estimate that the market might have included the visual narratives from as many as a hundred thousand makers. More than 11.4 million copies of amateurs' *dōjinshi manga* were delivered to the Big Sight venue and perhaps their makers sold as many as 8.7 million copies by the end of the market. Add to this literally thousands of other *dōjinshi* comic markets large and small held in Japan and throughout Asia each year, and one begins to sense the gigantic enterprise that Yonezawa, his colleagues, *dōjinshi* artists, and fans initiated.

It is nearly impossible to convey the scope and scale of COMICMARKET. The catalogue for the market Masami Toku and I attended in August 2000 contained one thousand, four hundred pages filled primarily with postage-stamp-sized images of the characters *dōjinshi* artists either created themselves or parodied from *manga*

Figure 8.19 *Get Me Power.* These two pages are from a Japanese kid's *dōjinshi*, titled *Get Me Power.* In its forty-two pages, I counted more than fifty different cyborgs, fitting into every one of my ten classifications.

sources. In following just one of the many hundreds of strands of character types, as we did with 'Boys' Love' (Wilson and Toku, 2004: 94–103), the richness of the enterprise becomes evident.

8.6. 'Boys' Love'

Teenage Japanese girls have found ways to explore their emerging sexuality using boys as surrogates. In 1976, when Keiko Takemiya created the pretty young French boarding school student Gilbert Cocteau, who couldn't resist falling into bed with other boys and men too, her enormously popular and influential series (she told us that her publisher had initially resisted) opened the floodgates for boy-with-boy love *manga* (Wilson and Toku, 2004; Schodt, 1983: 101–103). Now a large percentage of the *dōjinshi manga* sold at comic markets is devoted to 'Boys' Love' and '*Yaoi*'. And yet when I quizzed *dōjinshi* creators and *otaku* consumers by asking variations on the question, 'is this about gay love?' the answer was always an emphatic 'No!' 'Gay love is reality; this is fantasy!' And what they meant was that 'Boys' Love' *dōjinshi* provided a narrative space in which amateur female creators and their readers could explore, ironically, dimensions of femininity. In the girls' *dōjinshi*, males serve as female surrogates that permit girls to experiment with and experience vicariously what it is like to be the submissive or dominant partner, to explore a spectrum of masculine and feminine roles and identities, to be unburdened by fears of pregnancy and to escape from the traditional role of childbearing and mothering, and perhaps, symbolically, to gain power and control over males (Wilson and Toku, 2004: 100–101; Wilson, 2005b: 45). This is, of course, only one of many fictional surrogates through which kids can explore human potential.

8.7. Cyborgs

Japanese kids use cyborgs to explore power – and just about every other human and inhumane potential. I became fascinated by cyborgs while examining a stack of fifteen *dōjinshi manga* published by members of university *manga* clubs.[14] These *dōjinshi* provided a useful and convenient way of broadly sampling the *dōjinshi* phenomenon. In three hundred and seven university *dōjinshi* club stories I examined, I discovered, among a vast array of characters, lots of cyborgs. These cyborgs were distinguished by a strangeness that invited a closer analysis. Consequently, I developed a classification scheme consisting of ten cyborg types. It included:

1. whole-body (usually 'muscular') mechanical superhero and super-nemesis types (6%);
2. cyborgs with mechanical prostheses – usually mechanical arms, many of which were weapons (7%);
3. cyborgs with mechanical accoutrements – various additions to bodies that provided powers and protections (5%);
4. biological assemblages; cyborgs that were apparently cobbled together from human parts in the manner of Frankenstein's monster (2%);
5. mutants: a great variety, that reminded me of the bar scene characters in the first *Star Wars* film (16%);
6. post-mortals: characters with wings – and of course the ability to fly (8%);
7. human and animal combinations – often humans with animal ears, tails, etc. (19%);
8. characters that appeared cyborgian because of the costumes and outfits they wore that appeared to give them unusual power or status (the class is probably pre-cyborgian) (20%);
9. ghosts and other characters having skulls and appearing in shrouds (7%); and
10. other cyborg-like characters not fitting into any of the nine previous classifications (these characters came in a variety of shapes and sizes – pocket monsters, ciphers, which is to say, characters that were nearly featureless, etc.) (30%).

To present these data in another way, in the university students' *dōjinshi*, there was an average of 1.2 cyborgs in each story or feature. I must quickly add that in other *dōjinshi* it is possible to find a much greater number of cyborgs. For example, in a forty-two-page *dōjinshi* titled *Get Me Power*, I counted over fifty distinct cyborgs fitting into every one of my ten classifications!

The question that prompted my analysis of cyborg types was, in effect, 'what do they reveal about Japanese adolescents' notions of humanity?' In other words, did the fictional attachments, extensions, and alterations to humanoid bodies reveal something of human longing to be more than we are and do more than we do now? My conclusions were only tentative – and more negative than positive. For example, when young people created mechanical musclemen, it seemed like misguided masculinity. Virtually the only thing these creatures are good for is combat. And whom do they battle? It's usually other mechanical cyborg monsters. One monster makes it necessary to create a counter-monster, and so on ad infinitum. A greater cyborg monster on one side begets an even greater monster on the other side. In their efforts to 'protect' themselves, they destroy others, who in turn try to destroy them. What should we think of these young makers of mechanical monsters who take such delight in destruction?

And then there are cyborgs in the *dōjinshi* narratives with troubling prosthetics such as knives, hooks, and other weapons in place of hands; good, perhaps for fighting and injuring, but not so good for caressing or reaching gently out to others. In the twenty-first century, reality has thankfully transcended the fiction of these crude appendages. The young people who drew these prosthetic limbs already had devices 'attached' to their own hands – cellphones that allowed them to reach out to others – and they would soon possess smartphones that were like little chunks of their brains that they could hold in their hands and that would permit them to gather worlds without end with the flick of fingers and thumbs – so much more useful than knives and hooks.

Mutants and combinants were puzzling. The associations could be positive or negative. Was it radiation messing up our genes or invasive genetically altered organisms destroying our planet? Of course the cyborgs may have been mere expressions of human desire. Bird-people – who wouldn't want to fly? And as for the blending of male and female, perhaps it's a way of creating a better human. And what of ghosts and angels – perhaps these post-mortals were signs of longing for immortality. There seems almost no end to the over-approximations of human potential depicted by Japanese children in their visual narratives (Wilson and Wilson, 1987: 22).

9. A nation of visual narrators: distributed pedagogy

What I find so intriguing about the Japanese visual narrative enterprise is how it functions as a vast informal pedagogical system in which innovation is found at all levels with contributions being made by both amateurs and professionals. I am especially fascinated by the complex sets of exchanges and influences that occur between the *dōjinshi*-producing kids, *manga* artists, publishers, pedagogues and consumers. The way in which they collaboratively drive innovations and continually reshape visual narrative output is a story yet to be satisfactorily told – and I can only begin to point to the bare outlines of the phenomenon here.

My colleague Masami Toku and I were interested in exploring how young people became *mangaka* and the ways in which they were identified and nurtured. We were also interested in exploring relationships between amateur *dōjinshi* artists and professional *mangaka*. To this end, we conducted extensive interviews with editors and *manga* school directors from eleven major Tokyo *manga* publishers and the directors of independent and university-related *manga* schools. We also interviewed some of Japan's most famous *mangaka*, including Keiko Takemiya, Machiko Satonaka, Takao Saito and the great animator Hayao Miyazaki – exploring relationships between their childhood drawing experiences and their career choices. To analyse relationships between *dōjinshi* artists and professional *mangaka*, we interviewed artists who had been employed as professional *mangaka* before reverting to a semi-professional status working as *dōjinshi* artists, as they explained in essence, in order to have more freedom to follow a personal vision. In Taiwan in 2002, I interviewed the members of *dōjinshi* groups regarding their histories, motives, goals, activities, group structures, working relationships, and finances.

Here is a brief summary of the workings of the Japanese (and Taiwanese) visual narrative systems at the turn of the twenty-first century. There is a large and eager group of young people who aspire to become *mangaka*, and commercial publishers of *manga* who wish to identify and groom them. Each of the major publishers has organized schools and established contests to attract a steady flow of talent. The very best aspirants – one school director estimated it at perhaps as few as 1% – are assigned to editors. They are coached as they prepare stories, which, if deemed promising, are printed in one of the publisher's magazines; and, if the stories are received positively by fans, the young artist is invited to develop a series. If such a series should be successful, it could then become volumes.

But what if the young aspirant is not so successful? She or he can create *dōjinshi*. Indeed, many of the aspirants who compete for the attention of *manga* publishers are already members of *dōjinshi* groups, and when they do not achieve success with publishers they continue to develop their characters, their plots, their stories, and attract fans by presenting their works in the thousands of comic markets held throughout Japan each year. In other words, comic market venues provide an outlet for talent judged not quite good enough for the big time. Some *dōjinshi* artists actually develop fan bases sufficiently large to provide a steady income. And some *mangaka* choose to leave commercial publishers so that they can pursue semi-professional careers in the *dōjinshi*/comic market arena. Now the internet provides an additional venue where *dōjinshi* creators can reach a worldwide audience.

Every *dōjinshi* collective has its own story. Nevertheless, as I interviewed members of these groups I began to see patterns. Typically, they formed their groups in high school or college. Often, there was a passionate leader who invited friends to join. The groups encouraged, supported, and capitalized on the talents of members. They planned their publications together, assigned themselves tasks – one of the most important being that of producer/editor who oversaw the publication by selecting and arranging stories, making sure submissions met the group's standards, and getting the issue to a printer and delivered to a comic market. *Dōjinshi* members often led double lives, sometimes having careers relating to graphic design but engaged in other occupations too. One was a primary school teacher who dared not let her students know that she was a famous *dōjinshi* artist. When I asked members who were in their late twenties and early thirties how long they planned to continue producing *dōjinshi*, their answers were often that they didn't know, but that they would continue as long as they received satisfaction. One famous Taipei *dōjinshi* artist in her thirties was working on a psychological trilogy about infantile behaviour and crime that could take her years to complete – and I had no doubt that she would see the project to the end.

Many of the *manga* publishers denied that there were important relationships among *dōjinshi* artists and their work, comic markets, and their own publishing empires. Typically, in interviews, they dismissed *dōjinshi* as amateurish and claimed that *dōjinshi* artists seldom achieved success as professional *mangaka* – which is true, but they ignored the fact that artists leave publishers in order to sell their work in *dōjinshi* markets. It is also worth noting that CLAMP, a highly successful *manga* phenomenon, started as a *dōjinshi* group. More importantly, I think that the publishers failed to see *dōjinshi* artists as a part of a vast visual narrative system – one that is almost ecological and rhizomatic in character with innumerable relationships that make the system dynamic and feed innovation.

To illustrate the kinds of interactions that transpire within the system, let me return to the 'Boys' Love' phenomenon. When Keiko Takemiya got an idea for a boys' love narrative, she pressured her reluctant publisher to print the story. It became a sensation; hundreds of thousands of amateur girls and young women picked up on the idea and created their own versions of boys' love that they sold to millions of fans in comic markets that came into being because adults like Yoshihiro Yonezawa wanted to provide a venue for those kids to show and sell their *dōjinshi*. What remains unmapped – and what is probably impossible to map – is how boys' love began to mutate within *dōjinshi* publications. New characters drove sexual experimentations, symbolically at least, in new directions and it was not only visual narratives and visual culture that changed; in all likelihood, Japanese culture changed, too – and those changes are probably reflected in commercial *manga*. Perhaps the changes were important and perhaps they were not, but changes they were.

Of course, the system is too complex for us to fully understand how the changes that occur within *dōjinshi* affect the ways commercial *manga* editors and publishers guide their *mangaka* and direct their publications. Nevertheless, within the system countless professionals and amateurs – adults, teenagers, and little kids – have created many hundreds of thousands of *manga* and *dōjinshi* characters, and these characters play their roles and thus instruct the inhabitants of the nation regarding what to think about themselves and to speculate about the sorts of selves they might become. These communally created character types pose myriad prospects and possibilities for being and behaving in the world. It's a vast collaborative enterprise – both enlightened and dystopian – in which kids and professionals alike play important roles.

10. The end – for now

What story have I told? It's that kids who live in visual narrative cultures teach themselves to read comics and to create comics. Without formal instruction by adults, kids in America and Europe and especially in Asia make their own sequential visual narratives. That so many children living in visual narrative cultures created amazingly coherent sequential narratives when I invited them to do so – even if they had never before drawn a story – still amazes me. I'm somewhat less surprised that kids draw their stories in the styles of the comic worlds they inhabit. They can only depict/speak in the visual languages and dialects they see around them – whether it is the simple intrinsically biased graphic depictions of other children or the styles of the comics they read. Of course, the task I have given kids in different parts of the world – asking them to draw sequential stories in six empty frames – made the task relatively easy if visual cultural models were available. They weren't available in the Egyptian village where the children drew single and related vignettes more than sequences – and therefore they used the simple formulaic styles of other children.

The kids' story drawings I have collected and studied reveal the enormous differences between the few simple skills children need in order to draw a static picture and the complex confluence of visual, narrative and compositional skills that must be present if they are to plot, design and produce story-length visual narratives (Cohn, 2013; McCloud, 1993). Nevertheless, kids in visual narrative-saturated cultures such as Japan, Korea, Taiwan, and to a lesser extent in Western cultures, willingly undertake the arduous task of producing their own story-long and book-length visual narratives. They produce their self-initiated visual narratives because there is also a confluence of visual cultural, social and literary factors. Kids work within well-established visual narrative traditions that continually evolve in popular commercial publications and in the works of many thousands of amateur producers. Visual narrative cultures entice kids to produce their *dōjinshi* and comics – and the production and quality is highest when they organize themselves into groups, encourage and teach one another, when commercial printers cater to amateur producers, and when comic markets provide venues for them to show and sell their works. All these factors comprise a kind of cultural ecology of the visual narrative – indeed, I've likened the *dōjinshi* visual culture to an impossible-to-map rhizome (Wilson, 2003b). Like biological evolution, new and

Figure 8.20 *Planet in a Box*. Does making *manga* make Japanese kids smarter than, say, Egyptian village kids, who have no access to comics and do not draw sequential visual narratives? I don't know the answer to this question. Nevertheless, when I asked a fifteen-year-old Osaka girl to draw a story, she drew 'The School for Gods'. In the first frame, the students are asked if they have completed their assignments – to create a planet in a box – and in the second frame one apprentice god proudly presents her project. In the third frame, another student reluctantly shows her project – because it is a failure. And then when asked what she was going to name her failed planet, she explains that she was going to call it 'Earth'. The story is exquisitely drawn, with cropping, changes in implied distance, and beautifully integrated text, and it also exemplifies how visual narratives provide some kids with a marvellous way to express complex ideas that they care deeply about.

novel features may appear almost anywhere in the visual cultural 'ecosystem'. What really counts is how these novel features are adopted and adapted to take visual narratives to new heights. In Asia, at least, kids are important players in the visual narrative system.

I've answered most of the questions that have arisen during my four decades of studying kids' visual narratives – the questions that I posed at the beginning of this chapter. Still, I'm left with an incomplete answer to the one big 'why' question that arose early in my studies. Why do kids like J. C. Holz draw their own comics? Why do so many Japanese kids create *dōjinshi*? Yes, I have concluded that it is for the personal, social, cognitive and aesthetic satisfaction they receive. But surely it is more than this? There is an even bigger question: does producing enough *dōjinshi* to fill thousands of comic markets each year make Asian kids smarter than kids in other parts of the world (Wilson, 2005b)? Or stated more broadly, do highly productive young visual narrators, creating anywhere in the world, have cognitive powers, personal and interpersonal knowledge, societal and cultural insights, superior prophetic visions of the future, and greater possibilities for adapting to changing moral and ethical climates than other kids? What I do know is that in advanced visual narrative cultures kids use adult artists' comics as models, and without much encouragement or assistance from adults, they teach themselves and other kids to produce visual narratives – graphic stories that are both visually exciting and astonishingly profound in content. I'm convinced that, in their versions of comics and *manga*, kids have adopted an important form of pedagogy that they use for their own purposes. In their visual narratives, kids decide for themselves which aspects of themselves and their worlds, their futures and their ways of behaving, they want to explore symbolically. All they need are models from the visual cultures that surround them, something like a pen to make a mark, some paper (or a computer, printer, and the internet) and their imaginations. Through their visual narratives they educate themselves amazingly.

Notes

1. It is ironic that the copying of comics disdained by many art educators actually accelerated children's drawing development because the comics provided a plethora of models geared to a range of developmental steps.
2. Neil Cohn, the editor of this book, writes (personal communication): 'when I was ten years old, I actually formed a full "comic company" through which I sold (via mail-order catalogue) comics created by myself and a childhood friend (other friends of mine were the Board of Directors, me being the Chairman). I still have giant boxes full of the various different series we created. We were very serious about it! By the time I was thirteen, I was doing a full professional-style process, first doing thumbnails and then drawing pages on 11 × 17 inch Bristol board, using blue line pencils, and doing full pencils and inks.'
3. Now, four decades after our initial case studies, we know that some of our subjects have become artists and designers. Michael became a highly successful graphic designer who has done work for the Metropolitan Museum of Art and the Art Institute of Chicago; Kelly became a chef; and Dirk is a paediatric cardiologist. Young prolific visual narrators do not necessarily become artists. For some kids, producing lots of visual narratives serves its purpose for a limited period of time and then they move on to other pursuits.
4. We discussed with the Krietlers the cognitive orientation functions for kids who produced graphic narratives primarily for themselves and showed how Wilson (1976) had applied their hypotheses to an analysis of the novelist Julian Green's autobiographical account of the explicit sexual content in his boyhood copying and reworking of the nudes in Gustav Dore's illustrations for Dante's *Inferno*. The Kreitlers encouraged us in broadening the application of their theory to children who created visual narratives.

5. Teachers work with students throughout the elementary and middle school grades to teach the basic elements of written composition and storytelling. Nevertheless, high school and college instructors complain that students cannot write coherent compositions. School instruction in visual narration is rare to non-existent and yet young children produce visual narratives that are both coherent and complex beyond even their verbal storytelling – and they do so without formal instruction. It appears that the visual narrative has pedagogical and cognitive developmental potential largely unrecognized and untapped by schools and society.

6. The samples were small: ninety-three children from Boston, a hundred from Adelaide, sixty-nine from Cairo, and fifty-eight from Helsinki. Although we analysed the drawings for themes, the visual and stylistic differences between the Egyptian children's drawings and those in the other three samples was strikingly different.

7. These classifications of narrative disequilibration are taken from Vladimir Propp's (1968) *Morphology of the Folktale.*

8. I lived in Cairo from January to April 1982, during a sabbatical leave from Penn State. The primary purpose of my visit was to collect Egyptian children's story drawings. Dr Nabil Husseini at Helwan University assisted me in every aspect of the inquiry, making contact with schools, translating children's descriptions of their drawings, and discussing interpretations of their narratives. I submitted a two-hundred-and-seventy-five-page report of my sabbatical research to the Penn State provost, but the full results of my research have not been published (Wilson, 1982).

9. Children in the three neighbourhoods viewed television – including American cartoons – certainly a common form of visual culture. Animated cartoons appeared to have little influence on how Egyptian children drew stories. The influence of printed comics and other illustrations, however, is an entirely different matter.

10. The Nahia sample was comprised of ninety-five third- and seventy-seven sixth-grade children, the Embabba sample had sixty-four third- and eighty-six sixth-graders, and the Zamalak sample had sixty-eight third- and eighty sixth-graders.

11. Ten compositional patterns were analysed and all were significantly different among the Nahia village and Zamalak children (five p < .001, two at p < .01, and three at p < .05).

12. Now I regret that I did not compare Cairo's wealthy Zamalak children's drawings with those of the Osaka children in order to provide another set of insights. At the time, I was interested primarily in extreme differences.

13. I see young peoples' self-initiated drawings and other art-like activities (undertaken to please themselves and to fulfil personal interests) as the first pedagogical site. Schools and other hierarchically structured educational institutions where students are required to fulfil teachers' assignments (in contexts that range from coercive to collaborative) for the purpose of meeting educational and societal goals comprise the second pedagogical site. When kids and interested adults voluntarily come together (at the margins of schooling and in settings like comic markets or on the internet) to collaboratively facilitate the production of art-like products and to replicate art-world-like functions comprise the third pedagogical site (Wilson, 2008; Wilson and Wilson, 2009: vi–ix).

14. I purchased these *dōjinshi* at the 2000 COMICMARKET for a variety of reasons: they had lots of original characters – in other words, they appeared to contain fewer parodies of commercial *manga* characters than most of the *dōjinshi* in the market; they were inexpensive – I assumed that they were subsidized partly by universities; they had lots of pages and stories – one had 634 pages and 53 stories, and they contained a broad cross-section of narrative, design and drawing skills.

References

Arnheim, R. (1978). Expressions. *Art Education,* 31(3): 37–38.

Arnheim, R. (1997). A look at a century of growth. In: A. M. Kindler (ed.), *Child Development in Art* (pp. 9–16). Reston, VA: The National Art Education Association.

Cohn, N. (2013). *The Visual Language of Comics: Introduction to the Structure and Cognition of Sequential Images.* London: Bloomsbury.

Cole, N. R. (1966). *Children's Arts from Deep Down Inside.* New York: The John Day Company.

Efland, A. (1976). The school art style: a functional analysis. *Studies in Art Education,* 7(2): 37–44.

Gardner, H. (1980). *Artful Scribbles: The Significance of Children's Drawings.* New York: Basic Books.

Goodman, N. (1978). *Ways of Worldmaking.* Indianapolis, IN: Hacket Publishing.

Kreitler, H., and Kreitler, S. (1972). *Psychology of the Arts.* Durham: Duke University Press.

Lowenfeld, V. (1957). *Creative and Mental Growth* (3rd edn). New York: Macmillian.

McCloud, S. (1993). *Understanding Comics: The Invisible Art.* New York: HarperCollins.

Piers, M. W. (1972). *Play and Development.* New York: Norton.

Propp, V. (1968). *Morphology of the Folktale* (first edition translated by L. Scott, with an introduction by S. Pikova-Jakobson; second edition revised and edited with a preface by L. A. Wagner and new introduction by A. Dundes). Austin, TX: University of Texas Press.

Ricci, C. (1887). *L'Arte die bambini.* Bologna: Nicola Zanichelli. (Tranlated by Maitland, in *Pedagogical Seminary,* 1894(3): 302–307.)

Schodt, F. L. (1983). *Manga! Manga!: The World of Japanese Comics.* Tokyo, New York, and San Fransisco, CA: Kodansha International.

Sully, J. (1896). *Studies of Childhood.* London: Longmans, Green.

Ulbricht, J. (2005). J. C. Holz revisited: from modernism to visual culture. *Art Education: The Journal of the National Art Education Association,* 61(2): 12–17.

Wilson, B. (1974). The superheroes of J. C. Holtz plus an outline of a theory of child art. *Art Education,* 16(1): 2–9.

Wilson, B. (1976). Little Julian's impure drawings. *Studies in Art Education,* 17 (2): 45–62.

Wilson, B. (1982). Benign and threatening worlds: the themes, compositions, and styles of the story drawings of Egyptian village, working-class, and upper-middle-class children. Unpublished sabbatical leave monograph, the Pennsylvania State University, University Park, PA.

Wilson, B. (1992). Primitivism, the avant garde, and the art of little children. In: D. Thistlewood (ed.), *Drawing: Research and Development* (pp. 14–25). Harlow, Essex: Longman.

Wilson, B. (1997). Types of child art and alternative developmental accounts: interpreting the interpreters. *Human Development*, 40: 155–168.

Wilson, B. (1999). Becoming Japanese: *Manga*, children's drawings, and the construction of national character. *Visual Arts Research*, 25(2): 48–60.

Wilson, B. (2000). Empire of signs revisited: children's manga and the changing face of Japan. In: L. Lindstrom (ed.), *The Cultural Context: Comparative Studies of Art Education and Children's Drawings* (pp. 160–178). Stockholm: Stockholm Institute of Education Press.

Wilson, B. (2002). Becoming Japanese: *Manga*, children's drawings, and the construction of national character. In: L. Bresler, and C. M. Thompson (eds), *The Arts in Children's Lives: Context, Culture, and Curriculum* (pp. 43–55). Dordrecht, Netherlands: Kluwer Academic Publishers.

Wilson, B. (2003a). Three sites for visual cultural pedagogy: honoring students' images and imagery. *The International Journal of Arts Education*, 1(3): 107–126.

Wilson, B. (2003b). Of diagrams and rhizomes: visual culture, contemporary art, and the impossibility of mapping the content of art education. *Studies in Art Education*, 44(3): 114–129.

Wilson, B. (2004). Child art after modernism: visual culture and new narratives. In: E. W. Eisner and M. D. Day (eds), *Handbook of Research and Policy in Art Education* (pp. 299–328). Mahwah, NJ, and London: Lawrence Erlbaum Associates and the National Art Education Association.

Wilson, B. (2005a). More lessons from the superheroes of J. C. Holz: the visual culture of childhood and the third pedagogical site. *Art Education: The Journal of the National Art Education Association*, 61(2): 18–24.

Wilson, B. (2005b). Does manga make the Japanese smarter than the rest of us? In: M. Toku (ed.), *Shoja Manga: Girl Power* (pp. 43–46). Chico, CA: Flume Press at California State University.

Wilson, B. (2008). Research at the margins of schooling: biographical inquiry and third-site pedagogy. *International Journal of Education through Art*, 4(2): 119–130.

Wilson, B., and Toku, M. (2004). 'Boys' love', *yaoi*, and art education: issues of power and pedagogy. In: D. L. Smith-Shank (ed.), *Semiotics and Visual Culture: Sights, Signs, and Significances* (pp. 94–103). Reston, VA: National Art Education Association.

Wilson, B., and Wilson, M. (1976). Visual narrative and the artistically gifted. *The Gifted Child Quarterly*, xx(4): 432–447.

Wilson, B., and Wilson, M (1977). An iconoclastic view of the imagery sources in the drawings of young people. *Art Education*, 30(1): 4–12.

Wilson, B., and Wilson, M. (1979a). Children's story drawings: reinventing worlds. *School Arts*, 78(8): 6–11.

Wilson, B., and Wilson, M. (1979b). Drawing realities: the themes of children's story drawings. *School Arts*, 78(9): 12–17.

Wilson, B., and Wilson, M. (1982). The persistence of the perpendicular principle: why, when and where innate factors determine the nature of drawings. *Review of Research in Visual Arts Education,* 15: 19–32.

Wilson, B., and Wilson, M. (1984a). A tale of four cultures: the story drawings of American, Australian, Egyptian and Finnish children. In: R. Ott and A. Hurwitz (eds), *Art and Education: International Perspectives* (pp. 31–38). University Park, PA: The Pennsylvania State University Press.

Wilson, B., and Wilson, M. (1984b). Children's drawings in Egypt: cultural style acquisition as graphic development. *Visual Arts Research*, 10(1): 13–26.

Wilson, B., and Wilson, M. (1987). Pictorial composition and narrative structure: themes and the creation of meaning in the drawings of Egyptian and Japanese children. *Visual Arts Research* 13(2): 10–21.

Wilson, M., and Wilson, B. (1982a). The case of the disappearing two-eyed profile: or how little children influence the drawings of little children. *Review of Research in Visual Arts Education*, 15: 1–18.

Wilson, M., and Wilson, B. (1982b) *Teaching Children to Draw: A Guide for Teachers and Parents.* Englewood Cliffs, NJ: Prentice-Hall.

Wilson, M., and Wilson, B. (2009) *Teaching Children to Draw: A Guide for Teachers and Parents*, 2nd edn, revised. Worcester, MA: Davis.

Part III

Visual Narratives across Cultures

9

The Walbiri Sand Story[*]

Nancy Munn

Fundamental to Walbiri graphic art is narration in the sand. Here I consider the most elaborate genre of this practice, a mode of storytelling, which also provides a basic medium for analysing the internal structure of the larger graphic system. As will be seen, ancestral designs[1] cannot be understood as isolates, but must be examined in relation to the graphic forms emerging in everyday narration.

The areas of bare sand characteristic of central Australia provide a natural drawing board permanently at hand. Since any continuous conversation is generally carried

[*] This chapter is a shortened and slightly altered version of Chapter 3 in *Walbiri Iconography: Graphic Representation and Cultural Symbolism in a Central Australian Society* (University of Chicago Press, 1986; first published by Cornell University Press, 1973; copyright Nancy D. Munn, 1973, 1986). The research for this book was carried out among the Walbiri (now transcribed 'Warlpiri') people of Yuendumu settlement, central Australia, in the late 1950s, and the study reflects Walbiri culture as I knew it at that time.

on by persons sitting on the ground, marking the sand readily becomes a supplement to verbal expression.

Walbiri often contrast their own mode of life with that of the white Australian's by remarking with pride, 'We Walbiri live on the ground' (*walya-ngga ga-liba nyina*, ground-on we sit). They regard sand drawing as part of this valued mode of life, and as a characteristic aspect of their style of expression and communication. To accompany one's speech with explanatory sand markings is to 'talk' in the Walbiri manner.

The graphic elements that are used in this way are culturally standardized and, as this study attempts to demonstrate, belong to the same basic system of forms utilized in the designs. Indeed, as we shall see, designs or distinctive features of particular designs may also emerge in storytelling or conversation. With some few exceptions, all standardized graphic configurations in the Walbiri repertory exhibit the same characteristic 'building block' structure:[2] they consist of one or more discrete, irreducible elements such as a circle, line, or arc. These 'ultimate constituents' are combined into standardized arrangements of varying complexity that I call 'figures'. Each constituent is semantic; that is, it refers in any given usage to some particular item of meaning.

In these contexts, graphic forms are media of social interaction in a different sense than they are in ritual contexts: they form part of the discourse through which information is exchanged or experiences and events communicated. The forms themselves are not *wiri* – they are not 'condensation symbols' like the ancestral designs, or if they happen to be designs, they are functioning essentially as sign vehicles in narrative communication.

1. The sand story

Both men and women draw similar graphic elements on the ground during storytelling or general discourse, but women formalize this narrative usage in a distinctive genre that I shall call a *sand story*. A space of about one to two feet in diameter is smoothed in the sand; the stubble is removed and small stones plucked out. The process of narration consists of the rhythmic interplay of continuous running graphic notation with gesture signs and singsong verbal patter. The vocal accompaniment may sometimes drop to a minimum; the basic meaning is then carried by the combination of gestural and graphic signs. The gesture signs are intricate and specific and can substitute on occasion for a fuller verbalization.[3]

Walbiri call stories told by women in this fashion by the term for any traditional story about ancestral times, *djugurba*. They point out that only women tell stories in this manner, although all Walbiri are familiar with the method. While the technique is elaborated most systematically in narrations of events ascribed to ancestral times, women also use it in a more fragmentary way to convey personal experiences or current gossip. As a mode of communication it can be activated in narration generally, irrespective of whether the content is supposed to refer to ancestral times or the present. A 'proper' *djugurba*, however, is thought to refer to ancestral events.

The social context of storytelling is the casual, informal life of the camp, unhedged by secrecy or ritual sanctions. The women's camps are a common location. An average group at one of the camps might consist of three to ten women with their small children and numerous camp dogs. Even in the hottest weather the women tend to sit close together; without changing her position or making any special announcement, a woman may begin to tell a story. Occasionally an older woman can be seen wordlessly intoning a story to herself as she gestures and marks the sand, but ordinarily a few individuals in the group will cluster around the narrator, leaving whenever they wish regardless of whether the story is finished or not. At any time, the narrator herself may break off the story and go to perform some chore, or even go to sleep in the process of narration.

Although my presence undoubtedly increased the frequency of storytelling, there were few married women at Yuendumu who did not have at their command a number of such stories and who could not recount them with fluency, expressiveness, and a skilled use of the sand graphs and gesture signs. Each woman had a fund of stories that she may have learned from any female kin or from her husband. When asked, women sometimes suggested that tales should be transmitted from mother to daughter, but in fact there are no specific rights over these stories; as women said, 'everybody' teaches them these tales.

Walbiri children do not tell sand stories as a pastime, but at the age of about five or six they can make and identify the basic graphic forms used in narration. If asked, they can demonstrate this narrative method, but without employing gesture signs. A small child or baby may sit on its mother's lap while she tells a sand story; the observation of sand drawing is thus part of early perceptual experience. Sand drawing is not systematically taught, and learning is largely by observation.[4]

At the age of about eight or nine, a child can quite readily tell narratives of his or her own invention. As a girl grows older, she becomes increasingly fluent in storytelling and may use the sand story technique (largely without gesture signs according to my observation) to communicate narratives about personal experiences or that she has herself invented. She may occasionally tell such tales to other girls or younger children. Older boys are more reluctant to use the technique since it is identified with feminine role behaviour.

2. Vocabulary

Figure 9.1 sets out the graphic elements used in the storytelling, and the meaning ranges of each. As it shows, there are about twelve or thirteen elements regularly used, although coinage should not be thought of as entirely closed; in addition, some

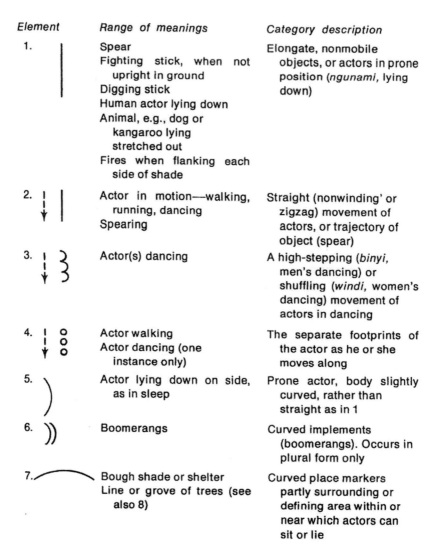

Element	Range of meanings	Category description
1.	Spear Fighting stick, when not upright in ground Digging stick Human actor lying down Animal, e.g., dog or kangaroo lying stretched out Fires when flanking each side of shade	Elongate, nonmobile objects, or actors in prone position (*ngunami*, lying down)
2.	Actor in motion—walking, running, dancing Spearing	Straight (nonwinding' or zigzag) movement of actors, or trajectory of object (spear)
3.	Actor(s) dancing	A high-stepping (*binyi*, men's dancing) or shuffling (*windi*, women's dancing) movement of actors in dancing
4.	Actor walking Actor dancing (one instance only)	The separate footprints of the actor as he or she moves along
5.	Actor lying down on side, as in sleep	Prone actor, body slightly curved, rather than straight as in 1
6.	Boomerangs	Curved implements (boomerangs). Occurs in plural form only
7.	Bough shade or shelter Line or grove of trees (see also 8)	Curved place markers partly surrounding or defining area within or near which actors can sit or lie

Figure 9.1 Sand story vocabulary.

1–2. In the wider system, the action line (2) and a line for elongate items tend to blend together.

2–4. Arrows indicate motion. Footprints (4) are made by 'walking' the fingertips along the sand. I have no record of this use of dot series to depict footprints in Walbiri ancestral designs, but they do appear in designs in other parts of central Australia. See Spencer and Gillen, 1938; Roheim, 1945: 242–243.

5, 7, 9. Arcs vary considerably in deepness, but the tendency is for 9 to be a deep arc, and for 7 to be comparatively shallow, although there are instances in which 7 is fairly deep and overlaps visually with 9. In the wider system, it is more difficult to make a distinction between these two 'place' markers, and unfortunately I do not have explicit contrasts by informants to resolve this problem.

Element	Range of meanings	Category description
8. ~~~	Grove of trees	Place marker used for trees only, usually for depicting shade in which a kangaroo is lying
9. ◠ ⊐	Hut	Enclosure for living
10. 〜	Actor sitting Actor standing	Actor in static position, i.e., in contrast to 2, 3, 4, but not prone (in contrast with 1)
11. /𝓂 ‖‖	Creek bed Blanket or "bed"	A striated or somewhat crumpled space on which actor may rest
12. ⬭	Food or water scoop Baby carrier Shield Spear thrower Oval "bed" (ngura), hollow in ground for sleeping	Oval, hollow containers, and related forms

10. The preferred form of the U-shape is a deep arc with a slightly pointed end, but the shape may vary away from this expressed preference in the flow of narration. When a number of individuals sitting in a line are shown, slurring often takes place, and the U elements are joined together yielding a shape rather like that of no. 3. The more usual meaning for this element is 'sitting', but it is also used to depict standing persons. In both cases, the ends of the U-shape are the legs. Occasionally, a shift from sitting to standing position is expressed by a sort of U mark in which the hand simulates the act of getting up from the sand.

11. The element is drawn with the fingers spread out, and either parallel or zigzag type marks may emerge, although the latter is more usual for the 'blanket'. The string figure that women regard as representing a bed also shows a zigzag type of configuration.

12, 13. An oval form is also used to represent a large water hole or rock hole, and as an alternate for a nest or hill, when these are supposed to be large and elongate. A 'nest' can take a slightly rectangular form; a 'hut' can also vary in this way – curved to angular – without any semantic change. It seems likely that there is no significant contrast between angle and curve in the system, although the curved form is the more usual: the angular shape appears as an occasional variant of the circle, or oval.

(Continued)

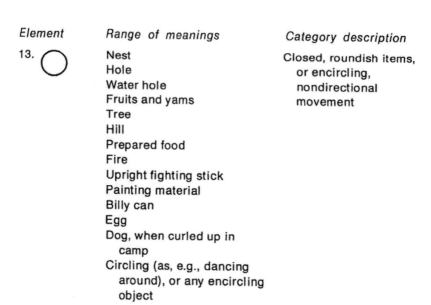

Element	Range of meanings	Category description

13. ◯	Nest
	Hole
	Water hole
	Fruits and yams
	Tree
	Hill
	Prepared food
	Fire
	Upright fighting stick
	Painting material
	Billy can
	Egg
	Dog, when curled up in
	    camp
	Circling (as, e.g., dancing
	    around), or any encircling
	    object
		Closed, roundish items,
		    or encircling,
		    nondirectional
		    movement

Figure 9.1 continued.

13. The circle is usually plain – i.e., not spiral or concentric – but spiral forms occur occasionally, especially, according to my observations, for trees or fire. When concentric circles occur in the sand story they constitute a construction of circles nested inside each other, each with a separate meaning: for example, a line of women dancing around an upright fighting stick.

Yams. An alternate form for a yam is a circle with wavy strings attached to it – the yam 'strings'. This little figure specifies a yam and does not have a wide application as does the circle alone.

Fire. A common alternate for the circle in representing fire is a small mound of sand brushed into place by the middle and index fingers. An earth oven may also be simulated by digging a hole; a gesture then indicates the placement of meat in the hole; finally, sand is placed over this and a small mound is created.

elements such as a meander line widely used in other 'dialects' of the graphic system occur occasionally in sand story usage.

Each element covers a range of possible meaning items (the second column of the chart); the breadth of these ranges varies for the different graphs, but the over-all tendency is toward a relatively high degree of category generality. For instance, the sand story provides a term for elongate items (actors or elongate objects) in a prone position. The particular class of items meant – such as a spear, a kangaroo, or a man lying down – depends upon narrative context, and specification takes place within the storytelling process.

Various cues besides the verbal may aid in pinpointing the specific meaning in any given usage. For example, two or more straight lines partly enclosed in an arc representing a bough shade (as in Figure 9.2, no. 1) are always actors lying down in camp, and not objects. Narrative context or verbal commentary may provide the information as to the identity of these actors. If one line is considerably smaller than the other, it is a child and the line beside it a woman. On the other hand, if a number of elements of a U-shape are shown grouped around a line (as in Figure 9.3A, no. 18), this figure in itself does not tell us whether the line is an actor or one of the elongate objects for which the element is also used.

The circle is one of the most widely used and most general in the sand story vocabulary; it may serve for any item that can be included in a category of roundish or closed, nonelongate forms. Such items are, for example, the hole of an animal, a water hole, a hill, a particular variety of wild fruit, and so on. Only one such item is relevant in any given usage.

The same class of objects can sometimes be represented by different graphic elements. For instance, a fighting stick when placed upright in the ground is depicted by a circle, but when laid down, as a line. Another sort of variation is due to the availability of more specific alternate terms for a particular item as well as a more inclusive general graph. Thus a circle may be used to specify a yam, but occasionally women draw a circle plus wavy lines (representing the strings or roots) to depict this item.

Graphic elements with a more specific meaning range than the more typical categories of the sand story do occur. Element no. 8 in Figure 9.1, for instance, refers only to a shade or grove of trees and in fact has a limited distribution; it usually appears in a scene showing a kangaroo lying down in the shade while a hunter is stalking him.

In sum, the relatively high degree of category generalization typical of most of the story vocabulary increases the number of different classes of things that can be conveyed in graphic form while maintaining a relatively small repertory of elements; it also leads to greater dependence upon the storytelling process for the specification of meaning in each usage. Nevertheless, it is apparent that certain kinds of information cannot be carried by the graphs. Some basic, recurrent activities like eating, cooking, and talking have no direct graphic representation.

This fragmentary, dependent character of the graphic signs highlights the fact that they are interlocked with more articulate mediums of communication. In the telling of a story, the graphic channel of communication establishes a kind of visual punctuation of the total narrative meaning.

3. The flow of graphic scenes in storytelling

As I have pointed out, a sand story begins with the clearing of a space. This action prepares the 'screen' on which the graphic figures will appear and also serves as a kind of 'curtain raiser'; children sometimes respond to this preparation by exclaiming, *'djurgurba!'* – that is to say, 'Look, a story!'

As the story is recounted, successive graphic elements appear on the sand, their sequence bound directly to the flow of narrative action. But while the sequence of elements reflects the temporal order of the narrative, the arrangement of elements on the sand reflects the spatial positions of actors and objects (Figure 9.2). The spatial assemblage constitutes a graphic scene; division between scenes is marked by *erasure*, and a graphic story develops through the continuous cycling of scenes in the manner of a movie.

Each scene is a unified physical setting within which actions take place. As Figure 9.2 suggests, it is usual to set the scene by drawing in an object or objects signifying the setting, such as a bough shade, water hole, or grove of trees.

1. Camp

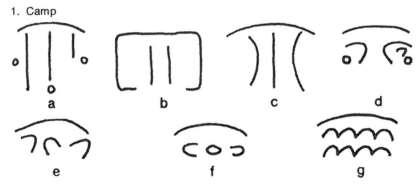

1. Camp: a. Man, woman and child sleeping in front of a bough shade. The woman is always beside the child (small line). O = fire. b. A hut with two persons sleeping in it. The rectangular form is illustrated. c. A man and two women (one on each side of him) sleeping in camp. This is a standard way of representing a man and two wives. d. A man and woman sitting in camp are often shown facing in different directions. (The arc = bough shade.) A baby (small U-shape) sits on the woman's lap. O = fire or food. e. Three people sitting in camp. f. Two people – e.g., man and wife – sitting in front of fire, eating. g. Large number of persons sitting in men's or women's camps.

1A. Ceremonial camp

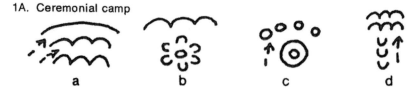

1A. Ceremonial camp: a. Women dancing with a line or grove of trees behind them. b. Women dancing around a fighting stick with a grove of trees in the background. c. Same as b; line of trees is shown by small circles. d. *Bulaba* ceremonial scene. The men are shown dancing in the foreground; singers – men and women – sit facing them.

Figure 9.2 Sand story scenes – types of scenes and sample graphic settings.

(Continued opposite)

2. Juncture, and movement to and from scenes with settings

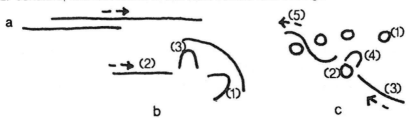

a   b   c

2. Juncture, and movement to and from scenes with settings: Juncture, that is, a scene shift, may be marked by erasure of the previous scene; path lines need not be entered next, but the narrator may go directly into the camp or food-gathering scene. Otherwise path lines (a) are shown – a man's path ahead of a woman's. b, c. Movement to and from scenes with settings. b. Individual sitting in camp (1); another person comes in (2) and sits down (3). c. When a man and woman are eloping and hurrying on from one place to the next, or a man is following a game animal, scenes of this kind may occur. (1) Line of trees; (2) water hole. An individual comes in (3), sits down by the water hole (4), and hurries away through the line of trees (5).

3. Foraging

a   b   c

3. Foraging: a. A characteristic way of showing a number of women digging for honey ants in the roots of trees. b. Z = the creek bed; O = water hole in the creek; OO = trees. UO = woman with water scoop, for example beside her, drinking from the water hole, or digging it. c. Standard depiction of a man spearing a kangaroo. U = man; / = spear being thrown; – = kangaroo lying in the shade.

4. Finale. Going into the ground

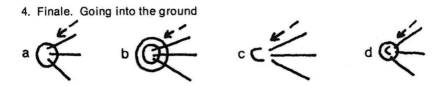

a   b   c   d

4. Finale. Going into the ground: Finale scenes need not always occur, but when they do, they always represent actors coming together and going into the ground. a. O = hole. ///= paths of actors converging on the hole. b. If more than one circle is shown, each circle has a meaning: for example, the inner circle might be a water hole, the outer one a circle of trees. c. U = dead man in the ground. People converge on burial place. d. Dead man in a hole, with people converging on burial place.

The narrator often states the name of this object as she draws it;[5] the word has a deictic function, as if she were pointing to the object saying, for instance, 'Here is a bough shade'. Transitions between scenes ('junctures') may be marked by the movement of actors after the scene has been erased, but the graphs used in these 'junctures' do not include a scene setting.

Within a scene, erasure does not usually occur. Thus it sometimes happens that graphic elements may overlay each other. This is most common in my experience in camp scenes where actors may first be shown sitting and eating, and then lying down to sleep (or the reverse sequence, eating after sleeping). In these cases, one layer of elements may be drawn over the other, but erasure does not ordinarily intervene.

Generally speaking, the scene (or sometimes the episode within one scene) functions as a configurative unit displaying the spatial relations of actors and objects; but when the scene shifts this set of relations is obliterated. Since by the use of erasure an indefinite number of scenes can be conveyed without expanding the pictorial space (the sand 'screen'), the medium itself does not impose limits on the number of scenes that can be depicted for any single story. Accordingly, the number of narrative-graphic scenes in a story may vary indefinitely according to the storyteller's whim. As we shall see, the structure of a narrative is such that a woman may spin the tale out lengthily, or present only the core of incidents, as she wishes.

Since the sand graphs disappear as the scene is changed, the visual, extrasomatic channel is no more time binding than the verbal and gestural ones; all are characterized by 'rapid fading'. A particular story can never be looked at as a unitary whole, and no retelling is likely to reproduce the exact arrangements and scene cycles again. No doubt, this feature in itself reinforces the binding of the act of graphic construction or picture-making to the act of narration, for the graphic stories produced at one time cannot be used mnemonically later to evoke the larger narrative content.

4. Types of scenes

The scenes regularly recurring in a sand story can be classified into a few basic types: camp scenes (men's, women's, and family camps) marked usually by a bough shade or hut; ceremonial camps or clearings sometimes including a ceremonial prop, such as an erect fighting stick in the case of women's ceremonies; scenes outside the camp involving food foraging and hunting or digging for water, and often marked by a grove of trees or a water hole; scene juncture (showing movement from place to place and lacking a 'setting'); and a finale, which I call a 'going-in scene', always marked by a hole in the ground or the depiction of a dead man inside the ground. Figure 9.2 illustrates these scene types and gives examples of characteristic graphic configurations.

There is no introductory formula for a sand story: any type of scene may be used, but camp scenes are common. The formulaic ending, although not a required part of the narration, is of particular interest: both the motif it introduces and the associated iconography have ramifications in Walbiri cosmology. At the end of a tale, 'all the people' of the story come together and go into the ground. A circle is drawn and the path lines of the actors converge within it. Often, a death in the story precedes this event. If this is so, then a U-shape may be drawn and the path lines of the actors directed into its open end. Sometimes a particular item relevant to the story – a tree, hill, or fighting stick – may be the object into which the actors enter. In one instance, concentric circles depicted a woman's breast and the actors went into the nipple. The standard verbal expression associated with this finale scene is 'they became nothing then' (*lawa-djari-dja-lgu*). This means they died; the tale has come to an end.

5. Scene cycling and narrative content

A regularly occurring type of scene sequence consists of a camp scene, departure from camp (juncture); foraging, hunting, and related scenes; and return to camp. This cycle represents the time period of a day, and revolutions of the cycle suggest the passage of time. In fact, some stories consist of little more than revolutions of this basic cycle with minor variations in content. In others, this cycle may function as a kind of framework to spin out the more specific plots. The following example, a fraction of a longer account, suggests the sorts of events that might be contained in the basic cycle and the way in which the cycle can revolve:[6]

> Here is a fire burning in a hut. A Djungarai man, two Nangala women and a child are sleeping. They get up. They eat meat. They go hunting. The women dig for yams. Putting meat and yams in the containers, they go to camp. The fire is burning. They cook the yams. Having cooked them, they eat them. They put the meat in the hut. They go for water. They drink the water. They give meat to their mother. [After sleeping in their camp and waking up] they go to their mother. They go hunting. Here are yams. The mother digs for yams. [All are shown digging for yams.] They go off to camp. The fire is burning. They sleep. They wake up. The man hurries off hunting. Here stands a tree. The kangaroo is lying down. He spears it. He cuts it open and takes out its intestines. He takes it to the shade. Here is the tree. He digs a hole. He throws twigs into the hole and lights a fire. He cuts off the tail; he cuts the two legs. The meat is cooking [in the earth oven.] He takes the meat off the fire and puts it down. He cuts the two thighs – the two good parts. He takes it to camp. He walks along. Here stands the camp. The fire is burning. Nangala is sitting. Djungarai comes walking and puts down the meat. He cuts it up. They eat … [this continues in a similar vein with particular emphasis upon the cutting up of the different parts of the kangaroo].

In most stories, more particularized plots are built into this general framework: after the cycle has been repeated for a number of turns, these incidents intervene and shift the cycle or give it a more 'unique', specific cast. The plot having run its course, a storyteller may then return to this basic cycle. Sometimes she repeats it for a time and then again embarks on a series of specific events. In the following tale of an emu hunt, the entrance of the emu into the ground marks the end of this incident; usually such an event would end the story, but in this case the storyteller considered events following it to be a part of the same tale. This 'serial' treatment is facilitated by the cyclical framework.

> Here are yams. A woman walks up and puts down her food container. She digs for yams. She puts the food in the container and walks to the shade. She returns with another woman [her co-wife] to camp. Here is the hut. The woman sits down. She puts down the container with food. A man [the woman's husband] comes in. He sits down. He lies down to sleep. The man sleeps. The two women sleep. The man sleeps by his spears. [After they wake up] the man goes off hunting. The women go off hunting. An emu comes along. The man spears it. Here are many trees with the emu's nest. The man takes the emu eggs. He puts them down. He takes up the emu and the eggs and he carries them off. The man goes to the hut. The two women now sleep. [The next day] the man and women go hunting. The women go off for vegetable food. An emu sits on its nest. The man comes and throws a spear at it. The emu flees. The man sings to catch the emu. After pursuing the emu, the man grows tired and lies down to sleep. He [wakes and] follows the same emu. Through a creek bed the emu flees. The man pursues. [This is repeated for a few times to indicate the length of the pursuit]. Here is a big pool of water. The emu goes into it forever. The man goes into it forever.
>
> One of the man's wives follows behind him. She comes upon the same place where the man slept. Here is the water to which the emu fled. The woman goes crying and beating herself in grief for her husband. Some other women come hunting. They ask her why she is crying. [She answers]: 'I have lost my husband.' Now she is single. She goes along to the [women's] camps where there are many people. She sits down weeping. Many other women come weeping. They make 'sorry cuts' on their heads with digging sticks. [Afterward] she marries another man. They sit in camp. The man sleeps, the woman sleeps. Here is the fire. They wake up. The man hurries off hunting. The woman goes hunting with many of her 'sisters-in-law.' They dig for yams. They dig and dig. They go to a shade. They go back to camp. The man comes. He sits down. He gives meat to the woman. The woman sleeps. The man sleeps . . . [incomplete].

The actors of the typical sand story are for the most part anonymous persons referred to by the subsection labels, as for example, Djangala or Nangala or simply as 'man' and 'woman'. Occasionally, they are called by some typifying name characterizing their role in the story, such as 'the immoral one'. These individuals are simply ancestral people – the people who lived in those times rather than identifiable ancestors. Stories are not associated with any particular totemic species or ancestors, and they are not localized in geographical space. As the narrator of the emu story said, when asked where the events of her tale took place, 'No place – *djugurba*'.

While most of the actors are human beings, some have extrahuman characteristics. Tree women, for example, emerge from a mother tree and are somewhat more powerful than ordinary women. *Ginggi* is an evil sprite in human guise, a cannibal and something of a trickster. There is no single *ginggi* or tree woman whose actions are elaborated in a number of different tales; rather, numerous representatives of each appear in different tales. Much less commonly actors appear who are personifications of nonhuman animal species. These usually have special powers but interact with ordinary human beings.

Occasional tales include behaviour of an extraordinary kind, such as the transformation of a man into a snake, which Walbiri do not believe happens today; but such occurrences are exceptional. A large part of story behaviour consists simply of the action patterns of daily life: food acquisition, mourning rites, ceremonies of various kinds. Others are the individual case type, the substance of gossip: love affairs, fights, personal quarrels, and immoral behaviour (particularly incest) and its punishment. Emphasis is placed on activities in which women play a central role. Moreover, food exchanges between a man and his wife (and to a lesser extent, her mother) are reiterated in the sand story as part of the daily round of hunting, gathering, and food consumption.

While all these stories are regarded as traditional accounts of ancestral activities, it is obvious that we have here a narrative projection of the cyclical day-after-day experience of daily routine and a recounting of the sorts of incidents and behaviour also possible for the most part in the ongoing present of Walbiri daily life.[7] It is, in effect, this repetitive daily existence that is going under the label *djugurba*, ancestral way of life.

6. Figure types and story contexts

We can turn now to considering in more detail some features of the sand story iconography of special relevance to the larger graphic system. For this purpose, I abstract from the story configurations certain important types of figures (that is, types of element combinations) that recur with high frequency in the graphic narration. These types are found also in other genres of the graphic art, where they may communicate more complex, cosmological notions. Before the significance of these more complex messages can be understood, we have to examine the use of these figures to convey events and contexts of ordinary, daily experience; for it is in such 'casual' usages that the semantics of the former are grounded.

Figure 9.3 provides examples of certain element combinations regularly appearing in sand stories, which I have classed as instances of two different types of figures, or what I shall refer to as 'figure types'. The most pervasive of these is what I have called the 'actor-item' type (Figure 9.3A). The U-shape in these constructions signifies some individual – an 'actor' – in either a sitting or standing position (sitting is the more usual meaning). Another element oriented in front of or behind the actor and

A. Actor-item figures

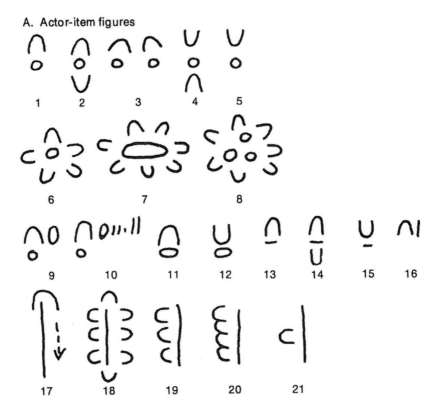

Figure 9.3 Actor-item and enclosure figure types in the sand story.

A. Actor-item figures

1. A man or woman sitting at a water hole; a woman sitting digging for yams, etc. 2, 3. A man and woman sitting at fires; two women digging for yams, etc. 4, 5. Actors sitting with backs to the 'item'.

6. A number of actors – for example, women dancing around a fighting stick or people sitting at a fire. 7. Actors sitting around large rock hole (elliptical form of the circle). 8. Women plucking fruit – circles in a group are not likely to be water holes.

9. A woman sitting with water carrier at her side and water hole in front of her, digging for water; a man with his shield, etc. 10. A set of weapons at the side indicates the actor is male. 11. A shield or receptacle in front of the actor. 12. A shield or receptacle at back. 13-16. A stick or spear shown in different positions relative to the actor.

17. An action line: for example, a man throwing a spear. 18-21. Different arrangements of actors around or beside another actor lying down, or, less commonly, around some elongate object (e.g., a large fighting stick). 18. A common way of depicting dancers and singers grouped around an actor (the sleeper) in a dream. 20. Slurring of U element is common when a line of persons is shown.

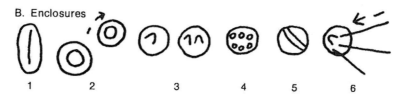

B. Enclosures

1   2   3   4   5   6

Figure 9.3 continued.

B. Enclosures

1. Sleeper lying in an oval depression such as characterizes traditional sleeping arrangements, sometimes called 'bed' in English. The enclosing line may also be a blanket.

2. Water running around a hill: inner O = hill; outer O = water. The enclosing circle may also be a motion line, for example, paths of actors dancing around a pole.

3. Birds sitting in a nest, or people sitting on a hill, etc.

4. Eggs in a nest.

5. Characteristic way of depicting a dead person laid in a tree (tree burial), but may also have other meanings.

6. An enclosure of the type in final scenes. See above Figure 9.2, no. 4d. A dead man in a hole with actors converging on the hole, and 'going in'. The hole-path figure that results has analogues in other parts of the graphic system.

sometimes between his legs (the ends of the U-shape) refers either to some object in the actor's immediate vicinity with which he is concerned at the time, or less commonly to an action in which he is engaged. The general meaning of the first sort of figure may be summarized as 'actor in relation to object' and of the second as 'actor-action'.

In figures of the latter sort, the action may also involve an object: for instance, a line drawn swiftly out from between the legs of the actor can serve to represent a man standing, throwing a spear (Figure 9.3A, no. 17). The line is both the spear and the act of throwing it. Thus there is no clear distinction between actor-action and actor-object constructions, and it is convenient to link them both in one overarching figure type with a general meaning that can be stated as 'actor (in relation to)-item' ('actor-item').

While the kernel of this figure type is a U-shape and another element (most commonly a circle or a line, but also other elements where relevant), the figure can be pluralized;[8] two or more actors may then appear in various arrangements (see Figure 9.3). (The 'item' can also be in plural form, as when a number of emu eggs are the focus of the actor's interest, but this is rarer.)

An actor-item figure is sometimes combined with an additional attributive element or subsidiary figure representing one or more of the actor's implements such as a wooden dish or digging stick, or weapons laid beside him (Figure 9.3A, nos. 9, 10, 16).

Table 9.1 Actor-item figures and narrative situations

Actor	Item	Narrative situation
Two women sitting	Honey ant hole	Two women digging for honey ants.
Wife, husband	Food	A man and wife eating in camp.
Woman	Fire (food on fire)	A woman cooking food at midday, while out foraging.
Many women dancing	Fighting stick	Some women dancing at a *yawalyu* ceremony to attract lovers.
Man sitting	Water hole, shield, spears	A man with spears and shield beside him drinking at a water hole while out hunting.
Three wives	Husband lying down	A man's wives sitting around him while he is sleeping in camp.
Man standing	Spear (being thrown)	A man throws a spear during a fight.
Man sitting	Penis	A man sends his penis underground to have intercourse with a number of distant women. (Incident in one narrative).

These items can also imply the sex of the actor. For instance, an oval representing a baby carrier placed beside a U-shape indicates that the actor is a woman, while lines and arcs depicting spears and boomerangs, respectively, placed in the same position would indicate that the actor is a man. In addition, figures in which an action is depicted often include an object. For example, a kangaroo shown lying down may be the object of the spear being thrown by an actor (Figure 9.2, no. 3c).

The actor-item figure commands a wide range of specific situational contexts, for in one or another of its variant forms it is used to convey much of the action of the sand story. In any given instance, it denotes a specific meaning relevant to the story being told. The sorts of specific meanings and narrative situations that these figures might articulate in particular instances of use are exemplified in Table 9.1, and still others are suggested by the commentaries accompanying Figures 9.2 and 9.3.

We have here then a relatively homogeneous and simple iconographic formulation for a wide variety of daily activities, essentially activities within a single place or scene. Activities connected with food gathering, hunting and eating, and sexual intercourse can be conveyed by this figure type, which also occurs in all the categories of ancestral designs (Figure 9.4). In each of these design categories, the figure type tends to take on meanings characteristic of that category. For example, in men's *ilbindji* designs (see Figure 9.4B), actor-item figures always carry sexual connotations and may include additional elements specifying male and/or female sexual characteristics. In *guruwari* designs, the figure usually carries a reference to the ancestral camp site (see Figure 9.4C and also Chapter 6 in *Walbiri Iconography*, which discusses the 'site-path' figure type.)

A second type of graphic figure that can be observed in the storytelling, and that is of general importance in the system as a whole, consists of a circle enclosing another element or figure. This configuration carries the meaning 'a closed or roundish item enclosing another item or items' (Figure 9.3B). I refer to it as an *enclosure*.[9]

An enclosure may occur independently or may function as the 'item' in certain actor-item figures; that is, it has the same privileges of occurrence as the circle or other elements standing for the 'item' in this figure type. Actor-item figures, on the other hand, can also occur inside circle enclosures when the story sense warrants it. The enclosure most commonly carries the meaning 'in' or 'inside' but it may also mean that the enclosed items are 'on' a particular object. For instance, a U-shape inside a circle could mean an actor sitting on a hill, or an actor sitting inside a hole. Where an oval encloses a straight line representing an actor lying down, this often specifies the actor lying asleep in a shallow oval sand depression such as is found in front of the windbreak in the traditional Walbiri camp. In each instance, the hill, the hole, the shallow depression circumscribes the actor, and indicates a place or locus within which he is situated.

In the sand story finale, this type of figure is associated with death: it may be used to represent the dead person sitting inside the ground. In these contexts, the lines (paths of the 'people') going toward the circle imply 'going in'; although the figure itself need not always involve an enclosure, it implies this notion (Figure 9.2, no. 4; Figure 9.3B, no. 6).

A. Yawalyu. After pencil drawing (1); after body paintings (2, 3).

| 1. Wallaby | 2. Opossum | 3. Fighting stick |

A. *Yawalyu.*

1. Thigh design. O = rock hole. UU = Wallabies drinking.

2. Thigh design. UU = two opossums sitting. According to the associated story, the elements specify a male and female opossum. In the story, the dreamer – a man – and his wife are identified with the opossums. O = meat. The two opossums sit eating meat. This is probably also an allusion to sexual intercourse for which 'eating' is a standard metaphor. No explanation was given for the surrounding ovals.

3. U = woman sitting at a *yawalyu* ceremony. / = fighting stick lying down behind her.

Figure 9.4 Actor-item figures in designs.   (*Continued overleaf*)

B. *Ilbindji* and related designs. After man's pencil drawings.

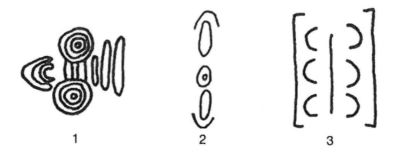

1   2   3

C. *Guruwari*. After pencil drawing (1); after sand drawing (2).

1. Two Walingari men   2. Lizard

B. *Ilbindji.*

1. Outer U = man. Inner U = woman. OO = woman's breasts; the lines between are the man's cicatrices. Long ovals = man's arms 'pulling up' the woman. The informant associated the design with a rain ancestor, but my impression is that an *ilbindji* design of this kind could actually be associated with different ancestors depending on a man's own lodge affiliations.

2. A Manguru design. Only part of the design drawn by the informant is shown. U = woman. Long oval = man, i.e., penis. O = navel of the man and woman – 'naval' is probably a euphemism for the genitals. Cf. Roheim 1945:102. Cf. ⟵ ☰ an instance of a woman's story notation showing a man having intercourse with a number of women sleeping in a women's camp.

3. [ ] = shade or hut. UU = women sitting around a man who is lying down. / = the man. Cf. Figure 9.3, no. 18.

C. *Guruwari.*

1. UU = the two men sitting back to back (repeated top and bottom). O = the water hole they came out of, and also their camp. – = shield, // = spears.

2. O = hill, and also the fruit the lizards are eating. UU = lizards sit eating fruit. After they eat, the hill emerges, and they go inside it. ⁾⁾ = boomerangs. (On notions of metamorphosis and multiple meanings for design elements, see Chapter 6 *Walbiri Iconography*.)

Figure 9.4 Continued.

A type of enclosure of special interest is a circle-within-circle scheme. Although not very common in the sand story, it may occur in various contexts; for example, a circle enclosing a smaller circle may serve to represent women dancing around a ceremonial pole. An example mentioned above in connection with 'going-in' scenes involved a circle-within-circle scheme used to represent a woman's breast, with the inner circle as the nipple, and surrounding outer circles representing the breast. The circle does not always carry static meanings, but sometimes may convey the notion of circling movement (in contrast to extended, directional movement conveyed by the line).

Certain recurrent configurations are highly idiomatic. An example is the kangaroo hunting scene illustrated in Figure 9.2, no. 3c. This figure (one that is especially familiar to children) has a fixed specific meaning: it always represents a kangaroo lying down in the shade with a hunter throwing his spear. To my knowledge it does not recur, however, in the design genres, but is prominent only in the sand story. On the other hand, another idiom – two shallow arcs placed symmetrically on either side of a straight line, representing two women sleeping on either side of a man (Figure 9.2, no. 1c) – recurs as a design in women's *yawalyu*. Thus it serves as one example of the structural continuity between the sand story graphs and *yawalyu* designs.

7. Discussion

In sand storytelling, the speaker does not enact the events to which a tale is thought to refer, but creates fleeting graphic images of it on the sand as part of the narrative processes. Graphs emerge as 'attributes' of the sand in close relation to, but detached from, the body of the speaker, and typically as part of a social process in which information said to refer to the ancestral world is communicated. Unlike speech or gesture signs, the graphs are objectivated outside the speakers and listeners in a concrete spatial field that forms the visible focus of their interaction.

The process of forming the graphs is almost wholly absorbed by the temporal process of narration. This 'absorption' undoubtedly accounts in part for the simplicity of the elements and the 'productivity' of the graphic structure: with a relatively few, standardized elements an indefinite range of meanings and situational contexts can be graphically expressed. The simplicity also enhances speed and ease of production.

Nevertheless, the graphs are arranged as 'pictures'; that is, they are organized not simply in a linear way following speech sequence as is characteristic of a script, but also as images in pictorial arrangements. Moreover, the elements themselves are 'iconic' in the sense that they pick out simple perceptual qualities of the forms of objects and acts that they denote, and 'translate' these into a graphic medium. In fact, the graphic art as a whole can be described as a system of relatively simple iconic elements with the capacity for productivity in communication; in different ways it is always closely linked with verbal expression.

In the sand story, the graphs serve in the communication of a reality that, while labelled as ancestral, actually blends with the ongoing pattern of daily life (especially pre-settlement life). Notable here is the anonymity of the typical actors: they are not specific individuals around which varied tales are built, but simply represent classes of persons who seem to flow through the stereotyped habitual activities of daily life characterizing the sand story events; they are essentially depersonalized 'types'. Such stories are primarily tales about the *way* ancestors lived (which is essentially the way traditional Walbiri lived), rather than being about *particular ancestors*. The cosmic significance of these stories is limited: reality tends to be presented on the same level as the reality of everyday life, and the stereotypic framework itself expresses the microtemporal cycling of daily life.

Thus in the sand story we see the graphic system bound to meanings connotative of everyday experience. Since this use of the graphs is open to children, exposure to these associations occurs in a casual atmosphere from childhood. If one considers the repetitiveness of typical figures and scenes, one can see how graphs may become redolent of the content and rhythms of the daily life experiences that they denote, and so can come to objectivate them in the imagination.

Notes

1. I use the term 'design' here to refer only to ritual forms of the graphic art. These can be broadly categorized as *Yawalyu* (graphic designs over which women exert control); *Ilbindji* (designs that men create for the purpose of attracting women as lovers); and *Guruwari* (designs over which men exert control). *Guruwari* is also the general term for all ancestral designs. Designs may be painted on the body and oval wooden boards. Men also paint designs on the ground and incise them on boards or stones.

2. I have illustrated a few of these exceptions in an earlier paper on graphic representation (Munn, 1966, Fig. 1a).

3. The term *yira-ni* (to 'put', put down, or mark) is used to refer to the process of sand marking. The term for story (*djugurba*, see below) also refers to the sand pictures in this context, although the Walbiri do have a general term for mark, *yiri*. The latter is more commonly employed, however, in connection with ancestral symbols like designs and songs. Gesture signs are called ṟaga ṟaga (ṟaga, hand); Walbiri women make a more elaborate use of these signs than do men. The verbal patter is referred to as 'speaking' (*wangga*), not singing (*yunba-ni* or *yiri-ma-ni*). When I first heard women telling these stories, they seemed to me to be singing; but Walbiri songs have a distinctive structure, and it is these forms that are 'sung'.

4. I observed only one instance of conscious teaching. In this case, I noticed a mother casually teaching her small son gesture signs and sand graphs. I doubt if this was a regular procedure.

5. My impression is that women verbalized more of the story when I was taking notes on it than they would have ordinarily, or than they did when I was just listening and not trying to record the account in full.

6. Occasionally a storytelling provides the particular plot elements without the use of the cyclical frame, and such stories are likely to be brief accounts. The cycle facilitates not only the stretching out of a single plot, but also a kind of additive process in which it is possible to add more specific plots together into a single tale. The two stories in the text are free translations of Walbiri accounts that I have condensed slightly.

7. In the late 1950s, Walbiri at Yuendumu did not go out hunting and gathering everyday; rather, these activities took place largely on weekends and work holidays. At the time, Walbiri depended for most of their food on government rations. However, Walbiri settlement at Yuendumu did not begin until 1946–1947; and much of the Walbiri pre-settlement culture and social organization (with, of course, adjustments and ongoing changes) was an active part of their lives in the period I was there. (See also Chapter 1 in *Walbiri Iconography*.)

8. Any element may be pluralized, since number is a feature of the graphs. In sand stories, arrangements consisting simply of several U elements are common (e.g., loose arrangements of these elements representing a number of women sitting in mourning). A number of actors sleeping in camp appear as parallel lines that may look like the lists Walbiri use in tallying items (see Chapter 6, *Walbiri Iconography*). Dual forms of 'actor' elements are common: for example, two actors sitting back to back or sleeping in camp. When one U-shape faces the other, there is usually a shared object such as food or a water hole between them.

9. Enclosures may have various spatial values: for example, the enclosed item may be inside or underneath the surface depicted by an enclosing circle, or it may be on top of this surface, and so on.

References

Munn, N. D. (1966). Visual categories: an approach to the study of representational systems. *American Anthropologist*, 68(4): 936–950.

Roheim, G. (1945). *The Eternal Ones of the Dream*. New York: International Universities Press.

Spencer, B., and Gillen, F. J. (1899). *The Native Tribes of Central Australia*. New York: Macmillan, 1938.

10

Alternative Representations of Space:

Arrernte Narratives in Sand*

David P. Wilkins

1. Introduction

The research reported in this chapter emerges out of the Space Project of the Max Planck Institute for Psycholinguistics, Nijmegen. The goal of that project is to investigate the nature of spatial description and conception from a cross-linguistic and cross-cultural perspective. A basic position taken within the Space Project is that

* This chapter originally appeared as a paper in *Proceedings of the CLS Opening Academic Year 1997–1998*, edited by M. Biemans and J. van de Weijer, pp. 133–164 (Nijmegen: Nijmegen/Tilburg Center for Language Studies).

it is not sufficient to just examine the conceptual organization encoded in language, one must also study other behaviours that are directly focused on spatial issues. As Levinson (1992: 8, emphasis mine) notes:

> we now have enough information about cultural and linguistic difference to show that generalizations about how humans conceive of, talk about and operate in space are not going to be easily made. *Field-working anthropologists and linguists have a real role to play here by describing systems of language, thought and action in the spatial domain from very different cultural traditions.*

Based on my own fieldwork among the Arrernte, a Central Australian Aboriginal desert-dwelling group, I will describe a very different form of spatial representation from a very different cultural tradition. As in other communities inhabiting the desert region of Central Australia, traditional Arrernte narratives to young children were typically accompanied by drawings in the sand and by the use of an auxiliary sign language. Although neither sand drawing nor the Arrernte auxiliary sign language could, on their own, convey a complete narrative, when combined these two forms of representation could supplant the use of language altogether. Indeed, in certain contexts, whole narratives were often rendered in sand and sign without the support of spoken language. My focus here will be sand drawing.

For most Aboriginal communities in Central Australia, the majority of day-to-day social interactions and discursive practices take place while seated or reclining on the ground. As Munn (1986: 58) observes, '[t]he areas of bare sand characteristic of central Australia provide a natural drawing board permanently at hand', and most forms of talk can be, and often are, illuminated by drawings in the sand. The following quote from an Arrernte person shows that the integration of sand drawing and narrative recounting is seen by the Arrernte themselves as a particularly characteristic traditional practice.

1 Tyerrtye-le   ayeye   altyerre-nge-arle   ane-ke   akerte   ile-me,
   person-ERG   story   Dream-ABL-REL   be-past   PROPR   tell-pres

   apmere   akerte.   Ayeye   arratye   ile-me   nthakenhe   apeke-arle
   place   PROPR   story   true   tell-pres   how   maybe-REL

   irre-ke   akerte.   *Altyerre   ahelhe-ke*   *ile-me*   *arrwekelenye-le*
   happen-past   PROPR   Dream   ground-DAT   tell-pres   front-ERG

   areye-arle   *ile-rrirre-tyarte*   *arteke.*
   plural-REL   tell-pl.S-rem.past.hab   SEMBL

Aboriginal people tell stories about the Dreamtime and about the land, and they tell true stories about things that have happened. *They tell stories onto the ground like the old people used to.*

(Henderson and Dobson, 1994: 471, my morphemic analysis, glossing and emphasis)

In relation to the Warlpiri, Munn (1986: 58) has similarly commented that '[t]o accompany one's speech with explanatory sand markings is to "talk" in the Walbiri manner'. Although all Arrernte speakers (men and women, young and old) can, and do, make use of sand-drawing conventions, the most elaborated and systematic use of this mode of representation appears to be in women's recountings of traditional narratives to young children.

In this study, I will focus on two aspects of these narratives: (1) the spatial properties of sand drawing (i.e., how sand drawing is used as an iconic system for representing events as they unfold in space), and (2) the developmental effects that appear to be related to early exposure to sand drawing.

2. The spatial properties of sand drawing

The description in this section is a synthesis of my own observations together with those of other researchers who have worked in Central Australia. For the Arrernte, there are only sketchy accounts of sand drawing to be found in C. Strehlow (1913), T. G. H. Strehlow (1951, 1964), Róheim (1974), and Seagrim and Lendon (1980). The most extensive account for this region is Munn's (1986 [1973]) treatment of Warlpiri sand drawing, based on field research undertaken in the late 1950s. Munn's main focus in that work, however, was not sand drawing *per se*, but the system of graphic representation that appears in a number of different media and contexts, not just narratives in sand. For instance, the same stock of basic iconic elements and the same core representational 'grammar' that are found in sand drawing are also used in women's body painting, in the preparation of ceremonial grounds, on men's sacred objects, and, more recently, in the acrylic 'dot' paintings produced for sale in the contemporary art market. Still, there is much about sand drawing and its dynamic production that remain outside this shared, 'medium independent', representational core and is in need of closer description.

One very important unresearched issue, that will barely be touched on here, is the question of how sand drawing, spoken narrative and sign are all integrated into a coherent narrative whole. Or, to put the question another way, how do the different semantic potentials embodied in each communicative system combine to give a final 'full' narrative interpretation? Such a question itself presupposes that we already understand the semantic potential of sand drawing. In this section, I begin an assault on this issue by outlining some of the spatial properties of sand drawing. Since it is a medium of visual communication which has a dynamic temporal aspect, sand drawing clearly has different representational constraints and different representational potentials when compared to spoken language.

The Arrernte term for the act of sand drawing is *impatye-ile-me* (track-CAUSE-pres), literally 'causing tracks' or 'making tracks'. It can also be referred to *as impatye ahelhe-ke mpware-mele ayeye ile-me* (track ground-DAT make-SS while story tell-pres) 'telling a story while making tracks on the ground' (cf. Henderson and Dobson, 1994: 369).[1] A narrator, seated on the ground, will prepare to tell a story by smoothing out the sand in front of her and removing any bits of foreign matter (rocks, sticks, leaves, etc.) that are likely to impede fluent drawing. This smoothed out space is the bounded surface upon which drawing will take place. The defined drawing space, together with the sign language and gesture space of the narrator, constitute the locus of visual attention for the audience.

Into the drawing space, the narrator will place various conventional iconic signs. These are referred to in Arrernte as *impatye* 'tracks' and people themselves remark that the shape of the icons tend to be the same as (or, at least, idealized versions of) the impressions that would be left by an object if it were placed on the sand.[2] For example, Figure 10.1 presents a 'grab' from a video of sand drawing, and in it we see a woman (the narrator) sitting in front of a completed story scene that she's just drawn into the smoothed out space in front of her. To help clarify the representational depiction in Figure 10.1, Figure 10.2 provides a labelled sketch of the same drawing. The narrator is facing south, and on the eastern edge of the drawing space (narrator's left) she has drawn a long shallow arc which represents a windbreak – a crescent-shaped shelter made of branches which people often sleep in at night. In the middle of the arc is a circular depression which indicates the central stump, pole or bush around which the windbreak is built. The presence of a windbreak automatically indicates that we have a camp scene. The 'U'-shapes in the drawing represent seated people – this is roughly the shape which people who are sitting cross-legged leave in the sand. The two people

Figure 10.1 A scene from an Arrernte sand drawing ('grabbed' from video).

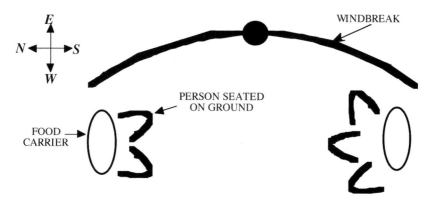

Figure 10.2 Labelled sketch of the sand-drawing scene in Figure 10.1.

seated in the north are sitting with their backs to three people seated in the south, indicating that we have two different family groupings. Each group is seated facing an oval shape. The oval represents a 'food carrier', a kind of wooden dish which women use to collect food and water in, and which is oval in shape when looked at from above. The configuration of people and food carrier suggests that people are having a meal.[3]

The very preliminary introduction to sand drawing that has just been sketched should provide sufficient background for understanding the discussion of the spatial properties which now follows. Of the more than one dozen general spatial properties that are key to understanding Arrernte sand drawing, only six will be treated in this chapter. These six provide the necessary background for the later discussion of the developmental consequences of exposure to sand drawing.

2.1. Only visible features drawn (no marks of the invisible)

The narrator will only represent things that would be visible in the narrated scene in their drawing. There is no representation of things that would be invisible, such as the wind, noises, speech (i.e., there is nothing like 'speech bubbles' in cartoons), odours, etc. (cf. Nash, 1995).[4] In fact, the entities represented are typically tangible. Thus, while shade and shadows are frequently referred to in the narration, they tend not to be represented, although I do have one example where the shadow cast by a person is drawn in. Similarly, the smoke from a fire, even when referred to in narration, is not usually instantiated in the drawing space. Invisible and intangible entities can often be inferred from aspects of the drawing. When a figure is drawn lying next to a tree (drawn as something like: O()), it is possible to infer, from standard desert practice, that the person was sleeping in the shade of a shady tree. Similarly, even if the wind is not represented, its effects may be (e.g., the pattern it makes on the ground, or its blowing coals out of a fire onto someone sitting by the fire).

In Figure 10.1, all the entities in the depicted scene are visible and tangible objects in the created storyworld – windbreak, five people, and two food carriers. As a rule, any concrete entity mentioned in the spoken version of the narrative will be drawn into the scene, however, it often happens that entities are drawn into the scene that are not explicitly mentioned in the spoken version. This is usually the case for objects that can be inferred as being present, either on the basis of the general type of scenario which is being talked about (e.g., camp scene vs. hunting scene vs. travelling scene), or on the basis of the roles played by different people in the scene. For instance, in the spoken versions of the same story as that depicted in Figure 10.1, there is never any spoken (or signed) mention of the windbreak or of the food carriers, only the people are referred to directly in speech. But, having established in the spoken narrative that we have a camp scene, the inclusion of the windbreak in the drawing fleshes this out. Moreover, stating in the spoken version that the people are eating, leads to the natural inference (from an Arrernte perspective) that food carriers would be present in the scene, and, indeed, this inference on the basis of speech is given overt representation in the drawing.

2.2. Things that move necessarily leave a trail of tracks

Among the visible entities that are drawn during narration are paths and trails of tracks. In much of the desert region, the surface of the country tends to preserve the marks of events that have recently transpired in a place. Traditionally, tracking abilities were critical for survival, and researchers like T. G. H. Strehlow (1951, 1964) explicitly tie tracking abilities to the form of representation in sand drawing.

> *Aranda art showed a scene as viewed through the eyes of a native people whose whole existence had depended largely on their tracking ability. . . .* A Central Australian native used to read the ground like a book. . . . Centuries of acute observation had similarly taught him to tell from tracks not only what kind of birds and animals were in his neighbourhood, but also what they had been doing before his arrival and what they were likely to be doing at the moment.
>
> (Strehlow 1951: 3, emphasis mine)

In the representation system, as in the reality of Arrernte experience, anything that moves along the ground leaves a trail of tracks. So, in the course of narration, when motion (along the ground) is predicated of an entity, its path will be marked in the sand and/or modelled in gesture and sign.[5] The path can be as simple as a line drawn in the sand or as complicated as a full representation of actual foot prints (with numerous possibilities in between). In Figure 10.1, we have five people statically located, hence no paths, but when a person gets up and leaves, the static representation is rubbed out and a path is drawn from his/her prior location towards the direction s/he is travelling. No representation of an entity in motion is given except its trail of tracks. Once the entity stops, however, it is again given a static representation. To get a better sense of how this works in practice, consider the following excerpt from T. G. H Strehlow's (1964: 46) description of a Western Arrernte girl telling a story while sand drawing:

> . . . Next the boy would be shown approaching: the story-teller would walk her fingers across the sand, leaving behind a series of dots. The U-figure would now be rubbed out, to show that the *njunju* [i.e. the evil monster woman] had got up to chase the boy. The story-telling fingers would stride rapidly from the fire across the sand to the point where the boys tracks had ended. The chase would begin – round and round the camp-fire; and the index finger would indicate the trail and the pace of the pursuer and pursued by drawing a narrowing spiral more and more rapidly around the central circle that stood for the camp-fire. . . .

2.3. The longer a mobile entity is statically located, the deeper its 'track'

Although sand drawing can largely be treated as a form of 2-D representation, there are certain important cases where the possibilities of 3-D 'modelling' in sand are exploited. For instance, the difference in weight of two people may be represented by making a deeper impression in the sand for the heavier person. Similarly, a seated person already drawn as a 'U' figure may later be retraced several times, creating an increasingly deeper impression, in order to emphasize that a significant amount of time has passed while the person has remained seated in that place. Indeed, just as heavier objects placed on sand do tend to make a deeper impression, so it is the case that when mobile entities are statically located in one place for a long time, their 'track' becomes deeper (often due to minor bodily shifts as they perform whatever activities they are engaged in while statically located). Here, we have a nice example where, in the representation system, spatial aspects can be manipulated to indicate (via a combination of iconicity and metonymy) the passage of time. Critically, this is instantiated by moving beyond the 2-D properties of the system and utilizing 3-D aspects of the medium (in this case, depth).[6]

2.4. The perspective on objects and events is from above; sand drawings present an aerial view of events

T. G. H. Strehlow (1951, 1964) has suggested that the traditional reliance on tracking abilities, as discussed earlier, is directly responsible for the conventional perspective taken in sand drawings, and in Arrernte art more generally. He argues that the skill of reading real world events off the ground was a crucial skill that was drilled from an early age, and became second nature after much practice.

As a result the Aranda people had, naturally enough, developed in their pictorial art the habit of looking down upon a landscape from above and not from the side as we do.

(T. G. H. Strehlow 1951: 3)

Noting that most iconic signs in sand drawing have the same shape as the impression they would leave in the sand when canonically placed will only get us so far. For instance, it does not explain the representation of landforms and fixed objects, like waterholes, hills, trees, creek beds, and so on. For these, it is more accurate to say that the relation between the real object and the representation in the sand is an iconic outline of the object as it would appear 'from above'. When a real hill or waterhole is talked about, drawers may take great pains to get the exact contour line right, but this is often not important to the story and, as a result, such entities are commonly represented in idealized fashion as circles or ovals.

The 'aerial perspective' is not only relevant to object representation, but also to the representation of the spatial relations between objects, and to the representation of event actions. Central Australian art has often been described as presenting an idealized map of place and country. In sand drawing, we get 'floor plans' of scenes, complete with motion tracks.

For mobile or moveable objects, representation of the object in sand drawing will depend on the object's general orientation in the scene and the (idealized) view from above that that orientation would give. Figure 10.3 shows sand drawings of two different objects in different orientations – a person in three different orientations (seated, lying and walking) and a digging stick in two different orientations (lying and upright in ground).

Munn (1973: 219) has argued against the claim that this form of representation takes an 'aerial view' perspective. She writes:

I avoid here such descriptions as 'bird's eye view' which imply that the solution is derived from a particular way of looking at the object, or that it shows us the object form a particular perspective. My implication is rather, that the solution derives from the internal structure of the representational system, and that we cannot automatically 'read off' from the structure a perspective from which the object is being viewed.

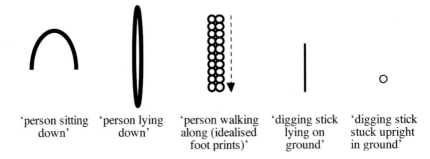

'person sitting   'person lying   'person walking   'digging stick   'digging stick
down'   down'   along (idealised   lying on   stuck upright
                                    foot prints)'   ground'   in ground'

Figure 10.3 Representation of changing object orientations shows 'aerial view'.

She has certainly touched on two important points which should not be forgotten – firstly, that the drawing is not to be taken as a representation of the narrator's or the protagonists' perspective on the events in the story world, and secondly, that the form of drawing does not reflect people's habitual way of looking at the objects represented. Still, this does not negate the position that the drawing as a form of representation has a conventional perspective (from 'above') and requires a form of 'thinking for drawing' that makes no claims about narrative perspective *per se* (narrative perspective itself being derived at the semantic and pragmatic level from the interaction of communication systems in context). It is impossible to ignore the fact that this form of representation varies perspectivally from the form of side-view drawing which is commonly used to accompany story narratives in contemporary English books and magazines. Moreover, Strehlow's hypothesis is only that Arrernte art conventions developed on the basis of analogy to the reading of tracks in the sand on the ground. This does not require any claim about the typical perspective taken on objects themselves, only the perspective on the traces the objects leave behind which can be used as 'icons' to invoke the total concept. Further, in extending the system, there is no claim that an accurate representation of the contour of a hill, for instance, is derived from having seen it from above. Indeed, it is most likely to have been derived from walking around the base and/or from side-on visual encounters. Still, Arrernte narrators themselves often talk about such representations as being what the thing would look like from above: **impatye akertne-nge-ntyele are-me-arteke** (track/mark top/above-ABLATIVE-onwards see-pres-SEMBLATIVE) 'it's like seeing the track/mark right from above'. In the section on developmental consequences of exposure to sand drawing, there will be further reasons given for recognizing that sand drawing embodies a convention of representing objects, spatial relations and events in 'bird's-eye view'.

2.5. Things in a story representation should be oriented as they would have been in the real world; things are represented in their absolute spatial orientation

As Munn (1986: 69) has observed, the order in which objects and events are drawn in the sand corresponds directly to the narrative chronology. She adds that, 'while the sequence of elements reflects the temporal order of the narrative, the arrangement of elements on the sand reflects the spatial positions of actors and objects'. Munn does not, however, tell us what spatial considerations determine how actors and objects are positioned and oriented within the drawing space, only that the representation is a 'spatial assemblage' constituting a 'graphic scene' in which intrinsic spatial relations between actors and objects are modelled. There is more that needs to be said.

With respect to Figure 10.1, I noted that the narrator, who was facing south, had placed the windbreak at the eastern edge of the drawing space. No matter which way the narrator had been facing the drawing space, she still would have drawn the windbreak on the eastern side with its back facing east and its opening facing west. For most of the year, the prevailing winds are from the east, and as a result windbreaks are most often built with the real world spatial orientation that was drawn in the sand. For stories, even made-up stories, a convention has developed that an unmarked camp scene will indeed be represented by first placing a windbreak in its canonical orientation as this narrator has done. However, this is just one example of a more far-reaching convention of spatial representation in sand drawing. Namely, that objects and events will be oriented as they would have been in the real world. This does not simply mean that objects and events in the story world will preserve roughly accurate intrinsic 'facing' relations with respect to one another (internally to the scene), it also means that they will be represented with roughly accurate cardinal point orientation (i.e., anchored to fixed bearings external to the scene). Thus, if in the spoken narrative a girl is said to have gone off towards the west, then her path must be drawn from real world east to real world west. This convention similarly applies to accompanying handsigns, so that a motion to the west must also be signed from east to west. Moreover, when real places are being talked about in the narrative, they will be 'mapped' onto the ground in such a way that their position in the drawing space has the same absolute directional orientation in relation to other objects in the space as the real places do – that is, if place A is north of place B in reality, then the drawn representation of place A will be placed to the north of that of place B in the drawing space (cf. Nash, 1995). Thus, an absolute frame of reference (i.e., the use of fixed bearings, or absolute coordinates, like north, south, east, and west, to locate objects) helps dictate the (horizontal) orientation with which objects and events are drawn into the space. This then constitutes another example of the preference many Australian Aboriginal groups show for using a geo-centred absolute frame of reference for spatial description and representation instead of a body-centred relative frame of reference (see Haviland, 1993; Levinson, 1996; Pederson et al., 1997).

2.6. Episodes that unfold in a single place–time location are 'tracked' into a single frame; erasure of the space signals a change of place–time location

This is the last spatial property of sand drawing to be discussed. Unlike the previous five properties, which all related to the creation of drawings within the drawing space, here we are concerned with the spatial significance of removing a depicted scene, or one of its parts, from the drawing space. As Munn (1986: 69–71) points out, '[e]ach scene is a unified physical setting within which actions take place'. That is, once a setting is established in the drawing (or, more accurately, *through* the coordinated acts of drawing and narration), all the actions that occur at the unified place–time location represented there will be mapped continuously into the scene. An episode builds up progressively within a single 'frame', and the narrator never erases fixed (immobile) entities, landforms, or places, nor does she erase tracks that have been laid down, until the episode at that place–time location is completed. The final result is a pictorial representation of the 'complete' episodic scene within a single 'frame'. Erasure of such a drawing, by smoothing out the sand so that a fresh drawing space is reestablished, not only signals the end of an episode, but also signals a change in place–time location within the narrative.

Usually total erasure means a change of place (i.e., a complete change of setting). For example, it is common for the wiping of a camp scene to be followed by the establishment of a hunting scene which involves some of the protagonists in the preceding episode now performing food-gathering acts at a place removed from the original camp. In this case, both place and time are shifted. The wiping may also signal a shift of focus to a different character in the story. For instance, a scene with two boys swimming at a waterhole may be wiped out and a new scene established which represents a monster in a cave preparing to go out and hunt for children. On the basis of the spoken narrative, we know that the monster's preparations are contemporaneous with the boys' swimming, and so the newly drawn scene represents a shift in place, but not of time. Less frequently, total erasure is used when there is no real place shift, but there is a temporal shift. Figure 10.4 presents a sketch of the scene that was wiped out before the 'breakfast episode' depicted in Figures 10.1 and 10.2 was constructed. Here, we have the same camp with the same windbreak, the same food carriers and the same five people (women and girls).

The scene in Figure 10.4 was the first episode to be constructed in the narrative and introduces us to the 'camp' and its inhabitants while they are sleeping at night.

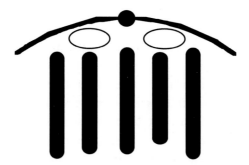

Figure 10.4 Initial place–time location in a narrative (just prior to total wipe).

The food carriers are stored within the windbreak, and local knowledge would tell us that all five people would be sleeping with their heads towards the windbreak. This whole scene gets erased, and the narrator then recreates the windbreak in the same place in the drawing space as it was before. Then the other objects are placed one by one to build the scene in Figure 10.1, as the narrator relates that the people woke up, got their food carriers and had breakfast. Thus, while there is a change in configuration of the movable and mobile objects in the camp, the camp location remains the same, and the major shift that is signalled by the wipe is the change from a 'nighttime sleeping episode' to a 'morning-time breakfast episode'. We have a change in place–time location by virtue of a significant (non-continuous) shift in time (and a change in actions that are time-related).

Total erasure serves yet another function, it is used like a visual 'The End' to signal that the story is over and the narration has finished. In this case, the wiping is often slower and more deliberate, and once the erasure is finished there is commonly a couple of 'definitive' flat-handed slaps on the drawing space. This final wipe re-establishes a 'pure' drawing space, and it often happens that, at the persistent requests of children in the audience, a new narrative will commence in this space. As Strehlow (1964: 46) observes, '[f]inally, the whole sand story would be wiped out, and some new tale would begin to take shape on the ground'.[7] The discussion now moves from the significance of complete erasure of a scene to the significance of partial erasure of a scene (i.e., erasure of only some elements within an established scene). With respect to her observations of Warlpiri sand drawing, Munn (1986: 72) has noted that '[w]ithin a scene, erasure does not usually occur'. My own observations suggest that, for the Arrernte, this claim concerning partial erasure is subject to individual and contextual variation. Individuals seem to vary as to how much of the narrative content they will convey in language and sign, and how much they will convey through drawing. Narrators who rely more heavily on drawing also seem to do more partial erasures, removing particular objects from within a scene. Further, as noted earlier, there are contexts where sand drawing and sign are used in the absence of speech. For instance, during a meeting, a woman may keep children quiet and entertained by conveying a whole narrative with just sand drawing and sign, and in such 'non-speech' contexts there appears to be a higher rate of erasure within a scene than in co-speech contexts. Of course these conditions are related, and it seems reasonable to say that the more sand drawing bears the role of principle means of communication, the more there are fine-grained nuances within scenes that involve partial erasure.

In all the cases of erasure within a scene that I've recorded, it is always a mobile or moveable entity that is wiped out and the erasure signals that the entity has changed place-location within the scene. For example, one narrator will regularly signal people getting up and leaving a scene by wiping out the U-shape which refers to a seated person and then re-drawing a new U-shape (representing the same person) which now faces in the exact direction the person will travel to, and then drawing or signing the travel path. In other words, the turning to move off is signalled by partial erasure and then re-establishing the person in a new orientation. As another common example of partial erasure, narrators will often erase an artefact that was drawn on the ground next to a person sign in order to indicate that the person has picked the object up (e.g., if a food carrier placed next to a U-shape is wiped out, it usually indicates that a woman has picked up the food carrier to do something with it).

3. The child's acquisition of sand-drawing conventions

In the preceding section, I have tried to sketch out how sand drawing is used as an iconic system for representing narrated events as they unfold in space. In particular, six spatial properties of sand drawing as a dynamic visual means of communication were discussed. These properties can be summarized as follows:

a Only visible features of a scene are drawn; there are no marks of the invisible.
b Things that move necessarily leave a trail of tracks. In the course of narration, when motion (along the ground) is predicated of an entity, its path will be marked in the sand (and/or modelled in gesture and sign).
c The longer a mobile entity is statically located in one place, the deeper its 'track'.
d This medium of communication represents objects and events as if they had been seen from above (i.e., sand drawings present an aerial view of events).
e Things in a story representation, entities or events, should be oriented as they would have been in the real world. That is, things are represented in their absolute (geo-centric) spatial orientation.
f Episodes that unfold in a single place-time location are drawn continuously into a single drawing space. Total erasure of the space signals a change of place–time location and a new focal episode. Erasure of a drawn symbol within a scene (partial erasure) signals a change in place of that object.

As I have already noted, these six properties are just a subset of all the spatial properties that one needs to be familiar with in order to interpret an Arrernte 'narrative in sand', but they will be sufficient for the purposes of the following discussion of the developmental effects of exposure to sand drawing.

Since sand drawing reaches its most elaborated form in women's narratives to young children, it seems reasonable to presume that it is designed to be accessible to children and that it is enacted in such a way as to hold a child's attention. Roughly speaking, a narrator sees her main audience as being any child between about eighteen months and ten years, although babies and adults are commonly present. As Munn (1986: 63) notes: 'A small baby or child may sit in its mother's lap while she tells a sand story; *the observation of sand drawing is thus part of early perceptual experience'* (emphasis mine).

How does this early perceptual experience evolve into an understanding of the conventions of sand drawing itself? In this section, I explore some aspects of Arrernte children's acquisition of sand-drawing conventions. In particular, I examine evidence for the 'internalization' of some of the spatial properties of sand drawing.

Based on observational evidence, the following is a tentative general developmental timetable for the production of sand drawing. This timetable presumes a more traditional lifestyle in which sand drawing continues to be a significant component of the Arrernte child's experience. Such conditions are, however, rapidly disappearing in most areas in which Arrernte people live.

- By eighteen months – children mimic sand-drawing behaviour and 'scribble' in sand in a fashion that caretakers respond to as drawing.
- By three years – children produce some of the basic iconic signs (including the U-shaped seated person sign), and recognize more signs than they produce.
- By five years – children produce all of the basic iconic signs and start producing more complex scenarios, they also start combining drawings and utterance in a form of proto-narration.[8]
- By ten years – children, especially girls, are actively telling stories using sand drawings, however they commonly fail to use absolute orientation, they often do not use total erasure to break up episodes, and they are not integrating handsigns into their narrative.[9]
- By twelve years – boys (now on the verge of initiation) no longer engage in what is seen as a woman's activity, although they will still use marks in the sand to annotate their discussions; girls continue to elaborate their sand-drawing and narrative skills.[10]
- By late teens (to early twenties) – usually after a woman has had her first child, young women are finally showing the most elaborated use of sand drawing with all the features previously described (including integration with handsigns).

In what follows, we will discuss children between the ages of three and ten. Three aspects will be briefly explored: (i) drawings of the human figure; (ii) perception of drawings by non-Aboriginal Anglo-Australians; and (iii) narrative behaviour with accompanying drawings.

3.1. Cultural differences in drawing

Until quite recently, psychological studies of children's drawings presumed that development in drawing skills was a fairly direct reflection of cognitive development. However, more recent studies have demonstrated that, even for the youngest children, there is little that can be concluded about the child's cognitive state on the basis of the form of their drawings (Bremner, 1996; Cox and Hill, 1996; Cox, 1992). Part of the evidence against the earlier position has come from cross-cultural explorations of drawing development. Bremner (1996: 512) identifies two main trends in current psychological research on children's drawings:

> Firstly, there is the move towards studying *the development of drawing as a more or less specific spatial skill.* . . . There clearly must be connections between drawing skills and other cognitive activities, but we are only just beginning to find out about these links. Secondly, there is now plenty of evidence against the notion of rigid stages in the development of drawing.
>
> (my emphasis)

One particularly well-explored area is children's drawings of the human figure (Cox, 1992; Freeman, 1975, 1977; Bassett, 1977; Kellogg, 1970). At least in Western cultures, one of the earliest recognizable forms to emerge in children's art is the drawing of a person. However, as has often been noted, the earliest drawings of the human figure are often 'incomplete', in that the trunk and/or arms are often omitted. In fact, there is often no distinction between the head and the trunk, with stick legs and stick arms drawn projecting directly from a round head. Such figures have come to be known as 'tadpole figures' (alternatively, 'tadpole people', 'tadpole forms' or 'tadpoles'), and a typical example is given in Figure 10.5.

Freeman (1977) argued that '[t]hese "tadpole people" are worthy of detailed attention, for they are extraordinarily common, if not universal'. Cox (1992) went a step further by hypothesizing that tadpole figures would show little, if any, crosscultural variation because all children, regardless of cultural background, would be dealing with the same spatial representational problem. She writes:

> Although there has been little cross-cultural work on tadpole figures, my guess is that the tadpole figures drawn by children in different cultures will be rather similar, whereas the conventional figures of older children will show more differences in style. The reason for this is that the tadpole drawer is grappling with the basic problem of how a real three-dimensional object might be represented in a two-dimensional medium. The basic problem is likely to be the same for all children, regardless of culture.
>
> (Cox, 1992: 69)

Figure 10.5 'Tadpole figure' by a non-Aboriginal Anglo-Australian preschooler.

The above formulation is somewhat problematic, since it already presumes the existence of tadpole figures that could be brought into cross-cultural comparison. But what if there was a culture in which children did not start with tadpole figures in their representation of people? This, in fact, would not falsify her hypothesis as stated, since it allows that if they were to draw tadpole figures, these figures would not be substantially different from that of a child in any other culture. This is not merely quibbling, as I hope to show in the following discussion.

In a recent article in the *The Times Higher Education Supplement* (9 August 1996), Cox and co-author Hill describe some of the consequences of being confronted with Warlpiri children's art from Central Australia. The subtitle of that article asks: 'What makes Aborigine [sic] children draw people as semi-circles when Western children draw stick figures?'. The careful reader, remembering the 'U'-shaped representations of seated human figures discussed for sand drawing above, is likely to provide the same sensible answer as Cox and Hill have: Warlpiri children are drawing a human figure according to the conventions of their culture. What is not clear from this brief article is the relevant ages being talked about, and their illustrations of pen and paper drawings are from children aged seven and eight, an age at which Cox (1992) has already conceded cultural differences are apparent.[11] But, as I have noted already, by the age of three Arrernte children (in more traditional situations) are producing 'U'-shaped human figures in the sand. There seems to be no 'tadpole' precursor. Could it simply be that children are not confronted with this particular problem 'of how a real three-dimensional object might be represented in a two-dimensional medium', because the culture provides a ready and easy conventional iconic 2-D solution? (driven in part by the readiness of adults to identify curved marks produced in the 'scribbles' of children as representations of the human figure). If so, then one might argue this is not a real counter-example to Cox's hypothesis, since culture circumvents the emergence of the problem that lies at the heart of it.

Illustrations from the Cox and Hill article also demonstrate that Warlpiri children are in fact merging two traditions of drawing due to contact with Anglo-Australian culture. This is similarly true of Arrernte children, as demonstrated by the following pictures from children attending the Aboriginal-controlled bilingual and bicultural education program at the Yipirinya School in Alice Springs.

In Figure 10.6, both pictures represent different scenes of being out bush in home country where elders are telling children from the school, and other members of the community, traditional stories. We see that, as far as trees and buses are concerned, we have a Western style representation, but when it comes to (statically located) people, we have the traditional Central Australian form of representation. In both cases, the traditional U-shaped icons are organized in such a way that they 'map' out the intrinsic seating arrangements of the people in the scene. In the first picture, the main storyteller sits under the tree to the left, facing the audience, while in the second picture the main storyteller sits with his back to the central bus and again the audience faces him. One

Figure 10.6 Artwork by children at the
Yipirinya School (1989) showing a merging of
drawing conventions. Both represent elders
telling stories to the kids.

nice touch in the first drawing is the small 'U' figures within larger 'U' figures towards
the periphery of the audience: this is a representation of adults (primarily mothers
and teachers from the school) holding babies and younger children on their lap.

These pictures show that these school-age children, exposed to the conventions of
Western drawing, are grappling with Cox's supposed problem of representing a real
three-dimensional object in a two-dimensional medium when it comes to trees and
buses, but are still relying on the traditional Central Australian two-dimensional
(aerial view) solution for drawing groups of seated people. This certainly presents an
easy and economical way of keeping things oriented as they would have been oriented
in the real world (one of the spatial properties of sand drawing), even if it is from an
intrinsic point of view rather than an absolute geo-centric point of view. In a sense,
the Western form of drawing seems to provide the background scene-setting of the
pictures, but it is the traditional form of representation which is used to render their
central theme (i.e., what and who the pictures are about).

The subtitle of Cox and Hill's article seems to imply that Central Australian
children do not draw stick figures. However, once again as a result of cultural contact,

they sometimes do, and the manner in which they approach the task is significant from a cross-cultural perspective. Figure 10.7 shows a five-year-old Arrernte girl's pen and paper drawing of a girl getting off a bus. The stick figure has been annotated to show the order in which she 'constructed' it. The initial element was a U-shape of the sort we have already, here treated as the legs. Then she drew the body line, then the arms and only at the end did she provide the head. From the perspective of research into Western children's drawings, this manner of construction is 'odd' for at least two reasons. Firstly, it is well reported that children from Western cultures overwhelmingly prefer to start by drawing the head. For instance, Bassett (1977) asked twenty-eight children, with a mean age of four years nine months (SD = 3.2 months), to draw a picture of a man on a plain sheet of paper, and all twenty-eight begin with the head. This Arrernte five-year-old, however, started with what may be interpreted either as the legs, or as the basic cultural icon of a human being, or both, and the head was the last element to be drawn. The second 'oddity' in the production of this drawing, is that the 'legs' are rendered in one stroke, as a 'U'-shape. Overwhelmingly, children from a Western tradition draw each leg separately. It seems likely that the Arrernte child is extending her earlier acquired representation of a human being, by using it as the basis of a stick figure representation, and this is stimulated by exposure to Western-style drawings (including Western-style children's drawings). How would Cox, at least in her 1992 incarnation, explain the difference between this Arrernte stick figure production and that of Western children? It seems that both are grappling with the same problem but have come to different solutions. Rather than suggest that the Arrernte child is influenced by culture and that Western children are reacting 'naturally' to a certain spatial problem, I'd prefer to see the premise of Cox (1992) brought into question. An alternative to suggesting that children are trying to represent a real 3-D object in a 2-D medium is to suggest that

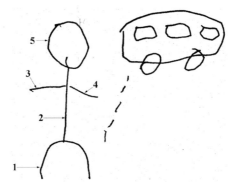

Figure 10.7 Drawing by a five-year-old Arrernte girl, annotated to show the order in which the stick figure was constructed.

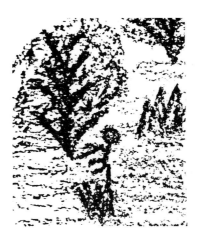

Figure 10.8 Detail from a
nine-year-old Luritja/Western
Arrernte girl's (1983) crayon
drawing, showing a woman
seated at a bush digging for
food.

they are trying to represent an object according to the 2-D drawing conventions they
have identified in their culture. Different cultural conventions in the spatial properties
of standard drawing representations might then influence children to attack the
problem of drawing the human figure in different manners cross-culturally.

Figure 10.7 is of further interest, because the girl who drew it said she had drawn a
girl walking away from a bus. In line with the Central Australian sand-drawing principle
that 'things that move necessarily leave a trail of tracks', she has presented a crude
representation of the motion path from the bus. However, compared to older Arrernte
children's stick drawings this representation is odd. While older children sometimes
also start with a 'U'-shape to begin their figures, it only ever occurs in the instance
where a person is represented as being seated, which is consistent with the significance
of the 'U'-shape in traditional representational uses. For example, Figure 10.8 presents
a detail from a nine-year-old girl's drawing in which we have a stick figure, again built
on a 'U'-shape, representing a seated woman using a digging stick to dig for food at the
base of a bush. However, when older children draw stick figures of people walking or
standing, they either draw the legs separately, or use an inverted-'V'.

A typical observation concerning children's drawings, even from children older
than ten years of age, is that they tend to mix multiple views or perspectives (e.g.,
providing part of a drawing in side view, and part in aerial view). Alternative views
tend to be attached at adjacent joints. Cox (1992: 86) provides a nice illustration in
which a girl aged seven years, seven months has depicted a horse and cart by presenting
the horse from a side view and presenting the cart to which it is attached (with all four
passengers) from an aerial view. A species of this tendency is a folding-over arrangement

Figure 10.9 Seven-year-old Western Arrernte girl's (1983) drawing of two vehicles, with aerial view of the inside projected onto/into the side of each vehicle.

in which 'the child is anxious to preserve the shapes on at least two planes at right angles to one another' (Cox 1992: 138), and this also often leads to a merged aerial view and side (or frontal) view. However, Figure 10.9 is an example of a type of merged perspective that seems to be unfamiliar in Western children's drawings, but is common in Arrernte drawings – an aerial view (floor plan view) is projected onto (or, perhaps more accurately, into) the sideview of a 'container' like a vehicle or a building.

In Figure 10.9, a seven-year-old Western Arrernte girl has drawn two vehicles travelling out together to go on a bush trip. We see the vehicles drawn in side view according to Western conventions, but the insides of the vehicles are presented in 'bird's-eye view' using Central Australian representational conventions to show the seating arrangements. The larger vehicle is a Toyota Troop Carrier, which has a large back cabin with bench seats running down each side. The U-shapes are the people on the seats – with three people on the front bench, seven on the right (i.e., 'upper') bench, and six on the left (i.e., 'lower') bench. Once again, we see a child seated on its mother's lap (on the left bench) and we also see a woman with a digging stick (towards the back of the vehicle on the left bench). In between the two long benches in the cabin are the crates and containers that are used to carry the food and tools for the bush trip. The second vehicle is a normal car, with people sitting in the front and back seats. Although the human figures are not elaborated, this is still a complex picture from the point of view of the way the perspectives are mixed and the amount of information given about the intrinsic spatial relations of the people and the objects in the vehicle.

In this subsection, we have dealt primarily with Arrernte children's drawings on paper. The five pictures reproduced in Figures 10.6 through 10.9 all reveal a merging of Central Australian and Western drawing traditions. Still, in every drawing, we see evidence of one or more of the spatial properties that are found in sand drawing as a representation system. The synthesis of the two traditions seems to hint at an emerging new tradition, which draws conventions of representation from both sources, but mixes them in a unique fashion. In a recent paper (Wilkins, 1997), I have demonstrated that in their spoken narratives 'Arrernte children show unique Adult-like channelling of attention which is very different from their English-speaking counterparts' and that they 'demonstrate certain adult patterns of 'thinking-for-speaking'.[12] I would similarly argue that Arrernte children's drawings also show channeling of attention which is like that of Arrernte adults and which replicates certain adult patterns of 'thinking-for-drawing'. The findings here strongly support the following observation by Cox and Hill, and suggest that cultural influences are already in effect from the time that children are beginning to produce their first drawings. Cox and Hill (1996) write:

> Children's artwork is a reflection of how they see and understand the world. It does not progress in isolation but is influenced by the images already used by the people in their culture.

3.2. Perception of Western drawing

The preceding section demonstrated cultural differences in picture production, but what about the Arrernte child's comprehension of drawings? Sandefur (1981: 18–24), reporting on work undertaken by Eirlys Richards among the Walmatjari, another desert-dwelling Aboriginal group, recounts a case in which 'some illustrations that had been drawn by a European artist' for a Walmatjari book 'were tested out before being printed'. The Walmatjari misperceptions of various drawings, and their explanations of what they thought was going on, were very revealing and gave further evidence of the fact that 'the perspective of traditionally oriented Aborigines is very different from that of Europeans' (Sandefur, 1981: 24). Of four drawings discussed, I found two particularly interesting. In one, the illustration showed a mother and calf running, but '[t]he Walmatjari thought the cows were lying down chewing their cuds' (Sandefur, 1981: 20), and in the other, a picture of the cow lying down in the shade, the cow was thought to be a mule, and 'the Walmatjari thought it was in running motion' (Sandefur, 1981: 23). This confusion of represented motion for stasis and represented stasis for motion intrigued me and led me to try my own little test.

I myself drew a much simpler picture of a running horse. This is given in Figure 10.10. I showed this drawing to ten non-Aboriginal Anglo-Australian children aged between five and ten, and each of them had no hesitation in declaring that it was a running horse. I then showed it to nine Arrernte children aged between four and

Figure 10.10 Author's 'running horse' as used in a test of picture interpretation.

seven. I worked with each child individually in the presence of one of the Arrernte teachers from the Yipirinya School.[13] Each child was questioned informally about the drawing in a manner that would not bias the child towards an active motion reading of the picture (i.e., by asking the Arrernte equivalents of 'What's this picture about?' or 'What do you see in this picture?', rather than 'What's happening in this picture?').

All nine Arrernte children recognized that Figure 10.10 was a picture of a horse, and five even recognized it as a running horse. The youngest, a four-year-old, offered no further observations beyond stating it was a horse and then going on to point at various body parts and naming them. Of the remaining three children, one (a five-year-old) said the horse was lying down, and the other two (a five-year-old and a seven-year-old) said that this was a picture of a dead horse. When questioned about the marks around the feet (intended to be a sign of the dust kicked up during running), the child who had said the horse was lying down reported that this was the wind blowing around the horse, while the seven-year-old who had said the horse was dead declared that these marks were evidence of crows having come down to eat the horse.

Of course, if one were to default to an aerial view perspective, as in sand drawing (or treat this drawing as the representation of an impression an object would leave in the sand), then this would lead to the interpretation that this horse was lying on the ground (or dead). That is, rather than seeing this as a side view representation, if it were instead taken as a 'bird's-eye view' representation, then we have a static lying horse, not an active moving horse. But, this is unlikely to be the full explanation. In discussing the findings with a number of adults, one woman in her sixties declared that the children who said the horse was dead were correct. She cited the way the legs were bent as evidence for this position. In Sandefur's report, the Walmatjari had similarly shown a sensitivity to the positioning of the legs in coming to their interpretation of the illustrations they were shown. Furthermore, a man in his late sixties observed that, although he knew that this was the way 'whitefellahs put running horses on paper', he himself always had to think hard to see it. He was disturbed by that fact that there were no tracks, and if there are no tracks, how could it be moving? Thus, there seems to be a potential complex of factors: no tracks leads to an inference that there is no motion; and to have no motion and still have the legs positioned as they are, leads to the inference that the horse can't be standing but must be lying (and, in fact, looking as if it were dead); and since the typical Central Australian form of representation is from an aerial view, then, in the absence of any information to the contrary, one can presume this is an aerial view representation.

Whatever the correct analysis of these responses, it seems clear that, even after years of cultural contact, there still seem to be some perservering cultural differences in the interpretation of Western drawing conventions. Moreover, two spatial properties of sand drawing as a representation system seem to be implicated in the alternative interpretations taken by some Arrernte children and adults – (i) aerial view perspective, and (ii) things that move leave a trail of tracks. Levinson (1992: 31) notes that:

> Cultures specialize in particular shapes, and cross-cultural psychologists even suggest that peoples are differentially susceptible to various spatial illusions according to their socialization in a 'carpentered world' of right-angles (as in Western architectural structures) or a 'bent and moulded world' of circles and spheres (as e.g. in many African houses and corrals).

Evidence in this subsection suggests that peoples socialized in a world of sand drawing and tracking would also show culturally determined susceptibilities to certain spatial illusions, just as they are predisposed to make certain culturally guided spatial interpretations of hand-drawn stimuli.

4. Narrative behaviour with accompanying drawings

In this final section, I'd like to briefly address one possible consequence of the manner in which sand drawing narratives are broken into episodes punctuated by total erasure. Remember that in sand drawing, one narrative episode builds up progressively within a single drawing frame, and the narrator never erases fixed entities or tracks, until the episode at that place-time location has been completed. It is not the final 'full' picture that accompanies and illustrates the narrative, it is the dynamic process – the accompanying running commentary in sand – which illustrates it. The final picture that emerges for each episode is a mnemonic for all the things, actions and events that occurred in the episode, and it is eradicated to make way for the next narrative unit.

That, for the Central Australian child, the wiped out drawing space is a salient 'frame' for episodic action is implied by the following quote from Munn (1986: 69).

a sand story begins with the clearing of a space. This action prepares the 'screen' on which the graphic figures will appear and also serves as a kind of 'curtain raiser'; children sometimes respond to this preparation by exclaiming, 'djugurba' – that is to say, 'Look, a story!'

I have already noted that, in terms of their own story telling, even by the age of 10 children are not using total erasure to break up episodes. Instead, they tend to tell the whole story, while progressively drawing it all in one space, and total erasure simply makes way for the next story. This, for example, is true of the Western Arrernte girl whom Strehlow (1964) describes. Of course, such a behaviour is not independent of the fact that children's stories also seem to be much shorter and less elaborated than their adult models. At any rate, whether the pattern is one episode per drawing space, as for adults, or one story per drawing space, as for children, the fact remains that a 'complete' picture is not a static snapshot inside an episode, it is the culmination of a dynamic, chronologically ordered set of representations of actions and events in sand.

All of this is necessary background to an observation I only made in passing in a previous publication (Wilkins 1991: 217). I quote the relevant passage:

> [some] young Arrernte children who are given a comic book to tell stories from, will expect each separate frame to tell a story rather than connecting one frame with the next. Educational Psychologists [assigned by the Northern Territory education department to assess Arrernte children's abilities, in the early 1980s] ... had used the story telling with comic books as evidence of an inability for Arrernte children to attribute causal relations and to identify thematic connections. Of course, they missed the fact that such relations and connections are typically present within a single frame of story telling for the Arrernte, not spread across the frames. This is purely a matter of convention.

In other words, presented with a standard elicitation paradigm in which a picture series of usually black and white drawings is used, some Arrernte children would build whole episodes or stories for each drawing, but not necessarily connect one supposedly related drawing to the next. Instead of arguing any form of deficiency on the Arrernte child's part, it seems more plausible to suggest that, through socialization into the Arrernte tradition of story narration with accompanying sand drawings, these Arrernte children construe picture-like configurations that are meant to accompany narration as the culminations of narrative action rather than as individual snapshots that are the building blocks of an episode or story.

5. Conclusion

For many Central Australian Aboriginal communities, like the Arrernte and the Warlpiri, using language in an appropriate manner requires a knowledge of how and when to accompany, or even replace, one's speech with sand drawings. To narrate stories in the Arrernte or Warlpiri fashion is to 'tell stories onto the ground like the ancestors used to'. Although the practice of sand drawing reaches its apex in women's stories to young children, that early exposure provides important foundations for various traditional adult cultural and communicative practices. As Strehlow (1964: 46) observes:

> Because of the practice they had gained as children in making running illustrations for their secular stories, the older men were fond of using sand drawings also when passing on the sacred myths to the younger initiated males.

In this chapter, I have focused narrowly on the spatial aspects of sand drawing, and the correspondence between those spatial properties and Arrernte children's culture-specific behaviours in the production and comprehension of drawings. Although there is much evidence that Arrernte children have been influenced by exposure to Western drawing conventions, it is interesting to see that these have not fully displaced the more traditional conventions found in sand drawing. In fact, children have synthesized the two traditions in production, and there seems to be some community variation as to which conventions are drawn upon in the interpretation of Western illustrations. Spatial principles like 'take an aerial view in event representations' and 'anything that moves (on the ground) leaves a trail of tracks' lie at the heart of sand drawing and its probable precursor, tracking, and were shown here to be significant both in Arrernte children's own art work and in their interpretation of non-Arrernte drawings. Moreover, there seems to be good evidence that the manner in which sand drawing is mapped to narrative structure (in terms of episodic chunking) can also have an effect on the interpretation of Western-style picture series (as in comics). The research presented in this chapter helps to elucidate the following unsubstantiated comment I made in Wilkins (1997: 307):

> In Central Australia, narratives of all sorts tend to be supported and augmented by two other semiotic systems, sand-drawings and absolutely oriented gestures. Either system, or both together, could draw a child's attention to certain aspects of the rhetorical structuring of narrative and lead them to hypotheses concerning the critical features of adult-like 'thinking-for-narrating'.

In discussing the unique aspects of Australian Aboriginal forms of spatial thinking, especially those of Central Australian groups, Levinson (1996: 377) has claimed:

> Gesture and language and handsign and sand-drawing are deeply intertwined. Although the complete picture has yet to be painted . . .

I have tried to paint a corner of that picture by concentrating on just one of these four representation systems. This is not the end of the story, a move will need to be made towards detailing how the four systems integrate with one another, and to examining whether, for instance, they present a unified picture of spatial conceptualization or whether each system embodies a different, medium-specific, view of the spatial domain.

Acknowledgements

This should be considered only a work-in-progress. I would especially like to thank the members of the Arrernte-speaking community who have patiently worked with me for over fifteen years now. In particular, the Yipirinya School and the Intelyape-lyape Akaltye project have been extremely helpful and supportive of my research. Margaret Heffernan, more than any other person, has taught me about the wonders of sand drawing. In preparing this chapter, I have been given very good advice by Melissa Bowerman, Penny Brown and Barbara Villanova. I look forward to further comments.

Notes

1. Munn (1986: 61) observes that the Warlpiri term for 'the process of sand marking' is *yirrarni* 'to put; to place; to set down', and the term *jukurrpa* 'story; dream; Dreaming totem' also 'refers to the sand pictures' in the context of women narrating traditional stories.
2. Referring to the stock of iconic signs used in Arrernte art generally (including sand drawing), Strehlow (1964: 47) notes that '[t]he basic figures themselves were undoubtedly stylized representations of the actual marks of persons, animals, and objects left behind on the surface of the ground'.
3. In fact, in the narrative which this is taken from, the camp is an *arlwekere*, a 'single women's camp'. The five people are women and girls, and they are seated to have breakfast before they go off hunting. The pair of people in the north are key protagonists in the story, a girl (the more westerly figure) and her maternal grandmother (the slightly larger 'U'-shape to the east).
4. In his description of the manner in which senior Aboriginal people of the arid regions of Central Australia use drawings, including sand drawings, to represent ('map') country, Nash (1995) notes that invisible entities like 'wind direction, arrows for directions, unmarked borders, [and] views/aspect' are not represented. Furthermore, he reports that 'when using European maps, invisible features (contour lines, isogals, grid lines) can sometime by dismissed as *kanunju/kantu* 'inside' ~ 'underground'.
5. Nash (1995) observes that in producing maps of country, Warlpiri and Warlmanpa people will include Dreaming tracks (i.e., the paths of travel of totemic ancestors) and also traditional routes of travel (in historical times), even if tracks would now be obliterated. This might be considered a partial counter-example to the first spatial property of sand drawing discussed (i.e. 'only visible features drawn, no marks of the

invisible'), however, it is my own experience that at the time of drawing such tracks and routes, people commonly enter the perspective (narrative world) of the time when the tracks would have been 'fresh'. It is important to remember that the objects that are represented would be visible and tangible in the time-world of the account.

6. The need to recognize certain 3-D properties of sand drawing is a minor corrective to Munn's (1973: 206) claim that : 'the spatial grammar with which we are dealing is strictly in accord with the rules of the two-dimensional country 'Flatland''. Here, she is referring to Rudolf Arnheim's (1954) concept of 'Flatland' and quotes favourably his observation that in 'Flatland' 'the relationship between flatness and depth is undifferentiated' (Arnheim 1954: 60). As we have seen, however, this is not strictly true in sand drawing (at least, not in the Arrernte sand drawings I have studied).

7. Nash (1995) observes that a 'map' of country sketched in the sand is 'erased on completion of discussion', and this contrasts to "signpost' *jururru*, indicator 'map' left on ground for those following'.

8. This is consistent with Munn's (1986: 63) observation for Warlpiri children that 'at the age of about five or six they can make and identify the basic graphic forms used in narration. If asked, they can demonstrate this narrative method, but without employing gesture signs.'

9. From his field work among the Western Arrernte in 1929, Róheim (1974) reports a play session with a ten-year-old boy, Depitarinja, and two younger children. These children incorporate sand drawing as part of their play. He writes: 'Depatarinja had by this time taken charge of the proceedings. He brought another little boy and girl to take place of the absentees. The children sat and played in the sand. Their game was in the mythological style. . . . They made marks in the sand. 'This is a soakage. Now an euro comes to drink. There is a hut. Now the goat wants to drink water.' . . . The game was extraordinarily similar to the *altjiranga* (ancestor) stories of the adults, both in the geographical representation of everyday events and, in places, the similarity of the symbols used.'

10. In describing the Western Arrernte community at Hermannsburg in the late 1960s and early 1970s, Seagrim and Lendon (1980: 45) write: 'School-age children seemed to keep to sex-segregated groups, the girls generally sitting not far from the adults, telling stories accompanied by sand tracings or looking after younger children. The boys were generally more active, kicking footballs around, out in the bush presumably hunting small game, or simply indulging in boisterous play.'

11. To clarify the Cox and Hill (1996) position further, note that with respect to the widespread commonalities in tadpole figures across Western cultures they argue that: 'just because we see a similar pattern of drawing development in a number of western cultures, it does not follow that this pattern is necessarily "natural" in some innate or inevitable sense. . . . When we compare western children's figures with those in many other cultures we find a number of differences'. Let me emphasize again, however, that they do not indicate at what age significant differences begin to emerge.

12. Here, I am using Slobin's (1996) notion of 'thinking for speaking'. He writes (1996: 76) that 'the expression of experience in linguistic terms constitutes *thinking for*

speaking – a special form of thought that is mobilized for communication.' Later, I
introduce two analogous notions 'thinking for drawing' and 'thinking for narrating'.
13. This testing took place in 1984 when I was employed by the Yipirinya School as
Linguist and Literature Production Supervisor.

References

Arnheim, R. (1954). *Art and Visual Perception*. Berkeley: University of California Press.
Bassett, E. M. (1977). Production strategies in the child's drawing of the human figure:
towards an argument for a model of syncretic perception. In: G. Butterworth (ed.),
pp. 49–59.
Bremner, J. G. (1996). Children's drawing and the evolution of art. In: A. Lock and
C. R. Peters (eds), *Handbook of Human Symbolic Evolution* (pp. 501–519). Oxford:
Clarendon Press.
Butterworth, G. (ed.) (1977). *The Child's Representation of the World*. New York: Plenum
Press.
Cox, M. (1992). *Children's Drawings*. London: Penguin Books.
Cox, M., and Hill, R. (1996). Different strokes. *The Times Higher Education Supplement*.
9 August, p. 18.
Freeman, N. (1975). Do children draw men with arms coming out of the head? *Nature*,
254: 416–417.
Freeman, N.H. (1977). How young children try to plan drawings. In G. Butterworth
(ed.), *The child's representation of the world* (pp. 3–29). New York: Plenum Press.
Haviland, J. (1993). Anchoring, iconicity and orientation in Guugu Yimithirr pointing
gestures. *Journal of Linguistic Anthropology*, 3: 3–45.
Henderson, J., and Dobson, V. (1994). *Eastern and Central Arrernte to English Dictionary*.
Alice Springs: IAD Press.
Kellogg, R. (1970). *Analyzing Children's Art*. Palo Alto, CA: Mayfield.
Levinson, S. C. (1992). Primer for the field investigation of spatial description and
conception. *Pragmatics*, 2(1): 5–47.
Levinson, S. C. (1996). Language and space. *Annual Review of Anthropology*, 25: 353–382.
Levinson, S. C., and Brown, P. (1994). Immanuel Kant among the Tenejapans:
anthropology as empirical philosophy. *Ethos*, 22(1): 3–41.
Munn, N. D. (1973). The spatial presentation of cosmic order in Walbiri iconography.
In: A. Forge (ed.), *Primitive Art and Society* (pp. 193–220). London: Oxford
University Press.
Munn, N. D. (1986). *Walbiri Iconography: Graphic Representation and Cultural
Symbolism in a Central Australian Society*. Chicago, IL: University of Chicago Press.
Nash, D. G. (1995). Notes towards a draft ethnocartographic primer (for central
Australia), unpublished manuscript.
Pederson, E., Danziger, E., Levinson, S., Kita, S., Senft, G., and Wilkins, D. P. (1997).
Semantic typology and spatial conceptualization. Cognitive Anthropology Research
Group, MPI. Working Paper No. 40.

Róheim, G. (1974). *Children of the Desert: The Western Tribes of Central Australia.* Volume One (edited and with an introcution by W. Muensterberger). New York: Basic Books.

Sandefur, J. L. (1981). Cultural considerations in vernacular literacy programmes for traditionally oriented adult Aborigines. *Literacy in an Aboriginal Context.* Work Papers of SIL-AAB, Series B, Volume 6: 1–30.

Seagrim, G. N., and Lendon, R. J. (1980). *Furnishing the Mind: A Comparative Study of Cognitive Development in Central Australian Aborigines.* Sydney: Academic Press.

Slobin, D. (1996). From 'thought and language' to 'thinking for speaking'. In: J. J. Gumperz and S. C. Levinson (eds), *Rethinking Linguistic Relativity* (pp. 70–96). Cambridge, MA: Cambridge University Press.

Strehlow, C. (1913). *Die Aranda- und Loritja-Stämme in Zentral-Australien* IV, I: *das Soziale Leben der Aranda und Loritja.* Frankfurt am Main: Joseph Baer.

Strehlow, T. G. H. (1951). Foreword. In: R. Battarbee (ed.), *Modern Australian Aboriginal Art* (pp. 1–7). Sydney: Angus and Robertson.

Strehlow, T. G. H. (1964). The art of circle, line and square. In: R.M. Berndt (ed.), *Australian Aboriginal Art* (pp. 44–59). Sydney: Ure Smith.

Wilkins, D. P. (1991). The semantics, pragmatics and diachronic development of 'Associated Motion' in Mparntwe Arrernte. *Buffalo Papers in Linguistics*: 207–257.

Wilkins, D. P. (1997). The verbalization of motion events in Arrernte (Central Australia). In: E. Clark (ed.), *The Proceedings of the Twenty-Eighth Annual Child Language Research Forum*, Stanford, CA: CLSI: 295–308.

11

Sequential Text–Image Pairing among the Classic Maya

Søren Wichmann

and Jesper Nielsen

1. Introduction

Visual narratives have enjoyed much recent attention, particularly those used in comics and graphic novels. Even historically oriented studies often begin no earlier than with the publications of the first American comic strips in the late nineteenth century (e.g., Fuchs and Reitberger, 1978: 13; Hegerfors and Åberg, 1996: 5), and hence concentrate on the last hundred years' history of comics. However, the use of sequential images to convey narratives extends back throughout human history. Occasionally, references are made to prehistoric or other early cultures that used combinations of text and image. Oft-mentioned examples are Egyptian and Mesopotamian reliefs or the famous medieval Bayeux tapestry (Fuchs and Reitberger, 1970: 10–11; Hegerfors and Åberg, 1996: 5). A notable exception to this trend is Scott McCloud's *Understanding Comics* (1993), which in some detail describes principles of text–image pairing not only among the ancient Egyptians, but also among the fourteenth- to sixteenth-century Mixtec of Mexico, who painted narratives on screenfold books of bark paper.

This chapter aims to cover new ground in the relatively neglected area of research into pre-modern pictorial narratives, focusing on the Classic Maya. As early as the first century AD, scribes and artists of the Preclassic Maya society realized that the combination of text and image offers unique possibilities for relating series of events. Maya sequential art painted on ceramics and stuccoed walls or engraved on limestone tablets and lintels make use of a broad range of expressive features, many of which recur in the better-studied modern comics. The aim of this chapter is to discuss and delimit the definitorial properties of what we have termed Maya *sequential text–image pairing* as a neglected subcategory within the broader category of Maya visual communication (see also Nielsen and Wichmann, 2000; Martin, 2006; Stone and Zender, 2011: 13–28). Most of the examples we will discuss are found on exquisite ceramic drinking vessels, and narrate mythic stories, some of which will be in focus in the current chapter. More generally, this preliminary investigation seeks to throw some light on the development and practice of text–image pairing in a culture historical perspective.

2. The cultural context and media of Maya text–image pairings

Before moving on to a description of the subcategory of sequential text–image pairing, a short introduction to the Maya and the media of sequential art is needed. The pre-Columbian Maya civilization flourished between about 250 BC and the arrival of the Spaniards in AD 1519. The Maya are documented archaeologically in southern Mexico, Belize, Guatemala and the westernmost part of Honduras, and they constituted one of the cultures of major importance in Mesoamerica. Maya culture shared a number of traits with other Mesoamerican cultures, for example temple-pyramids, a special ballgame, human sacrifice and a ritual calendar of two hundred and sixty days (see Sharer and Traxler, 2006; Martin and Grube, 2008). In several ways, however, the Maya were unique. Most significantly, they produced more written texts than any other Mesoamerican culture, using a logophonetic writing system, which, even if it was not invented by the Maya, certainly was developed to an unmatched degree of sophistication by the Maya themselves. They also developed a tradition of producing elite polychrome ceramics decorated with text-image pairings of a quality and expressivity unequaled in Mesoamerica (Coe, 1973, 1982; Robiscek and Hales, 1981; Kerr, 1989, 1990, 1992, 1994, 1997; Reents-Budet, 1994; Just, 2012). The majority of known vessels of this sort were produced in the Classic period, more specifically between AD 600 and 900, a time span known as the Late Classic.

Since only four Maya screenfold books (or codices) have survived to this day, polychrome vessels and plates are by far the richest source for studying sequential art. More than a thousand vessels with text–image pairings have been published in photographic reproduction, and many more are known or expected to exist. Unfortunately, most of the known vessels are unprovenanced, as they have come to the light of day by the sacking of elite tombs by looters. The four aforementioned codices are sacred almanacs, which, due to their function, contain only few examples of sequential art, but it must be assumed that this genre was also represented in bark paper books. Ceramics and books are generally closely related media. Thus, polychrome vessels have been described as the 'ceramic codex' (Robiscek and Hales, 1981: 13). The best evidence that ceramics and books were treated by the Mayas as closely related media are square vessels which in height and width echo the codex format (Reents-Budet, 1994: 222; Taube, 1994). By turning such a vessel, you literally proceed to a new 'page' in the ceramic codex. Vessels produced for carrying text–image pairings took on very simple shapes as compared to vessels not used as 'paper'; there is a general absence of curving walls, handles, ornamental additions, and so on. The simple ceramic forms possibly 'reflect the artists' desire for as much pictorial space as possible (. . .); the simpler the shape, the easier it is to adapt a flat pictorial composition to the vessel' (Reents-Budet, 1994: 16). The idea of vessels as ceramic 'paper' is also suggested by the hieroglyphic texts on the vessels, which in many cases refer to the vessels by means of the word *jich*, meaning 'surface' or 'page' (Reents-Budet, 1994: 113, 127).

What then, was communicated by way of polychrome ceramics and what role did they play in Maya society? Dorie Reents-Budet (1994: chapter 6) has identified three major categories of pictorial themes found on Maya ceramic vessels, each having several subcategories: (*a*) the natural environment; (*b*) historical scenes, including subcategories with some of the most frequent themes being palace scenes, warfare, ballgame, and sacrificial or ritual scenes, and finally, (*c*) supernatural beings and events. The scope of text–image pairings on vessels is markedly larger than that of monumental stone inscriptions, which primarily deal with events in the lives of the ruling elite and which are usually accompanied merely by a sculptural portrait of a ruler, sometimes involved in a specific act relating to ritual or conquest. There is ample evidence that finely decorated vessels had a utilitarian function, namely for drinking chocolate or maize gruel (e.g., Beliaev et al., 2010), but their function as a social currency may have been of greater importance. Vessels played a central role in political negotiations and alliance-building between city-states and in rituals, and are likely to have been the most common and important type of object in ritual gift-giving (see the vessels K5094[1] and K6059 for possible examples). According to Reents-Budet (1994: 89), 'one of the necessary criteria enabling a vessel to function as social currency is that it be a special object such as a vase finely painted by a well-trained artist'. Thus, the value of the vessel was enhanced if the text–image decoration was made by a true master of the arts, and since master scribes and painters usually came from the upper stratum of society (Coe and Kerr, 1997: 97–99), sometimes even from the ruling family, the status of the painter no doubt also lent additional value to a vessel. Through signatures on vessels we now know the names of a few of the master painters. *Aj Maxam* was the name of the principal vessel painter of the king of Naranjo called *K'ahk' Tiliw Chan Chaak* ('Rain god who fire-burns the sky'), and a vessel from his hands has been found in a royal tomb in the neighbouring city of Buenavista, possibly indicating its original role in a ceremonial gift-giving (Houston et al., 1992; Reents-Budet, 1994: 300–305; Martin and Grube, 2008: 74–77). Although *Aj Maxam* worked with themes, types of images, and compositional conventions already established by tradition, he did not always have to sign his work, since his individual style, easily recognizable in the calligraphic quality of the hieroglyphs and images, would immediately reveal the identity of the creator of the vessel.

Several terms have been proposed for the type of object which we are studying here. Will Eisner (1990, 1996) has used the term *sequential art* and McCloud (1993: 5–9; see also Cohn, 2013a) introduced the more elaborate term *juxtaposed pictorial and other images in deliberate sequence*. We will generally stay with the term *sequential text–image pairing*, where *sequential* alludes to narrative patterns.

3. Sequential text–image pairing as a new subcategory of conjoined text and image

Four major categories of visual communication were used by the ancient Maya: (*a*) discrete texts; (*b*) images; (*c*) conjoined text and image, that is, text and image occurring together but spatially separated from one another; and finally (*d*) embedded texts, where textual elements merge with images (Berlo, 1983). When discussing text and image within the confines of Classic Maya ceramics, it should be pointed out that the term *image* encompasses both natural representations and more stylized iconographic images. The term *text* refers to words written with hieroglyphic signs in the Maya logophonetic writing system (see Coe and van Stone, 2001; Kettunen and Helmke, 2010, for general introductions). All of the hieroglyphic texts which we shall be citing in the following were written in an early form of Ch'olan[2], as were most monumental inscriptions. Texts on vessels can be divided into two groups: a standardized row of hieroglyphs bordering the upper rim of the vessel, known as the Primary Standard Sequence (Coe, 1973), or PSS, for short. The PSS states that the vessel was dedicated and painted or engraved, what type of vessel it is (drinking cup, gourd, etc., see Houston et al., 1989), and what kind of drink it was designed to hold (a specific type of cacao drink, maize gruel, etc.). Furthermore, the PSS often tells us who owned the vessel, the owner's status and affiliation, and sometimes even who painted the vessel (Grube, 1986; Reents-Budet, 1994). The second category of text, which is less homogeneous, comprises all the remaining types of messages written on the vessels. The contents of these texts, labelled Secondary Nonrepeat Texts by Coe (1973), ranges from the names of supernatural beings and small excerpts of myths to descriptions of historical battles, accessions and ritual events.

Let us now return to the four major categories (*a–d*) of visual communication: The so-called discrete texts (*a*) are texts written with Maya hieroglyphs that are not accompanied by any images. Such 'pure' and image-independent texts are extremely rare in the extensive corpus of hieroglyphic inscriptions. Equally rare are examples of the second category, (*b*), which comprises 'pure' images, such as the panels from X'telhú, where no hieroglyphic text is present to provide the names of the agents, the time of the event or information about the provenance of the captives. A couple of factors help to explain why category (*b*) is so rare. One is the strong historical awareness of the Maya. When depicting a contemporary ruler, for instance, they wished to also maintain a record of the ruler's identity and his or her major deeds for future generations, much for the same reason that monuments in the modern cityscape that refer to historical events or people usually come with at least some minimal information like names and dates. Another factor may be that the Maya wished to reserve at least a part of the message for the literate upper classes. But in general, it simply seems to be typical of the Maya style of visual communication to be multimodal, something which developed into a cultural style and may not be in need of any special explanation.

By far the most commonly used type of visual communication and artistic expression among the Maya was that of conjoined text and image (*c*). Janet C. Berlo (1983) has shown that with respect to this type the images are not necessarily simply illustrations of the event described in the text. Text and image elaborate on each other, and in order to receive the complete message of a vessel, a stela or a page in a codex, one has to read, and combine, the information of both text and image (Figure 11.1). According to Berlo, 'sometimes our overreliance on textual information causes blindness to the other modes of communication, although it is clear that to the Maya artist it was the complementarity of these modes that provided the maximum means

Figure 11.1 Through the combination of text and image (exemplifying the AxBy type) the famous 'Regal Bunny Pot' (K1398) narrates two sequences of a larger mythic cycle. Note also the so-called PSS hieroglyphic text running along the upper rim of the vessel. (Photo © Justin Kerr).

of expression' (Berlo, 1983: 10). Thus, Maya visual communication never suffered the radical separation of text and image that is, or at least has been, characteristic of the Western world. For a long time, this separation resulted in a conception of 'high' art as being either 'pure' text or 'pure' images, whereas the combination of the two were regarded as inferior and best suited for advertising, entertainment and types of 'low' art (McCloud, 1993: 140–151). To Maya artists, on the contrary, the combination of text and image was the most expressive and hence preferred kind of visual communication. Category (*d*), embedded texts, transcends the boundaries between text and image and is realized by integrating or embedding hieroglyphic signs into images in subtle ways. This is mainly possible due to the close relationship between Maya hieroglyphic signs, which to a high degree are representational, and iconography (Stone and Zender, 2011). Embedded texts could be used to signal what material objects were made of, to indicate place names or personal names, etc.

The subcategory of sequential text–image pairing belongs within the broad category of conjoined text and image, and has sequentiality as its most distinctive and recurrent feature. The juxtaposition of images and text in sequence enables the artist to indicate movement and temporality and to describe a series of ongoing events. Hitherto, sequentiality in Maya art has received surprisingly little attention (Robiscek and Hales, 1981: 113; Schele and Miller, 1986: 38; Reents-Budet, 1989), and the emphasis has been on other types of narrativity, such as 'monoscenic' and 'simultaneous' narrative (Schele and Miller, 1986: 38; Reents-Budet, 1989).[3] We now turn to a more detailed description of how the Maya expressed and used sequentiality.

Before that, however, some words on the composition of the vessel paintings in general, including the non-sequential ones, are appropriate.

4. The organization of images

Unlike Maya texts, which have a fixed reading order combining left-right and top-down, Maya images are not necessarily decoded in a specific order. Furthermore, the artists who produced the painted vessels did not use any overt means for linking images together in a specific order, such as arrows, which are common in a modern context, or footprints, a device often used in Postclassic central Mexican screenfolds. Nevertheless, in subtle ways that were specific to the medium of cylindrical vessels, the artists could direct the decoding of the images such that the viewer's attention more or less unconsciously would focus according to the intentions of the artists. Nowadays the images of Maya painted vessels are most often photographically reproduced by means of the roll-out technique invented by Justin Kerr. This allows for reproducing a cylindrical image as if it were painted on a single, flat page. It is a definite advantage for the student to have a complete overview of each vessel, but when studying these roll-outs one tends to forget that this is not the way the Maya viewer would confront them.[4] As a preparatory step towards studying the composition of the cylindrical images it is instructive to look at compositions intended to go with cylindrical containers in our own culture, such as the labels on wine bottles or those on containers for spices, pills etc. In doing this, one discovers that one is never in doubt as to where the front is, even though the front is never overtly marked as such by any specific means, but rather by a number of different cues, such as more salient decoration, a larger label, colours, etc.

When one confronts a real-life Maya vessel, any given part which is clearly visible in one gaze corresponds to somewhat less than half of the total diameter of the vessel. This visible stretch more or less corresponds in size to the minor part of the roll-out image when divided by the golden section (aka the golden ratio).[5] Thus, a natural way of utilizing the space for painting would be to place three or four evenly spaced images or scenes around the vessel wall. This pattern, which we shall call A B C, is indeed a common one (Figure 11.2a). We include under this type also vessel paintings that have two, or more than three or four images, since the criterion is not the number of images, but rather that the characters depicted turn in the same direction, that no particular image stands out as central, and that there are no heavy frames separating the images. Another layout which is even more common is for there to be a front, suggested by an artistically elaborated or thematically central image, and a back, constituted by back-to-back figures. In this type, the front and the sides are not separated. Thus, the scene of the front 'spills' over into the sides, but usually only that part of the scene which is relatively minor in importance. Thus, in a palace scene, the front may be constituted by a ruler or other major political figure sitting in an elevated place with rows of subordinates to either side of him. The subordinates sitting last in each row will meet back to back on the side of the vessel opposite to that of the ruler and constitute the back of the vessel painting. Although palace scenes may be more common with this type, which we shall name bAd, we have chosen as an example a scene of an action-oriented nature (Figure 11.2b). The different subvarieties could be symbolized abAdf, bABd, bd, etc., depending on the number of central and secondary images, but we

Figure 11.2a An example of the ABC type of utilization of the surface provided by the vessel (K2023), in this case showing three *wahy* creatures each accompanied by a hieroglyphic caption. (Photo © Justin Kerr).

Figure 11.2b Characteristic of the bAd type is the central figure, typically a ruler in a palace scene, or event flanked by secondary or assistant individuals who will meet back to back on what can be called the back of the vessel (K558). (Photo © Justin Kerr).

Figure 11.2c The AxBy type divides the total image into four spaces, two large ones with equally important and often near-identical images and two smaller ones, frequently quadrangles containing glyphs or decoration. This example (K2702) shows two identical, seated individuals and two rows of pseudo-glyphs. (Photo © Justin Kerr).

prefer to stick to the general label only in order not to complicate the use of symbolic conventions. A third common organizational pattern consists in a division of the total space into four images, two large ones which are equally important, in fact often near-identical, and two smaller ones, that is, quadrangles extending more in the vertical dimension, which contain glyph rows or decoration. We shall name the resulting type AxBy (Figure 11.2c, see also Figure 11.1). Although it is a salient type, we do not agree with Reents-Budet (1994: 7) that this is the most common organizational pattern.

We stress that this is not intended as an exhaustive typology although a greater part of the corpus fits these major types perfectly or with some allowances for deviations and combinations.[6]

5. Narrative sequentiality in Maya imagery

Maya artists narrated series of actions and events by presenting images and text in sequence. This seemingly simple device was used in two slightly different ways. One, which we call *broad sequentiality*, expresses a series of events in progression. Between each sequence enough time has passed for a markedly different situation to obtain. Thus, a story is told. It bears remarking that very similar ways of narrating stories and myths were employed by the Moche culture in Peru (AD 100–800) on beautifully painted vessels (e.g., Donnan and McClelland, 1999). A seminal study by Jeffrey

Quilter explores this dimension of what he terms the 'narrative approach' to Moche iconography (Quilter, 1997). The other type of sequentiality encountered among the Maya is *narrow sequentiality*. What is important here is movement. By making very small changes in the position of, say, a person's arm or a bird's wing, the representation of motion is achieved. Unlike cases of broad sequentiality, no actual course of events is narrated, but, as with early modern forms of animation, the images are made to appear as if they are moving (see also below). The sequences sometimes appear to be recursive such that the movement would continue indefinitely as the vessel is continuously turned, but in other cases they have natural starting and ending points. Whereas broad sequentiality is not common (we have so far only identified about a couple of dozen examples), it is common enough to allow for some generalizations.

How may we distinguish sequentiality in Maya art? Only in a few cases is sequentiality found with the type AxBy, where a division between the sequences is clearly marked by a frame or a column of hieroglyphic text separating the different scenes (K1398, K1440, K1670). In other cases, the means for separating sequences are less apparent. On a roll-out photo, the entire image may appear as one single scene, but, as already mentioned, we need to remember that the Maya did not see the paintings in this way. Rather, when holding a vessel in front of you, it is only possible for the human eye to see a restricted part, so one must rotate the vessel to see the next part. Thus, sequentiality can be obtained simply by turning the vessel, and explicitly drawn frames are not needed. This technique bears resemblance to the *emaki* ('picture scrolls') which appeared from the eleventh to sixteenth centuries in Japan and are credited as being precursors to Japanese *manga* (Schodt, 1983). Readers would unfurl different scenes in a handscroll, but only a portion of the narrative would be visible at a time. A similar principle of achieving sequentiality was also used in optical toys such as the *zoetropes* and *phenakistoscopes* invented in Europe in the first half of the nineteenth century. The zoetrope 'contained a series of drawings on a narrow strip of paper inside a revolving drum [with slots to look through]' (Thompson and Bordwell, 1993: 4–5). Such 'moving pictures' are often regarded as forerunners of the cinema, but they are also very close to how we think Maya vessels were 'read'. Thus, neither zoetropes nor Maya vessels need lines or frames to separate each drawing; the effect of sequentiality is obtained simply by turning or revolving the vessel or drum. A wonderful example of narrow sequentiality can be found on a vessel from the collections of the Popol Vuh Museum in Guatemala City (Chinchilla Mazariegos, 2011: 60–61, Figure 15). It portrays the Maize god performing a dance, and shows three different, brief moments of the dance. This is most clearly seen in the position of the legs and feet, and turning the vessel literally makes the youthful Maize god swirl in his dance.

An example of broad sequentiality can be seen on an Early Classic vessel (K6547), now in Museum für Völkerkunde in Berlin (Figure 11.3). One half of the vessel shows a Maya lit-de-parade with mourning figures, and the other half is a resurrection scene showing the deceased reborn into the world of his ancestors. The 'Regal Bunny' vessel (Figure 11.1; to be further discussed below) is another excellent example. A

Figure 11.3 With its two scenes showing the death and subsequent resurrection of a Maya ruler, the so-called 'Death Vase' (K6547) exemplifies broad sequentiality (The Museum für Völkerkunde, Berlin, Germany). (Photo © Justin Kerr).

unique combination of broad and narrow sequentiality appears on K4151 (Figure 11.4), which shows two successive hunting scenes involving the Hero Twins well known from the K'iche' epic *Popol Wuj* (Christenson, 2003; see also Coe, 1989). The first scene captures the moment when one Hero Twin has just issued a clay pellet from his blowgun. Notice that the pellet is still hanging in the air. The target, a heron-like water bird, unaware of the danger, is about to swallow a fish. Note the wings of the flying bird above the blowgun, as well as the bird below it. When the vessel is turned, the action moves forward in time about one second. As the clay bullet strikes the heron, its long neck is thrown back by the power of the shot, and it drops the fish, which is then immediately taken by the bird below the blowgun. By changing the position of the wings of the flying bird, the illusion of flapping wings is achieved. The scene, then, is presented in ultra-slow motion, so to speak.

It is useful to refer to the three types of organizing vessel paintings that were introduced in the preceding section (bAd, AxBy, ABC) when discussing sequentiality, since the artist's choice of a given type will naturally affect whether and how sequential

Figure 11.4 Perhaps one of the most creative examples of Classic Maya vase painters' use of the round shape of the drinking vessel is the 'Blowgunner Vessel' (K4151), where turning the vessel results in seeing the heron being hit by the pellet fired by the Hero Twin. Note that the left-side image is the first in the sequence. (Photo © Justin Kerr).

effects are obtained. The three types follow from the natural limitations of the round medium with its typical size appropriate for a drinking vessel. There can maximally be three main images, as in the ABC type, if each is to fully occupy the range of a gaze. The AxBy type results when, instead of three main images, the artists chooses to have just two and to use the rest of the space for decoration or text. Finally, the bAd type offers itself in the situation where the artist prefers a single, main image. Vessels where major parts are left undecorated are never found. Thus, what determines the patterns are a combination of limitations on the medium, limitations on human visual perception, and artistic conventions.

The bAd type is most commonly used for palace scenes showing the handing over of tribute or other tokens of respect to a ruler. This type is structurally incompatible with sequentiality – at least in its pure form – but other features known from modern sequential art do occur, such as direct speech and gestures indicating the nature of the relationship among the characters depicted.

The AxBy type is often decorational, having identical A and B images. Sometimes the difference between A and B is just a movement of part of the image. The points in time that separate A and B may be further removed, however, allowing for A and B to show two highlights in for instance a mythological story or the historical narrative of a battle.

The ABC type is usually reserved for images of a rather decorative nature, e.g., depictions of animals (different or similar). Although one might expect the ABC type to lend itself to short narratives along the lines of a three-panel modern comic strip, sequentiality is actually usually restricted to one or two images and mostly occurs with the AxBy type.

Although we have implied in this section that the individual vessel is the typical medium for painted narratives, it is important to point out that there are stories which seem to extend over several vessels, each telling its part of the story. Prominent examples of this phenomenon, which, for want of a better term, we might call *network sequentiality,* are the stories of the sacrifice of the Jaguar Baby and that of the snake, the old man, and the woman (Robiscek and Hales, 1981: 113–118, 1988; Rivera and Capistrán, 2013). Unfortunately, it is difficult to know how such thematically related vase paintings functioned in the lives of the ruling elite – we do not even know how they functioned in their deaths. In other words, although we may assume that the known examples have been sacked from elite tombs, we do not know whether a particular series come from the same tomb.

6. Determining the directional decoding of sequential text–image pairing

For the modern student of Maya vase paintings, who has only vague insights into the stories they tell, it is often a problem knowing which scene comes first. There are, for instance, cases where two persons are shown going through a series of rituals. In order to fit the description into the limited space of the wall of the vessel, the artist does not show both persons going through all parts of the ritual, however, but instead shows each person going through one part of the ritual only (K5445, K4151). In these cases, it is very difficult to determine the starting point. Since the reading order of horizontally organized text is from left to right one might suppose that visual messages on vessels were normally decoded in the same direction, that is, by turning the vessel clockwise.[7] Indeed, in a rare example of the ABC type where the images seem to be ordered sequentially (Figure 11.7, discussed below) the direction is clockwise. As mentioned in the previous section, however, the vast majority of visual narratives consist of just one or two images. In a situation with just two images, the sequence will be the same whether the vessel is turned clockwise or counterclockwise. So sequential images alone do not provide safe evidence for the direction in which vessels were turned when images were decoded. As already mentioned, the Maya artists did not use any special devices (such as arrows or numbered frames) for helping the viewer determine the direction of decoding. Nevertheless, there are often thematic, visual or textual clues by which the viewer may be helped. We will exemplify these in turn.

Since stories told by vase paintings are apparently always part of the shared cultural knowledge of the Maya elite, the *theme* of the painting provides clues as to where decoding should start. In some cases, such as paintings referring to the theme of the resurrection of the Maize god, even the modern student knows enough of the content from related pictorial materials and orally transmitted myths to be able roughly to identify a particular sequence in the larger story. In other cases, which are unfortunately rare, the action is of such a common nature that the cultural boundaries do not obstruct the interpretation of sequentiality (see Figures 11.3, 11.4).

The *visual* clues to directionality are diverse and subtle. Sometimes there is an overall 'line' in the composition (K2352), sometimes the glance of a central person appears to indicate the direction (K511), and often the confrontation of two figures will indicate where the centre of the scene is (as in the bAd type).

Finally, *texts* may give a clue to where the sequence starts. As mentioned, texts are of two types, either they are linked to the images (Secondary Nonrepeat Texts), in which case they may occur anywhere, or detached from the image (Primary Standard Sequence, or PSS). The presence or absence of a PSS is not correlated with any type of vessel painting, be it types as defined by style, theme or otherwise. Interestingly, although the PSS is thematically and spatially (it nearly always occurs on the top rim) detached from the rest of the vessel painting, it may interact subtly with respect to alignment. Thus, the beginning of the text, represented by the so-called Initial Sign, more often than not occurs roughly over the central or first image of the vessel painting (Figure 11.3). With bAd types the Initial Sign is often aligned with image A, and with the AxBy and ABC types, whose formal structures do not otherwise indicate which scene is the hierarchically or temporally primary one, the Initial Sign of the PSS sometimes seems to indicate where decoding should start.

7. The techniques and idioms of Maya sequential art

Having demonstrated that the Classic Maya developed sequential art, we shall now be concerned with a number of formal traits of a more specific nature within this Maya subcategory of visual art. It is convenient to compare them with the much better studied modern comics. The following is a list of the most common forms of expressive features, idioms, graphic conventions or 'vocabulary' (a term from Eisner, 1990: 7; see also McCloud, 2006) that are found both in modern comics and in Maya sequential art. It should be kept in mind that although these traits are characteristic of both, they do not necessarily have definitorial status, since most also occur in 'monoscenic' and 'simultaneous' text–image pairings.

7.1. Conjunction of text and image

Although sequential art without texts does exist, it is fair to say that it is through the combination of image and text, i.e. of showing and telling, that the genre most markedly distinguishes itself from other art forms and achieves a special form of expressivity. McCloud (1993: 152–155) lists a number of categories of text–image combinations found in today's comics. Two of these categories, the *additive* and the *interdependent* combinations can be found in Maya sequential art. The *additive* combination occurs when 'words amplify or elaborate on an image or vice versa' (McCloud, 1993: 154). Although we have not yet found good examples, these types surely occur, since additive combinations are the rule in Maya non-sequential art represented by stelae and codices. More common is the *interdependent combination* where 'words and pictures go hand in hand to convey an idea that neither could alone' (McCloud, 1993: 155). In such combinations, hieroglyphic texts arranged in conventional columns, sometimes serving as boundaries between the scenes, in many cases provide important background information on the depicted scenes. Thus, texts can sometimes serve the dual purpose of conveying messages and contributing to the visual organization of images. Furthermore, text placed in front of the characters, often attached to the mouth by speech-lines, tells us what the actors of the event say, sometimes even expressed in first person (see our analysis of the 'Regal Bunny' vessel below). Thus, text and image go together in complementary ways to tell and show the entire story. An example is provided by a Late Classic vessel (K1196) that shows an old teacher instructing two young men in the scribal arts and mathematics (Figure 11.5).

Figure 11.5 An elderly teacher with god-like attributes corrects his pupils (K1196). Note the use of speech-line connecting the mouth of the teacher with the glyphic captions. (Photo © Justin Kerr).

A fine line from the old man's mouth leads to glyph compounds in front of him. The text contains the words *tat bihil* meaning 'the line is thick' (Wichmann, 2004b). Apparently, the old master is reproaching his young student for his lack of calligraphic skills (additional examples on K625, K5094, and Robiscek and Hales, 1981: nos. 30 and 87). With this technique, the Maya may be said to have invented what could be called a speech-line, a functional equivalent of the 'tail' (Cohn, 2013b) of the modern speech-balloon (see also Nielsen, 2014). Since the Maya did not make use of speech balloons as containers for signs, they also did not develop the various modern expressive variations of speech balloons and thought bubbles modifying or adding to the contents of messages written inside such balloons that are known from modern comics (Cohn, 2013b; Forceville, 2013). Nevertheless, at least one example of an expressive balloon without writing inside does occur, cf. the discussion of Figure 11.9 in the next section. The speech-line may have been around as a pictorial convention in Mesoamerica long before the Classic Maya to judge from a cylinder seal dated to around 650 BC from the Olmec site of San Andrés, near La Venta. Here, lines emanating from the beak of a bird connect to what seems to be hieroglyphic signs (Pohl et al., 2002).

Finally, a third type of text–image combination used by the Maya, the so-called *embedded text*, will be touched upon. As already mentioned, the integration of elements from the writing system into images is a common phenomenon in Maya art. In contrast, it is relatively rare in modern comics, although there are well-known examples such as Uncle Scrooge with $ signs in his eyes. Such examples would probably be more common if logograms, that is, single signs representing entire lexemes, were more common in the writing systems of European languages. In contrast, many Maya hieroglyphs and images are closely related because of the logographic component of the Maya writing system, whereas our alphabetic signs are arbitrary signs with no apparent resemblance to objects in the world.

7.2. Pictorial representations of motion, sound and smell

As already mentioned, the Maya were able to give their images a 'movie-like' appearance. This kind of sequentiality, which we have called *narrow*, was achieved by changing the positions of the arms, legs, or head of the characters depicted in the scenes. A couple of examples will illustrate the principle, which is closely related to how the zoetrope works. A group of vessels show rulers engaged in a ritual dance similar to the example of the Maize god already mentioned. Most of these vessels have two scenes which at first glance appear to be identical, but there are small variations (Figure 11.6). The dancer's leg and arm positions are changed in subtle ways, presumably in order to create an impression of the movements of the dancer (see also K4619, K4649). Another example comes from a vessel decorated with a scene showing supernaturals drinking. In three sequences, we are able to follow the movement of the drinking cup (Figure 11.7). In the

Figure 11.6 Narrow sequentiality in use on K4989. Two slightly different positions in a dance performed by two richly attired Maya rulers are presented. (Photo © Justin Kerr).

Figure 11.7 Three seated individuals engaged in what seems to be a ritual drinking ceremony (K4377). Note how the position of the drinking cups are changed from right to left, producing a movie-like effect. (Photo © Justin Kerr).

first scene, it is close to the large jar which probably holds the liquid and it is held almost vertically. In the next scene, the cup is raised, now slightly more tilted towards the mouth of the character. In the last scene, the cup is in a drinking position. When rotating the vessel clockwise, we almost see a fully animated sequence (for additional examples, see: K3649, K3844, K5371, K5421, K5454, and Robiscek and Hales, 1981: Figure 17b). Examples can also be found outside the medium of ceramics. On the magnificent wall paintings of Structure 1 at Bonampak (Room 1), five gourd-rattle players are shown. The players 'make different movements, almost showing a frame-by-frame cinematic record of how such rattles are shaken' (Miller, 1988: 321).

A device to illustrate motion within the same picture may be found on a vessel showing a ballgame in progress (K5435, Figure 11.8). Reents-Budet (1994: 269) argues that the undulating lines or curlicues that float around the scene are speech-lines tying the figures to the glyphic captions. A closer look, however, reveals that the scene contains eight figures, twelve glyphic captions and nineteen curlicues. Thus, Reents-Budet's interpretation is questionable, and an alternative function of the lines would be one similar to that of the curlicues found in, for instance, Hergé's *Tintin*, where they indicate speed or quick motion when occurring in such positions as behind a running man (cf. Forceville, 2011). Such a function fits well a depiction of a ball-game scene, where speed and motion are central ingredients. As for the representation of sound, only a few possible examples can be found, not counting the combination of glyphic text and speech-lines described above. On K4613, two jaguar-like felines appear to be roaring or exclaiming fierce words, since speech-balloons with a flame-like outline emanate from their mouths (Figure 11.9, see also K3924). If our interpretation is correct, this is a unique example of the shape of a speech-balloon having been changed in order to indicate the character or emotion expressed by the voice. In contrast, this technique is very common in modern sequential art (Eisner, 1990: 26–27; Cohn, 2013b; Forceville, 2013; Forceville et al., 2010). Two additional ways of indicating sound or breath can be seen in association with animals.

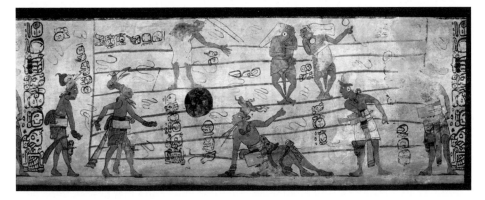

Figure 11.8 Ballgame scene (K5435) with very rare examples of curlicue-like lines, presumably added to the scene to add the impression of speed, movement and ongoing action. (Photo © Justin Kerr).

Figure 11.9 Two feline beings, probably either supernatural creatures or human impersonators, roar with flame-like speech balloons (K4613). (Photo © Justin Kerr).

Sometimes small undulating lines are seen emanating from the nostrils of deer (e.g. K1398, cf. Figure 11.1; Robiscek and Hales, 1981: no. 43 and Figure 64); on K5367, smoke-like scrolls emanate from the mouth of a bat; and on a vessel published by Robiscek and Hales (1981: Figure 17a) a deity appears to be screaming out or perhaps rather vomiting a very large and strange personified speech-scroll. Finally, we shall consider how smell could be visualized. Occasionally the skeletal inhabitants of the feared underworld-place Xib'alb'a are shown with various coloured smoke-like scrolls emerging from either their bellybuttons or their behinds. Presumably, this is a way of depicting the foul smell of the more or less decayed creatures of Xib'alb'a (Figure 11.10; see also K718). Such 'indexical lines' (Cohn, 2013a, cf. also McCloud, 1993) are also found in modern comics.

Figure 11.10 Among several frightening creatures in a scene that seems to be set in the Maya Underworld, a partly skeletonized figure (number four from the left) emits large smoke-like scrolls from his belly to signal the gasses and foul smell of decay (K3924). (Photo © Justin Kerr).

7.3. Scene-over-setting

In Maya imagery, characters and objects always appear in the foreground, normally tied to a *ground line* (Schele and Miller, 1986: 36; Reents-Budet, 1994: 9). As a pictorial device, this is similar to the principle of *scene-over-setting* (our term), which is a common trait in modern comics, as noted by Fuchs and Reitberger (1978: 48). The scene-over-setting principle operates in a great many painted ceramics, and appears almost never to be deviated from. Other than persons and animals, the outlines of palace walls, a stylized mountain, curtains, the steps of a ballcourt, vessels or the like may occur in the foreground, but never very prominently and often only partially depicted so as to suggest the setting of the scene (Figure 11.11; see also Reents-Budet, 1994: Figures 3.4 and 4.44). As noted by Robiscek and Hales (1981: 9), the background is usually vacant (represented by monochrome colouring) – only rarely is a naturalistic and detailed background with a landscape, trees, temples, crowds of people etc. presented. In our survey, we have in fact only encountered one clear example. On the Early Classic vessel from Berlin mentioned earlier (Figure 11.3), the resurrection scene has a complete background with mountains, a temple, and trees with animals among their branches. The result is a crowded image where it is difficult to distinguish the individual elements – a stark contrast to the vessels with scene-over-setting composition where the viewer's attention is not distracted in any way.

7.4. Gesture and positioning of human and animal figures

Almost all types of emotions and attitudes can be expressed graphically by what Will Eisner calls a 'non-verbal vocabulary of gestures' (1990: 100). In modern comics,

Figure 11.11 A detailed palace scene (K5445) shown taking place on a basic ground line, representing the stuccoed floor of the room, and with bound-up curtain hanging down from above. (Photo © Justin Kerr).

gestures, body language and other visual signs help us to easily recognize and understand the characters' moods (cf. Forceville, 2005, on the representation of anger, for instance). Gestures and body positions were important to the Maya as well, and the meaning of some of the gestures appears to be shared between the Maya and us (cf. the vessel from Berlin in Figure 11.3 with individuals that are clearly crying and expressing their grief and sadness). However, some gestures are culture-specific and most of the many different Maya gestures and bodily positions are not yet well understood (Kurbjuhn, 1980: 117–184). The meaning of a few specific types of gestures and positions can, however, be determined with some certainty; among them is 'the posture of royal ease' (Schaffer, 1986), a position in which rulers sit legs crossed on thrones, sometimes with one leg hanging over the throne, and with hands gesticulating towards a lesser noble, scribe, or other subordinate. No doubt this was a position associated with powerful and influential persons (e.g. K5353, K5450, K5453); additionally, there is a subordinate attitude (left hand raised to touch the right shoulder), which presumably expresses respect for higher-ranking individuals (e.g. K4959, K5082; see also God L in Figure 11.1). Still, there are plenty of other examples which at the present are difficult to associate with specific emotions, rank, etc.

By changing body proportions from normal to abnormal, modern comic artists make humans and animals appear funny. According to Fuchs and Reitberger, the proportion between head and body of figures in humoristic comics thus frequently changes from 1:8 to 1:3 (Fuchs and Reitberger, 1978: 50). Similar changes in body proportions can be found in Maya sequential art, although not necessarily in the ratio 1:3. The characters that undergo these changes are always supernatural beings, such as the so-called animal companion spirits (*wahy*) or the denizens of Xib'alb'a, the Maya underworld (Figure 11.12;

Figure 11.12 Three fantastic creatures blending features of various animals with human attributes depicted with a change in body proportions, probably to emphasize their supernatural quality (K4947). (Photo © Justin Kerr).

see also K3450, K4011). These characters are sometimes weird mixtures of humans and animals or various species of animals, which is clearly another hint at their supernatural nature (e.g., Robiscek and Hales, 1981: nos. 49–53; Grube and Nahm, 1994; Helmke and Nielsen, 2009). It is possible that the Maya intended to ridicule the creatures of the Otherworld, but other explanations for the distorted body proportions are more plausible. The abnormal bodies seem to be a trademark of supernatural beings, and they likely convey something which is scary and threatening, as one might imagine the world of spirits and gods to have been for the ancient Maya.

7.5. Colour and light

The broad spectrum of colours used for painting the polychrome vessels served mainly to enhance the realism of the representations. Some colours, like red, had symbolic values, and could be associated with various religious concepts, deities, etc. (Houston et al., 2009; Nehammer Knub, 2013), but colours were apparently never used in the expressive manner that we know so well from modern comics, such as when an envious man turns green, a sick one yellow or a freezing one blue. We do find variation in skin colours, but it seems to serve other purposes. Skin colours may range from light brown to dark brown and near black (K791, K4412, K4549, K5453). Although some of the variation may be due to body-painting, it might also possibly indicate different ethnic groups or rank.

Practically no examples of the use of light effects and shadows to produce an impression of volume or three-dimensionality of persons and objects are known (Schele and Miller, 1986: 35). For some unknown reason, the Maya did not develop this technique. Not even in scenes that clearly take place at night, in dark chambers or caves and where torches are in use, do we find the use of shadows (e.g. K5445, and Reents-Budet, 1994: Figure 5.9). A number of other traits that are common in sequential art of today are absent or very rare in that of the Maya. Thus, the Maya only used normal perspective in their images and never the bird's or worm's eye view, and persons and objects were always depicted two-dimensionally. As Schele and Miller (1986: 36) observe, 'spatial illusion in two-dimensional art was severely limited, and the optical devices used to imply position in space were very few.' Any impression of perspective or relative position in space was indicated only by overlapping, the basic orientation point being the groundline (e.g. K767, K3413, and K3814).

It is equally rare to see an expressive use of the frame-line and the size of the frames. If present, the frames serve mainly as neutral devices to delineate the scenes – to indicate the passing of time, or, as in modern comics, to contain and transport the look of the reader (see Eisner, 1990: 43–44). Maya frames are generally of a very simple rectangular shape and of uniform size, although at least one notable exception can be found. Thus, K5351 has a sequence with the so-called Paddler gods in their canoes (Figure 11.13). The images have rounded cruciform-shaped frames that allude

Figure 11.13 An unusual example of modified frames on K5351. The so-called Paddler Gods appear in cruciform-shaped frames cuing their journey from one realm of the cosmos to another. (Photo © Justin Kerr).

to a variant of the Maya logogram for 'cave', and here they probably symbolize the entrance point to the watery Underworld, which is exactly the place where the Paddler gods are going: as we see in one of the images, the canoe is tilting and about to sink. In this unique example, the frame indicates where the scene takes place.

8. A sample analysis: the 'Regal Bunny Pot' (K1398)

In this analysis, we shall exemplify many of the categories and observations made in the preceding sections. The vessel, which has been nick-named the 'Regal Bunny Pot' by epigraphers, is an exceptionally rich and beautiful example of Maya sequential art (Figure 11.1).

Composition   The painting is organized according to the pattern AxBy. It is topped by a Primary Standard Sequence (PSS) whose contents has nothing to do with the contents of the rest of the painting. Nevertheless, the Initial Sign (glyph block 4 from the left) seems to be aligned with what could be the first image in a two-part sequence, suggesting that the story begins in the left field of the roll-out photo. In that image, we see a rabbit holding a walking stick and a bird-shaped hat in his left hand and some rolled-up clothes (probably a loin cloth) under his right arm. In front of the rabbit is a nude old man, holding his right arm to his shoulder, a well-known gesture of reverence. The Maya viewer would surely recognize the story, while we may only guess that the rabbit has bereaved the old man of his outfit which identifies him as God L, one of the most important gods of the Maya underworld (Taube, 1992: 79–88). In the scene in the right part of the photo, the rabbit seems to be hiding from

God L behind a personage whose facial features and the logogram for *k'in* 'sun, day' on his shin and upper arms reveal his identity as the Sun god. God L is again making reverence, this time kneeling. The composition follows the scene-over-setting principle: there is nothing in the backgrounds. The story is told by way of broad sequentiality.

Text–image types   Of the four text–image types discussed previously, as many as three are represented. The PSS may be considered a *discrete text*, since its contents in no way interacts with the images. The columns, as we shall see shortly, do interact with the images, as do the short texts attached by curving lines to the mouths of the characters and appear to function essentially as the tails of speech balloons. The columns and the 'speech lines' together with the images are examples of *conjoined text and image*. The *k'in* signs on the body of the Sun god are examples of *embedded texts*, as are the grape-like markings of the monstrous heads at the base each of the two panels. These markings recur in the signs for *tun* 'stone' and *witz* 'mountain'. The monstrous heads thus represent anthropomorphized mountains.

Text   For years, epigraphers have struggled with the complex and highly unusual features of the additional glyphic texts on the vessel, but during the last decade collaborative efforts of several epigraphers have cast new light on the contents (see Stuart, 1993; Beliaev and Davletshin, 2006; Helmke, 2012: 179–184). Here, we have decided not to focus on the two long vertical columns of texts (which mainly provide background information to the story), but rather turn our attention to the texts linked to the 'speech lines' accompanying the rabbit, God L (twice) and the Sun god. To the far left, we have the words of the rabbit, which confirm that he has stolen the regalia of God L, including his broad-rimmed hat. His insulting words read as follows (see Helmke, 2012: 181–183):

> *Pulu ajo'l, uhtz'un awitz, k'ulis, itzamaat.*
> Burn your head, smell your sweat, paunch, Itzamaat [wizard-penis].

There are still parts of God L's response that resist complete decipherment, but his answer clearly refers to his missing clothes and the lack of his hat:

> *Ilik hat . . . nimam, bay nibuhk . . . nibaah?*
> Let it be seen that you . . . my elder, where are my clothes . . . my head?

The narrative continues in the right-hand scene where God L now kneels before the mighty Sun god, complaining:

> *Ajaw! Ahch'al(?) t'uhl uch'amaw niyuhal, nibuhk, nipatan.*
> Lord! The mud (?) rabbit has taken my jewellery, my clothes, my tribute.

The reply from Sun god is that the rabbit is not with him (although it hides behind his back):

Mahchaj ahch'al(?) t'uhl ta hiin, nimam, huliiy . . . xaman ixuh.
The mud (?) rabbit has been taken from me, my elder, he arrived here . . . to the north, Lady moon.

From other vessels, we know that the rabbit and the Moon goddess did indeed have a close relationship. For example, a vase partially reproduced in an auction catalogue (Sothesby's 1993) shows a scene where a rabbit is holding God L's broad-rimmed owl hat and is, in turn, being held by the Moon goddess. There are other thematically related vase paintings. Helmke (2012: 179–181) suggests that another earlier scene in the narrative may be present on the so-called Princeton Vase (K511), where the rabbit appears to be spying at the underworld court of God L. K559 and K796 also show the rabbit together with the moon goddess. On K1485, the Sun god and the Moon goddess are together, receiving something from various God N's and what seems to be their female companions. On K1560, a dwarf seems to be substituting for the rabbit in a scene where an old man is being undressed, a scene very suggestive of the Regal Bunny story. Unfortunately, we are not able in each case to determine whether there is a relationship of *themes* (parts of narratives) or *types* (whole narratives) (a distinction used in the classification of folk tales, cf. Thompson, 1973). Partly, this is due to the very nature of Maya vase paintings, since these are designed to tell only a theme or two per item. It is only in cases where the type is shared that we may speak of network sequentiality proper. Christophe Helmke has recently suggested a new analysis of the Regal Bunny story, including the Moon goddess' relation to the main characters of K1398. He summarizes the essence of the plot as follows: '[i]t is precisely because of the close relationship between the rabbit and the Moon goddess, that we can surmise that the two are in cahoots, the rabbit quite likely acting on her behalf. The Sun god, evidently harbouring a known felon, is plainly shown lying to God L and sending him on a proverbial wild goose chase. As such, the substance of the narrative is the deliberate disgrace of God L' (Helmke, 2012: 183). Thus, the Regal Bunny vase seems to enter into network sequentiality with the vessel sold at Sothesby's. The additional information given to us by the latter is that the rabbit hands over the outfit of God L to the Moon goddess. The vessel from Sothesby's suggests that the rabbit is acting as trickster who has fooled both God L and the Sun god.

9. Conclusions

In this preliminary investigation, we have attempted to identify some of the principles by which Maya sequential art works and to sort out useful categories and establish some terminology that ought to be useful when analysing Maya visual communication in general and sequential art in particular. In addition to presenting these analytical tools, our objective has been to contribute to the discussion of visual narratives from a broader culture historical perspective than is usually provided in the literature. Our study has revealed many similarities between Maya sequential text–image pairing and modern comics, but there are also salient differences. For instance, the stories that the Maya artists tell are few in number and abbreviated to one or two scenes. In contrast, the number of Western comics is massive and they always tell whole stories. We attribute this phenomenon to the fact that the Maya were more unified in terms of shared cultural knowledge than are members of Western society. For the ancient Maya, the messages existed before the medium, that is, as orally transmitted myths and stories, and the artists would elaborate on, but not create narratives. By combining the techniques of narrow and broad sequentiality more consistently, the Maya could easily have told whole stories the way Western comics do, but as far as we know they did not, apparently because there was no need for it. Great artistic achievements exist both in Maya sequential art and Western comics, for reasons that are somewhat similar. The painted Maya vessels were a form of 'social currency' (Reents-Budet, 1994: 88) in an exchange network of goods and prestige, whereas Western comics are commercial. The former were exchanged for prestige (of the donor), the latter for both money and prestige (of the artist).

While we find many similarities at the level of visual narrative techniques – similarities that reveal shared cognitive features across cultures – 'Western' and Maya sequential text–image pairing are radically different from a more sociological point of view. From the eighteenth century and onwards, the combination of and interplay between text and image was, in Western society, considered a debased form of communication. Only artists who directed themselves towards a mass audience, prominently including the lower classes, dared venture into text–image pairing. The ancient Maya, however, considered the combination of text and image the most exquisite and exclusive form of artistic communication, and, as far as we know, reserved it for elite consumption. Thus, under these diametrically opposed social conditions, art forms arose more than a thousand years apart in radically different cultures, art forms that nevertheless share an incredible amount of minute technical detail. With these observations we hope to have contributed a little to filling one of the holes of the official history of art.

Acknowledgements

An earlier version of this thoroughly revised article is contained in the volume *Comics and Culture: Analytical and Theoretical Approaches to Comics* published in 2000 by the Museum Tusculanum Press in Copenhagen. We thank the editors, Anne Magnussen and Hans-Christian Christiansen, as well as the publisher for their kind permission to publish a revised version in the present volume. Warm thanks go to

Christophe Helmke for helpful comments, references and suggestions, to Neil Cohn for inviting us to contribute to this volume and providing comments, and also to Justin Kerr for his permission to reproduce the images used here.

Notes

1. Throughout this chapter, we shall make many references to different vessels, using, whenever possible, the numbering system of the most prolific publisher of Maya vessels, Justin Kerr. Kerr numbers are introduced by 'K'. Most of the vessels are published in Kerr's *Maya Vase Book* series that number 6 volumes to date (Kerr, 1989, 1990, 1992, 1994, 1997, 2000, but can also be easily accessed and searched via Kerr's online Maya Vase Data Base at http://research.mayavase.com/kerrmaya.html. Other rich sources are Robicsek and Hales (1981), Reents-Budet (1994), and Coe (1973).
2. A group within the Mayan family of languages. Another group, namely Yucatecan, is represented, though mainly in the inscriptions of Northwestern Yucatan and on so-called Chocholá-style ceramics. The codices may be bilingual. See further Lacadena and Wichmann (2002), and Wichmann (2004a, 2006).
3. The term 'monoscenic narrative' refers to single images 'wherein one scene from the total event is portrayed and stands for the whole' (Reents-Budet, 1989: 189). Monoscenic narratives often express 'collapsed time', such as when a ruler is shown on the battlefield; grabbing an enemy by the hair as if he is in the middle of the act of capturing him, and yet the captive is already dressed as a sacrificial victim (we have this example from Peter Mathews, personal communication, 1999). 'Simultaneous narrative' shows several actors and actions, not necessarily interacting with each other, in a single scene. This kind of narrative is said by Reents-Budet (1989: 190–191) not to be uncommon on painted ceramics from the Late Classic.
4. It is likely that the artists made sketches on bark paper before painting the vessel itself, since examples of artists running out of space or leaving blanks because of bad planning are surprisingly rare.
5. Mathematically defined, the golden section along one dimension of an object is where the ratio of the lengths of the two segments is the same as the ratio of their sum to the larger of the two segments. This ratio is always 1.61803. Euclid is the first to have provided the mathematical definition. There is a long 'Western' tradition recognizing the aesthetic importance of the golden ratio. For instance, as is well known, 'Western' books are traditionally most often designed such that the proportion between the length of the vertical side and that of the horizontal side approximates the golden ratio (Livio, 2002).
6. Not only do the three patterns cover most of the tokens, deviations from the patterns also seem to be significant. In other words, the exceptions may sometimes be said to confirm the rule(s). On K1092, a scene with drunken people is shown. This painting does not fit any of the patterns. It seems as if the painter intentionally chose a disorderly general organization in order to convey disorderliness. Other examples are K1182, K1558, and a number of vessels paintings showing *wahy*, that is, supernatural

spirits; in the latter instances it is as if the deviation from the organizational pattern conveys a supernatural world, fit for the supernaturals that inhabit it (see Helmke and Nielsen, 2009).

7. This directionality might be comparable to what Cohn (2013c) calls 'navigational structure' – how readers physically navigate the content of a visual narrative. Comics more often than not follow a left-to-right, top-down path (the 'Z-path') just like alphabetically based writing systems, but there are nevertheless often departures from this pattern.

References

Beliaev, D., and Davletshin, A. (2006). Los sujetos novelísticos y las palabras obscenas: Los mitos, los cuentos y las anécdotas en los textos mayas sobre la cerámica del período Clásico. In: R. Valencia Rivera and G. LeFort (eds), *Sacred Books, Sacred Languages: Two Thousand Years of Religious and Ritual Mayan Literature* (pp. 21–44). Markt Schwaben: Acta Mesoamericana, Vol. 18, Verlag Anton Saurwein.

Beliaev, D., Davletshin, A., and Tokovinine, A. (2010). Sweet cacao and sour atole: mixed drinks on Classic Maya ceramic vases. In: J. F. Staller and M. D. Carrasco (eds), *Interdisciplinary Approaches to Food, Culture, and Markets in Ancient Mesoamerica* (pp. 257–272). New York: Springer.

Berlo, J. C. (1983). Conceptual categories for the study of texts and images in Mesoamerica. In: J. C. Berlo (ed.), *Text and Image in Pre-Columbian Art: Essays on the Inter-Relationship of the Verbal and Visual Arts* (pp. 1–39). Oxford: BAR International Series.

Chinchilla Mazariegos, O. (2011). *Imágenes de la mitología maya*. Guatemala City: Museo Popol Vuh, Universidad Francisco Marroquin.

Christenson, A. J. (2003). *Popol Vuh: The Sacred Book of the Maya*. Winchester: O Books.

Coe, M. D. (1973). *The Maya Scribe and His World*. New York: The Grolier Club.

Coe, M. D. (1982). *Old Gods and Young Heroes: The Pearlman Collection of Maya Ceramics*. Jerusalem: The Israel Museum.

Coe, M. D. (1989). The Hero Twins: myth and image. In: J. Kerr (ed.), *The Maya Vase Book, Vol. 1.* (pp. 161–184). New York: Kerr Associates.

Coe, M. D., and Kerr, J. (1997). *The Art of the Maya Scribe*. London: Thames and Hudson.

Coe, M. D., and Van Stone, M. (2001). *Reading the Maya Glyphs*. London: Thames and Hudson.

Cohn, N. (2013a). *The Visual Language of Comics: Introduction to the Structure and Cognition of Sequential Images*. London: Bloomsbury Academic.

Cohn, N. (2013b). Beyond word balloons and thought bubbles: the integration of text and image. *Semiotica*, 197: 35–63.

Cohn, N. (2013c). Navigating comics: an empirical and theoretical approach to strategies of reading comic page layouts. *Frontiers in Psychology*, 4: 186. doi:10.3389/fpsyg.2013.00186.

Donnan, C. B., and McClelland, D. (1999). *Moche Fineline Painting: Its Evolution and Its Artists.* Los Angeles, CA: UCLA Fowler Museum of Cultural History.

Eisner, W. (1990). *Comics and Sequential Art.* Revised edition. New York: Poorhouse Press.

Eisner, W. (1996). *Graphic Storytelling and Visual Narrative.* New York: Poorhouse Press.

Forceville, C. (2005). Visual representations of the idealized cognitive model of *anger* in the Asterix album *La Zizanie. Journal of Pragmatics*, 37: 69–88.

Forceville, C. (2011). Pictorial runes in *Tintin and the Picaros. Journal of Pragmatics*, 43: 875–890.

Forceville, C. (2013). Creative visual duality in comics balloons. In: T. Veale, K. Feyaerts, and C. Forceville (eds), *Creativity and the Agile Mind: A Multi-Disciplinary Study of a Multifaceted Phenomenon* (pp. 253–273). New York: Walter de Gruyter.

Forceville, C., Veale, T., and Feyaerts, K. (2010). Balloonics: the visuals of balloons in comics. In: J. Goggin and D. Hassler-Forest (eds), *The Rise and Reason of Comics and Graphic Literature* (pp. 56–73). Jefferson, NC, and London: McFarland.

Fuchs, W. J., and Reitberger, R. C. (1970). *Comics: Anatomie eines Massenmediums.* München: Heinz Moos Verlag.

Fuchs, W. J., and Reitberger, R. C. (1978). *Comics-Handbuch.* Hamburg: Rowohlt Taschenbuch Verlag, GmbH.

Grube, N. (1986). An investigation of the primary standard sequence on Classic Maya ceramics. In: V. M. Fields (ed.), *Sixth Palenque Round Table, 1986* (pp. 223–232). Norman, OK and London: University of Oklahoma Press.

Grube, N., and Nahm, W. (1994). A census of Xibalba: a complete inventory of *Way* characters on Maya ceramics. In: J. Kerr (ed.), *The Maya Vase Book,* Vol. 4 (pp. 686–715). New York: Kerr Associates.

Hegerfors, S., and Åberg, L. (1996). *100 År Med Tegneserier.* København: Carlsen Comics.

Helmke, C. (2012). Mythology and mythic time. In: M. Didrichsen and H. Kettunen (eds), *Maya III, Life • Death • Time* (pp. 160–185). Helsinki: Didrichsen Museum of Art and Culture.

Helmke, C., and Nielsen, J. (2009). Hidden identity and power in Ancient Mesoamerica: supernatural Alter Egos as personified diseases. *Acta Americana*, 17: 49–100.

Houston, S., Stuart, D., and Taube, K. (1989). Folk classification of Classic Maya pottery. *American Anthropologist*, 91(3): 720–726.

Houston, S., Stuart, D., and Taube, K. (1992). Image and text on the 'Jauncy Vase'. In: J. Kerr, *The Maya Vase Book*, Vol. 3 (pp. 499–508). New York: Kerr Associates.

Houston, S., Brittenham, C., Mesick, C., Tokovinine, A., and Warinner, C. (2009). *Veiled Brightness: A History of Ancient Maya Color.* Austin, TX: University of Texas Press.

Just, B. R. (2012). *Dancing into Dreams: Maya Vase Painting of the Ik' Kingdom.* New Haven, CT and London: Princeton Art Museum.

Kerr, J. (1989). *The Maya Vase Book: A Corpus of Rollout Photographs of Maya Vases by Justin Kerr,* Volume 1. New York: Kerr Associates.

Kerr, J. (1990). *The Maya Vase Book: A Corpus of Rollout Photographs of Maya Vases by Justin Kerr,* Volume 2. New York: Kerr Associates.

Kerr, J. (1992). *The Maya Vase Book: A Corpus of Rollout Photographs of Maya Vases by Justin Kerr,* Volume 3. New York: Kerr Associates.

Kerr, J. (1994). *The Maya Vase Book: A Corpus of Rollout Photographs of Maya Vases by Justin Kerr,* Volume 4. New York: Kerr Associates.

Kerr, J. (1997). *The Maya Vase Book: A Corpus of Rollout Photographs of Maya Vases by Justin Kerr,* Volume 5. New York: Kerr Associates.

Kerr, J. (2000). *The Maya Vase Book: A Corpus of Rollout Photographs of Maya Vases by Justin Kerr,* Volume 6. New York: Kerr Associates.

Kettunen, H., and Helmke, C. (2010). *Escritura jeroglífica maya.* Madrid: Acta Ibero-Americana Fennica, Series Hispano-Americano 8, Instituto Iberoamericano de Finlandia.

Kurbjuhn, K. (1980). *Die Sitze der Maya. Eine ikonographische Untersuchung.* Dissertation zur Erlangerung des akademische Grades Doktor der Philosophie. Universität Tübingen.

Lacadena, A., and Wichmann, S. (2002). The distribution of Lowland Maya languages in the Classic Period. In: V. Tiesler, R. Cobos, and M. Greene Robertson (eds), *La organización social entre los mayas. Memoria de la Tercera Mesa Redonda de Palenque,* Vol. II (pp. 275–314). México D.F.: Instituto Nacional de Antropología e Historia and Universidad Autónoma de Yucatán.

Livio, M. (2002). *The Golden Ratio.* New York: Broadway Books.

Martin, S. (2006). On Pre-Columbian narrative: representation across the word-image divide. In: J. Quilter and M. Miller (eds), *A Pre-Columbian World* (pp. 54–105). Washington, DC: Dumbarton Oaks Research Library and Collection.

Martin, S., and Grube, N. (2008). *Chronicle of the Maya Kings and Queens,* revised edition. London: Thames and Hudson.

McCloud, S. (1993). *Understanding Comics: The Invisible Art.* New York: Harper Collins.

McCloud, S. (2006). *Making Comics: Storytelling Secrets of Comics, Manga and Graphic Novels.* New York: Harper Collins.

Miller, M. E. (1988). The boys in the Bonampak Band. In: E. P. Benson and G. G. Griffin (eds), *Maya Iconography* (pp. 318–330). Princeton, NJ: Princeton University Press.

Nehammer Knub, J. (2013). Earning your stripes: an iconographic analysis of war paint among Mesoamerican cultures. In: J. Nielsen and C. Helmke (eds), *The Maya in a Mesoamerican Context: Comparative Approaches to Maya Studies* (pp. 93–121). Markt Schwaben: Verlag Anton Saurwein.

Nielsen, J. (2014). 'To Sing Arrows': observations on the representations of sound in the writing and iconography of Teotihuacan. In: C. Helmke and F. Sachse (eds), *A Celebration of the Life and Work of Pierre Robert Colas* (175–191). Markt Schwaben: Acta Americana, Verlag Anton Saurwein.

Nielsen, J., and Wichmann, S. (2000). America's first comics? Techniques, contents, and functions of sequential text–image pairing in the Classic Maya period. In: A. Magnussen and H.-C. Christiansen (eds), *Comics and Culture: Analytical and Theoretical Approaches to Comics* (pp. 59–77). Copenhagen: Museum Tusculanum Press, University of Copenhagen.

Pohl, M. E. D., Pope, K. O., and von Nagy, C. (2002). Olmec origins of Mesoamerican writing. *Science*, 298: 1984–1987.

Quilter, J. (1997). The narrative approach to Moche iconography. *Latin American Antiquity*, 8(2): 113–133.

Reents-Budet, D. (1989). Narrative in Classic Maya art. In: W. F. Hanks and D. S. Rice (eds), *Word and Image in Maya Culture: Explorations in Language, Writing, and Representations* (pp. 189–197). Salt Lake City, UT: University of Utah Press.

Reents-Budet, D. (1994). *Painting the Maya Universe: Royal Ceramics of the Classic Period.* Durham and London: Duke University Press, in association with Duke University Museum of Art.

Robicsek, F., and Hales, D. M. (1981). *The Maya Book of the Dead: The Ceramic Codex. The Corpus of Codex Style Ceramics of the Late Classic Period.* Charlottesville, VI: The University of Virginia Art Museum.

Schaffer, A.-L. (1986). The Maya 'Posture of Royal Ease'. In: V. M. Fields (ed.), *Sixth Palenque Round Table, 1986* (pp. 203–216). Norman, OK and London: University of Oklahoma Press.

Schele, L., and Miller, M. (1986). *The Blood of Kings: Dynasty and Ritual in Maya Art.* New York: George Braziller, in association with the Kimbell Art Museum, Fort Worth.

Schodt, F. L. (1983). *Manga! Manga! The World of Japanese Comics.* New York: Kodansha America.

Sharer, R. J., and Traxler, L. P. (2006). *The Ancient Maya*, 6th edition Stanford, CA: Stanford University Press.

Sothesby's (1993). *Pre-Columbian Art, including Property from The St. Louis University Art Collection, The Manoogian Collection, The Collection of the late Edwin Janss, Jr., The Estate of Elizabeth Halsey Dock.* New York [auction catalogue for 17 May].

Stone, A., and Zender, M. (2011). *Reading Maya Art: A Hieroglyphic Guide to Ancient Maya Painting and Sculpture.* London: Thames and Hudson.

Stuart, D. (1993). Breaking the code: Rabbit Story. In: G. Stuart and G. Stuart (eds), *Lost Kingdoms of the Maya* (pp. 170–171). London: National Geographic Society.

Taube, K. (1992). *The Major Gods of Ancient Yucatan.* Washington, DC: Dumbarton Oaks Research Library and Collection.

Taube, K. (1994). The Birth Vase: natal imagery in Ancient Maya myth and ritual. In: J. Kerr (ed.), *The Maya Vase Book*, Vol. 4 (pp. 650–685). New York: Kerr Associates.

Thompson, K., and Bordwell, D. (1993). *Film History: An Introduction.* New York: McGraw-Hill.

Thompson, S. (1973). *The Types of the Folktale: A Classification and Bibliography.* [=FF Communications, 184]. Helsinki: Suomalainen Tiedeakatemia.

Valencia Rivera, R., and García Capistrán, H. (2013). In the Place of the Mist: analysing a Maya myth from a Mesoamerican perspective. In: J. Nielsen and C. Helmke (eds), *The Maya in a Mesoamerican Context: Comparative Approaches to Maya Studies* (pp. 35–50). Markt Schwaben: Verlag Anton Saurwein.

Wichmann, S. (ed.) (2004a). *The Linguistics of Maya Writing.* Salt Lake City, UT: University of Utah Press.

Wichmann, S. (2004b). El concepto de camino entre los mayas a partir de las fuentes epigráficas, iconográficas y etnográficas. In: M. Montes de Oca (ed.), *La metáfora en Mesoamérica* (pp. 13–32). México, DF: Universidad Nacional Autónoma de México, Instituto de Investigaciones Filológicas.

Wichmann, S. (2006). Mayan historical linguistics and epigraphy: a new synthesis. *Annual Review of Anthropology*, 35: 279–294.

12

Linguistic Relativity and Conceptual Permeability in Visual Narratives:

New Distinctions in the Relationship between Language(s) and Thought

Neil Cohn

Chapter Outline

1. Introduction

In the early twentieth century, American linguists became fascinated with the disparity between the structure of European languages and the Native American languages that they had begun to study with seriousness. This pervasive variation in linguistic structure led them to question whether such differences impacted something deeper: would the structures of the language a person speaks influence the way in which they think?

Along with over a half-century of serious sign language research, the recent proposal of 'visual language' raises another contrast with spoken languages that again challenges the way we think about the relationship between language and thought: What is the relationship between different modalities of expression (verbal–auditory, visual–bodily, visual–graphic) and how do they relate to deeper facets of cognition? Thus far, few researchers have examined these questions with regard to the structure and cognition of drawings and visual narratives. This chapter seeks to further clarify the boundaries of this research and offers a broad survey of how the visual–graphic modality fits into research on the relationship between language and thought.

1.1. Visual language theory

Human beings as a species are biologically predisposed to use three methods of expressing concepts (Cohn, 2013): creating sounds from our mouths, moving our bodies (especially hands and faces), and creating images by manipulating the world around us (i.e., drawing). Whenever any of these conceptually expressive modalities (verbal–auditory, visual–bodily, visual–graphic) uses a system of rules and constraints that gives order to these expressions (i.e., a grammar), the result is a type of language. Thus, meaningful structured sequential sounds become *spoken languages*, structured sequential body motions become *sign languages*, and structured sequential images literally become *visual languages*. These visual languages are most commonly associated with the visual narratives found in comics of the world, which may use culturally distinct visual languages depending on their origin: American Visual Language used in superhero comics ('Kirbyan') differs in structure from Japanese Visual Language often found in *manga*. Thus, like spoken languages, visual languages are not universal and may manifest in culturally distinct ways.

Even when any of these systems does not fully develop into a 'language' it still persists in its ability to convey meaning, rendering it a 'resilient system' that lacks a full grammar and consistent lexicon (Cohn, 2012; Goldin-Meadow, 2003). For example, even though a person might not learn a sign language, their ability to *gesture* persists as an expressive system. Gestures often use novel gesticulations that do not belong to a stored lexicon and they do not use a combinatorial grammatical system to constrain their output. Indeed, most gestures accompany speech at a rate of roughly one per spoken clause, but do not combine with each other (Clark, 1996; McNeill, 1992). Nevertheless, this modality still allows meaning to be conveyed, despite being diminished in comparison to a full sign language. Similarly, though a person might not learn a full visual language – with the ability to draw coherent sequential visual narratives using a consistent visual vocabulary – most people retain the ability to draw individual images with some basic proficiency (Cohn, 2012, 2013). These people do not necessarily draw a full visual language, but the graphic system persists as a resilient, yet comparatively impoverished, communicative modality.

Intrinsic to this broader theory is the idea that all of these expressive modalities – whether as full 'languages' or simple systems (without a grammar) – combine together to create multimodal interactions. This is reflected in gestures that accompany speech and drawings that accompany text. In fact, within this broader framework, multimodality is considered to be the *normal* and *predisposed* state of human communication, and all expressive modalities are assumed to connect to the same underlying conceptual structure of meaning.[1] Each modality thus has unique schematic 'lexical' and grammatical structures which serve as 'handles' for commonly shared conceptual structures[2] (Jackendoff, 1987, 2012). However, each modality affords different functional advantages and disadvantages for the way in which they package conceptual information. For example, the dominantly symbolic verbal modality differs in its affordances from those of the dominantly iconic visual–graphic modality – due to the fact that sound and light intrinsically vary in how they convey information (Cohn, 2013).

Overall though, this view of 'language' holds that all three modalities belong to a *single communicative system of conceptual expression* that uses three modalities in combination to accomplish maximal communicative effectiveness. Within this system, development may determine which modalities become full 'languages' (in the sense of having a lexicon and a grammar), and which merely persist as resilient expressive domains. Regardless of how each modality may develop, the overall tripartite architecture reflects the entirety of the 'human expressive system.'

Given this overall architecture between conceptual structure and the modalities of expression, this raises an interesting question: What is the relationship between these expressive modalities *to each other*? Since they all share a common source of meaning, do these different modalities also share similar ways in which those concepts are expressed? In other words, what does the relationship between these expressive systems tell us about the relationship between language and thought?

1.2. Relativity and permeability

It is hard to find a topic more controversial in the linguistic sciences than the relationship between language and thought, because it directly questions the roles of *nature* and *nurture* in our understanding and perception of the world (Lucy, 1992).

We might characterize there being three basic positions about the relationship between language and thought.

First, a *nativist* perspective attributes conceptualization to be genetically endowed, and all languages express the same concepts through their varying vocabularies (e.g., Fodor, 1975; Pinker, 1994). The extreme version of this view is that all languages can or do express all concepts equally and the structure of those languages makes no noticeable impact on the fairly innate specified meanings. Under this view, we should therefore expect that other non-linguistic functions (perception, categorization, attention, etc.) should also be consistent across all people, no matter what language they speak (or sign, or draw).

The complete opposite viewpoint would be a *deterministic* perspective, whereby the brain comes as a blank slate and all meaning is acquired from experiential and linguistic sources. In the extreme version of this view, the language *determines* a person's concepts because they receive those meanings from the language they learn. Thus, every language offers a unique and different set of meanings on the world. This in turn allows the structuring of a particular language to affect all other aspects of cognition: A person may see, categorize, and experience the world very differently as a speaker of one language versus another.

A somewhat middle-ground (yet still controversial) viewpoint is a *relativistic* perspective, which says that – no matter the degree to which conceptual structures are innate or externally acquired – languages may offer a unique 'lens' by which a person experiences the world (e.g., Whorf, 1956). Here, languages of the world may predominantly express the same meanings (and indeed, all could use similar underlying conceptual primitives), but the patterned way those meanings are structured within varying linguistic systems might predispose a person to think in different ways. This view is particularly compatible with Slobin's (1987, 1996) notion of 'thinking for speaking', which shifts focus away from 'language' structuring 'thought' as solid and static cognitive states. Rather, the system a person uses for 'speaking' habituates a person for a certain type of 'thinking' – a dynamic process. Here, the repeated usage of patterns in a language might provide a certain predisposition for particular conceptualizations, which may in turn impact other facets of cognition.

Over the past several decades, a renewed interest in the relationship between language and thought has yielded several research programs investigating numerous semantic dimensions expressed by languages, including: space, time, motion, substance and form, as well as others (e.g., Boroditsky, 2006; Gumperz and Levinson, 1996; Lucy, 1992). This research has suggested at least some relativistic influence between specific languages and thought. We might characterize support for this relationship coming from two types of evidence:

Type 1: Evidence from studies of other expressive modalities.
Type 2: Evidence from studies of perception, attention, behaviour, etc.

The first type of evidence shows how conceptual framings from spoken language influence non-verbal modalities, most often gesture. For example, many languages locate objects in space in terms of cardinal directions (a system of *absolute* space), rather than in terms of the egocentric viewpoint of a speaker with words like left, right, front, and back (a system of *relative* space) (Levinson, 1996). For example, a napkin could be described as 'south of the plate' in an absolute system, but 'left of the plate' in a relative system. Thus, the same arrangement on the opposite side of the table would change to 'north of the plate' in an absolute system, but would remain 'left of the plate' no matter which side it was on in a relative system. Researchers have observed that the gestures of speakers of absolute systems of direction, such as the Australian Aboriginal language of Guugu Yimithirr, also are anchored into absolute space (Haviland, 1993; Majid, Bowerman, Kita, Haun and Levinson, 2004). That is, when they speak of events, their gestures orient towards the directions that the events *actually happened*. This reinforcement of cardinal directions is consistent with the absolute system of spatial reference in their speech, therefore suggesting a connection between the conceptualization of space in the language and in their gestures.

Another example is the gestures related to time. Núñez and Sweetser (2006) observed that the South American language of Aymara situates space in the opposite direction from that of English. While English-speakers typically speak of the *past being behind them* and *looking ahead to the future*, Aymara uses the reverse directions: the past is in front and the future is behind. This conceptualization is reinforced by deictic gestures by speakers of Aymara, who point rearward when speaking of the future and forward when speaking of the past. Here again, the patterns of encoding concepts found in speech arise in a different modality of expression, namely gestures, which are used as evidence for the relationship between language and thought.

The second type of evidence for relativistic effects comes from experiments looking at non-expressive perception and behaviour. For example, in order to examine the effects of absolute versus relative spatial systems, researchers take individuals into the wilderness and asked them to point towards significant locations, such as large cities that may be several miles away (Levinson, 1997). When speakers of languages that use relative space attempt this task (like English or Dutch), their pointing is fairly random and highly inaccurate. However, speakers of absolute systems are able to point within a few degrees of accuracy to the actual locations of these landmarks. This accuracy is attributed to their attending to cardinal directions more readily than speakers of languages with relative space: if you need to talk and gesture about cardinal directions, you should have a greater ability to situate landmarks within that spatial knowledge. This task therefore illuminates that this knowledge is not necessarily tied to a person's communicative expressions. It is important to note that, while these observations are gathered with regard to pointing gestures, the gestures themselves are not naturally elicited as a reflection of the conceptualization; here they are merely an elicited response to the questions of the task (i.e., indicating a direction).

Other examples of this second type of evidence come from tasks observing how people categorize objects. For example, languages like English allow for plural nouns of objects (*candles*), but not for substances (**waxes*). In contrast, languages like Yucatec Mayan encode most all nouns with information about substance, and counting those objects uses a classifier that describes that overall substance or form (e.g., *two long thin wax*) but not a pluralization of the unit itself (i.e., not *two candles*). In a non-verbal experiment, participants were given three objects (e.g., combs made of plastic or wood, with or without a handle) and were asked to non-verbally group them together (Lucy and Gaskins, 2001, 2003). Speakers of English were more likely to match objects in terms of their shape (combs with handles), though their materials may have differed (wood and plastic), whereas speakers of Yucatec Mayan were more likely to match in terms of substances (both plastic), while their shape differed (handle and no handle). Such results indicated that the encoding of material and shape in nouns influence the perceptual categorization of those actual objects.

Similar findings have appeared with regard to investigations of grammatical gender, since many languages differentiate objects by encoding them as either masculine or feminine. In one study, speakers of Spanish and German viewed objects that were masculine in one language, but feminine in the other (Boroditsky, Schmidt and Phillips, 2003). They found that objects were rated to be more masculine or feminine depending on the gender in their language. In addition, speakers described these objects with traits reflecting the gender of their language. For example, German speakers described bridges (feminine in German) as 'beautiful, elegant, fragile, pretty, slender . . .' while Spanish speakers (where bridges are masculine) described them as 'big, dangerous, strong, sturdy, towering . . .' Since this categorization is not manifest in an alternative expressive modality than speech, they are Type 2 evidence. The effect of gender on conceptualization has also been shown through artwork. Segel and Boroditsky (2011) found that personified objects in artwork from Italy, France, Germany and Spain matched the encoding of gender for those objects in the artists' spoken languages. Because this distinction emerges in a different form of expression (drawing) to express the same conceptualization found in spoken language, it is therefore Type 1 evidence.

Let's now consider these findings in light of the theory of the communicative system that we have previously outlined. With this tripartite architecture, 'Type 1' evidence for linguistic relativity is categorically different from 'Type 2' evidence. As discussed, visual language theory argues that all expressive modalities are tied to a common conceptual structure and that the verbal, bodily/manual, and visual–graphic modalities are naturally different channels of a singular human communicative system. If this is the case, evidence of similar conceptualizations in different modalities is *not* necessarily a relativistic effect, but of the natural connections within the *singular communicative system* resulting from a shared common conceptual structure (whether influenced by one of those external systems or not).

Given this, we can further distinguish the relationship between language and thought into two distinct categories: 1) relativity and 2) permeability, now schematized in Figure 12.1:

1 *Linguistic/conceptual relativity* – when the framing of a conceptualization by an expressive system (i.e., language in *any* modality) influences behaviour in a non-expressive domain (i.e., perception, attention, etc.).
2 *Linguistic/conceptual permeability* – when the framing of a conceptualization in one expressive modality influences and/or is shared by the framing of that conceptualization in other expressive modalities.

The idea of permeability is that the sensorial 'packaging' of form-meaning pairings stored in long-term memory for one modality influences the conceptual packaging in other modalities (which in turn may or may not influence non-expressive modalities – that is, may have relativistic effects). In this framing, neither relativity nor permeability manifest because of a one-way influence of the spoken modality onto other modalities. Rather, framing from any modality could hypothetically influence any other modality (or external system). In addition, especially in the case of permeability, influence may not necessarily be 'causal' from one modality to another. Shared conceptualization across modalities could also arise through co-development of those systems or through 'cultural' influence acting on multiple systems at the same time.

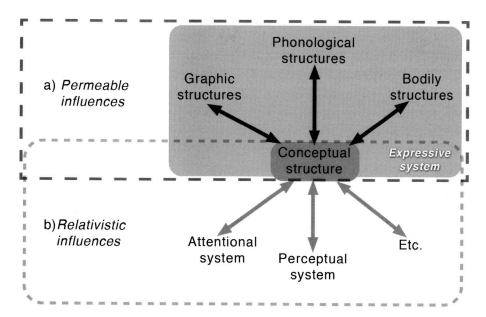

Figure 12.1 Conceptual structures in relation to a) the three modalities of human expression and b) other systems of cognition.

This distinction thereby changes how we might characterize the previously discussed findings. The evidence that speakers of Yucatec Mayan are more inclined to focus on substance than English speakers who focus more on shape is a *relativistic* effect, because the patterns of a language lead to different attentional and perceptual categorization – non-expressive domains. In contrast, the finding that speakers of Aymara gesture rearward to express the future is an example of *permeability*, because it demonstrates how one expressive modality (verbal) shares a conceptualization with another expressive modality (bodily). Both types of evidence arise in the encoding of absolute space: speakers' natural gestures reflect absolute directions (*permeable*) while they maintain absolute space in non-expressive spatial orientation tasks like dead-reckoning (*relativistic*).

With this distinction in place, we can now ask several questions about *relativity* and *permeability* with regard to visual language specifically. What evidence do we have of permeability between different expressive systems? Is there evidence of shared underlying conceptualizations beneath the expressions in visual languages with verbal or signed languages? Is there evidence that visual languages might influence the structures of non-expressive forms (i.e., linguistic relativity)? Is there evidence that cognitive orientations of non-expressive forms have manifestations in the expressive forms, visual language in particular (i.e., 'reverse relativity')?

As we progress to addressing such questions, it is worth bearing in mind that few studies have explicitly examined these types of cross-cultural issues with regard to drawing systems. The subsequent discussion thus provides a broad survey of *potential* evidence from the existing literature as well as outlines potential areas of future study. Any substantial claims that are sought to be made about these overall relations thus must be followed by rigorous empirical investigation.

2. Permeability and relativity in basic lexical items

In the simplest form, we find permeability between shared expressions in the vocabularies of verbal, signed, and visual languages. For example, there are several 'morphemes' in American Visual Language that borrow directly from English idioms, like when the path of a person's vision shows knives going towards another person, directly depicting 'staring daggers' at someone. The convention of stars floating above a person's head to show dizziness derives from the expression 'seeing stars', while stars replaced for someone's eyes to show a desire for fame relates to the idiom of someone having 'stars in their eyes' (Cohn, 2013), as depicted in Figure 12.2a. A visual language may have a reverse influence though. For example, conventions from the Japanese Visual Language used in *manga* have been

Figure 12.2 Visual morphology tied to idioms (a), transferred to sign language (b), invoking possible relativistic effects (c), or tied to conceptual metaphors (d and e).

appropriated directly into the sign language of Japan (Takeuchi, 2012), such as large eyes for surprise or a series of vertical lines across the forehead to show anxiety (Cohn and Ehly, in preparation), as in Figure 12.2b. In this case, the influence runs from visual language to sign language, rather than the aforementioned direction of verbal to visual.

Instances like these are not necessarily 'deep' permeability effects related to conceptualization, though they are evidence of the influence of one domain on another. In this case, one domain fully replicates the meaning found in another modality by also transferring its form. Showing stars *as* someone's eyes for the expression 'stars *in* their eyes' is a direct graphic depiction of a verbal expression. Of course, visual morphemes do not necessarily need to reference a verbal idiom; they could stand alone as visual conventions without someone knowing their origins. This type of permeability does not show profound restructuring or shared conceptual resources, but it does show that 'borrowing' not only occurs from 'language contact' between verbal languages alone, but also between modalities.

Some visual morphology may be tied to relativistic effects as well. One study looked at how the affixation of a lightbulb floating above someone's head to commonly mean 'inspiration' (Figure 12.2c) might translate to actual insight. Participants were found to be more 'inspired' to solve logic puzzles when working in a room with a bare lightbulb, compared with participants who only received lighting from overhead florescent lights (Slepian, Weisbuch, Rutchick, Newman and Ambady, 2010). These results suggested that lightbulb affixes above a head can have relativistic effects on general intelligence and problem solving. Nevertheless, critics of these findings have argued for other explanations of these results, such as various levels of lighting in general priming more creative inspiration, and not lightbulbs specifically (e.g., Steidle and Werth, 2013). Regardless of the specific results, this study suggests that basic aspects of visual morphology can at least be tested for connections to relativistic and embodied aspects of cognition.

3. Conceptual metaphor

Another place where different modalities might employ common conceptual resources in their expressions might come from domain-general conceptual metaphors. Conceptual Metaphor Theory has posited that one domain of knowledge is understood in terms of another domain, such as when a career is understood in terms of a journey, manifested in phrases like *Climbing the corporate ladder* and *His career reached a crossroads* (Lakoff, 1992; Lakoff and Johnson, 1980). Under this view, certain entrenched correspondences between conceptual domains exist across various cultures' spoken languages. In the case of the above metaphor, that mapping is between the associated conceptual information about careers and journeys. By extension, if these metaphorical schemas are integral to human thought across languages, we might expect them to also permeate expressions in non-verbal domains; and, in fact, research has shown conceptual metaphors abound in the visual languages from various countries and historical time periods (Díaz Vera, 2013; Forceville, 2005; Shinohara and Matsunaka, 2009).

From the view of permeability, we might expect that the same conceptual metaphors might underlie both verbal and visual expressions. A well-studied example of this type is the idea that ANGER IS A HOT FLUID IN A PRESSURIZED CONTAINER (Lakoff, 1992). This mapping arises in expressions like *He blew his top* or *She was steaming mad*, which conceptualize anger as a hot fluid that is bursting forth from the container of the person (or their head, specifically). This metaphor arises in the visual form with the conventionalized representation of steam blowing out of someone's ears, their head being the container, as in Figure 12.2d. In fact, many other visual expressions convey this same metaphor, ranging from steam emanating from the top of a character's head to them bouncing up and down due to the building pressure of the anger (Eerden, 2009; Forceville, 2005; Shinohara and Matsunaka, 2009). In addition, this metaphor – and many others – appears to transcend cultural boundaries, as it is found in depictions of anger in both European comics (Forceville, 2005) and Japanese *manga* (Shinohara and Matsunaka, 2009). The manifestation of similar metaphors across domains implies that these are permeable conceptualizations.

These examples show how metaphoric mappings transcend cultural boundaries, but some work has also implied that visual languages might invoke culture-specific morphology to depict conceptual metaphors. Abbott and Forceville (2011) document a specific convention in a Japanese *manga* where characters' hands turn into stumps when they lose control over a situation, as depicted in Figure 12.2e. They argue that this representation invokes the metaphor LOSS OF CONTROL IS LOSS OF HANDS, possibly connected to a superordinate metaphor of EMOTION IS BODILY CHANGE. So far, no work has explored whether a similar metaphor underlies morphology in other visual languages, and/or if it also appears in the spoken Japanese language. Thus, while there may be evidence of metaphors specific to particular visual languages, it is unclear whether this diversity is independent or tied to the metaphors of spoken languages (i.e., whether it is permeable or isolated to its specific modality).

Here we find an important direction for further research on Conceptual Metaphor Theory: to articulate the degree of universality and diversity of these metaphors and their expressions across modalities. Are there metaphors that we should expect to occur in all visual languages of the world? Are there metaphors that only occur in certain systems? Are there conceptual metaphors thought to be specific to certain verbal languages that also occur in the visual languages of the same cultures, and yet do not appear in other visual languages? These types of questions related to the permeability of conceptual metaphor across domains will be important to address as the literature on this field progresses.

4. Paths and motion events

One fruitful area of research that has been explored in studies of linguistic relativity has been the trajectory and characteristics of path actions. The linguist Len Talmy (1985) observed that languages typologically differ in how they code information related to the path of an action – its movement from source to goal (i.e., *going, entering, exiting*) – and its manner – the way by which it traverses that path (i.e., *bouncing, wiggling, sauntering*, etc.). In a *satellite-framed* construction, both manner and motion might be encoded into a verb (*go, run*), while the path is encoded in a 'satellite' of a preposition (*out*, *in*), as in *He **ran out** of the house*. In a *verb-framed* construction, the motion and path can go together in a verb (Spanish: *salir*–'exit', *entrar*–'enter'), while information about its manner must go into an additional verb (*corriendo*–'running'), as in *He **exited** the house **running***. Talmy then pointed out that different languages prefer certain types of expressions over others, with satellite-framed 'S-languages' allowing for a main verb to contain information about manner of motion, and verb-framed 'V-languages' expressing this in a separate verb. S-languages include English, German, Dutch, Mandarin and others, while V-languages include Spanish, French, Japanese, Hebrew, and others. Corpus analysis has confirmed that S-languages use far more manner of motion verbs than V-languages (see Slobin, 2003, for summary).

Because this typology distinguishes ways in which motion, path, and manner might be expressed by different languages, researchers targeted it as a possible place to show relativistic effects. Slobin (2000, 2003) argues that, because S-languages consistently draw focus to the manner of paths, this should increase the salience of paths in the conceptualization of motion events. The reasoning is that every clause must have a main verb and if that slot is allocated to a path (as in V-languages), extra effort and attention is required to add an expression of manner in a separate verb. In contrast, S-languages allow for manner to appear within the obligatory main verb and thus should come more readily in conceptualization.

This difference in salience manifests in several domains, including mental imagery, translation, and – most relevant to our broader discussion – narration (often studied in experiments where participants describe the events in wordless visual narratives). In general, narratives told by S-language speakers focus explicitly on manner of motion and unitization of successive events, while those by V-language speakers often provide the setting and environment wherein motion events happen, though both paths and their manner may be left to inference (Slobin, 2000, 2003). For example, it is easy in an S-language to provide a main verb, and extend the path across several event segments (*He ran **out of** the house, **across** the street, **into** the bar*) where the manner persists throughout the entire path (all involve *running*). V-languages would describe a path in the main verb of each clause (*He exited the house, crossed the street, entered the bar*), and to specify manner would require an added verb (*running*) to each segment repeatedly.

In addition, authors of fiction in S-languages tend to provide more information about manner of movement than authors of books in V-languages. Other research looked at translations of books between English (S-language) and Spanish (V-language). Spanish translations tended to retain less manner of motion verbs than their English originals, but English translations retained nearly all original verbs and even *added* new ones. These diverse findings provide converging evidence for differences in conceptualization offered between S- and V-languages regarding motion and events (again, see Slobin, 2003, for summary of these studies).

Few studies have examined whether the path/manner distinction arises in visual languages. However, in one study, Tversky and Chow (Tversky, 2010; Tversky and Chow, 2009) extracted random panels from comics from China, America, Japan and Italy. These choices cut across distinctions of culture – Western (America and Italy) vs. Eastern (China and Japan) – as well as across linguistic coding of path and manner – S-languages (Chinese and English) vs. V-languages (Japanese and Italian). They reasoned that, because S-languages should have more verbs of motion compared to V-languages, these cultures should depict more 'active' representations. American and Japanese participants then rated the panels on a scale of 'action' vs. 'setting the scene.' Comics from China and America (S-languages) were rated as having more action than those from Japan and Italy (V-languages). Nevertheless, within these contrasts, a second trend occurred: Panels from Eastern countries (China, Japan) were judged to be more action-oriented than those from Western countries (America, Italy).

These results provide preliminary evidence for a distinction between S- and V-languages with regard to the depictions of action, suggesting that path information encoded in verbs of motion could impact the drawing systems of speakers of those languages. However, this study had a fairly small sample size and used only a random sample of panels from a single comic per culture. Also, it did not directly examine paths in these visual languages, but used participants' interpretations of 'degree of action' as a proxy for such a distinction.

In recent work, we examined this same distinction by coding the component parts of paths (i.e., path segments) directly in panels from various comics. We coded for each of the three path segments: a source (the start of the path), the goal (the endpoint of the path), and the trajectory (the path traversed). As depicted in Figure 12.3, these path segments could all be present in a single image. However, a panel could frame only individual segments of this overall path (imagine if each dotted box in Figure 12.3 represented a panel border, or used combinations such as source-trajectory or trajectory-goal alone). Note also that the arc of the trajectory and the impact stars also provide information about the manner of the ball's path: it is *bouncing*.

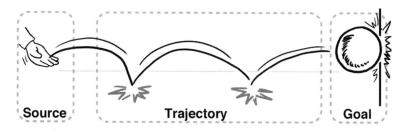

Figure 12.3 A motion line divided into its component parts.

Following Slobin, we reasoned that panels from visual languages by speakers of S-languages (like English) should depict more paths in general than those by speakers of V-languages (like Japanese). In particular, they should depict more trajectories, since that is where the manner of a path occurs. We therefore compared panels in fifteen books of three types of visual narratives: mainstream superhero comics from the United States, Japanese *Shonen manga* (boy's action/adventure comics), and action-oriented OEL *manga* (Cohn, Wong, Pederson and Taylor, in preparation b). Original English Language (OEL) *manga*, are comics created by English-speaking individuals across the world in the style of, or at least influenced by, Japanese *manga* (Brenner, 2007). That is, these speakers of English aim to draw these works in Japanese Visual Language (or a visual language influenced by it).

If paths depicted in OEL *manga* resemble those in American comics, and are unlike those in Japanese *manga*, it would imply a permeable influence of their spoken S-language that might contrast with the structure of their appropriated visual language. In contrast, if OEL *manga* trend more like Japanese *manga* and unlike American comics, it would imply no influence from their native spoken language and would instead suggest that they fully acquire the conventions of Japanese Visual Language.

Our results seemed to be more consistent with a permeable effect of the spoken language on the structures of the visual languages. Figure 12.4 depicts the proportion of panels per book where path segments were isolated (i.e., they were the only path segment depicted in that panel). On the whole, goals and especially trajectories – the path itself – were depicted more often than the source of the path. This is broadly consistent with observations that the endpoints of paths are more salient than starting

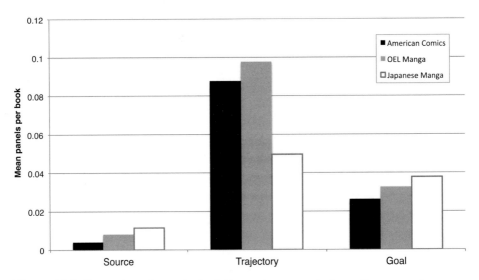

Figure 12.4 Proportion of panels depicting only one part of a path segment (source, trajectory, or goal) per book.

points, which occurs in both verbal language, and perception and attention (Lakusta and Landau, 2005; Regier, 1996, 1997). Between groups, though, both American comics and OEL *manga* depicted more trajectories than Japanese *manga*. This distinction is consistent with the prediction that English (S-language) speakers – regardless of drawing in the visual language associated with American superhero comics or *manga* – would be more likely to depict information about paths than speakers of Japanese (V-language). This therefore implies a permeable influence of the spoken language on whichever visual language is used by those speakers.

Finally, some additional evidence may speculatively be provided from translated comics. Recent work has discussed that translations of Marvel Comics into French in the late 1960s faced stringent French censorship laws, which led to the alteration of many images (Deluxe, 2012; Depelley and Roure, 2009). While some changes related to lessening aspects of violence (like omitting blood splatter, or characters being stabbed), other alterations seem more unusual. Perhaps these changes connect to cross-cultural preferences related to visual languages (i.e., translation from one visual language to another)? For example, dynamic motion lines were omitted from the

American version   French version

Figure 12.5 Page altered in the translation between American and French versions of the same comic (original American publication was *Daredevil #43*, August, 1968. Written by Stan Lee with art by Gene Colan and Vince Colletta). Artwork and characters owned and copyright © Marvel Entertainment, Inc. and its subsidiaries.

American English versions (S-language) when the French versions (V-language) were created, along with 'impact stars' depicting the endpoint of the path where one figure strikes another, as depicted in Figure 12.5. From the view of American superhero comics, without these representations, characters' postures no longer imply that one character hit another, but rather that one character dodged the punch of another. In addition, sound effects were often omitted, which often functionally provide information about the manner of motion.

These alterations in French versions of the comics are consistent with claims about differences in the usage of motion lines between American and French comics (Shipman, 2006), and align with the findings that manner of motion verbs decrease in translations of fiction from S-languages to V-languages (Slobin, 2003). Perhaps these changes actually reflect a translation between the 'Kirbyan' superhero dialect of American Visual Language to be closer to a French Visual Language? Perhaps these influences also align with permeable effects from English and French? Again, both experimental and corpus research could aid in differentiating whether such changes are incidental or actually reflect something deeper about cognitive systems between these cultures.

5. Windowing of attention

Many of the previous examples of how paths might differ in their depiction revolved around the way in which panels function to frame a scene in different ways. Sentences can often provide a 'window of attention' for what information they highlight on a scene (Talmy, 2000). Path and manner languages essentially 'frame' motion events in different ways, but other types of framing might focus less on motion than the componential parts of a scene. Consider the sentences below.

   a The bicycle leaned against the side of the house, across from the grocery store.
   b The bicycle leaned against the side of the house.
   c The bicycle was across from the store.
   d The bicycle leaned against the house, across from the grocery store.
   e The bicycle leaned against the house, across from the store.

The sentence in (a) provides the 'full' view of the overall scene, while each of the sentences in (b–e) omits particular portions of the overall scene. The result is that the 'window' of attention in describing the scene emphasizes or de-emphasizes different information.

Panels serve a similar function for framing the visual information of a graphic scene, here acting like a 'window' for a reader on whatever is happening in the full fictitious environment of a visual narrative (Cohn, 2007, 2013). Because of this, we can categorize the *attentional framing* of panels based on how much information they contain. A *Macro* panel contains multiple interacting entities, often showing the

Macro
Multiple interacting entities

Mono
Single entity

Micro
Less than a single entity

Amorphic
No active entities

Figure 12.6 Framing of information across different attentional types of panels.

full scene. A *Mono* contains just a single entity, no matter the framing (full body, bust, head, etc.). A *Micro* shows less than a single entity, usually through a close-up that frames only a portion of the overall person or object. Finally, an *Amorphic* panel has no entities at all – it only shows elements of the background or environment which do not play an 'active' role in the broader visual sequence.

With this categorization, we can distinguish how cultures might differ in the way that they frame the entities in a scene. In our first study (Cohn, 2011), we coded these dimensions across panels in American comics and Japanese *manga* from 1985 to 2000. American comics had substantially more Macros than Monos with very few Micros, while Japanese *manga* used a nearly equal amount of Macros and Monos with substantially more Micros. Thus, while American comic panels primarily focused on a broader scene, Japanese *manga* showed less than a full scene over half the time, using mostly Macros and Monos.

Our next studies asked whether variation in genres might change these initial findings. Our first follow-up coded panels in American mainstream comics, American independent comics/graphic novels, and Japanese *manga* (*Shonen* and *Seinen*) from 1991 to 2008 (Cohn, Taylor-Weiner, and Grossman, 2012). As depicted in Figure 12.7, mainstream and independent American comics did not differ from each other, and both used near comparable amounts of Macros and Monos, with few Micros and Amorphic panels. In contrast, panels from Japanese *manga* used twice as many Monos as Macros, and substantially more Micros and Amorphic panels than American comics. Thus, we again found a clear cross-cultural distinction between panels in comics from America and Japan.

Recent work has also examined differences between panels in four genres of *manga*: *Shonen* (boys'), *Shojo* (girls'), *Seinen* (men's), and *Josei* (women's). By and large, we found the same trends as in our previous findings of *manga* (Cohn, Wong, Taylor, Huffman and Pederson, in preparation): more Monos and Macros with less Micros and Amorphic panels. The trend of more Monos than Macros seemed to be most pronounced in adult *manga* (*Seinen*, *Josei*), while *manga* ostensibly aimed at younger readers (*Shonen*, *Shojo*) did not show a statistical difference between these attentional

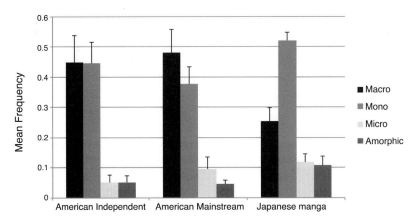

Figure 12.7 Framing of attention in American mainstream comics, American independent comics, and Japanese *manga* (Cohn, Taylor-Weiner and Grossman, 2012).

types. Overall, marginal differences appeared in the framing between genres of *manga*, which implied at least some consistent framing persisting across the 'dialects' of Japanese Visual Language.

These findings in the framing of information via panels may find similarities with the differences that arise between Western and Asian cultures with regard to perceptual attention. As has been demonstrated in research on cross-cultural psychology (Nisbett, 2003; Nisbett and Masuda, 2003; Nisbett and Miyamoto, 2005), on average, individuals from American culture tend to look more at the primary figures involved in a scene while neglecting aspects of the surrounding environment. In contrast, individuals from Asian cultures tend to focus equally on the surrounding environment as much as the primary figures. These findings have also been echoed in studies of photography and artwork. Images from Western cultures tend to emphasize the focal objects and figures while images from East Asia put more focus on the broader environment (Masuda, Gonzalez, Kwan and Nisbett, 2008; Nisbett and Masuda, 2003).

The differences that we found in our coding of attentional categories of visual language panels seem to support these differences in cross-cultural perception. Insofar as panels frame visual information, they can simulate how an individual may view a scene, with panels depicting only the information captured by a 'spotlight of attention' (Levin and Simons, 2000). Panels from Japanese *manga* thus depict individual characters (Monos), their parts (Micros), and environmental information (Amorphic) because these panels focus their attention on the specific relevant information, similar to the way that the eyes of Japanese individuals might move across a scene. In contrast, American panels do not use this type of 'simulated attention' and instead depict a full scene (Macro) because American readers will more readily pick out the relevant features without needing panels to focus their attention, since their perception tends to focus on the primary figures anyhow. Thus, panels in Japanese *manga* will be more likely to provide a 'subjective viewpoint' on a scene (i.e., panels show the viewpoint of characters) than panels in American comics, as has been theorized (McCloud, 1993) and supported with corpus data (Cohn, 2011).

These findings motivated us to compare these distinctions in visual narratives that have been influenced by Japanese *manga,* though are not found in Japan (Cohn, Wong, Taylor, Huffman and Pederson, in preparation a). As mentioned above, OEL *manga* use the visual style (i.e., graphic structure) of Japanese Visual Language, but are created by English-speaking individuals. In addition, Korean *manhwa* have also appropriated the same graphic structure as the Japanese Visual Language (Lent, 2010), but remain within the cultural context of Asia (unlike OEL *manga*). We therefore asked: would these systems maintain the same type of framing as panels from 'native' *manga* in Japan? Here, we again found that mainstream (superhero) American books used more Macros (~51%) than Monos (~39%), with few Micros or Amorphic panels (~5%). Japanese *manga* (Shonen) were also the same as earlier studies, and had almost identical framing as Korean *manhwa*: more Monos (~45%) than Macros (~35%), with decent amounts of both Micros and Amorphic panels (~10%). Panels from OEL *manga*, however, appeared in between those from 'native' American comics and Japanese *manga*. Monos and Macros were roughly equal (~43%), with some Micros and Amorphic panels (~7%). These findings suggest that the framing of space in OEL *manga* are not entirely like the structure of Japanese *manga*, nor are they entirely like American comics. Rather, they appear to be a hybrid of the two systems (a pidgin?), meaning that any potential influence of the culture on the graphic system is not deterministic.

Without additional cross-cultural evidence from language, these corpus analyses appear to be 'reverse relativistic' in relation to the findings of cross-cultural attention. That is, the windowing of attention in perception appears to be reinforced in the visual language (but not inevitably), rather than the graphic system influencing the cognitive system. Providing relativistic evidence would require experimental data observing how readers of comics view scenes, and whether the types of visual narratives they read would influence these eye movements. Studying creators of OEL *manga* and non-Asian readers of *manga* may be enlightening on this point: does reading (or drawing) Japanese *manga* change a person's perception and attention?

Finally, with these gross differences between 'Western' and 'Eastern' direction of attention, should we expect these broad distinctions of 'culture' to override factors such as permeable or relativistic differences coming from language? Indeed, with regard to motion verbs alone, English is more similar to Mandarin and Japanese is closer to French, despite cutting across these 'East/West' divisions. Exploring these intertwined issues of culture and language(s) can provide more insight to factors involved with such cross-cultural comparisons.

6. Spatial orientation

Finally, perhaps the best evidence for both permeability and relativity with regard to all three modalities comes from a context removed from the visual languages found in comics. In Central Australia, Aboriginals use a system of drawings in the sand that can accompany speech and signing/gestures. While the most complex sand drawings appear in the telling of narratives by women, parts of this system are also used in daily conversation by both sexes, similarly to co-speech gestures (Green, 2014; Munn, 1986; Wilkins, this volume). The ability for this extensive use of drawing in communication is facilitated by the ubiquity of sand in the environment of these communities, on which speakers sit and interact as part of daily life.

As was mentioned previously, many of the languages used by Aboriginals in Australia have systems of absolute spatial reference – they locate space with words related to cardinal directions. This is distinctly different from systems of relative space that focus on words relative to a speaker's body, such as left, right, forward, and back. Research has shown that Aboriginals also encode these absolute spatial orientations in their gestures (e.g., Haviland, 1993; Majid et al., 2004). If they are gesturing about events that occurred along a north-south dimension, their gestures will maintain this north-south axis no matter what direction their body is facing. This is a permeable effect, since the gestures created in conversation reflect the absolute directions coded in the spoken languages.

In previous work, this orientation in the gestures has been taken as one point of evidence for more widespread relativistic effects of these languages with regard to spatial orientation. As discussed, speakers of absolute systems are more accurate in locating unviewable landmarks than speakers of languages with relative space (Levinson, 1997). In other experiments, participants face a table with numerous objects on it (say, an arrow facing to their left, pointing to the south), and then turn 180° to another table where they then must choose objects that match those from the first table (Levinson, 1996, 1997; Majid et al., 2004). Speakers of relative systems choose objects that maintain the same orientation relative to their body (arrows still facing to their left, but now pointing north), while speakers of absolute systems choose objects maintaining the same orientation in environmental space (arrows facing right of the participant, but still pointing south). Thus, relativistic effects on perception and behaviour with regard to spatial understanding extend beyond the permeable effects of gestures alone.

If absolute space is fully permeable across all domains, then we might also expect it to appear in sand drawings, which is indeed the case. Because sand drawings unfurl across time in interactive communication, the actual meaningful signs are economical enough to be conveyed quickly. They use simple lines and shapes to depict fairly polysemous expressions. For example, a simple line may be a spear, a person lying down, the path of someone's movement across the ground, or the path of a thrown spear (Green, 2014; Munn, 1986, this volume). These meanings must be disambiguated through context.

Unlike the visual languages used in comics, sand narratives do not become segmented in spatially distinct units with an inferred time between them, but rather unfurl in a single space across real-time. This single space is situated within an aerial, 'bird's eye view' perspective, and most of the drawings are said to represent 'tracks' or the imprints made in the sand. For example, a person is shaped roughly like the letter 'U', because that is iconic to the imprint a person makes when sitting in the sand (Green, 2014; Munn, 1986, this volume). Tracks are also important to sand drawings to indicate movement. Wilkins (this volume) presented Aboriginals with a drawing of a horse that, under a Western point of view, would be interpreted as running, being depicted from a lateral side-view with puffs of smoke to indicate movement. However, they viewed the horse as lying down or dead, because, from their perspective the horse was not viewed from a lateral viewpoint, but from an aerial viewpoint – meaning it was lying on its side. Additionally, since the drawing had no 'tracks' to indicate movement, the puffs of smoke were interpreted as crows, nibbling on the 'dead' horse.

This fixed aerial viewpoint also means that all representations are locked into absolute space: If a character moves North to South in a sand story, they are represented as moving from actual North to South in the drawings. This interpretation of absolute space appears to be fairly robust. Green (2014) describes experiments where Aboriginals sat in a room viewing videoed sand narratives on a computer. In these experiments, the spatial orientation of the actual narrative in the sand drawings (on the screen) did or did not align with the orientation in which the participants saw the screen (i.e., with an interpretation of the screen being 'flattened' into absolute space). In several cases, participants would mistakenly attribute the directions within the videoed narratives to the real-life absolute directions they were facing, even if it yielded odd interpretations of the motions in the story (such as placement of objects canonically to the East now strangely placed to the North). That is, participants interpreted the sand stories more in terms of the physical, real-world orientations than those intrinsically implied by the drawings themselves.

Finally, it is worth observing that the aerial viewpoint is the only way that an absolute space could possibly be maintained in a drawing system. A lateral viewpoint of objects like that used in other visual languages would have no way to orient cardinal directions. Thus, the structure of the sand drawings is tailored to reinforce these absolute spatial directions, as is the lateral directions for speakers of relative directions. Whether such reinforcement recurs cross-culturally is a question for anthropological and corpus research.

In sum, because these Aboriginal cultures maintain absolute spatial orientations in speech, gestures, and drawings, this reinforcement perhaps shows the best evidence of permeable effects across all expressive domains. Meanwhile the non-linguistic experimental tasks beyond expressive modalities show further evidence of relativistic effects for this conceptualization on various aspects of cognition and behaviour.

7. Conclusion

This chapter has provided a survey of the various relationships between expressive modalities (verbal–auditory, visual–manual, visual–graphic), thought, and culture. In line with the idea that all expressive modalities are inherently connected within a broader conceptual system, I have introduced a new notion of 'permeability' that describes the influence and/or sharing of the structuring of concepts in one modality with another modality. This distinction differs from relativistic relations of language and thought, where the structure of an expressive modality influences other facets of the cognitive system (perception, attention, categorization, etc.).

As should be evident by this survey of research, only a limited number of studies have begun to look at these complex relationships in the visual–graphic modality and this line of research remains in its infancy. Given the scant targeted research examining such phenomena, further research will be needed to confirm whether the observations herein hold up to additional empirical scrutiny. With the broad theory of visual language now laid out, an important first step would be to learn more about the properties of existing systems across the world. Using large-scale corpus analyses to code across various dimensions of this visual language structure, we can begin to understand how these systems might differ and/or overlap. These structures can then inform additional targeted experiments examining the impact of such structures on perception and behaviour.

Acknowledgements

Thanks go to Dan Slobin for the feedback on previous drafts and to Lera Borodistky and her lab for helpful discussions of these ideas.

Notes

1. Note that we could also attribute a separate 'conceptual structure' to each modality, which would then be linked together within the broader conceptual system. However, it should not alter this overall framework and the distinctions made throughout.

2. Here, I include all aspects of 'meaning' into my use of 'conceptual' structures. I collapse here a notion of algebraic type meaning as 'conceptual structure' and a 'geometric' type of meaning as 'spatial structure' – roughly corresponding to Marr's (1982) 3-D model (Jackendoff, 1983, 1987, 2002, 2012), as well as notions of image schemas (Johnson, 1987; Talmy, 2000). It should be noted that the extended version of Jackendoff's conceptual structure also interfaces into the motor system and other sensory channels (Jackendoff, 1987), as in theories of embodied cognition. For simplicity, I refer to both of these together as 'conceptual structures', while acknowledging that more subtle and complex interactions between these components exist in expression.

References

Abbott, M., and Forceville, C. (2011). Visual representation of emotion in manga: loss of control is loss of hands in *Azumanga Daioh*, Volume 4. *Language and Literature*, 20(2): 91–112. doi: 10.1177/0963947011402182

Boroditsky, L. (2006). Linguistic relativity. *Encyclopedia of Cognitive Science* (pp. 917–921). London: John Wiley.

Boroditsky, L., Schmidt, L. A., and Phillips, W. (2003). Sex, syntax, and semantics. *Language in Mind: Advances in the Study of Language and Thought*: 61–79.

Brenner, R. E. (2007). *Understanding Manga and Anime*. Westport, CT: Libraries Unlimited.

Clark, H. H. (1996). *Using Language*. Cambridge: Cambridge University Press.

Cohn, N. (2007). A visual lexicon. *Public Journal of Semiotics*, 1(1): 53–84.

Cohn, N. (2011). A different kind of cultural frame: an analysis of panels in American comics and Japanese manga. *Image [&] Narrative*, 12(1): 120–134.

Cohn, N. (2012). Explaining 'I can't draw': parallels between the structure and development of language and drawing. *Human Development*, 55(4): 167–192. doi: 10.1159/000341842

Cohn, N. (2013). *The Visual Language of Comics: Introduction to the Structure and Cognition of Sequential Images*. London: Bloomsbury.

Cohn, N., and Ehly, S. (in preparation). The vocabulary of manga: visual morphology in dialects of Japanese Visual Language.

Cohn, N., Taylor-Weiner, A., and Grossman, S. (2012). Framing attention in Japanese and American comics: cross-cultural differences in attentional structure. *Frontiers in Psychology – Cultural Psychology*, 3: 1–12. doi: 10.3389/fpsyg.2012.00349

Cohn, N., Wong, V., Taylor, R., Huffman, R., and Pederson, K. (in preparation). A cross-cultural analysis of attentional framing structure in visual narratives: framing attention in Japanese, American, and Korean comics.

Cohn, N., Wong, V., Pederson, K., and Taylor, R. (in preparation). Cross-cultural differences in the depiction of paths across visual narratives.

Deluxe, J.-E. (2012). Marvel 14: the incredible history of France's censorship of Marvel Comics, translated by L. Barbarian. In: J. Rovnak (ed.), *Panel to Panel: Exploring Words and Pictures*.

Depelley, J., and Roure, P. (2009). Marvel 14: les Super-Héros contre la censure. France: Metaluna Productions.

Díaz Vera, J. E. (2013). Woven emotions: visual representations of emotions in medieval English textiles. *Review of Cognitive Linguistics*, 11(2): 269–284. doi: 10.1075/rcl.11.2.04dia

Eerden, B. (2009). Anger in Asterix: the metaphorical representation of anger in comics and animated films. In: C. Forceville and E. Urios-Aparisi (eds), *Multimodal Metaphor* (pp. 243–264). New York: Mouton De Gruyter.

Fodor, J. (1975). *The Language of Thought*, Vol. 5. Cambridge, MA: Harvard University Press.

Forceville, C. (2005). Visual representations of the idealized cognitive model of anger in the Asterix album *La Zizanie*. *Journal of Pragmatics*, 37(1): 69–88.

Goldin-Meadow, S. (2003). *The Resiliance of Language: What Gesture Creation in Deaf Children Can Tell Us about How All Children Learn Language*. New York and Hove: Psychology Press.

Green, J. (2014). *Drawn from the Ground: Sound, Sign and Inscription in Central Australian Sand Stories*. Cambridge, MA: Cambridge University Press.

Gumperz, J. J., and Levinson, S. (1996). *Rethinking Linguistic Relativity*. Cambridge: Cambridge University Press.

Haviland, J. (1993). Anchoring, iconicity, and orientation in Guugu Yimithirr pointing gestures. *Journal of Linguistic Anthropology*, 3(1): 3–45.

Jackendoff, R. (1983). *Semantics and Cognition*. Cambridge, MA: MIT Press.

Jackendoff, R. (1987). *Consciousness and the Computational Mind*. Cambridge, MA: MIT Press.

Jackendoff, R. (2002). *Foundations of Language: Brain, Meaning, Grammar, Evolution*. Oxford: Oxford University Press.

Jackendoff, R. (2012). *A User's Guide to Thought and Meaning*. Oxford: Oxford University Press.

Johnson, M. (1987). *The Body in the Mind: The Bodily Basis of Meaning, Imagination, and Reason*. Chicago, IL: University of Chicago Press.

Lakoff, G. (1992). The contemporary theory of metaphor. In: A. Ortony (ed.), *Metaphor and Thought*, 2nd edn Cambridge, MA: Cambridge University Press.

Lakoff, G., and Johnson, M. (1980). *Metaphors We Live By*. Chicago, IL: University of Chicago Press.

Lakusta, L., and Landau, B. (2005). Starting at the end: the importance of goals in spatial language. *Cognition*, 96: 1–33.

Lent, J. A. (2010). Manga in East Asia. In: T. Johnson-Woods (ed.), *Manga: An Anthology of Global and Cultural Perspectives* (pp. 297–314). New York: Continuum Books.

Levin, D. T., and Simons, D. J. (2000). Perceiving stability in a changing world: combining shots and intergrating views in motion pictures and the real world. *Media Psychology*, 2(4): 357–380.

Levinson, S. (1996). Language and space. *Annual Review of Anthropology*, 25: 353–382.

Levinson, S. (1997). Language and cognition: the cognitive consequences of spatial description in Guugu Yimithirr. *Journal of Linguistic Anthropology*, 7(1): 98–131. doi: 10.1525/jlin.1997.7.1.98

Lucy, J. A. (1992). *Language, Diversity, and Thought: A Reformulation of the Linguistic Relativity Hypothesis*. Cambridge, MA: Cambridge University Press.

Lucy, J. A., and Gaskins, S. (2001). Grammatical categories and the development of classification preferences: a comparative approach. In: M. Bowerman and S. Levinson (eds), *Language Acquisition and Conceptual Development* (pp. 257–283). Cambridge: Cambridge University Press.

Lucy, J. A., and Gaskins, S. (2003). Interaction of language type and referent type in the development of nonverbal classification preferences. In: D. Gentner and S. Goldin-Meadow (eds), *Language in Mind: Advances in the Study of Language and Thought* (pp. 465–492). Cambridge, MA: MIT Press.

Majid, A., Bowerman, M., Kita, S., Haun, D. B. M., and Levinson, S. (2004). Can language restructure cognition? The case for space. *Trends in Cognitive Science*, 8(3): 108–114.

Marr, D. (1982). *Vision*. San Francisco, CA: Freeman.

Masuda, T., Gonzalez, R., Kwan, L., and Nisbett, R. E. (2008). Culture and aesthetic preference: comparing the attention to context of East Asians and Americans. *Personality and Social Psychology Bulletin*, 34(9): 1260–1275. doi: 10.1177/0146167208320555

McCloud, S. (1993). *Understanding Comics: The Invisible Art*. New York: Harper Collins.

McNeill, D. (1992). *Hand and Mind: What Gestures Reveal about Thought*. Chicago, IL: University of Chicago Press.

Munn, N. D. (1986). *Walbiri Iconography: Graphic Representation and Cultural Symbolism in a Central Australian Society*. Chicago, IL: University of Chicago Press.

Nisbett, R. (2003). *The Geography of Thought: How Asians and Westerners Think Differently . . . and Why*. New York: Nicholas Brealy Publishing.

Nisbett, R., and Masuda, T. (2003). Culture and point of view. *Proceedings of the National Academy of Sciences*, 100(19): 11163–11170.

Nisbett, R., and Miyamoto, Y. (2005). The influence of culture: holistic versus analytic perception. *Trends in Cognitive Sciences*, 9(10): 467–473.

Núñez, R., and Sweetser, E. (2006). With the future behind them: convergent evidence from Aymara language and gesture in the cross-linguistic comparison of spatial construals of time. *Cognitive Science*, 30: 1–49.

Pinker, S. (1994). *The Language Instinct: How the Mind Creates Language*. New York: Harper Collins.

Regier, T. (1996). *The Human Semantic Potential: Spatial Language and Constrained Connectionism*. Cambridge, MA: MIT Press.

Regier, T. (1997). Constraints on the learning of spatial terms: a computational investigation. In: R. Goldstone, P. Schyns, and D. Medin (eds), *Psychology of Learning and Motivation: Mechanisms of Perceptual Learning* (Vol. 36, pp. 171–217). San Diego, CA: Academic Press.

Segel, E., and Boroditsky, L. (2011). Grammar in art. *Frontiers in Psychology*, 1. doi: 10.3389/fpsyg.2010.00244

Shinohara, K., and Matsunaka, Y. (2009). Pictorial metaphors of emotion in Japanese comics. In: C. Forceville and E. Urios-Aparisi (eds), *Multimodal Metaphor* (pp. 265–293). New York: Mouton De Gruyter.

Shipman, H. (2006). *Hergé's Tintin and Milton Caniff's Terry and the Pirates: Western Vocabularies of Visual Language*. Paper presented at the Comic Arts Conference, San Diego, CA.

Slepian, M. L., Weisbuch, M., Rutchick, A. M., Newman, L. S., and Ambady, N. (2010). Shedding light on insight: priming bright ideas. *Journal of Experimental Social Psychology*, 46: 696–700.

Slobin, D. I. (1987). Thinking for speaking. *Proceedings of the Thirteenth Annual Meeting of the Berkeley Linguistics Society*: 435–444.

Slobin, D. I. (1996). From 'thought and language' to 'thinking for speaking'. *Rethinking Linguistic Relativity*, 17: 70–96.

Slobin, D. I. (2000). Verbalized events: a dynamic approach to linguistic relativity and determinism. In: S. Niemeier and R. Dirven (eds), *Evidence for Linguistic Relativity* (pp. 107–138). Amsterdam: Benjamins.

Slobin, D. I. (2003). Language and thought online: cognitive consequences of linguistic relativity. In: D. Gentner and S. Goldin-Meadow (eds), *Language in Mind: Advances in the Study of Language and Thought* (pp. 157–192). Cambridge, MA: MIT Press.

Steidle, A., and Werth, L. (2013). Freedom from constraints: darkness and dim illumination promote creativity. *Journal of Environmental Psychology*, 35(0): 67–80. doi: http://dx.doi.org/10.1016/j.jenvp.2013.05.003

Takeuchi, K. (2012). ASL manga: visual representation in storytelling. *Deaf Studies Digital Journal*, 3.

Talmy, L. (1985). Lexicalization patterns: semantic structure in lexical forms. In: T. Shopen (ed.), *Language Typology and Syntactic Description*: Vol. 3. *Grammatical Categories and the Lexicon* (pp. 36–149). Cambridge, MA: Cambridge University Press.

Talmy, L. (2000). *Toward a Cognitive Semantics* (Vol. 1). Cambridge, MA: MIT Press.

Tversky, B. (2010). Segmenting and connecting: from event perception to comics. *Human Computer Interaction Class at Stanford University*. http://www.youtube.com/watch?v=tSHZDfx86T0

Tversky, B., and Chow, T. (2009, 11/21/09). *Comics: Language and Culture Affect Action in Depictions*. Paper presented at the Psychonomics, Boston, MA.

Whorf, B. L. (1956). The relation of habitual thought and behavior to language. In: J. B. Carroll (ed.), *Language, Thought, and Reality: Selected Writings of Benjamin Lee Whorf* (pp. 134–159). Cambridge, MA: MIT Press.

Wilkins, D.P. (this volume). Alternative Representations of Space: Arrernte Narratives in Sand. In: Neil Cohn (ed.) *The Visual Narrative Reader* (pp. 251–279). London: Bloomsbury. Original edition (1997) M. Biemans and J. van de Weijer (eds) *Proceedings of the CLS Opening Academic Year '97 '98* (pp. 133-164). Nijmegan: Nijmegen/Tilburg Center for Language Studies.

Further Reading

Because most of the works in this collection summarize large bodies of literature, readers interested in learning more are directed towards the works cited in each chapter. However, below are listed some additional suggestions for 'recommended reading' categorized by topic in the order they appear in the collection.

On the cognitive structure of visual narratives

Cohn, N. (2013). *The Visual Language of Comics: Introduction to the Structure and Cognition of Sequential Images.* London: Bloomsbury.

This monograph provides a broad framework for 'visual language theory' and the integration of visual narrative into the cognitive and linguistic sciences. It covers all the main areas of structure, discusses initial forays into psychology experiments on sequential image comprehension, and outlines how cross-cultural research might frame the understanding of visual narratives from around the world (including Australian sand narratives).

Form, meaning and stylistics of images

Forceville, C., El Refaie, E., and Meesters, G. (2014). Stylistics in comics. In: M. Burke (ed.), *The Routledge Handbook of Stylistics* (pp. 485–499). London: Routledge.

While Lefèvre's chapter targets the stylistics of graphics alone, Forceville, El Refaie, and Meesters discuss stylistics across numerous levels of the structure found in comics.

Willats, J. (1997). *Art and Representation: New Principles in the Analysis of Pictures.* Princeton: Princeton University Press.

Willats, J. (2005). *Making Sense of Children's Drawings.* Mahwah, NJ: Lawrence Erlbaum.

The books by John Willats are excellent for their discussion of the cognitive structure of drawings. His 2005 book also formulates a rough developmental trajectory for how children learn to draw.

Conceptual metaphor and blending theory

Lakoff, G., and Johnson, M. (1980). *Metaphors We Live By*. Chicago, IL: University of Chicago Press.

Lakoff and Johnson's original, classic work arguing for conceptual metaphor theory.

Fauconnier, G., and Turner, M. (2002). *The Way We Think: Conceptual Blending and the Mind's Hidden Complexities*. New York: Basic Books.

Fauconnier and Turner outline their 'blending theory' for explaining the various ways that conceptualization maps across domains.

Forceville, C., and Urios-Aparisi, E. (eds) (2009). *Multimodal Metaphor*. New York: Mouton de Gruyter.

Forceville and Urios-Aparisi edit a broad collection of papers discussing metaphor and blending theory as applied to domains other than language. In particular, the central part of the book contains several chapters on visual narratives of cartoons and comics. See also individual papers cited in Forceville's chapter.

Discourse and visual narratives

Halliday, M. A. K., and Hasan, R. (1976). *Cohesion in English*. London: Longman.
Halliday, M. A. K., and Hasan, R. (1985). *Language, Context, and Text: Aspects of Language in a Social-Semiotic Perspective*. Victoria: Deakin University Press.

Halliday and Hasan's original works describing coherence relations in text, which both Saraceni and Stainbrook reference.

McCloud, S. (1993). *Understanding Comics: The Invisible Art*. New York: Harper Collins.

McCloud's original book on comics was an inspiration for many to pursue scholarship on visual narratives. While the approach is now a little dated, the chapter on panel transitions, and their variation across cultures, is especially worth reading to see the origination of much academic work on sequential images (and an early instance of using theory to guide corpus analysis).

Developmental research on visual narrative comprehension

Nakazawa, J. (2005). Development of *manga* (comic book) literacy in children. In: D. W. Shwalb, J. Nakazawa and B. J. Shwalb (eds), *Applied Developmental Psychology:*

Theory, Practice, and Research from Japan (pp. 23–42). Greenwich, CT: Information Age Publishing.

Nakazawa's 2005 paper is the only other work in English summarizing research from Japan on the development of *manga* comprehension. Outside of this paper, only scattered papers discuss the comprehension of sequential images from a developmental perspective. However, some of these include . . .

Pallenik, M. J. (1986). A gunman in town! Children interpret a comic book. *Studies in the Anthropology of Visual Communication*, 3(1): 38–51.

Trabasso, T., and Nickels, M. (1992). The development of goal plans of action in the narration of a picture story. *Discourse Processes*, 15: 249–275.

Trabasso, T., and N. L. Stein (1994). Using goal-plan knowledge to merge the past with the present and the future in narrating events online. In: M. M. Haith, J. B. Benson, R. J. Roberts Jr and B. F. Pennington (eds), *The Development of Future-Oriented Processes* (pp. 323–349). Chicago: University of Chicago Press.

Children's production of drawings and visual narratives

Wilson, B., and Wilson, M. (1977). An iconoclastic view of the imagery sources in the drawings of young people', *Art Education*, 30(1): 4–12.

Wilson, B., and Wilson, M. (1987). Pictorial composition and narrative structure: themes and creation of meaning in the drawings of Egyptian and Japanese children. *Visual Arts Research*, 13(2): 10–21.

Wilson, B. (1988). The artistic tower of Babel: inextricable links between culture and graphic development. In: G. W. Hardiman and T. Zernich (eds), *Discerning Art: Concepts and Issues* (pp. 488–506). Champaign, IL: Stipes Publishing.

Wilson's primary source materials are all excellent in their discussion of children's drawing development. Many of these are listed in the bibliography of his chapter. See also John Willats' *Making Sense of Children's Drawings*, mentioned above.

Cohn, N. (2012). Explaining 'I can't draw': parallels between the structure and development of language and drawing. *Human Development*, 55(4): 167–192.

Cohn, N. (2014). Framing 'I can't draw': the influence of cultural frames on the development of drawing. *Culture and Psychology*, 20(1): 102–117.

This pair of papers attempts to draw together research on drawing to explain its cognitive status and why so many people feel they 'can't draw'. Both papers highlight the interactions between biology and culture in the development of drawing, and incorporate many of Wilson and Willats' insights.

Australian sand narratives

Munn, N. D. (1986). *Walbiri Iconography: Graphic Representation and Cultural Symbolism in a Central Australian Society*. Chicago, IL: University of Chicago Press.

Chapter 9 excerpts only a chapter from Munn's book related to sand narratives specifically. For a full appreciation of the broader scope of graphic representation by the Walbiri, her original book is highly recommended.

Green, J. (2014). *Drawn from the Ground: Sound, Sign and Inscription in Central Australian Sand Stories*. Cambridge, UK: Cambridge University Press.

Green's work provides the most comprehensive approach to Australian sand drawings from any researcher. It has also expanded beyond observations about the sand narrative system, and offers a view of the global multimodal interactions in which sand narratives are embedded. It should be essential reading for those interested in finding out more about these systems.

Mayan paintings

Stone, A. J. (1995). *Images from the Underworld: Naj Tunich and the Tradition of Maya Cave Painting*. Austin, TX: University of Texas Press.

The standard reference work on the paintings and hieroglyphic texts found in caves in the Maya area, mainly from the Classic period. A seminal contribution that shows that the Ancient Maya used a broad spectrum of media for their visual communication – including cave walls.

Miller, M., and Brittenham, C. (2013). *The Spectacle of the Late Maya Court: Reflections on the Murals of Bonampak*. Austin, TX: University of Texas Press; Mexico: INAH.

A new, massive and impressively in-depth study of the famous Classic-period polychromatic murals from the site of Bonampak in Chiapas, Mexico. Provides detailed analyses of the complex narrative in the murals, the accompanying glyphs, and their architectural and historical contexts.

Relationship between language and thought

Sapir, E. (2004). *Language: An Introduction to the Study of Speech*. Courier Corporation.
Whorf, B. L. (1956). The relation of habitual thought and behavior to language. In:

J. B. Carroll (ed.), *Language, Thought, and Reality: Selected Writings of Benjamin Lee Whorf* (pp. 134–159). Cambridge, MA: MIT Press.

Sapir and Whorf's original writings on the relations between language and thought are important for an historical perspective on this issue, though much of their analysis is now considered outdated.

Lucy, J. A. (1992). *Language, Diversity, and Thought: A Reformulation of the Linguistic Relativity Hypothesis*. Cambridge, UK: Cambridge University Press.

Lucy provides an extensive look at the relations between language and thought with careful attempts to establish a solid methodology for its study.

Slobin, D. I. (1996). From 'thought and language' to 'thinking for speaking'. *Rethinking Linguistic Relativity*, 17: 70–96.

Slobin attempts to re-frame the issues related to linguistic relativity in a more dynamic and cognitively oriented way.

Jackendoff, R. (2012). *A User's Guide to Thought and Meaning*. Oxford: Oxford University Press.

While Jackendoff mentions linguistic relativity only in brief, this work provides a broad overview of the relationship between language and thought in a way that is particularly commensurate with the overall approach discussed in this chapter. The book is also fairly readable for a broad audience.

Index